REPORT

T0130723

Evaluation of the Arkansas Tobacco Settlement Program

Progress During 2004 and 2005

Donna O. Farley, John Engberg, Brian Carroll,
Matthew Chinman, Elizabeth D'Amico, Sarah Hunter,
Susan Lovejoy, Lisa R. Shugarman, Hao Yu,
James P. Kahan

Prepared for the Arkansas Tobacco Settlement Commission

The research described in this report was sponsored by the Arkansas Tobacco Settlement Commission under Contract No. 4500160544.

Library of Congress Cataloging-in-Publication Data

Evaluation of the Arkansas tobacco settlement program : progress during 2004 and 2005 / Donna O. Farley ...
   p. cm.
   Includes bibliographical references.
   ISBN 978-0-8330-4046-6 (pbk. : alk paper)
   1. Public health—Arkansas. 2. Tobacco use—Arkansas. 3. Tobacco industry—Law and legislation—Arkansas. 4. Health promotion—Arkansas. I. Farley, Donna.
   [DNLM: 1. Smoking—prevention & control—Arkansas—Technical Report. 2. Health Policy—Arkansas—Technical Report. 3. Health Promotion—methods—Arkansas—Technical Report. 4. Program Evaluation—Arkansas—Technical Report. 5. Tobacco Industry—legislation & jurisprudence—Arkansas—Technical Report. 6. Tobacco Use Disorder—prevention & control—Arkansas—Technical Report. WN 290 E9191 2007].

RA447.A7E93 2007
362.29'609767—dc22

2006035954

The RAND Corporation is a nonprofit research organization providing objective analysis and effective solutions that address the challenges facing the public and private sectors around the world. RAND's publications do not necessarily reflect the opinions of its research clients and sponsors.

RAND® is a registered trademark.

Published 2007 by the RAND Corporation
1776 Main Street, P.O. Box 2138, Santa Monica, CA 90407-2138
1200 South Hayes Street, Arlington, VA 22202-5050
4570 Fifth Avenue, Suite 600, Pittsburgh, PA 15213-2665
RAND URL: http://www.rand.org/
To order RAND documents or to obtain additional information, contact
Distribution Services: Telephone: (310) 451-7002;
Fax: (310) 451-6915; Email: order@rand.org

Preface

The Tobacco Settlement Proceeds Act, a referendum passed by Arkansans in the November 2000 election, invests Arkansas' share of the tobacco Master Settlement Agreement (MSA) funds in seven health-related programs. The Act also created the Arkansas Tobacco Settlement Commission (ATSC) to monitor and evaluate the performance of the funded programs. As part of its evaluation function, the ATSC contracted with the RAND Corporation in January 2003 to serve as an external evaluator. RAND is responsible for performing a comprehensive evaluation of the progress of the seven programs in fulfilling their missions, as well as the effects of the programs on smoking and other health-related outcomes. RAND submitted its first Biennial Report to the ATSC in July 2004, presenting evaluation results for the first biennium of the Tobacco Settlement program (Farley et al., 2005a), and it submitted a subsequent interim report in June 2005 (Farley et al., 2005b).

This document is the second official Biennial Report from our evaluation. It documents continued activity and progress by the ATSC and the seven funded programs through May 2006, as well as trends in relevant health-related outcomes. First, the report summarizes the history and policy context of the Tobacco Settlement funding in Arkansas and discusses the ATSC's activities and its responses to recommendations by RAND in the 2004 evaluation report. Then it evaluates the progress of each of the funded programs, including assessing progress in achieving long-range goals established by the programs in 2005, tracking the program's process measures, and assessing performance on a set of program management integrity criteria. The report also updates trends in outcome measures developed to monitor effects of the funded programs on smoking and other health-related outcomes. Finally, it provides both program-specific and statewide recommendations for future program activities and funding.

The contents of this report will be of interest to national and state policymakers, health care researchers and providers, and others concerned with the effect of the tobacco settlement funds on the health of Arkansans.

This work was sponsored by the Arkansas Tobacco Settlement Commission, for which Chiquita Munir served as project officer. This work was carried out within RAND Health. RAND Health is a division of the RAND Corporation. Abstracts of all RAND Health publications and full text of many research documents can be found at the RAND Health Web site at http://www.rand.org/health/.

CONTENTS

Figures

Tables

Summary

The Master Settlement Agreement (MSA), the historic agreement that ended years of legal battles between the states and the major tobacco companies, was signed on November 23, 1998. Under the terms of the MSA, Arkansas has a 0.828 percent share of the payments made to participating states over the next 25 years. Arkansas is unique in the commitment made to invest its share of the Tobacco Settlement funds in health-related programs. The Arkansas Tobacco Settlement Proceeds Act of 2000 (referred to hereafter as the Initiated Act), a referendum passed by the voters in the November 2000 election, established the Arkansas Tobacco Settlement Commission (ATSC) to oversee the spending of MSA monies on seven health-related programs:

- Tobacco Prevention and Education Program (TPEP)

- College of Public Health (COPH)

- Delta Area Health Education Center (Delta AHEC)

- Arkansas Aging Initiative (AAI)

- Minority Health Initiative (MHI)

- Arkansas Biosciences Institute (ABI)

- Medicaid Expansion Programs (MEP)

The Initiated Act was explicitly aimed at the general health of Arkansans, not just at the consequences of tobacco use. Only one of these programs, TPEP, is completely dedicated to smoking prevention and cessation; it does, however, receive about 30 percent of Arkansas' MSA funds. Some programs primarily serve short-term health-related needs of disadvantaged Arkansas residents (AAI, Delta AHEC, MEP, MHI); others are long-term investments in the public health and health research knowledge infrastructure (ABI, COPH). Table S.1 shows the legislative appropriations and actual funding for support of these programs.

Table S.1

Appropriations and Funding for the Programs Supported by the Tobacco Settlement Funds and the Tobacco Settlement Commission

Funded Program	FY2004		FY2005		FY2006		FY2007	
	Appropriation	Funding	Appropriation	Funding	Appropriation	Funding	Appropriation	Funding[a]
Tobacco Settlement Commission	$2,417	$1,226	$2,429	$454	$638	$969	$641	TBD
Tobacco Use Prevention and Education	18,979	17,401	19,022	$15,070	17,451	15,097	15,179	13,729
AR Bioscience Institute	15,765	12,555	15,765	10,873	15,765	10,892	15,765	9,906
Medicaid Expansion[b]	20,064	16,410	20,087	14,211	27,554	14,237	13,833	12,947
College of Public Health	3,487	2,871	3,487	2,487	3,486	2,491	3,486	2,265
Delta AHEC	2,324	1,914	2,324	1,658	2,324	1,661	2,324	1,510
AR Aging Initiative	2,324	1,914	2,324	1,658	2,324	1,661	2,324	1,510
Minority Health Initiative	2,012	2,001	2,016	1,733	1,967	1,736	1,972	1,579
Total for programs	64,955	55,067	65,026	47,689	70,872	47,774	54,884	43,446

SOURCE: Arkansas Tobacco Settlement Commission.

a. Funding amounts for FY2007 are projected: actual amounts were provided on July 1, 2006, after the date this report was completed.

b. Amounts for the Medicaid Expansion represent only the Tobacco Settlement funding; these amounts are matched by federal funding according to cost sharing provisions of the Arkansas Medicaid program, which also are reflected in its total appropriations.

As part of its evaluation function, the ATSC contracted with the RAND Corporation to perform a comprehensive evaluation of the progress of the programs in fulfilling their missions, as well as their effects on smoking and other health-related outcomes. This report, the second in RAND's series of evaluations, addresses the following research questions:

- Have the programs achieved the goals that were set for them for the past two years?

- How did the programs respond to the recommendations made in earlier evaluations?

- How do actual costs for new activities compare to the budget; what are sources of any variances?

- How do the programs function with regard to the major program management process functions of governance, strategic decisionmaking, monitoring, quality improvement, financial management, and contracting?

- What effects do the programs have on improving the health of Arkansans in terms of smoking behavior, health outcomes related to tobacco use, and other health outcomes the programs address?

The answers to these questions serve to generate recommendations for how the programs, the ATSC, and other Arkansas agencies might better fulfill the aims of the Initiated Act.

SUMMARY OF PERFORMANCE THROUGH FISCAL YEAR 2006

Overall, the seven Tobacco Settlement programs have continued to refine and grow their program activities. In Chapters 3 through 9, we present assessments of each program's progress. Here, we summarize results across programs, signaling observed problems.

Achievement of Initiation and Short-Term Goals Specified by the Act

The Initiated Act stated basic goals to be achieved by the funded programs through the use of the Tobacco Settlement funds. It also defined indicators of performance for each of the programs—for program initiation, short-term, and long-term actions. In the 2004 evaluation report, we reported that MEP and MHI had not achieved the planned goals.

MEP had not achieved its initiation goals because the AR-Adults expansion program had not been approved by the federal Centers for Medicare and Medicaid Services (CMS). Additionally, MEP was underspending on two of the other three expansion programs. In the past two years, the AR-Adults expansion program has been approved and is starting up. However, underspending is still occurring for other programs within MEP.

MHI had not yet prepared a list of priority health problems for minority populations nor put together the biographical database that the act specified. Since then, MHI has released a list of priority health problems for African Americans; however, it has not provided a list for other minority populations in Arkansas, nor has it assembled the biographical database.

Program Progress on Self-generated Short-term Goals

RAND worked with each of the programs to specify short-term actions to be accomplished during FY2006. These are reported in detail in the respective evaluations of the seven programs (Chapters 3 through 9) and summarized here. This year, four programs—TPEP, COPH, Delta AHEC, and ABI—have met all of their goals and subgoals, while three programs have not. AAI fell short on the goal of putting together a database of funding opportunities. MHI did not submit an application for survey funding, increase enrollment in the Hypertension Initiative, or expand the Eating and Moving for Life Initiative. MEP did not achieve desired utilization of benefits in the AR-Seniors program or increase enrollment in that program.

ASSESSMENT OF PROGRAM MANAGEMENT PROCESSES

For the 2006 evaluation cycle, we introduced a management and governance process evaluation component, based on a questionnaire sent to all of the funded programs in advance of the in-depth interviews conducted in April 2006. The template for this form is Appendix C of this document. With this form, we requested information regarding four critical aspects of each program of the ATSC.

Our orientation for using this questionnaire is that, after four years of funding, the overall structures of the programs are largely in place, and our attention should turn to how the programs are functioning (i.e., process evaluation). While direct assessment of desired outcome measures is becoming more and more relevant, there is still a need for the major part of the evaluation to look at whether the processes necessary to promote successful outcomes are in place. Our examination covered information regarding the process of the four following components of program functioning:

- Governance leadership and strategic direction
- Monitoring and quality improvement
- Financial management
- Contract management

For each of these four components, we asked for each component in turn what the program had in place to administer the component, and then how well the processes in place were doing.

Governance Leadership and Strategic Direction

The diversity of the programs is reflected in their wide variety of governing bodies. Now that the start-up period is over, the governing bodies should play active roles in guiding the future strategic direction for the programs. These bodies also provide an important vehicle for linking a program to its environment so the program hears the views of its stakeholders and has access to vital resources. We asked each program to specify what governing and advisory boards it has and to rate the degree of involvement of these boards in performing oversight, monitoring program performance, and providing an interface with communities. These ratings are provided in the individual chapter reports of the programs and are summarized in Table S.2.

Table S.2
Governance and Advisory Boards

Program	Governing Board	Advisory Boards
TPEP	None	TPEP Advisory Board. Mostly advises on community needs and interactions
COPH	University of Arkansas Board of Trustees (from a distance)	None
Delta AHEC	University of Arkansas Board of Trustees (from a distance)	Advisory boards at each site mostly advise on community interfaces
AAI	University of Arkansas Board of Trustees (from a distance)	Reynolds Institute Community Advisory Board and boards at each regional Center on Aging advise, with considerable variation on degree of involvement
MHI	Arkansas Minority Health Commission exercises considerable oversight	Medical Advisory Board for the Hypertension Initiative, which is only minimally involved
ABI	ABI Governing Board of ex-officio appointees exercises considerable oversight	Scientific and Advisory Committees concern themselves with goals and priorities and monitor quality
MEP	None	None

The natural differences among governance patterns make simple generalization among all the programs difficult. None of the programs has much board involvement in fundraising; as budgets tighten, this could be an area where assistance could be helpful. Given the crucial role of raising funds beyond MSA amounts, boards could and perhaps should take on a greater (and often traditional) role in raising funds. Those programs that are several levels down in the organizational hierarchy from their official oversight organs can find themselves at the mercy of policies that have nothing to do with themselves, without recourse to effective intervention. Those programs that do not have advisory groups should consider forming some groups as vehicles for eliciting community input, developing strategy on pertinent issues, and identifying potential funding opportunities.

Monitoring and Quality Improvement

As of the end of FY2004, few of the programs had internal accountability mechanisms for regular monitoring and providing feedback on their progress; or, where mechanisms were in place, they relied on local program staff, who often did not have sufficient training or resources to fully comply. Such a monitoring process, when well implemented, enables programs to perform regular quality improvement and assess how well each program component is meeting its goals. This capability also can help the programs fulfill their external accountability for performance to legislators and other state policymakers. Table S.3 summarizes the quality management processes by program.

Table S.3
Quality Management

Program	Formal Quality Management Process	Monitoring capability
TPEP	Occasional external evaluations	Data collection and evaluation mechanisms in place to monitor work of contractors and grantees
COPH	Formal process in place since inception	Monitoring in place to support quality management
Delta AHEC	No overall formal process. Process for Diabetes Clinic	Some monitoring capability, but could be improved
AAI	No overall formal process. Informal tracking of activities for each Center on Aging	Little monitoring capability
MHI	No overall formal process. Process in place for Hypertension Initiative but not for others	Little monitoring capability, even for Hypertension Initiative
ABI	Formal process in place since inception	Monitoring in place to support quality management
MEP	No formal process	Monitoring capability for service delivery. Could benefit from monitoring consumers' experience

The information provided by the programs on their quality improvement activities is uneven and reflects the tradition of quality within the type of agency running the program. The more purely academic programs (COPH, ABI) have mature processes; line agencies within departments (TPEP, MEP, Delta AHEC) have no formal processes but have reporting requirements that could be the basis of processes; and specialized agencies (AAI, MHI, ATSC itself) would benefit from establishing official quality improvement regimes.

Financial Management

Our earlier evaluations showed that several of the programs have been lacking in some aspect of the accounting and bookkeeping skills needed for effective financial management. We recommended in these instances a local automated accounting system, along with additional training and support to strengthen staff ability to document spending accurately and to use this information to guide program management. Table S.4 summarizes the results of this year's assessment.

Table S.4
Financial Management

Program	Global System in Place	Program Capability for Components
TPEP	The state financial management system	Monitors program components, subcontracts, and grants through separate accounts. Staff qualified
COPH	The UAMS financial system	Monitors program components, but not separately. Staff qualified
Delta AHEC	The UAMS AHEC financial system	Monitors program components, but not separately. Staff qualified
AAI	The UAMS AHEC financial system	Components centrally monitored. Staff qualified
MHI	The state financial management system	Components not fully monitored. Staff not fully qualified
ABI	Each of the member universities has its own financial system	Program components self-monitored (as per Initiated Act). Staff qualified
MEP	The state financial management system	Monitors program components through separate accounts. Staff qualified

Contract Management

We asked each of the programs to provide information about how they manage contracts for services. Only TPEP and MHI have contracts. Both contract for expertise, while TPEP also issues subgrants for service delivery, and MHI contracts for treatment initiatives. TPEP has monthly financial tracking, monitors the quality of performance of contractees, and regularly compares contractee spending to reported activities. By contrast, MHI has monthly financial tracking only for the Hypertension Initiative, with annual financial tracking for other contracts. There is some monitoring of quality of performance, and there is no comparison of spending to activity.

PROGRAM EFFECTS ON OUTCOMES

An important part of any evaluation is examining the extent to which the programs being evaluated are having effects on the outcomes of interest. We assessed both effects on smoking outcomes and other program effects on nonsmoking outcomes.

Program Effects on Smoking Outcomes

Our analysis of smoking behavior in Arkansas provides evidence of the continued effectiveness of the Tobacco Settlement programs (primarily TPEP) on smoking outcomes, especially for the most vulnerable populations, such as young people and pregnant women. Smoking prevalence measures are largely taken from the Arkansas Division of Health Youth Tobacco Survey, the national Behavioral Risk Factor Surveillance System survey of adults, and the Arkansas Adult Tobacco Survey. Our main findings regarding smoking outcomes are summarized as follows:

- Smoking has decreased substantially among middle school and high school students since programming began.

- Tobacco Settlement programming has reduced smoking among young people, compared with what would be expected based on pre-program trends.

    o Young adults ages 18 to 25, are smoking less than previously.

    o Pregnant teenagers are smoking less than previously.

    o Pregnant women ages 20 to 29 are smoking less than previously.

- The dramatic improvement in compliance with laws prohibiting sales of tobacco products to minors has continued and has been verified by federal auditors.

- Adult smoking prevalence declined in 2005, following a slight increase in 2004, but we cannot yet confirm that this recent decline is a real effect.

- Our analysis of the variation in smoking by county does not provide evidence that people who live in areas where the TPEP activity was focused are less likely to smoke.

- There have been improvements in the rates of a variety of diseases that are affected in the short term by smoking and by secondhand smoke. The evidence is strongest in the cases of strokes and acute myocardial infarctions (heart attacks).

As in past years, our analysis of smoking rates for young adults, pregnant adults, and pregnant teenagers shows conclusively that these groups are smoking less than would be expected if there had been a continuation of the trends in rates that preceded the Tobacco Settlement programming. However, we did not observe definitive evidence of reduced adult smoking.

Program Effects on Nonsmoking Outcomes

Highlights of our findings regarding effects of the Tobacco Settlement programs that have a direct impact on health outcomes other than smoking are as follows:

- *Delta AHEC Teen Pregnancy Programming.* The Delta AHEC has made progress on collecting participant data, including satisfaction and health outcomes information. However, progress has been slow on the management and analysis of these data. We encourage the program to direct additional resources toward ensuring that data are collected and stored in a manner that lends itself to analyses that can be used to monitor program progress and evaluate participant outcomes.

- *Minority Health Initiative.* The MHI has data on outcomes for two out of three counties for its hypertension program participants, but no data for its Eating and Moving for Life initiative. RAND analysis demonstrates a possible effect of the hypertension program on blood pressure. MHI should improve its data collection in both programs and improve its data analysis capabilities.

- *Arkansas Aging Initiative.* There is some evidence that the Centers on Aging have reinforced the decline in avoidable hospitalizations in the counties where they are located. AAI data collection and analysis initiatives are making some progress toward providing useful evaluation of their programs.

- *Medicaid Benefits for Pregnant Women.* We continue to find that the expansion of benefits for pregnant women has led to increased prenatal care. We find **no** evidence that the expansion has reduced smoking among pregnant women or increased birth weights of their babies. Both of these effects would have been expected from increased care for pregnant women.

- *Expanded Medicaid Hospital Benefit.* We find some evidence that one component of the expanded hospital benefits is associated with increased access to hospital care for conditions requiring very short stays. The other component that reimburses for hospital days 21 through 24 appears to be reducing the amount of unreimbursed care rather than increasing the amount of care.

- *Expanded Medicaid Seniors Benefit.* There is weak evidence that the AR-Seniors program has accelerated the decline in avoidable hospitalizations among the elderly. We will monitor this incipient trend in future years.

For the two academic programs, COPH and ABI, we did not look at direct impact on health outcomes but instead used more traditional academic outcome measures.

- *College of Public Health.* The COPH's number of high-quality scholarly publications has increased substantially. Independent reviews of two of its leading projects confirm that the COPH is making major contributions toward the health of Arkansans.

- *Arkansas Biosciences Institute.* The ABI's publication of research findings in top-quality scholarly journals has increased dramatically over the past three years. Its research is being disseminated in respected journals in a wide variety of scientific subjects. Independent reviews of two recommended projects provide detailed verification that the major ABI projects are making significant contributions in their field.

COMMON THEMES ACROSS PROGRAMS

Our analysis identified two common themes across programs meriting attention: collaborative activities among the programs and the matching of appropriations and funding. We summarize here the discussion of these themes in Chapter 12.

Collaboration and Coordination across Programs

Collaborative activities among the programs strengthen their ability to serve the goals of the Initiated Act, to use the Tobacco Settlement funds efficiently, and to enhance needed health services for Arkansans. Different programs have different bases of expertise and can address common populations and common problems more effectively if they collaborate. Some programs have been working together since early in the program, and others have gradually increased their collaboration. Still, there is room for even more effort in this regard.

Appropriations Process and Fund Allocations

During the initial budgeting and appropriations process, several programs had appropriation allocations across expense classifications that did not fully match their operational needs. The program leaders were reluctant to make substantial changes to the fund allocations in the second biennial appropriations because doing so brought the risk of opening up the entire package to funding changes or reductions. Thus, the spending constraints experienced by the programs in the first two fiscal years were perpetuated in the FY2004–2005 biennial appropriations, which hindered several programs from using their funding effectively. We therefore recommended that the state should provide the programs with clear definitions of the appropriation line items as well as guidance for the budgeting process, so that programs understand clearly how they can use funds in each line item to support their activities.

The programs that were having the greatest problem with poorly allocated appropriations were the four programs that are part of the University of Arkansas for Medical Sciences (UAMS) system: AAI, COPH, Delta AHEC, and the UAMS portion of the ABI. UAMS submitted a proposal for reallocation of the FY2005 budgeted line items for these programs to the Peer Review Committee of the General Assembly, which approved the reallocation. For the FY2006–2007 biennial appropriations, which were completed in April 2005, the programs modified their line item allocations as needed. This step should help ensure that future program appropriations do not place artificial constraints on the programs' ability to spend according to operational needs.

TOBACCO SETTLEMENT COMMISSION

Although the primary focus of RAND's evaluation activities is on the funded programs, we have also examined the Arkansas Tobacco Settlement Commission itself. The ATSC is directed by the Initiated Act to conduct monitoring and evaluation of the funded programs "to ensure optimal impact on improving the health of Arkansans and fiscal stewardship of the

Tobacco Settlement" and "to justify continued support based upon the state's performance-based budgeting initiative."

ATSC Monitoring and Evaluating Activities

The Initiated Act directs the ATSC to develop measurable performance indicators to monitor programmatic functions that are state-specific and situation-specific and to support performance-based assessment for government accountability. In its second Biennial Report, submitted on August 1, 2004, the ATSC referenced, included as an attachment, and responded to RAND's first evaluation report covering 2002–2004 (Farley et al., 2005a). We summarize here the actions taken by the ATSC in response to each of our recommendations.

- *Quarterly Reports.* The commission should modify the content of the regular quarterly reports from the programs to require routine reports on their progress in addressing the issues identified in this evaluation. In response, the ATSC has changed the format of the quarterly reports submitted by the programs to incorporate the provisions listed in the recommendation. The programs are now submitting this information to the ATSC regularly, and the programs also are being asked to provide this information in their presentations at commission meetings.

- *Financial Reporting.* The commission should work with the state finance office and the funded programs to ensure that the programs are correcting the inadequacies of the accounting and financial management processes that this evaluation has identified. In response, the ATSC office is working to develop a financial reporting format that can provide uniformity in reporting across programs. In addition, the ATSC office has been monitoring actions by the programs to correct problems with inaccurate allocation of funds across appropriations line items. Now, all programs submit financial reports to the ATSC each quarter.

- *Technical Support.* The commission should earmark a modest portion of the Tobacco Settlement funds ($150,000 to $200,000 each year) to establish a mechanism that makes technical support available to the funded programs. This support should be targeted to help the programs correct some of the issues identified in this evaluation. The ATSC responded by developing this function as an integral part of the ATSC strategic plan. A portion of the ATSC budget was reserved to fund these activities. However, because of ceilings in the appropriations for the commission, it has been unable to purchase technical support in any significant quantity. The commission intends to request an increase in appropriation in order to implement these activities.

- *Expectations for Governing Bodies.* The commission should establish expectations for the performance of the governing bodies of the funded programs with respect to providing policy and strategic guidance for their programs, as well as monitoring program performance. The commission has not yet responded to this recommendation but is considering what to do, given the diversity of boards, commissions, and advisory groups among the various programs.

- *Enhancing Outcome Evaluations.* As the programs mature further, and more longitudinal information becomes available on outcomes, the commission should ensure that outcome evaluation work continues to document the extent of those effects. Meanwhile, the commission should interpret early outcome information with caution to ensure that conclusions regarding the programs' effectiveness are grounded on sufficient data. In response, the ATSC has emphasized to legislators that it will take time to begin to see outcomes.

Community Grants

According to the Initiated Act, if the deposits into the Arkansas Tobacco Settlement Commission Fund exceed the amount necessary to pay its expenses, then the ATSC may make grants, within its appropriation limits, to support community activities. In FY2004, the ATSC awarded its first set of 16 grants under this provision for a total of $353,678 in grants to community organizations. In the second round of community grants, awarded in FY2005, the ATSC funded 22 grants for a total of $487,522, with amounts ranging from $8,000 to $24,998. The ATSC established a requirement of quarterly reporting for the community grants, including both provision of information on progress, challenges, and successes in implementing the funded activity and reporting on grant expenditures.

Because the ATSC chose to use some of its available funds for technical support to the seven funded programs, it did not award new community grants for FY2006. Instead, it identified two existing awardees and renewed their grants.

RECOMMENDATIONS

Finally, we present our recommendation for the ATSC and for each program separately. Elaboration of the recommendations is provided in Chapter 12 for the policy issues that overarch the programs and in Chapters 3 through 9 for the individual programs.

Overall Recommendation Regarding Continued Program Funding

We again recommend this year that Tobacco Settlement funding continue to be provided to the seven funded programs. At the same time, performance expectations for the programs should be maintained actively through regular monitoring of trends in their process indicators, progress toward the newly established long-term goals, and trends in impacts on relevant outcomes. As stated in the 2004 evaluation report, we believe the programs supported by the Tobacco Settlement funds provide an effective mix of services and other resources that respond directly to many of Arkansas' priority health issues. With additional years of operation, the programs have achieved their initiation and short-term goals defined in the Initiated Act, with but one exception. The programs' impacts on health needs also can be expected to grow as they continue to evolve and increasingly leverage the Tobacco Settlement funds to attract other resources.

Overarching Policy and ATSC Recommendations

- **Aggressively seek funding to supplement the Tobacco Settlement funds.** To the extent that funding cannot be maintained, potential revisions to the funding allocations of Tobacco Settlement funds should be considered.

- **Leverage Tobacco Settlement funds.** Especially given the anticipated funding crunch, there is a need to rethink the direct service delivery components of programs that have them, and either justify the contribution of these components to people beyond the direct recipients, or eliminate these components.

- **Develop data collection and analysis plans and dedicate resources for implementing these plans.** The ATSC should provide funds for the training of program staff to accomplish these goals. These funds should be appropriated in the next General Assembly appropriations cycle.

- **Intensify the collaboration among the seven Tobacco Settlement programs.** This is most beneficial where programs experience challenges that can benefit from expertise that other programs possess.

- **Install formal quality improvement processes in each program.** Each program and the ATSC itself should have a documented formal quality management program as well as a complete reporting package through which the funded programs provide the ATSC with performance information on both their program activities and spending.

Tobacco Prevention and Education Program

- **Raise funding levels for the nine components of a comprehensive statewide tobacco control strategy to the minimums recommended by the Centers for Disease Control and Prevention (CDC) for Arkansas.** The funding share for tobacco prevention and cessation activities should be at least the percentage share stated for such activities stated in the Initiated Act.

- **Change the process TPEP uses to budget its funds to be in line with the other Tobacco Settlement programs.** Because the legislature funded an Arkansas Rainy Day Fund by shifting the first year of funds out of TPEP, budgeting is more complicated for TPEP than for the other programs receiving Tobacco Settlement funding.

- **Provide evaluation technical assistance for subcontractors and grantees.**

- **Evaluate the statewide media campaign** both in terms of output (public service announcements and community events) and focus, given that a statewide workplace smoking ban went into effect in July 2006.

- **Strengthen communication between TPEP staff and the TPEP Advisory Committee.** The TPEP Advisory Committee has a great deal of expertise that is not being fully utilized.

College of Public Health

- **Continue efforts to meet the new accreditation requirements by December 2007.** Such efforts include expanding full-time faculty for doctoral and master's programs, recruiting students for the new doctoral programs, and obtaining funding to support the additional salaries.

Delta Area Health Education Center

- **Continue to increase resources to conduct program evaluation activities.** Evaluation should be built into future programs and processes.

Arkansas Aging Initiative

- **Make fundraising across all regions one of its highest priorities**, identifying and pursuing funding opportunities through the state and federal governments, foundations, and the private sector. It may be some time before the local Community Advisory Committees are capable of the level of fundraising necessary to guarantee the long-term sustainability of the local Centers on Aging.

- **Ensure that each Center on Aging (COA) establishes and maintains a formal quality improvement process.** Systematic performance monitoring of the COAs is necessary and can be facilitated by the uniform database for tracking activities at the local level.

Minority Health Initiative

- **Improve the financial and quality management activities for all activities.** Most MHI activities continue to lack proper oversight and quality management.

- **Improve the program's capacity to carry out program activities funded by the Act and performance-monitoring activities.** The program needs to build or buy capacity to monitor both its internally funded and contracted activities.

- **Continue efforts to develop a database and design it in consideration of quality improvement processes.** The Initiating Act's mandate to create a database that includes biographical data, screening data, costs, and outcome has yet to be implemented.

- **Continue to study racial and ethnic health disparities and prioritize needs.** Prioritized needs for minorities other than African Americans have not yet been established.

- **Continue strategies to reach target populations** (i.e., minority Arkansans) across the state. MHI needs to know what part of the population its awareness efforts are reaching and if there are ways to increase health education dissemination.

- **Reassess MHI (as opposed to the normal annual cycle of assessment).** If, at that time, performance has not improved to the point where there is confidence that full functionality of the program can be achieved in a reasonable amount of time, then the MHI programming should be redistributed to other programs within the Tobacco Settlement framework. MHI is uniquely positioned to address directly the health needs and priorities of the state's minority populations. It has made some real progress in programming growth and financial reporting during FY2005, and it is spending more of its available funds than it had in the previous biennium. However, as discussed in Chapter 7, issues of declining enrollments, quality problems, and extremely high unit costs have been identified. While MHI has improved slightly on all fronts in the past year, it is still not functioning adequately. We are reluctant to repeat recommendations that have not been fully followed in the past. At the same time, the inherent value of much of the MHI programming and the important role filled by the Arkansas Minority Health Commission (AMHC) make us reluctant to recommend closing the program or moving it elsewhere. We therefore have adopted a compromise recommendation.

Arkansas Biosciences Institute

- **Be prepared to accommodate potentially severe cuts in funding.** ABI needs to continue to obtain grant funding at a level that can support the infrastructure that has been established at the different universities.

Medicaid Expansion Programs

- **Allocate funds to educate newly enrolled and current enrollees on a regular basis in the Pregnant Women's Expansion program and in the AR-Seniors program** regarding the services they are eligible to receive.

- **Initiate an outreach campaign to inform both potential enrollees and providers about the availability of the Medicaid Expansion Programs.** Enrollment trends for the Pregnant Women's Expansion have exceeded expectations but still lag behind projections. More troubling is that income-eligible elderly individuals are overlooked for enrollment in the AR-Seniors program because they are not applying for Qualified Medicare Beneficiary status.

- **Intensify efforts to meet spending targets for the expansions they support.** While the Medicaid programs are to be applauded for their intense effort in bringing the four expansion program on board, they should ensure that all four programs spend the funds available.

DISCUSSION

The Arkansas General Assembly and Tobacco Settlement Commission continue to have much to be proud of in the investment made in the seven programs supported by the Tobacco Settlement funds. COPH and ABI are particularly to be acknowledged for their contributions to improving the public health skills of Arkansans and increasing the national and global visibility of Arkansas as a locus of research applied to improving the health of the population. All programs continue to make substantial progress in expanding and strengthening the infrastructure to support the health status and health care needs of Arkansas residents. We have begun to observe effects on smoking outcomes, and with time, we believe the prospects are good for the programs to achieve observable impacts on other health-related outcomes over the next few years.

Arkansas has been unique among the states in being responsive to the basic intent of the Master Settlement Agreement by investing its funds in health-related programs with a focus on reducing smoking rates. We encourage state policymakers to reaffirm this original commitment in the Initiated Act to dedicate the Tobacco Settlement funds to support health-related programming. To do justice to the health-related services, education, and research these programs are now delivering, they must have the continued support and time they need to fulfill their mission of helping Arkansas to significantly improve the health of its residents. In addition, they must take the actions needed to ensure that issues identified in this evaluation are addressed to reinforce the effectiveness of Arkansas' investment in the health of its residents.

Acknowledgments

We acknowledge with pleasure the thoughtful participation by numerous people in the evaluation process as RAND gathered information on the context, history, and progress of the seven funded programs initiated by the Tobacco Settlement Proceeds Act. These included the members of the Arkansas Tobacco Settlement Commission (ATSC), members of the Arkansas General Assembly, and program directors and staff at the Department of Health, College of Public Health, Arkansas Biosciences Institute, Centers on Aging, Arkansas Minority Health Commission, Delta Area Health Education Center, and state Medicaid offices. These individuals participated in group and individual interviews, sharing their experiences in the history, context, and progress of the funded programs. They also engaged with RAND in the development of long-range program goals and outcome measures.

We would also like to acknowledge the assistance and guidance of the Arkansas Tobacco Settlement Commission during the execution of our evaluation, including those of Chiquita Munir; General William Lefler, commission chair; and the commission members. Their support derives from a commitment to objective evaluation that continues to reinforce our evaluation work.

We obtained valuable constructive criticisms of earlier drafts of this report from the ATSC and its programs, as well as Charles L. Gruder, executive director of Special Research Programs, University of California Office of the President, and RAND colleagues James Zazzali and Suzanne Wenzel.

Abbreviations and Acronyms

AAA	Area Agencies on Aging
AAI	Arkansas Aging Initiative
AASIS	Arkansas Administrative Statewide Information System
AATS	Arkansas Adult Tobacco Survey
ABI	Arkansas Biosciences Institute
ACH	Arkansas Children's Hospital
ACS	American Cancer Society
ADA	American Diabetes Association
ADFY	Arkansans for Drug-Free Youth
ADH	Arkansas Department/Division of Health
ADHE	Arkansas Department of Higher Education
AFMC	Arkansas Foundation for Medical Care
AGEC	Arkansas Geriatric Education Center
AHA	American Heart Association
AHEC	Area Health Education Center
AMHC	Arkansas Minority Health Commission
ARCHES	Arkansas Cardiovascular Health Survey
AR-GEMS	Arkansas Geriatric Education Mentors and Scholars
Arkansas INBRE	Arkansas IDeA Network of Biomedical Research Excellence
ASNB	Arkansas Safety Net Benefit
ASU	Arkansas State University
ATCB	Arkansas Tobacco Control Board
ATSC	Arkansas Tobacco Settlement Commission
BRFSS	Behavioral Risk Factor Surveillance System
CAB	Community Advisory Board
CAC	Community Advisory Committee
CBPR	Community-Based Participatory Research
CDC	Centers for Disease Control and Prevention

CEPH	Council on Education for Public Health
CHART	Coalition for Healthy Arkansas Today
CHC	Community Health Center
CHIP	Children's Health Insurance Program
CJRW	Cranford, Johnson, Robinson, Woods
CMH	Crittenden Memorial Hospital
CMS	Centers for Medicare and Medicaid Services
CoA	Center of Aging
COA	Center on Aging
COANE	Centers on Aging Northeast
COPH	College of Public Health
CPR	Cardiopulmonary resuscitation
CPS	Current Population Survey
CTFA	Coalition for Tobacco-Free Arkansas
CY	Calendar Year
DCO	Division of County Operations
DEC	Dean's Executive Committee
Delta AHEC	Delta Area Health Education Center
DEQ	Department of Environmental Quality
DFA	Department of Finance Authority
DHEC	Delta Health Education Center
DHHS	Department of Health and Human Services
DHS	Department of Human Services
DMS	Division of Medical Services
DrPH	Doctor of Public Health
EMFL	Eating and Moving for Life Initiative
EPSCoR	Experimental Program to Stimulate Competitive Research
FFP	Federal Financial Participation
FFY	Federal Fiscal Year
FORECAST	Formative Evaluation, Consultation, and Systems Technique
FPL	Federal Poverty Level

FTE	Full-Time Equivalent
FY	Fiscal Year
GEC	Geriatric Education Center
HETC	Health Education and Training Center
HPPR	Health Promotion and Prevention Research
HRSA	Health Resources and Services Administration
HSR	Health Systems Research
ILC	International Longevity Center
ISI	Institute for Scientific Information
JD	Juris Doctor
JIF	Journal Impact Factor
M&O	Maintenance and Operations
MASH	Medical Application of Science for Health
MEP	Medicaid Expansion Programs
MESH	Marianna Examination Survey on Hypertension
MHI	Minority Health Initiative
MISRGO	Minority Initiative Sub-Recipient Grant Office
MPH	Master of Public Health
MSA	Master Settlement Agreement
NIOSH	National Institute of Occupational Safety and Health
OCBPH	Office of Community-Based Public Health
PEPPI	Peer Education Program Promotes Independence
PharmD	Doctor of Pharmacy
PI	Principal Investigator
PSA	Public Service Announcement
QIO	Quality Improvement Organization
QMB	Qualified Medicare Beneficiary
RFP	Request for Proposals
SACOA	South Arkansas COA
SAMHSA	Substance Abuse and Mental Health Services Administration
SAP	Systems Applications Processes

SCCOA	South Central COA
SCHIP	State Children's Health Insurance Plan
SHC	Senior Health Clinic
SOS	Stomp Out Smoking
SSI	Supplemental Security Income
SURF	State Undergraduate Research Fellowship
SWAT	Students Working Against Tobacco
SWOT	Strengths, Weaknesses, Opportunities, and Threats
TPEP	Tobacco Prevention and Education Program
TRCOA	Texarkana Regional COA
UA	University of Arkansas
UALR	University of Arkansas Little Rock
UA-Ag	University of Arkansas, Division of Agriculture
UAF	University of Arkansas, Fayetteville
UAMS	University of Arkansas for Medical Sciences
UAPB	University of Arkansas at Pine Bluff
USDA	United States Department of Agriculture
YRBSS	Youth Risk Behavior Surveillance System
YTS	Youth Tobacco Survey

Chapter 1
Introduction and Background

The Master Settlement Agreement (MSA) that ended years of legal battles between the states and the major tobacco companies was signed on November 23, 1998. Under the terms of the MSA, the participating states will receive more than $206 billion in payments from the tobacco companies over the next 25 years. Following the agreement made by the attorneys general of the participating states, Arkansas has a 0.828 percent share of these payments, which it has been receiving since the agreement went into effect.

The state of Arkansas is unique in the commitment that has been made by both elected officials and the general public to invest its share of the MSA funds in health-related programs. A comprehensive program using the MSA funds to invest in the public health of Arkansans was established by the Tobacco Settlement Proceeds Act, a referendum passed by the voters in the November 2000 election (henceforth called the Initiated Act).

The Initiated Act created the Arkansas Tobacco Settlement Commission (ATSC), giving it the responsibility for monitoring and evaluating the performance of the funded programs. As part of its evaluation function, the ATSC contracted with the RAND Corporation to serve as an external evaluator. RAND was charged with performing a comprehensive evaluation of the programs' progress in fulfilling their missions, as well as effects of these programs on smoking and other health-related outcomes.

This report is the second Biennial Report from the RAND evaluation, which updates our findings presented in the first evaluation report (Farley et al., 2005a). An interim report was submitted to the ATSC (Farley et al., 2005b) in June 2005, updating our assessment of program progress during the year following the first Biennial Report. This second Biennial Report incorporates and updates findings provided in the 2005 interim report.

In the remainder of this chapter, we provide background information about the MSA, the basic orientation and content of the Initiated Act, and the methods used in the RAND evaluation. Chapter 2 addresses the policy context within which the Tobacco Settlement program operates, including activities and progress of the ATSC. Chapters 3 through 9 present evaluation results regarding the activities and progress of each of the seven funded programs. Chapters 10 and 11 present findings regarding trends in the programs' effects on smoking and other outcomes. Finally, Chapter 12 synthesizes evaluation findings and offers recommendations for program improvement and future spending of the Tobacco Settlement funds.

THE MASTER SETTLEMENT AGREEMENT

The MSA settled all legal matters alleged by the participating states against the participating tobacco companies, placed conditions on the actions of the tobacco companies, and provided for large payments from those companies to the states and several specific funds. All the states except Florida, Minnesota, Mississippi, and Texas are participants in the MSA, as are the District of Columbia and several U.S. territories.

1

Under the MSA, the tobacco companies are to make three types of payments to the states: up-front payments (1998–2003), annual payments, and payments to the Strategic Contribution Fund. In addition to the state payments, the MSA places other conditions on the tobacco companies, some involving additional payments and others placing constraints on their business practices, in particular with respect to marketing of tobacco products to youth.

The up-front payments totaled $12.7 billion, with $2.4 billion paid in 1998 and a like amount (adjusted for inflation) paid annually for the next four years. The annual payments to the states currently are supposed to total $183.7 billion. These payments are supposed to ramp up over time, with payments specified in the MSA of $4.5 billion in 2000, $5 billion in 2001, $6.5 billion in each of 2002 and 2003, and $8 billion annually in 2004 through 2007. Payments in 2008 through 2017 will be $8.1 billion annually, and payments in later years will be $9 billion annually. Starting in 2008 and continuing through 2017, the tobacco companies will pay $861 million annually into the Strategic Contribution Fund, for a total payment of $8.6 billion. Payments to the fund will be allocated to states based on a formula developed by the attorneys general. This formula reflects the contribution made by the states to resolution of the state lawsuits against the tobacco companies.

All of the payments to the states are subject to a number of adjustments, reductions, and offsets, so the actual payments the states receive differ from the base amounts defined in the MSA. These differences include adjustments for inflation, volume, nonsettling states' reduction, miscalculated and disputed claims offset, nonparticipating manufacturers, federal legislation offset, and litigation releasing parties offset. In fact, the ATSC anticipates—based upon its own experience—that the annual payments, rather than increasing over time, will be significantly reduced.

THE ARKANSAS TOBACCO SETTLEMENT PROCEEDS ACT

The Initiated Act (reproduced in this document as Appendix A) authorized the creation of seven separate initiatives to be supported by Tobacco Settlement funds, established short- and long-term goals for the performance of these initiatives, specified the funding shares to support the programs and a structure of funds for management and distribution of proceeds, and established the Arkansas Tobacco Settlement Commission to oversee the overall program. Subsequent legislation made slight modifications to some of the goals and programs, but all are essentially as they were originally intended.

The goals of the Initiated Act are (1) to reduce the initiation of tobacco use and increase its cessation, with the resulting health and economic impact; (2) to expand access to health care, especially for those who demonstrably lack access; (3) to develop basic and applied tobacco-related medical and agricultural research in Arkansas; and (4) to specifically address Targeted State Needs. From these goals the seven programs follow naturally:

- **Tobacco Prevention and Education Program (TPEP).** This program is to reduce the initiation of tobacco use and resulting negative health and economic impacts. It is managed by the Department of Health and Human Services (DHHS). It was originally called the Tobacco Prevention and Cessation Program and managed by the Arkansas Department of Health. A managerial change took place in 2005 when a government reorganization merged the Department of Health into the newly created DHHS.

- **Medicaid Expansion Programs (MEP).** This program is to expand access to health care through targeted expanded benefits packages that supplement the standard Arkansas Medicaid benefits. It is also managed by DHHS.

- **Arkansas Biosciences Institute (ABI).** This program is to develop new tobacco-related medical and agricultural research initiatives, to improve health of Arkansans, improve access to new technologies, and stabilize the economic security of Arkansas. The Initiated Act provides for ABI to be funded through separate appropriations to the participating institutions. The program's management reports to the ABI Board, which also was established by the Initiated Act.

The remaining four programs addressed the Targeted State Needs in the Initiated Act:

- **College of Public Health (COPH).** The college (originally called the School of Public Health in the Initiated Act) is a resource to provide professional education, research, and services to the public health community of Arkansas. It is a unit of the University of Arkansas for Medical Sciences (UAMS).

- **Arkansas Aging Initiative (AAI).** This program is to provide community-based health education for senior Arkansas residents, through outreach to the elderly and educational services for professionals. It is housed in the Reynolds Center on Aging, a unit of UAMS.

- **Delta Area Health Education Center (Delta AHEC).** This is an additional unit in the statewide Arkansas Delta AHEC system to provide clinical education; it was put into the Initiated Act to provide such services for the underserved and disproportionately poor Delta region of the state.

- **Minority Health Initiative (MHI).** This program is to identify the special health needs of Arkansas' minority communities and to put into place health care services to address these needs. It is managed by the Arkansas Minority Health Commission.

Only one of these programs, TPEP, is completely dedicated to smoking prevention and cessation; it does, however, receive one-third of the MSA funds. Some programs (AAI, Delta AHEC, MEP, MHI) primarily serve the current health-related needs of disadvantaged Arkansas residents; others (ABI, COPH) are long-term investments in the public health and health research infrastructure.

Long-term Performance Expectations for the Funded Programs

In addition to the overall goals, the act defined indicators of performance for each of the funded programs—for program initiation and short-term and long-term actions. In the 2004 evaluation report, we assessed the performance of the seven programs on their initiation and short-term indicators. It is premature to draw conclusions regarding the programs' long-term performance indicators because, as discussed in Chapter 10, it is still too early in the life of the programs to observe effects on many measures of health behaviors or health status. Refer to Chapter 12 for discussion of long-term performance goals.

Funding and Fund Flows

The act authorized the State Board of Finance to receive all disbursements from the MSA Escrow and to oversee the distribution of the funds as specified in the act. The fund structure and distribution of funding shares by programs are displayed graphically in Figure 1.1. The MSA disbursements are deposited into the Tobacco Settlement Cash Holding Fund, from which funds are to be distributed to other funds. The other funds consist of the Tobacco Settlement Debt Service Fund, the Arkansas Healthy Century Trust Fund, the Tobacco Settlement Program Fund, the Arkansas Tobacco Settlement Commission Fund, and the program accounts.

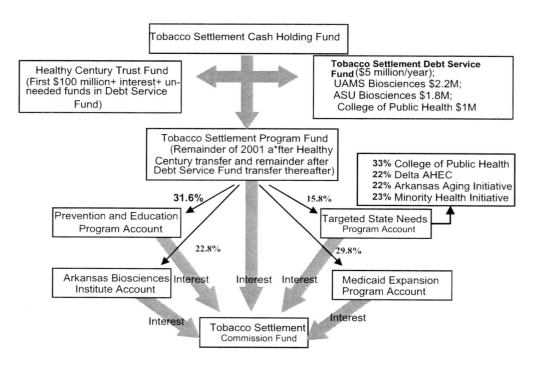

SOURCE: modified from 2001Arkansas Bureau of Legislative Research; Fiscal Review Division

Figure 1.1—Flow of Master Settlement Funds Received by Arkansas, as Defined in the Initiated Act

In calendar year 2001, $100 million of the first MSA funds received (mostly the up-front payments) were deposited in the Arkansas Healthy Century Trust Fund. This trust fund is intended to serve as a long-term resource to support health-related activities.

Interest earned by the fund may be used to pay expenses related to the responsibilities of the State Board of Finance, as well as programs and projects related to health care services, health education, and health-related research as designated in legislation adopted by the general assembly. Since then, no additional MSA funds have been placed in this trust fund.

The remainder of the 2001 funds and funds for each subsequent year have been deposited in the Tobacco Settlement Cash Holding Fund. Each year, the first $5 million in funds are transferred to the Tobacco Settlement Debt Service Fund, to pay the debt service on bonds for three capital improvement projects (debt service limits shown in Figure 1.1) for the University of Arkansas for Medical Sciences Biosciences Research building, College of Public Health building, and the Arkansas State University Biosciences Research building. The remaining amounts are transferred to the Tobacco Settlement Program Fund for distribution to program accounts for the funded programs, according to the percentages shown in Figure 1.1.

The programs, as well as the ATSC itself, receive biennial appropriations from the legislature. These appropriations are not cash allocations but are instead maximum amounts that the programs can spend, by category of spending. Programs have both years of each biennium to spend the Tobacco Settlement funds they receive (i.e., they are allowed to carry over unspent funds from the first to the second year of any biennium). However, any funds that remain unspent at the end of the biennium are returned to the Tobacco Settlement Program Fund and then are redistributed across all the funded programs according to the percentage distributions of funding established within the act. MEP is an exception to this provision because it has delayed payments of claims for health care costs incurred (Initiated Act, section 8[e]), and TPEP is an exception because of a shifting of the first year of funds, which has had cascading effects. These exceptions are discussed in the subsection immediately below.

The State Board of Finance invests all moneys held in the Tobacco Settlement Program Fund and the program accounts. Interest earned on funds in the Tobacco Settlement Program Fund is used to pay the expenses of the ATSC and is transferred to the ATSC on July 1 of each year.

If the deposits into the Arkansas Tobacco Settlement Commission Fund exceed the amount necessary for ATSC expenses, then the ATSC is authorized to make grants to nonprofit and community-based organizations for activities to improve and optimize the health of Arkansans and to minimize future tobacco-related illness and health care costs in Arkansas. Grant awards may be made up to $50,000 per year for each eligible organization, and funds are to be invested in solutions that work effectively and efficiently in Arkansas.

Emergency Provisions for Medicaid Expansion Programs and TPEP Program Shortfalls

Within a year following the Tobacco Settlement appropriations, Arkansas experienced a budgetary crisis that put the state Medicaid program at serious risk. In a special session in 2002, the general assembly declared an emergency and made two changes to the Initiated Act to provide emergency funding for the Medicaid program to mitigate the threat to its ability to provide adequate care to the state's neediest citizens.

The first change was a modification of the Medicaid Expansion Programs account so that funds in that account could also be used to supplement current general Medicaid revenues, if approved by the governor and the chief fiscal officer of the state for the Arkansas Medicaid Program. Funds could not be used for this purpose, however, if such usage reduced the funds made available by the general assembly for the Meals-on-Wheels program and the senior prescription drug program.

The second change was the funding of an Arkansas Rainy Day Fund by shifting the first year of funds out of the Tobacco Prevention and Cessation Program account. The purpose of the Rainy Day Fund is to make moneys available to assist the state Medicaid program in maintaining its established levels of service in the event that the current revenue forecast is not collected. As a result of this shift in funds, the DHHS has been placed in the position each year of borrowing funds to support its tobacco prevention and education activities, which then are repaid in the next cycle of Tobacco Settlement funds.

EVALUATION APPROACH

The ATSC Monitoring and Evaluation Function

The Initiated Act directed the ATSC to monitor and evaluate the funded programs to ensure optimal impact on improving the health of Arkansans and fiscal stewardship of the Tobacco Settlement. The evaluation is to assess the programs to justify continued support of the funded programs based upon the state's performance-based budgeting initiative. The act specified the following provisions for ATSC evaluation:

- Programs are to be administered pursuant to a strategic plan that encompasses a mission statement, defined programs, program goals with measurable objectives, and strategies to be implemented over a specific time frame.

- Evaluation of each program is to include performance-based measures for accountability that will measure specific health-related results.

- All expenditures from the Tobacco Settlement Program Fund and the program accounts are subject to the same fiscal control as are expenditures from state treasury funds.

- The chief fiscal officer of the state may require additional controls, procedures, and reporting requirements that are determined to be necessary to carry out the Act.

RAND Evaluation Methods

The evaluation approach we have designed responds to the intent of the ATSC to perform a longitudinal evaluation of the development and ongoing operation of its funding program. We employ an iterative evaluation process through which information is tracked on both the program implementation processes and any effects on identified outcomes. This information can be used to inform future funding considerations by the ATSC and general assembly as well as decisions by the funded programs regarding their goals and operations. The evaluation addresses the following four research questions:

- Have the funded programs developed and implemented their programming as specified in the Tobacco Settlement Proceeds Act of 2000 (taking into account any subsequent legislative modifications)?

- What factors are contributing to the programs' implementation successes or challenges?

- How do actual costs compare to budget; what are sources of any variances?

- What effects do the funded programs have on improving the health of Arkansans?

The logic model that guides our evaluation design is presented in Figure 1.2. This model identifies a two-tiered structure for the ATSC and its funded programs, which is mirrored in the evaluation design. On the left side of Figure 1.2, the ATSC itself is at the program policy level, providing advice to the general assembly in three major areas: selection of programs to fund, definition of goals for these programs to achieve, and monitoring effects of the funded programs' activities on the program goals. The second level is the funded programs, which perform activities to establish and carry out their work, monitor their progress toward goals, and assess their effects on outcomes of interest.

The evaluation, shown in the right side of the diagram, also consists of two levels—policy-level and program-level evaluations. Within the program evaluations, we perform a process evaluation to document the implementation processes, including relationships between the programs' goals and actions and the successes and challenges they experienced. We also perform an outcome evaluation to assess the extent to which the program interventions are achieving the intended outcomes for both program activities and the health status of the state population. This approach was taken to ensure that the evaluation of the programs is performed within the correct policy context, and that the results of the program-level evaluation are synthesized to generate usable information for future policy decisions by the commission and the general assembly. Further, the program evaluation results were designed to be useful to the individual programs for decisions on future program goals, strategies, and operational modifications. The evaluation components and methods are described further in Appendix B.

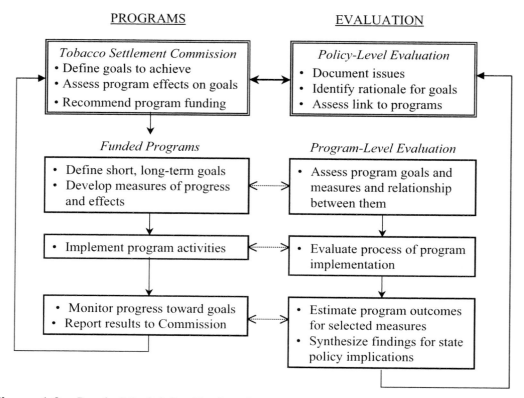

Figure 1.2—Logic Model for Evaluation of the Arkansas Tobacco Settlement Program

Implicit in this logic model is an important design principle that is central to most of the evaluations that RAND Health performs. In our view, the most effective evaluation is one that provides a vehicle for program leaders and participants to gain new knowledge that they can apply to strengthen the program for which they are responsible. We can learn from both successes and challenges in program operation. This principle is relevant to the Arkansas Tobacco Settlement Commission, which has been given the responsibility to oversee the Tobacco Settlement program and advise the general assembly and governor on future use of this funding. It also is relevant to the individual programs supported by Tobacco Settlement funding, which are expected to achieve the outcomes defined as priorities by the Initiated Act.

Process Evaluation Questionnaire

For the evaluation cycle of 2006, we introduced a governance and management process evaluation component, based on a questionnaire sent to all of the funded programs in advance of the in-depth interviews conducted in April 2006. The template for this form is Appendix C of this document. With this form, we requested information regarding four critical aspects of each program of the ATSC.

Our orientation for using this questionnaire is that, after four years of funding, the overall structures of the programs are largely in place, and our attention should turn to looking at how the programs are functioning (i.e., evaluation of process of program implementation, as shown in Figure 1.2). While direct assessment of desired outcome measures is becoming more and more relevant, there is still a need for the major part of the evaluation to look at whether the processes necessary to promote successful outcomes are in place. Our examination covered information regarding the process of the four following components of program functioning, namely:

- Governing and advisory boards
- Financial management and accounting
- Contracting and oversight
- Quality improvement.

For each of these four components, we asked for each component in turn what the program had in place to administer the components, and then how well the processes in place were doing. We did this with a combination of "circle the best answer" questions and short open-ended questions.

In addition to these four components, we asked for short answers with regard to two aspects of continuous program monitoring, namely:

- Progress on program goals (as specified in Farley et al., 2005b)
- Responses to RAND recommendations (as specified in that same document).

Whereas the four components are designed to apply to all ATSC programs, the continuous program monitoring and information we asked for were specific to the goals and RAND recommendations of each program.

Chapter 2
The ATSC Policy Context in 2005–2006

To effectively assess the performance of the Arkansas Tobacco Settlement program and the work of the funded programs, we must consider the program in the context of legislative and other events of the past two years. In this chapter, we first examine the funds received by Arkansas as its share of the Master Settlement Agreement and compare them to the planned payments in that agreement. We then look at the appropriations by the legislature to the ATSC and programs and compare them to the Tobacco Settlement funds actually received. Next, we turn to the government environment of the past two years and discuss the tobacco-related and other changes relevant to the mission of the ATSC. Finally, we discuss the activities of the Arkansas Tobacco Settlement Commission as it fulfills its mandate to provide oversight and monitoring of the performance of the funded programs as well as the funding of other community grants.

TOBACCO SETTLEMENT FUNDS RECEIVED BY ARKANSAS

According to the agreement made by the attorneys general of the participating states, Arkansas receives 0.828 percent of all funds paid to the states. From 1998 through 2002, Arkansas received $221,548,000 from the MSA, including both up-front payments and annual payments. Table 2.1 shows the amounts planned to be received and those actually received by Arkansas in subsequent years, after the annual payments were in full swing. The planned amount for FY2003 includes both the annual amount and the last installment of the up-front amount.

Table 2.1
Planned and Received Tobacco Settlement Amounts, FY2003-2007

Fiscal Year	MSA Planned Total Amount	Arkansas' Share (0.828 percent)	Received by Arkansas	Percentage Adjustment
2003	8,900	73.69	$62.18	-15.6
2004	8,000	66.24	60.07	-9.3
2005	8,000	66.24	51.50	-23.3
2006	8,000	66.24	52.77	-20.3
2007	8,000	66.24	48.45[a]	-27.9

SOURCE: Arkansas Tobacco Settlement Commission.

a. FY2003 MSA planned amount includes $2.7 billion in up-front payments.

Although under the terms of the MSA, fund receipts to Arkansas should remain stable for many years, the experience and future expectation is entirely different, as supported by Table 2.1. The discrepancy between the planned MSA amount and the actual amount paid is generally growing over time, and there are fears that the annual payments, rather than stabilizing in the $60–$70 million range, may fall to as little as half that amount.

According to the Initiated Act, funding to the programs is based on a percentage of Tobacco Settlement receipts, which means that when Arkansas fund receipts decline, all the funded programs share equally in the reduction of support. Worse, because the $5 million Debt Service Fund is taken as a flat subtraction from the MSA amount, the percentage reduction for each program is actually greater than that shown in Table 2.1. Impacts of funding reductions in the first few years were limited because the programs were just building their operations and were not yet spending all of the available funds. Now the programs are at full operation and, with a few exceptions, they are using all the funding available to them. The shortfall thus experienced has put observable constraints on the programs' ability to carry out their missions; the likely further reductions could jeopardize the very existence of some of the programs.

APPROPRIATIONS FOR THE FUNDED PROGRAMS

The Arkansas General Assembly has passed three biennial appropriations for the funds paid into the Tobacco Settlement program since the program's inception in FY2002 (July 2001). Although the percentage distribution of Tobacco Settlement funds are determined by the Initiated Act (see Figure 1.1), the appropriations need not match. Moreover, the legislative appropriations do not represent actual allocations of funds, but rather, spending ceilings for the programs.

Table 2.2 presents the appropriations and actual funding for the four most recent fiscal years FY2004 to FY2007, separately for each program, as well as for the commission itself. In examining this table, it should be kept in mind that the funds available for the programs are designated from the Tobacco Settlement funds received by Arkansas, whereas the commission is funded from interest earned on the Tobacco Settlement funds. Additionally, this table shows financial input to the programs and commission, not spending; program spending is detailed separately in the chapters of this report discussing the individual programs.

Within each biennium, the funded programs may carry over unspent funds from the first to the second year of the biennium. Therefore, in a given year, a program may underspend or overspend in comparison to the relevant annual appropriation, as long as the two-year appropriation limit is not exceeded. Exceptions to this biennial limit have been made for two programs—TPEP and the Medicaid Expansion Programs—because of circumstances unique to these programs. (See Chapters 3 and 9, respectively, for details on the exceptions.) In addition to the Tobacco Settlement funding, programs may (and are encouraged to) obtain and spend funding from other sources to further develop and sustain their programming; these sources are not included in either the appropriations or funding of Table 2.2.

Table 2.2
Appropriations and Funding for the Programs Supported by the Tobacco Settlement Funds and the Tobacco Settlement Commission

Funded Program	FY2004		FY2005		FY2006		FY2007	
	Appropriation	Funding	Appropriation	Funding	Appropriation	Funding	Appropriation	Funding[a]
Tobacco Settlement Commission	$2,417	$1,226	$2,429	$454	$638	$969	$641	TBD
Tobacco Use Prevention and Education	18,979	17,401	19,022	15,070	17,451	15,097	15,179	13,729
AR Bioscience Institute	15,765	12,555	15,765	10,873	15,765	10,892	15,765	9,906
Medicaid Expansion[b]	20,064	16,410	20,087	14,211	27,554	14,237	13,833	12,947
College of Public Health	3,487	2,871	3,487	2,487	3,486	2,491	3,486	2,265
Delta AHEC	2,324	1,914	2,324	1,658	2,324	1,661	2,324	1,510
AR Aging Initiative	2,324	1,914	2,324	1,658	2,324	1,661	2,324	1,510
Minority Health Initiative	2,012	2,001	2,016	1,733	1,967	1,736	1,972	1,579
Total for programs	64,955	55,067	65,026	47,689	70,872	47,774	54,884	43,446

SOURCE: Arkansas Tobacco Settlement Commission.

a. Funding amounts for FY2007 are projected; actual amounts will be provided on July 1, 2006.

b. Amounts for the Medicaid Expansion represent only the Tobacco Settlement funding; these amounts are matched by federal funding according cost sharing provisions of the Arkansas Medicaid program, which also are reflected in its total appropriations.

13

As shown in Table 2.2, the appropriations always exceeded the funding for every program and every fiscal year. Generally, but not always, the appropriations for the seven funded programs were close to proportional to the allocation proportions of the Initiated Act.

The appropriations and funding for the Medicaid Expansion Programs in Table 2.2 represent just the share covered by the Tobacco Settlement funds. After fairly stable appropriations through FY2005, the Medicaid appropriation for the third biennium increased to $27.6 million for FY2006 and decreased to $13.8 million for FY2007. The Tobacco Settlement funding for Medicaid is leveraged by federal matching at a rate of $3 for every state dollar for costs of medical services and a one-to-one match for program administration costs. This means that the total appropriation and funding for the Medicaid Expansion Programs are approximately 2.9 times the amounts shown in Table 2.2.

By contrast to the programs' appropriations, the ATSC appropriation in FY2006 and FY2007 was less than the amount of funding the commission actually received from interest in the Settlement funds. As a result, the commission could not spend all the funds it had available. This meant that the commission could not purchase the technical assistance for the programs that was recommended by RAND in the first biennial evaluation report—not because the funds were unavailable, but because the appropriation would have been exceeded.

The distribution of the appropriations across programs is shown graphically in Figure 2.1. The first year appropriation is only 40 percent of the FY2003 appropriation. This graph shows clearly the dominant shares of the appropriations for the three largest programs. The four Targeted State Needs programs together have only 16 percent of the total Tobacco Settlement appropriations through FY2005, and their share decreases to 14 percent in FY2006 and then increases to 18 percent by FY2007.

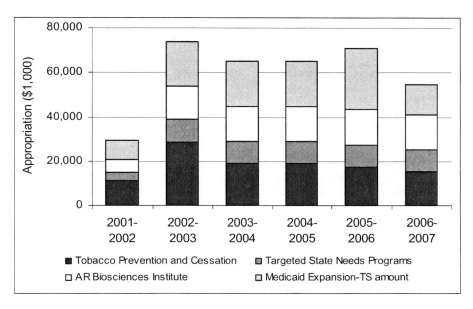

NOTE: Targeted State Needs programs consist of the College of Public Health, Delta AHEC, Arkansas Aging Initiative, and Minority Health Initiative.

Figure 2.1—Distribution of Annual Tobacco Settlement Appropriations across Funded Programs

LEGISLATIVE ACTIVITY AFFECTING THE TOBACCO SETTLEMENT PROGRAM

The Arkansas General Assembly held its 85th session during FY2005 and held a special session in April 2006, during which several bills were filed that could or did affect the Arkansas Tobacco Settlement program. They included several bills to establish smoke-free public places (some passed and some failed), a bill (failed) to use interest earned on Tobacco Settlement funds to support services by Community Health Centers in the state, and a bill (passed) to merge the state Department of Human Services with the Department of Health.

Controlling Use of Tobacco in Public Places

As discussed in the 2004 evaluation report and again in this report, state-level legislation controlling use of tobacco products in public places is an important "leg of a three-legged stool," in which the other legs are tobacco prevention and cessation programs (discussed in Chapter 3), and tax increases on tobacco products. The state legislature voted to increase cigarette taxes to 59 cents per pack in June 2003. While this represents a substantial increase from 34 cents per pack in July 2001, Arkansas is ranked 29th in the United States, and its tax rate is below the national average of 84.5 cents per pack. Making cigarettes more expensive through increased taxes continues to be an effective way to reduce and prevent tobacco use (Emery et al., 2001; Harris and Chan, 1998; Tauras, 2004). Interestingly, while tobacco use decreased in Arkansas after the increase in taxes, tobacco purchases increased in 2006 in the western part of the state, after Oklahoma voters passed a referendum to raise that state's cigarette taxes to $1.03 per pack.

During the 85th session of the Arkansas General Assembly, several bills were filed that would establish stronger rules for smoke-free environments in the state. Laws such as these have been found to reduce tobacco use. As shown in Table 2.3, only one of the bills was enacted during the regular session of the legislature; however, a special session of the general assembly called by the governor in April 2006 passed two bills. The strongest failed measure in the regular session was HB 1390, which would have prohibited sale or use of tobacco products in all public places. The other three failed measures passed the Senate but not the House. The only smoke-free environment bill enacted in the regular session was Act 135, which prohibits use of tobacco products in or on the grounds of medical facilities.

Even though the proffered bills were largely unsuccessful, the notion of protecting the public and employees from the increasingly recognized hazards of secondhand smoke was increasingly favored by public opinion. Several communities passed ordinances to restrict smoking in public places, but always in the face of claims by opponents that the economy (especially in the hospitality sector) would suffer (see Chapter 3 for details).

Matters came to a head during the first week of April 2006, when the governor called a special session of the general assembly. Included in the list of items for the special session was a major bill entitled the Arkansas Clean Indoor Air Act. This bill was rapidly and overwhelmingly passed by the Senate and—after only moderate resistance—also by the House, and it was sent to the governor, who signed it into law. Independently, a legislator offered an additional bill (passed and signed as Act 13 of 2006) that prohibits smoking in automobiles carrying a child who is restrained in a safety seat. Police are empowered to pull over and cite motorists they observe in violation of Act 13. However, fines may be waived if the motorist can prove that he or she is participating in a smoking cessation program (analogous to attending driving safety school when ticketed for a moving violation).

Table 2.3
Smoke-Free Environment Bills Proposed in the 85th Session of the Arkansas General Assembly

Bill Number	Status of Bill	Purpose of Bill
HB 1193	Enacted (Act 135 in 2005)	Prohibits the use of tobacco products in and on the grounds of all medical facilities in Arkansas
HB 1390	Died in committee	Would prohibit the sale of tobacco products and prohibit the use of tobacco products in public
HB 1883	Failed in House	Would prohibit the smoking of tobacco products in food service establishments in Arkansas
HB 2056	Failed in House	Would prohibit smoking in county-owned facilities
HB 2684	Failed in House	Would prohibit smoking in or near state buildings
SB 19	Enacted (Act 8 of 2006)	Prohibits smoking in most enclosed areas within places of employment; within any government-owned, -leased, or -operated space; and in most enclosed public places
HB 1046	Enacted (Act 13 of 2006)	Prohibits smoking in all motor vehicles carrying children who are restrained in safety seats

The Arkansas Clean Indoor Air Act

Passage of this act, especially after the failure of the various bills proposed in the 2005 session of the general assembly, represents a major step in tobacco control for Arkansas. This law applies to all types of businesses to prohibit smoking in enclosed areas within places of employment; within any government-owned, -leased, or -operated space; or in enclosed public places. The definition of "public place" is broad and covers almost all indoor or enclosed places where people might congregate except those where tobacco purchase or use is an expressed main activity. The act contains exceptions for very small businesses, as well as for restaurants and bars where people under the age of 21 may not be present. Hotels are largely smoke-free; 20 percent of rooms are to be designated for smoking, although hotels with fewer than 25 rooms may request exemption from the smoke-free requirement.

The act took effect on July 1, 2006. Its effect on smoking behaviors will be to a considerable extent determined by the nature and intensity of enforcement efforts. The act has consequences for TPEP, because previous efforts within the program to encourage local communities to enact smoking restrictions are no longer at issue; although the act does permit local governments to enact more stringent restrictions, the reality is that few such governments will feel the need to do so in the near future. Instead, efforts will go to enforcement of the provisions of the act. Data collection to measure the effects of the act will be crucial, and a number of the programs within the aegis of the Tobacco Settlement Commission (e.g., TPEP, College of Public Health) could play a significant role.

Proposed Use of Tobacco Settlement Funds to Support Community Health Centers

During the 85th session, the Community Health Centers of Arkansas sought state funding to help support the services delivered through subgrants to Community Health Centers for provision of primary medical, dental, mental health, pharmacy, and preventive services targeted to uninsured and underinsured Arkansans in medically underserved areas. Its original proposal, delineated in HB 1906, would have diverted $4 million in interest earned on the Tobacco Settlement funds invested in the $100 million Arkansas Healthy Century Trust Fund to create a Community Health Centers of Arkansas Fund to support these services. This bill did not pass, dying in House committee. An alternative bill (HB 1907) did pass, becoming Act 2309, which appropriated $5 million in general funds to support these services.

Merger of Department of Health with Department of Human Services

In April 2005, during its 85th session, the general assembly passed and the governor signed Act 1954, merging the Department of Health with the Department of Human Services, to create the Department of Health and Human Services (DHHS). The functions of the Department of Health have been taken over by the Division of Health within the new department. In addition, the State Board of Health was transferred to the new DHHS. This action was taken in order to "(1) improve the health of the citizens of Arkansas in an effective and efficient manner; and (2) provide for administrative cost savings in the delivery of health-related programs by combining overlapping functions and eliminating duplications of functions of the Department of Health and the Department of Human Services."

This consolidation of the two departments has direct implications for the Arkansas Tobacco Settlement Commission. First, TPEP has shifted from being administered by the Arkansas Department of Health to being a separate branch in the organizational chart of DHHS, and there is a different staff representing TPEP to the legislature; these changes could provide the possibility of more visibility for TPEP. Additionally, spending rules changes applied to DHHS mean that TPEP can no longer make advance lump-sum payments to grantees, which could have consequences for how coalitions pay community coalitions and therefore create cash flow problems for these coalitions.

The other Tobacco Settlement program administered by DHHS, the Medicare Expansion Programs, is not affected by this change. Medicaid was part of the Department of Human Services, and the organizational structure and staffing of that section was not altered.

Second, both the directors of the original Department of Health and the Department of Human Services are designated by the Initiated Act to serve on the Tobacco Settlement Commission. With the director of the Department of Health having been discontinued, it is not clear which position(s) should be appointed as commission members to represent these two functions.

THE TOBACCO SETTLEMENT COMMISSION

The Arkansas Tobacco Settlement Commission is directed by the Initiated Act to conduct monitoring and evaluation of the funded programs "to ensure optimal impact on improving the health of Arkansans and fiscal stewardship of the Tobacco Settlement" and "to justify continued support based upon the state's performance-based budgeting initiative."[1] Regular quarterly meetings of the commission have been held since its inception. In addition, special meetings have been scheduled when needed to carry out its functions effectively. For example, special meetings were scheduled for the commission to review and act on community grants that were awarded in 2003 and 2004. All of these meetings have been held in compliance with the state requirements for public meetings and related notices.

The work of the ATSC is guided by its strategic plan, which it has established pursuant to requirements of the Initiated Act (ATSC, 2004). This plan is currently under review and revision by the commission to establish a strategy to monitor and provide technical support for the funded programs.

ATSC Monitoring and Evaluating Activities

The Initiated Act directs the ATSC to develop measurable performance indicators to monitor programmatic functions that are state-specific and situation-specific and to support performance-based assessment for governmental accountability. Progress with respect to these performance indicators is to be reported to the governor and the general assembly for future appropriation decisions. The commission is to modify these performance indicators as goals and objectives are met and new inputs to programmatic outcomes are identified.

---

[1] Although the state has discontinued its performance-based budget initiative, its spirit continues to guide the ATSC.

The Initiated Act authorized the ATSC to hire an independent contractor to perform monitoring and evaluation of the program. The product of this evaluation is to be a biennial report to be delivered to the general assembly and the governor by August 1 preceding each general session of the general assembly. The report is to be accompanied by recommendations from the commission as to the continued funding for each program.

As specified in the act, the ATSC contracted with the RAND Corporation to perform the program evaluation, including tracking of expenditures made from the program accounts. The contract was effective January 1, 2003, for a two-year term, which was extended another two years for 2005–2006. This report is the second biennial evaluation report, which presents an update to the first biennial evaluation report submitted in 2004 as well as an interim report submitted in 2005. This report covers recent program activities, spending, program responses to recommendations, and assessments of program outcomes.

On August 1, 2002, the ATSC submitted to the general assembly and the governor a biennial report that reviewed the early progress of the funded programs in the first 12 months after receipt of Tobacco Settlement funding (July 2001–June 2002). Its assessment focused on indicators for program initiation, which are stated in section 18 of the act (ATSC, 2002). The ATSC recommendations for future appropriations were based on the following considerations:

- Reported performance is compared with initiation indicators only.

- It is recognized that most program components within the act are new programs requiring a period of deployment before short- and long-term objectives can be achieved.

- All programs received partial funding during the first year.

In its first report, the ATSC submitted recommendations regarding future appropriations for the programs. The ATSC recommended continued funding with no conditions for five of the seven programs, based on findings that the programs had been initiated successfully. It recommended "continued funding with concerns" for TPEP and the Minority Health Initiative.

In its second report, submitted on August 1, 2004, the ATSC referenced, included as an attachment, and responded to RAND's first evaluation report covering 2002–2004 (Farley et al., 2005a). The responses to the evaluation are presented later in this chapter.

Community Grants

According to the Initiated Act, if the deposits into the Arkansas Tobacco Settlement Commission Fund exceed the amount necessary to pay its expenses, then the ATSC may make grants, within its appropriation limits, to support community activities. Funded activities must meet the following criteria:

- Organizations must be nonprofit and community based.

- Proposals should be reviewed using criteria based upon the following principles:
  - All funds should be used to improve and optimize the health of Arkansans.
  - Funds should be spent on long-term projects that improve the health of Arkansans.

- o Future tobacco-related illness and health care costs in Arkansas should be minimized through this opportunity.

- o Funds should be invested in solutions that work effectively and efficiently in Arkansas.

- Grant awards are to be restricted to amounts up to $50,000 per year for each eligible organization. In practice, the ATSC set an upper limit of $25,000 for each grant, with actual grants awarded ranging in amounts from $5,000 to $24,998.

In FY2004, the ATSC awarded its first set of 16 grants under this provision for a total of $353,678 in grants to community organizations. In the second round of community grants, awarded in FY2005, the ATSC funded 22 grants for a total of $487,522, with amounts ranging from $8,000 to $24,998. The grants awarded for FY2005 are shown in Table 2.4.

Table 2.4
Community Grants Awarded by the ATSC for FY2005

Program Funded	Grant Amount
Youth Media Training and Cessation Support	$ 24,998
Murfreesboro Nutrition	11,770
Lighted Walking Trail	20,000
Healthy Lifestyles	24,998
Enhancing Healthier Lifestyles	24,340
Student Tobacco Objection (STOMP)	15,548
Know Your Numbers	24,260
Oral Cancer Screening	24,998
Breathe Easy	24,212
Kids for Health Video	24,998
St. John's Nicotine Addiction Treatment	20,790
CHOICES	24,165
Healthy Connections QUIT	24,533
Good Samaritan Clinic	24,998
Healthy Boone County	24,998
Healthy Hampton	8,000
Move It or Lose It	24,993
Empowering Arkansans to Optimize	24,998
Community Cares Christian Drug Program	24,998
UALR – You Know You Want To	24,998
Asthma Med Camps	21,280
White River Youth Tobacco Prevention	18,649
Total funding for community grants	$487,522

The ATSC established a requirement of quarterly reporting for the community grants, including both provision of information on progress, challenges, and successes in implementing the funded activity and reporting on grant expenditures. Each year, a small number of the grantees failed to carry out their activities, and some proceeded more slowly than planned. The ATSC monitored these issues, and was prepared, if necessary, to discontinue grants for programs that were not carrying out the funded activities.

Because the ATSC chose to use some of its available funds for technical support to the seven funded programs, it did not award new community grants for FY2006. Instead, it renewed the grants of two existing awardees. The renewal awardees were Healthy Boone County, which continued its program, and the Data Analysis Reporting for Tobacco effort, which was a successor to the QUIT program of Healthy Connections. Both programs received new grant amounts of $24,998. These two programs were chosen because they were deemed to have performed well in serving community needs and were thus the most deserving of the additional funding for continued support of their development work.

Looking beyond FY2006, the ATSC looked at the performance history of previous grantees and, with assistance from the RAND evaluation team, identified some candidate programs for additional support and some modification of its grant applications procedures. In considering new and continuing grant applications, it will ask each to submit a work plan for the coming year that is to include a list of measurable outcomes expected from the grantee's community activities.

Responses to Recommendations for the Commission in the 2004 Evaluation Report

The Tobacco Settlement Commission has an important role in ensuring the effective use of the financial resources that the Tobacco Settlement has provided to Arkansas. As the programs move forward, it will be important for the commission to hold them to uniformly high standards of performance and results. In Chapter 12 of its 2004 evaluation report, RAND made several recommendations for ATSC actions to help strengthen its role in oversight, support, and evaluation of the programs receiving Tobacco Settlement funding. We summarize here the actions taken by the ATSC in response to each of our recommendations.

Recommendation: The commission should modify the content of the regular quarterly reports from the programs to require routine reports on their progress in addressing the issues identified in this evaluation. Issues to be addressed include the following:

> Involvement of the programs' governing body (or advisory boards) in guiding program strategy and priorities
>
> Specific progress of the programs in achieving the goals and objectives of their strategic plans
>
> Actions being undertaken for continuous quality improvement and progress in improving services
>
> Actions being taken for collaboration and coordination among programs to strengthen programming
>
> The specific issues identified in the recommendations are at the end of each program's chapter in this report.

Commission Response: The ATSC has changed the format for the quarterly reports submitted by the programs to incorporate the provisions listed in the recommendation. The programs are now submitting this information to the ATSC regularly, and the programs also are being asked to provide this information in their presentations at commission meetings. The ATSC plans to increase its use of forums designed to enhance interactions between commission members and the programs to ensure both accountability and support for continuous strengthening of the programs. For example, the commission meeting locations are now being rotated among the locations of the programs based in Little Rock.

Recommendation: The commission should work with the state finance office and the funded programs to ensure that the programs are correcting the inadequacies of the accounting and financial management processes that this evaluation has identified.

> *Commission Response:* The ATSC office is working to develop a financial reporting format that can provide uniformity in reporting across programs. For example, the possibility is being explored of a financial reporting system to provide the same reports for all the programs. Work is proceeding carefully in this process to ensure that the format developed is useful and feasible for all the programs. In addition, the ATSC office has been monitoring actions by the programs to correct problems with inaccurate allocation of funds across appropriations line items, which were accomplished during the last legislative session.

Recommendation: To ensure that program spending is being monitored regularly, the commission should require the programs to submit quarterly financial statements of budgeted versus actual spending. The financial statements should be in sufficient detail to enable the commission to identify variances from budget, and explanations of variances should be provided. (These reports could be the same as those submitted to the programs' governing boards.)

> *Commission Response:* All programs submit financial reports each quarter to the ATSC. As discussed under the previous recommendation, this development work is underway, with plans to begin online reporting of program expenditures once the format and resources have been identified.

Recommendation: The commission should earmark a modest portion of the Tobacco Settlement funds ($150,000 to $200,000 each year) to establish a mechanism that makes technical support available to the funded programs. This support should be targeted to help the programs correct some of the issues identified in this evaluation.

> *Commission Response:* The technical support function is being developed as an integral part of the ATSC strategic plan that currently is being updated and revised. The State Department of Volunteerism has been identified as a resource to draw upon as the ATSC moves forward to support technical development work by the programs. This department is helping to identify what the programs need in the way of technical support by conducting a needs assessment. A portion of the ATSC budget was reserved to fund these activities. However, because of ceilings in the appropriation for the commission (and, notably, not unavailability of funds), the commission has been unable to purchase technical support in any significant quantity. The commission intends to request an increase in appropriation in order to implement these activities.

Recommendation: The commission should establish expectations for the performance of the governing bodies of the funded programs with respect to providing policy and strategic guidance for their programs, as well as monitoring program performance.

> *Commission Response:* This issue is being considered by the commission as part of its strategic planning process, so it has not yet provided the programs any written expectations for how they are to strengthen the roles of their governing bodies. It is a complex area, given the diversity of boards, commissions, and advisory groups of the various programs.

Recommendation: As the programs mature further and more longitudinal information becomes available on outcomes, the commission should ensure that outcome evaluation work continues to document the extent of those effects. Meanwhile, the commission should interpret early outcome information with caution to ensure that conclusions regarding the programs' effectiveness are grounded on sufficient data.

> *Commission Response:* In addressing the anticipated effects of the funded programs on health-related outcomes for Arkansans, the ATSC thus far has been relying on the RAND evaluation to provide the data and assessment of outcome trends. In testimony and discussions with legislators, commission members and staff have emphasized that it will take time to begin to see outcomes. As information emerges about program outcomes, the ATSC is gearing up to communicate the information proactively to leaders and citizens of the state.

Chapter 3
Tobacco Prevention and Education Program

PROGRAM DESCRIPTION

In August 2005, the Arkansas Department of Health was merged with the Department of Human Services to form the Department of Health and Human Services (DHHS). The new Division of Health's Tobacco Prevention and Cessation branch continues to offer programming supported by Tobacco Settlement funding—under the name of Tobacco Prevention and Education Program (TPEP)—according to the nine program components of what the national Centers for Disease Control and Prevention (CDC) recommends for statewide tobacco control programs (CDC, 1999a). Below are brief updates of activities for each of these programs.

Community Prevention Programs that Reduce Youth Tobacco Use. Twenty-nine community coalitions were funded for FY2005 (July 1, 2004–June 30, 2005) and 32 in FY2006. These coalitions continue to educate a wide range of audiences about the dangers of smoking and secondhand smoke, partnering with schools, churches, universities, hospitals, businesses, and a variety of media channels. The coalitions have also been active in trying to strengthen anti-tobacco policies in schools, businesses, hospitals, public festivals, and entire cities. These efforts have resulted in anti-smoking ordinances being passed in Fayetteville, Pine Bluff, El Dorado, and Fairfield Bay.

Local School Education and Prevention Programs in K–12. Seventeen consortiums of school districts or schools were funded for FY2005, and 19 were funded in FY2006. The school grantees have been working in schools to establish and strengthen infrastructure for tobacco prevention, including strengthening of school policies, implementing evidence-based tobacco prevention programs, promoting and referring to cessation services, and using media to disseminate anti-tobacco messages.

Enforcement of Youth Tobacco Control Laws. The Arkansas Tobacco Control Board (ATCB) continues to conducts compliance checks, with more than 7,500 done in 2004 and 6,700 in 2005. These checks are both new and follow-ups from complaints the ATCB receives or re-checks of previous violators. The ATCB has dramatically increased the amount of education it provides to merchants about compliance with the law. It conducted 24 trainings covering 157 employees in 34 stores in 2004, and it did 70 trainings covering 1,407 employees in 278 stores in 2005.

Statewide Programs with Youth Involvement to Increase Local Coalition Activities. The two statewide coalitions—Coalition for Tobacco-Free Arkansas (CTFA) and Arkansans for Drug-Free Youth (ADFY)—continue to pursue their anti-tobacco goals. CTFA continues to provide education and support local efforts to pass anti-tobacco ordinances, which aided the passing of the citywide bans and the statewide workplace ban in April 2006. ADFY has been cultivating a state-level group of youth, called the Tobacco Control Youth Board (also known as Arkansans for a Drug-Free Youth's Y.E.S. Team), to implement a multifaceted, statewide anti-tobacco media campaign in collaboration with a Little Rock media agency.

Tobacco Cessation Programs. In July 2005, the Arkansas College of Public Health (COPH) took over operation of the free statewide Quitline (1-866-NOW-QUIT) and science-based cessation counseling and pharmaceutical intervention program. The Quitline previously had been operated by the Mayo Clinic, and the treatment program had been operated by the Arkansas

Foundation for Medical Care (AFMC). COPH has expanded enrollment and is obtaining good quit rates.

Tobacco-related Disease Prevention Programs. The Arkansas Cancer Coalition used TPEP funds to support the University of Arkansas for Medical Sciences (UAMS) Smoke-Free Task Force's efforts to pave the way for implementing a completely smoke free campus at the University of Arkansas Medical School beginning July 4, 2004. The task force program was a multicomponent smoking cessation program for UAMS staff, for which the Cancer Coalition's grant helped support nonsmoking signage and a paging system to allow visitors to smoke off campus. TPEP funds were also used to support the Trails for Life program in collaboration with the Department of Parks and Recreation. In FY2004, about 7.5 miles of trails were built. These funds support an additional 1.5 miles of trail in FY2005 and an additional two miles in FY2006.

Public Awareness and Health Promotion Campaign. TPEP continued to work with the media agency Cranford, Johnson, Robinson, Woods (CJRW) to reinforce initiatives on smoking and secondhand smoke through print, radio, TV, partnerships, and sponsorship of local events around the state. Many events have been held in partnership with local sports teams, museums, festivals, concerts, and amusement parks. In June 2004, a redesigned Stomp Out Smoking (SOS)Web site was relaunched that is available in English and Spanish and includes youth-oriented information and activities, as well as information for parents, community partners, and medical professionals. The Web site has received several awards. In 2005, the SOS campaign sponsored several public events, started an e-newsletter, and ran radio, newspaper, magazine, and television advertising for general market, African-American, and Hispanic target audiences.

Minority Initiatives. TPEP funds the University of Arkansas at Pine Bluff (UAPB) to administer the Master's of Science in Addiction program and the Minority Initiative Sub-Recipient Grant Office (MISRGO). In 2004, the Addiction Studies program graduated all 21 students from its first class, 16 of whom have obtained addiction jobs in Arkansas. In 2005, eight more graduated, five of whom have obtained addiction jobs in Arkansas. MISRGO awarded 24 minority community-based grants for FY2004, 22 in FY2005, and 20 in FY2006. Targeting minority communities, these grants provide education on the effects of secondhand smoke; reduction of youth access; decrease in advertising and promotion of tobacco products; and promotion of cessation. MISRGO's new evaluator has facilitated several trainings with a focus on building grantee capacity to conduct self-evaluation.

Monitoring and Evaluation. TPEP has increased its evaluation requirements on all its grantees and contractors, and it monitors the CDC-identified four goals for tobacco control programs. From 2001 to 2005, TPEP contracted with the Gallup Organization to provide ongoing evaluations of the specific program activities. The Gallup contract was ended after FY2005 because it did not pass the Legislative Review Committee. TPEP has been developing a request for proposals (RFP) to secure the services of a replacement evaluator.

PROGRESS TOWARD ACHIEVING FIVE-YEAR AND SHORT-TERM GOALS

In 2005, RAND staff met with TPEP leadership to establish programmatic goals that define the program's vision for their future scope of activities. Five such goals, many of which cross program components as described above, were identified, and the TPEP progress in achieving these explicit goals is presented here.

Goal 1: For the school programs, achieve at least a 75 percent compliance rate with the CDC guidelines for school programs on tobacco prevention and cessation.

Progress on Goal 1: ON SCHEDULE. The CDC has seven guidelines for tobacco control in school programs: (1) enforce a school policy on tobacco use; (2) provide specific anti-tobacco instruction, (3) provide instruction K–12; (4) train teachers; (5) involve parents; (6) support cessation efforts; and (7) assess the tobacco-use prevention program. The guidelines are assessed by TPEP nurses who work in the schools. The funded school programs in FY2005 achieved an average rate of compliance of 75 percent of these guidelines (range 58–100 percent). This is up from 72 percent in FY2004 (range 50–100 percent).

Goal 2: Establish a state network of smoking cessation programs across the state with coverage such that people do not have to travel more than one hour to access a program (provided that funding is available).

Progress on Goal 2: ON SCHEDULE. The College of Public Health has taken over both the statewide Quitline and Cessation Network. The latter has 16 sites across the state. These sites, combined with the statewide Quitline, do provide coverage consistent with this goal. However, the intent was that the network of local programs to which people travel for services would provide this type of coverage. More sites need to be opened in order to achieve this goal.

Goal 3: Establish and maintain a mix of ads in the media campaign that emphasizes restricting smoking in public places (i.e., clean air) and smoking cessation in a 2:1 ratio.

Progress on Goal 3: ACCOMPLISHED. Although the statewide media campaign did focus heavily on smoking cessation, other entities funded by the TPEP program, namely the community and statewide coalitions, sponsored their own—TPEP-approved— campaigns that heavily focused on clear air. This resulted in about a 2:1 ratio. Now that a statewide smoking ban has been passed, this goal will need to be revisited.

Goal 4: By 2008, 25 percent of all Arkansans will live in communities that have legislated smoke-free environments that exceed levels of bans established by state legislation.

Progress on Goal 4: ON SCHEDULE. Taking into account the bans passed in Fayetteville, Pine Bluff, El Dorado, and Fairfield Bay, about 5 percent of Arkansans live in a community that has a smoke-free environment. The intent of this goal was to assess the percent of Arkansans who live in a smoke-free environment when the state overall had weak or little statewide restrictions. Now that a comprehensive statewide smoking ban has been passed, this goal may no longer be needed or useful, and TPEP resources may be better spent on other activities.

Goal 5: By 2008, 75 percent of Arkansas workers will be in a worksite with a smoke-free policy as assessed by the Census Bureau's Current Population Survey (CPS).

Progress on Goal 5: ACCOMPLISHED. According to the 2003–2004 CPS (the most recent data available), the percent of Arkansans working in a smoke-free workplace was 74 percent, an increase of about 10 percent since 2001–2002. Given that the statewide workplace smoking ban took effect in July 2006—the only exemptions are racetracks, dog tracks, hotels with fewer than 25 rooms, and establishments that only serve and employ those over 21—this rate should dramatically increase to close to 100 percent.

PERFORMANCE ON PROCESS INDICATORS

Ten indicators were selected to represent the overall progress of TPEP. These indicators are used to track progress on fulfilling the mandates in the act for the program to develop and monitor the nine components of the Tobacco Prevention and Cessation Program delineated in the Initiated Act. The program components for which indicators were established are the community coalitions to reduce youth tobacco use, local school education programs, enforcement of youth tobacco control laws, tobacco cessation programs, tobacco-related prevention programs, public promotion and health awareness campaigns, and minorities program. The current status of the TPEP program on these measures is summarized in Table 3.1. Refer to the appendix to this chapter for tables with detailed trend information.

Table 3.1
Process Indicators and Status over the Last Two Years

Indicators	Status
Number of community-level community changes initiated, especially newly enacted secondhand smoke policies	Activity increased in community changes, including the establishment of cessation referral networks, adoption of stronger anti-tobacco policies by schools, and smoke-free restaurants and multisite hospital systems
Percentage of CDC-recommended approaches put in place in each participating educational cooperative	Small overall improvement, up to 75 percent compliance
Number of stores checked by the Arkansas Tobacco Control Board (ATCB) for compliance with rules to not sell tobacco products to minors	ATCB checked somewhat fewer stores in order to provide more merchant education. The violation rate has continued to fall to a low of 6.5 percent.
Number of smokers enrolled in the Mayo Clinic Tobacco Cessation Service program	Enrollment in the Quitline declined but quit rates continued to be at or above the norm for such programs
Number of smokers enrolled in the statewide cessation program run by the AR Foundation for Medical Care (AFMC) program (now run by the College of Public Health)	Enrollment has been steady for the statewide cessation program and quit rates continued to be at or above the norm for such programs
Number of miles of hiking trails constructed in the Trails for Life program	Eighteen FY2004 grantees built about 7.5 miles of trail. FY2005 grantees are nearly done with another 1.5 miles
Number of public service announcements (PSAs) and community events to support tobacco prevention and cessation activities	Number of PSAs and events has declined somewhat since 2003
Percentage of media ad funds leveraged as donated funds from the media companies	The media contractor continues to leverage a significant amount of free media
Percentage of youth surveyed who recall the Stomp Out Smoking (SOS) media campaign	Recall of the SOS campaign has increased slightly since the last evaluation report
Percentage of graduates from UAPB Addiction Studies who obtain an addiction-related job within Arkansas after graduation	Since its inception, 21 out of all 29 graduates (72 percent) have obtained an addiction-related job in Arkansas

PERFORMANCE ON MANAGEMENT INTEGRITY CRITERIA

Types and Performance of Governing and Advisory Boards

In principle, the Arkansas State Board of Health is the governing board for the Division of Health, within DHHS, and TPEP is part of the Division of Health. TPEP receives minimal

29

oversight from this board. However, TPEP does have oversight from the TPEP Advisory Committee, which was established by the Initiated Act.

The TPEP Advisory Committee meets quarterly. The committee membership is specified by the Initiated Act. Table 3.2 shows the TPEP Advisory Committee members, their employment, and what organization they represent on the board. All but two of the sixteen board members are appointed by the governor to represent certain organizations in the state. Of the two at-large members, one is appointed by the president pro tem of the Senate, and the other is appointed by the speaker of the House. No member can serve for more than two consecutive four-year terms. Arkansas Students Working Against Tobacco (SWAT) serve as youth advisers. The advisory committee does not have any standing subcommittees, but it does convene ad hoc subcommittees when needed. For example, a subcommittee was formed to help plan the FY2006 TPEP media campaign.

Table 3.2
Makeup of the TPEP Advisory Committee

Name	Occupation	Organization Represented
Connie Ash	Nurse	Arkansas Nurses Association
Mary Benjamin, Ph.D.	Vice Chancellor of Academic Affairs—UAPB	University of Arkansas at Pine Bluff
David Covey, M.D.	Physician	At-Large member
Jill Cox	Program Coordinator—ADAPT	American Cancer Society
Anthony Fletcher, M.D.	Cardiologist	Arkansas Medical, Dental, and Pharmaceutical Association
Cynthia Gregory	Management Project Analyst	Minority Health Commission
Thomas Hoffpauir	Social Worker—UAMS	Arkansas Drug Free Youth
Wilhelmina Houston	Self-Employed	Coalition for Tobacco-Free Arkansas
William Jones, M.D.	Physician	Arkansas Medical Society
Barbara Kumpe	Advocacy Director for AHA—Arkansas	American Heart Association
Jimmy Leopard	Chief Executive Officer—Arkansas Medical Hospitals	Arkansas Hospital Association
Lynn Russell	State Leader—Family and Consumer Sciences	University of Arkansas Cooperative Extension
Jim Shenep	Senior Vice President—Delta Trust Bank	American Lung Association
Craig Stotts	Professor—UTHSC	Arkansas Center for Health Improvement
Bob Trevino	Commissioner of Arkansas Rehabilitation Services	League of Latin American Citizens
Gary Wheeler, M.D. (Chair)	Physician and Professor	At-Large member
Currently vacant		Arkansas Association of Area Agencies on Aging
Currently vacant		Arkansas Department of Education

RAND staff asked TPEP leadership to rate the level of involvement by the TPEP Advisory Committee in three categories of management functions: oversight, monitoring program performance, and providing interface with communities. RAND staff then confirmed those ratings with interviews and document reviews. These ratings are shown in Table 3.3.

Overall, the level of involvement shown by the TPEP Advisory Committee in management of the TPEP program was low to moderate. In terms of oversight, the advisory committee was moderately involved in helping TPEP set its priorities. For example, discussions with TPEP staff and advisory committee members confirmed that the advisory committee strongly advocated for a greater emphasis on clean indoor air. The advisory committee was minimally involved in quality management, goals, or budgeting.

Regarding monitoring program performance, the advisory committee was most involved in reviewing quality performance. This usually took the form of reviewing reports produced by TPEP about its various program components and giving feedback in its quarterly meetings. The advisory committee was only minimally involved in reviewing progress toward TPEP's goals, mostly through presentations made by TPEP to the advisory committee at the quarterly meetings. The advisory committee did not review spending. In terms of providing interface with communities, the advisory committee has provided feedback about community needs TPEP should address, but it has not been involved at all in fundraising.

The observation that TPEP's advisory committee is not adequately engaged is important because boards should be among a program's primary stakeholders. Additionally, the committee could strengthen its involvement by a number of steps, including (1) hiring an organizational consultant who specializes in board relationships and (2) interviewing counterparts in some of the other states that have statewide tobacco control programs (e.g., Arizona, California, Florida, Minnesota, Washington).

Table 3.3
Involvement of the TPEP Advisory Committee

Management Functions	Rating[a]
Oversight	
Goals and planning	2
Priorities	3
Budget	2
Quality management	1
Monitoring program performance	
Progress toward goals	2
Spending	1
Quality performance	3
Providing interface with communities	
Community needs	3
Community interactions	3
Fund-raising	1

a. Definitions of ratings: 1 = not involved, 2 = minimally involved,
    3 = not intense involvement, 4 = fully considers, 5 = directive.

Quality Improvement Process

In this section, we review the comprehensiveness of TPEP's quality management process—defined here as a written process used to continuously improve program performance over time. Broadly, it involves collecting various types of performance data, analyzing them, formulating improvement plans based on the analysis, and performing monitoring and feedback on progress.

TPEP has put measures in place at various levels to gather the data needed to judge performance. At the individual contract or grantee level, all of its contractors and grantees are required to collect their own data and report them to TPEP. In addition, for some grantee programs (coalitions, school grants), TPEP conducts its own independent assessments of quality and gives individual feedback based on those assessments. Although consumer satisfaction is not relevant for many of TPEP's programs, for those in which it is (Quitline and media campaign), satisfaction data are collected and used to make improvements. At the TPEP-wide level, from 2001 through June 2005, TPEP had contracted with the Gallup Organization to assist in monitoring program indicators and produce an annual report card. An RFP is being developed to secure a new evaluation contractor. In addition, TPEP internally tracks its progress on key performance indicators recommended by CDC for measuring tobacco control programs' success (disparities in tobacco use among minorities, promoting quitting, reduce secondhand smoke exposure, prevent initiation of smoking). Data on these indicators are then reported to the CDC and made widely available.

TPEP is less developed in its process to synthesize the data on measures across multiple grantees for the purpose of drawing lessons that can be used for program improvement. For example, the community coalitions are required to evaluate themselves and send reports to TPEP, and TPEP conducts its own midpoint assessment and provides feedback. However, there is no process to synthesize all of the evaluation reports and coalitions assessments to improve the next round of coalition grantees. Having such reports would also facilitate communication with the TPEP Advisory Committee (presenting one report instead of 30) and other audiences. The same is true for the school grantees.

For the contracted programs of Quitline and Cessation Network, Arkansas Tobacco Control Board, statewide coalitions, and media campaign, there is no organized process by which data are reviewed with the multiple stakeholders involved. This situation may be the result of the fact that TPEP has no formal quality review committee. Although each grant and contract has well-specified targets in its work plans, it is unclear how past data are reviewed between TPEP and the contractor's staff. TPEP does a good job in disseminating data from many of its programs (e.g., media), and when it had an evaluator under contract, TPEP published regular report cards that provided data on all of its programs.

Financial Management Process

TPEP uses the state accounting system, called the Arkansas Administrative Statewide Information System (AASIS), to report spending both to the state for the Tobacco Settlement program and to the TPEP Advisory Committee. TPEP has three staff members in the program who know how to work on the AASIS system, including running and monitoring reports: a financial program support manager, budget coordinator, and accounting technician. TPEP provides financial reports to the advisory committee upon request.

A key issue in managing the financial information is whether TPEP has organized its financial data in a way that allows appropriate oversight. TPEP has established separate accounts according to the program components CDC recommends for statewide programs, allowing it to budget for and monitor spending by each CDC component. However, some funding allocated to one CDC program component may also be relevant in another. For example, evaluation and monitoring is one CDC component. Although TPEP uses this category for funds to pay for its overall evaluation contractor (previously Gallup), it also requires all its grantees and contractors to conduct their own evaluations. Thus, the dollar amount reflected in TPEP's evaluation component underestimates total spending for evaluation.

Contract Management

TPEP utilizes three types of financial mechanisms to disperse funds: subgrants, professional services contracts, and fund transfers. For each of these methods, we report information about performance specifications, financial reporting, quality performance and reporting, and payment structure.

Subgrants. This mechanism is used for funding the community coalitions, school-based programs, statewide cancer and tobacco-free coalitions, and the Minority Initiative Set-aside (15 percent of total TPEP funds are subgranted to the University of Arkansas at Pine Bluff for the Master's of Science in Addiction Studies program and MISRGO). In terms of performance specifications, TPEP requires the subgrantees to identify both the goals and objectives and the number of specific activities they commit to achieving when they apply for funding. To ensure that the subgrantees' work plans are being followed and their activities are addressing their stated goals and objectives, TPEP's quality performance and reporting system involves monitoring subgrantees through a Web-based reporting system using a structured protocol and a review of subgrantees' quarterly reports of their work plan activities and outcomes. For financial reporting, regional grant administrators review subgrantees' monthly billing invoices and conduct at least one site visit to review financial records to verify compliance with proper procedures. As part of the monthly financial review, TPEP compares actual to planned spending, (requiring explanations of reasons for variances from the budget) and compares spending to program activity. The payment structure for subgrants allows the subgrantee to request up to 25 percent of the total award in advance. MISRGO staff maintains the oversight of the subgrants awarded through the MISRGO. The MISRGO subgrants are monitored in the same manner as those awarded by TPEP.

Professional Services Contracts. This mechanism is used for funding the Arkansas College of Public Health for the Quitline and Cessation Network, and the marketing and media contract with Cranford Johnson Robinson Woods. In terms of performance specifications, TPEP requires the contractor to identify the number of specific activities it commits to achieving. For example, the Cessation Network contract specifies the number of referrals to cessation services and number of persons who will receive cessation counseling at work sites. The Quitline contract specifies all aspects of the Quitline operation, such as, the hours of operation and the availability of Spanish-speaking counselors. TPEP's quality performance and reporting system involves monitoring the contracts through face-to-face meetings and quarterly reports that specify activities performed. The director of TPEP now meets with the media contractor and the Cessation Network and Quitline director weekly. For financial reporting, TPEP staff reviews contractor invoices monthly. As part of the monthly financial review, TPEP compares actual to planned spending (requiring explanations of reasons for variances from the budget) and compares spending to program activity. In addition, the Department of Health and Human Services, Contract Support Section, makes an onsite visit to monitor contract activity and assist contractors in achieving and maintaining compliance with billing. The payment structure for all of these contracts is such that they specify aggregate budgets to cover the costs for services provided, not on a per-unit-of-service basis.

Fund Transfers. This mechanism is used to fund the Arkansas Tobacco Control Board and the Arkansas Department of Parks and Tourism for the Trails for Life program. Overall, the payment structure for all these initiatives involves TPEP transferring funding to another account or entity. For example, Act 1750 of 2001 established the Arkansas Trails for Life grant program, which began allocating $300,000 a year to build public access walking trails designed to stimulate greater physical activity among Arkansans.

More specifically, the ATCB agreement specifies the number of inspections the board will conduct. TPEP's quality performance and reporting system for ATCB involves quarterly reports that specify activities performed. In addition, ATCB now has on its Web site a searchable database of checks and violations. TPEP staff reviews ATCB's invoices monthly, focusing on a few selected months to verify compliance with proper procedures. As part of the monthly financial review, TPEP compares actual to planned spending (requiring explanations of reasons for variances from the budget) and compares spending to program activity. The payment structure for ATCB involves initiating a fund transfer upon a request from the ATCB for reimbursement of expenses.

The Trails for Life program receives the least amount of oversight by TPEP. After the funds are transferred to Trails for Life, TPEP receives irregular updates on the trails grants being awarded and progress of trail construction. However, the Department of Parks and Tourism (Parks Department) provides extensive oversight. Performance is specified when the subgrantees apply to the Trails for Life grant program for funding; the quality performance and reporting system involves Parks Department staff's monitoring the subgrantees through face-to-face meetings, quarterly reports, and site visits; Parks Department staff reviews receipts and conducts a monthly financial review; and the payment structure involves lump-sum payments from the Parks Department to its subgrantees only after the subgrantees have demonstrated they have conducted all the necessary site planning and hired a contractor.

ANALYSIS OF SPENDING TRENDS

Act 1572 of 2001, HB 1021 of 2003, and HB 2090 of 2005 appropriated funds to TPEP for the first three biennium periods of the Tobacco Settlement Fund Allocation. Table 3.4 details the appropriations and actual funds received, by fiscal year. Numbers in parentheses indicate the actual amount received for a particular category. After the first biennium, TPEP returned $6,591,842 to the master Tobacco Settlement Fund. During FY2004, TPEP learned that its total allocation would decrease to $14,694,000. TPEP then requested the carryover amount from the first biennium. Near the end of FY2004, TPEP received $6,360,422. As part of these carryover funds, TPEP received a total of $21,054,422 for FY2004. In FY2005, TPEP received

Table 3.4
Tobacco Settlement Funds Appropriated and Received for the TPEP,
by Fiscal Year

Item	Second Biennium		Third Biennium	
	2004	2005	2006	2007
(1) Regular salaries	$1,362,742	$1,399,537	$1,482,421	$1,524,750
(2) Extra help	50,000	50,000	50,000	50,000
(3) Personal service matching	370,280	377,129	415,915	424,263
(4) Maintenance and operations				
(A) Operations	206,536	206,536	399,271	282,655
(B) Travel	40,030	40,030	31,957	31,957
(C) Professional fees	1,700,000	1,700,000	1,257,165	1,257,165
(D) Capital outlay	–	–	–	–
(E) Data processing	–	–	–	–
(5) Prevention and cessation Programs	13,868,073 (13,516,335)	13,855,204	12,442,086	10,349,295
(6) Personal services and operating expenses				
(A) Public health nurses[b]	–	–	–	–
(B) Nutrition & Physical Activity Program	881,000 (800,000)[a]	893,869	872,569	758,951
(7) Transfer to breast cancer control fund	500,000	500,000	500,000	500,000
Funds carryover	2,508,499	4,226,343	6,570,142	
Annual Total	$18,978,661 (21,054,422)[a]	$19,022,305 (16,984,867)[a]	$17,451,384	$15,179,036
Biennium Total	$38,000,966 ($38,039,289)[a]		$32,630,420	

a. Numbers in parentheses indicate the actual amount received for a particular category.

b. Act 61 of 2003 (H.B. 1021) moved salary expenses for public health nurses into regular salaries starting in FY2004.

$16,984,867.46 and had a carryover of $4,226,342.65 from FY2004. The total received for FY2005 was $21,211,210.11.

The following analysis describes the Tobacco Settlement expenditures by TPEP from July 2001 through December 2005. Because December 2005 is in the middle of the first year of the third biennium, no year totals for FY2006 are presented, and it is not yet possible to fully detail expenditures in the third biennium.

Table 3.5 presents the total annual Tobacco Settlement funds spent by the TPEP during this time period, using the funds categories listed in Table 3.4. As in prior years, TPEP spent less than the total amount received for FY2005. The leftover funds, totaling $6,570,141.60, were carried over in FY2006. Although programs of the Tobacco Settlement program are not allowed to carry over funds in between bienniums, TPEP made a formal request to the Arkansas Department of Finance Authority (DFA), which approved the carryover between the first and second bienniums. In January 2005, the Initiated Act was amended to allow TPEP to carry over funds without asking for DF&A approval. Act 1872 of 2005, titled Act to Clarify the Proper Distribution of Master Settlement Agreement Funds, changed carryover requirements for the Tobacco Prevention and Cessation Program. It states, Moneys remaining in the account at the end of each fiscal year shall be carried forward and used for the purposes provided by law." Funds remaining at the end of FY2005 (second biennium) are carried forward into FY2006 (third biennium) under this new mechanism.

Creating a spending budget for each fiscal year is more challenging for TPEP than for the other programs receiving Tobacco Settlement funding, because TPEP is the only program required to borrow ahead by estimating how much it thinks it will receive, to spend its borrowed amount, and then get paid back by the funds. It is further complicated by the fact that appropriations represent upper limits of approved spending.

Table 3.5
Tobacco Settlement Funds Spent by TPEP, by Fiscal Year

Line Item	2003	2004	2005	2006[a]
(1) Regular salaries	$496,642	$1,246,702	$1,351,567	$579,716
(2) Extra help	29,468	25,840	15,465	6,145
(3) Personal service matching	129,852	347,474	377,779	178,939
(4) Maintenance and operations				
(A) Operations	256,258	342,896	215,248	133,809
(B) Travel	21,244	38,105	12,576	3,430
(C) Professional fees	1,141,081	861,115	1,184,642	119,088
(D) Capital outlay	11,161	0	0	0
(E) Data processing	0	0	0	0
(F) Grants/AIDS	0	0	0	1,090,387
(5) Prevention and cessation programs[b]	11,937,223	13,178,096	10,189,268	4,245,352
(6) Personal services and operation expenses				
(A) Public health nurses	973,302	0	0	0
(B) Nutrition and Physical Activity Program	0	496,495	794,521	169,088
(7) Transfer to breast cancer control fund	500,000	500,000	500,000	500,000
Annual total	$15,496,231	$17,029,459	$14,641,067	$7,025,954

a. Amounts spent by December 31, 2005.

b. Includes amounts spent on minority initiatives.

Figure 3.1 highlights the TPEP spending by quarter for three categories: (1) regular salaries, personal service matching, and extra help; (2) maintenance and operations; and (3) tobacco prevention and cessation programs. Spending for all of these categories reached a plateau at the end of FY2003 as the tobacco prevention and cessation programs became fully operational. Starting in FY2004, spending ranged between $2.3 and $5 million per quarter.

A considerable amount of Tobacco Settlement funds originally designated for TPEP tobacco cessation and prevention was allocated, primarily by legislative action, to programs that were not directly focused on tobacco cessation and prevention, including the breast cancer control fund, the Trails for Life program, the nutrition and physical fitness program (Act 1220), and an Addiction Studies program at the University of Arkansas at Pine Bluff. Figure 3.2 highlights the percentage of tobacco and cessation funds spent on non-tobacco cessation and prevention activities. That percentage has remained fairly consistent each fiscal year.

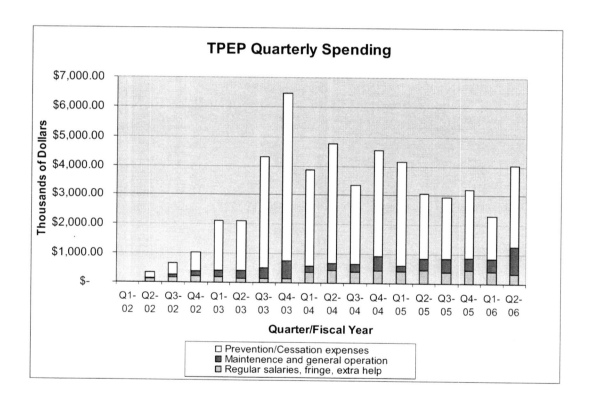

Figure 3.1—TPEP Tobacco Settlement Fund Spending, by Quarter of Fiscal Years

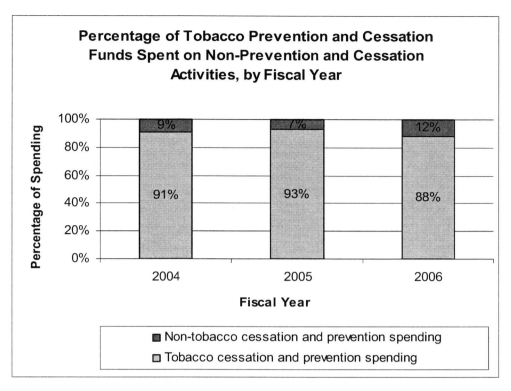

Figure 3.2—Percentage of Tobacco Cessation and Prevention Funds Spent on Non-Prevention and Cessation Activities, by Fiscal Year

The CDC has created guidelines for the amount of money each state should dedicate to various aspects of tobacco prevention and cessation (www.cdc.gov/tobacco). Table 3.6 highlights the recommended program components suggested by the CDC and compares the spending on these components in Arkansas in FY2002–2006, with the lower end of the funding criteria the CDC specifically designed for the State of Arkansas. In FY2005, TPEP's total spending fell below the lower end of the CDC-recommended total. While TPEP spent more than the recommended amount in one area, community programs, the CDC spending guidelines are lower end limits or the minimum amount that should be spent. TPEP's appropriations, however, do not account for the impact of inflation on its ability to meet CDC spending guidelines. The gap between what TPEP is able to spend and what the CDC recommends will continue to grow as long as TPEP's appropriations, and spending, remain constant or decline.

Although a large percentage of tobacco prevention and cessation funds has been spent for the intended purposes annually in 2003–2006, there are two concerns. First, the percentage spent on **nontobacco** activities thus far in 2006 is almost twice that in 2005. Second, TPEP stakeholders should be concerned with the very fact that the legislature has diverted these funds. When this happened in California, the expenditures for the earmarked programs became permanent and stable, even when revenue declined. Less than one-third of Arkansas' MSA funds are dedicated to tobacco prevention and cessation; the program's stakeholders should be urged not to let this level fall further.

Arkansas' TPEP spending should also be appreciated in a larger context. A recently released report from the American Heart Association, American Cancer Association, Campaign for Tobacco-Free Kids, and American Lung Association, titled *Broken Promise to Our Children: The 1998 State Tobacco Settlement Seven Years Later. A Report on the States' Allocation of the Tobacco Settlement Dollars* (2005), showed that most states have not spent their MSA funds on tobacco control. The report ranks Arkansas fifth in the United States in 2005 and 2006 in tobacco control spending, achieving—in its analyses—about 98 percent of the CDC minimum spending guides established for Arkansas (the states that have reached their spending guides are Maine, Colorado, Delaware, and Mississippi). While Arkansas should be applauded for its high rank on this measure, we note that it is still **below** the **minimum** standard. Moreover, this report overstates Arkansas' spending on tobacco control (it did not adjust the CDC minimum spending guidelines established in 1999 for inflation or account for the use of some TPEP funds for nontobacco programming).

Table 3.6
Tobacco Settlement Funds Spent on Tobacco Prevention Programs

Recommended Program Component[a]	Fiscal Year Spending				Lower End of CDC Funding Criteria[c]
	2003	2004	2005	2006[b]	
Community programs to reduce tobacco use	$3,209,286	$5,465,195	$4,177,303	$3,081,431	$3,065,191
Chronic disease programs	862,263	275,728	694,672	385,493	3,304,220
School programs	2,500,355	2,373,678	1,897,525	135,953	2,863,657
Enforcement	600,852	740,867	810,980	543,348	1,448,232
Statewide programs	1,070,338	1,213,322	1,057,956	217,542	1,183,426
Counter marketing	1,943,721	1,943,326	1,944,980	1,015,174	2,956,222
Cessation programs	2,137,104	2,455,559	1,591,896	316,538	3,422,562
Surveillance and Evaluation[d]	709,418	549,184	899,540	149,502	1,824,351
Administration and management	529,019	537,023	585,924	323,905	912,761
Total spent on tobacco-related programs	13,562,356	15,553,881	13,660,777	6,168,886	20,980,622
Total spent on non tobacco areas	1,933,875	1,475,578	980,291	857,071	

a. CDC-recommended program element budgets for tobacco prevention activities, from www.cdc.gov/tobacco.

b. Total monies spent by December 31, 2005.

c. These CDC estimates have been converted from 1999 to 2005 dollars using Consumer Price Index data from the Federal Reserve Bank of Minneapolis, found at http://woodrow.mpls.frb.fed.us/research/data/us/calc/hist1800.cfm.

d. TPEP builds evaluation into all of its contracts and grants. Because there is no way to quantify that built-in amount, the values in this row are underestimates of the amount that TPEP actually spends on evaluation.

RESPONSES TO EVALUATION RECOMMENDATIONS

Recommendation 1: Funding levels for the nine components of a comprehensive statewide tobacco control strategy should be raised to the minimums recommended by the CDC for Arkansas, and those programs that are not within the scope of tobacco prevention and cessation programming, as defined by the CDC guidelines, should be reevaluated for their contribution to reducing of smoking and tobacco-related disease.

> *Program Response:* Action on this recommendation is largely out of TPEP's control, as its funding is dependent on the status of the MSA payments. Further, programs that are not related to tobacco—Breastcare, Act 1220, Trails for Life, and the Addiction Studies program at University at Pine Bluff—are still being funded, accounting for 7 to 12 percent of the total TPEP budget from 2004 to 2006. Legislation states that all of these programs will be funded out of Tobacco Prevention and Cessation MSA funding.

Recommendation 2: Provide technical assistance and evaluation feedback to the community coalition and school grantees

> *Program Response:* TPEP grant administrators provided training for the community coalitions consisting of the following: utilizing the Web-based reporting system, effectively coding activities, and reporting on activities that are linked to their objectives outlined in their work plans. Follow-up training was provided on the system as well as evaluation. Technical assistance has been provided to the school cooperatives on various curricula, including a smokeless tobacco prevention curriculum. Training was provided on comprehensive tobacco policy that included the state and federal tobacco laws and enforcement issues for local school district educators. Also, the school health program analyst has been assisting schools and collaborating with school district advocates for the development of and changes to their comprehensive tobacco-free policy.
>
> TPEP has greatly increased its efforts in providing evaluation feedback to its community coalition and school grantees. Each of the grantees was assessed on its effectiveness using a structured protocol during a site visit and by reviewing final evaluation reports. After reviewing all community and school reports, TPEP met with each of the grant administrators and provided feedback (both verbal and written) on each community and school program within their region. The grant administrators shared the information with their grantees during a monitoring site visit.

Recommendation 3: Provide the ATCB additional financial resources to conduct merchant education.

> *Program Response:* The FY2006 contract was restructured to reduce inspections (from a minimum of 8,000 annually to 6,000) to make additional funds available for merchant education. As a result, the ATCB has dramatically increased its merchant education efforts (an increase from 24 trainings covering 157 employees in 34 stores in 2004 to 70 trainings covering 1,407 employees in 278 stores, in 2005). The reduction in the number of compliance checks does not appear to have negatively impacted the violation rate, as it continued to decline consistent with the previous reporting periods. The media contractor will assist with making training videos to be used by ATCB officers in FY2007.

Recommendation 4: Place stronger expectations on the statewide coalitions to evaluate their activities and the effects they are having across the state.

Program Response: TPEP held individual meetings with the directors of both statewide coalitions—the Coalition for Tobacco-Free Arkansas (CTFA) and the Arkansans for Drug-Free Youth (ADFY)—to discuss expectations regarding the services they provide and activities they complete. Trainings were provided on how these coalitions can report their activities effectively by utilizing the Web-based reporting system used by the community coalition grantees. Both ADFY and CTFA now use the system and have entered their activities. TPEP has also met with the CTFA director to discuss CTFA's work plan and its effectiveness and provided feedback on what CTFA can do to improve.

Recommendation 5: Make additional resources available for tobacco cessation programming, and better coordinate all cessation activities within the entire Arkansas Tobacco Settlement program to maximize those resources.

Program Response: Now that the contract for the Quitline and Cessation Network both reside with COPH (since July 2005), there is a possibility for greater synergy in utilization of resources.

Recommendation 6: Regarding the statewide tobacco media campaign, (1) continue at the same level of intensity; (2) increase its coordination with other anti-tobacco media campaigns being operated across the state; and (3) assess its effectiveness in reaching Arkansans and changing their attitudes about tobacco use.

Program Response: (1) The intensity of the output of the media campaign has declined somewhat since it first started, although recall of the SOS campaign has risen since its inception. (2) In addition to the media contractor, all other grantees or contractors that put out advertising must get TPEP approval of their advertising material. (3) The media campaign has focused on secondhand smoke and promoting cessation in FY2006. Before the new campaign was launched, media research—including focus groups and mall intercepts—was done to test the new advertising. Annual statewide surveys through 2005 have shown a steady increase in campaign recall and in anti-tobacco attitudes.

Recommendation 7: Provide more technical assistance to the Minority Initiative Sub-Recipient Grant Office on reporting, evidence-based activities, and evaluation.

Program Response: In November 2005, TPEP provided trainings to MISRGO grantees on methods to report their activities utilizing the Web-based reporting system. Prior to the training, TPEP met with the project coordinator of UAPB-MISRGO to discuss the details of the training. A follow-up training was provided to the UAPB grantees regarding the system as well as evaluation (February 2, 2006). Also, the MISRGO evaluator has provided technical assistance and training on evaluation to its grantees.

Recommendation 8: Finalize all of the evaluation mechanisms TPEP is using and provide adequate technical assistance to these mechanisms' end users.

Program Response: The Web-based reporting system has been finalized. The minority grantees and coalitions are using the reporting system. However, there is still some confusion among the grantees over the coding system being used. A review of the information submitted on the Web system revealed that many events that were coded as community changes (i.e., permanent changes in programs, practices, or policies with respect to tobacco, tracked in Table 3.1) were not community changes (the figures in Table 3.1 have been adjusted to reflect only true community changes).

Recommendation 9: Enhance TPEP's tobacco-related-disease efforts.

> *Program Response:* TPEP has made efforts to work more closely with the Chronic Disease Branch in this area. For example, the RFP being developed for an evaluator to evaluate TPEP also involved evaluation of the other chronic disease programs. In addition, a statewide chronic disease plan has been developed that includes tobacco control goals and objectives.

Recommendation 10: Change the process TPEP uses to budget its funds to bring it in line with the other Tobacco Settlement programs. Creating a spending budget for each fiscal year is more challenging for TPEP than for the other programs receiving Tobacco Settlement funding because TPEP is the only program required to borrow ahead by estimating how much it thinks it will receive, to spend its borrowed amount, and then get paid back by the funds.

> *Program Response:* This procedure is still in place. Changing it is largely out of TPEP's control and would require action by the state legislature. Although amending the Initiated Act allowing TPEP to carry over funds does help its budgeting situation, this process remains challenging.

RECOMMENDATIONS FOR PROGRAM IMPROVEMENT

Evaluation Summary

As a whole, the TPEP program continues to be extremely active in its prevention and cessation efforts. The community coalitions TPEP funds are effecting permanent changes in their communities (e.g., local restaurant going smoke-free) at an increased rate; and the passage of a statewide workplace smoking ban in April 2005 was in part due to the cumulative efforts of these groups. The educational co-ops funded by TPEP have been improving their implementation of evidence-based tobacco prevention programs and policies. Both the coalitions and co-ops still need to improve their tracking of the permanent changes in their communities, and TPEP ought to better synthesize the data coming from the local evaluations of these groups. The ATCB continues to make thousands of compliance checks of tobacco outlets all across the state and now provides merchant education. Violation rates have been steadily declining since 2002. TPEP continues to fund two statewide coalitions—CTFA and ADFY. ADFY engages youth to promote smoke-free lifestyles through media and education and has been participating more in required evaluation activities. CTFA has helped several communities promote clean air laws, but to date only a small number of cities (Fayetteville, Pine Bluff, El Dorado, and Fairfield Bay) have enacted these laws. The two cessation programs, the Mayo Quitline and the AFMC-run Cessation Network, have produced quit rates at or above the norm for such programs. In July 2005, the Arkansas College of Public Health took over operation of both, has expanded enrollment, and is obtaining good quit rates. Regarding links to chronic tobacco-related diseases; TPEP funds supported UAMS's move to a smoke-free campus and the Trails for Life program. TPEP is attempting to do more to link tobacco to other tobacco-related diseases. The media campaign has received less funding than when it first started, but despite the drop-off in intensity (i.e., less media and fewer community events), the SOS campaign continues to show improvements in recall among Arkansans and attract a large amount of free media contributions. The TPEP minority initiative has made considerable progress in its grant operations, and the grantees are receiving more assistance with their own planning and evaluation activities. Finally,

TPEP has greatly improved its evaluation activities across a number of its programs. TPEP's evaluation contractor, Gallup, was terminated in June 2005, and will need to be replaced.

Below are our recommendations for TPEP. Some recommendations are carried over from the last report, and some are new.

- **Raise funding levels for the nine components of a comprehensive statewide tobacco control strategy to the minimums recommended by the CDC for Arkansas.** (Continuation of a recommendation in the previous evaluation report.)

We continue to recommend that the CDC spending guideline for Arkansas be met in spending on funding for TPEP and other statewide tobacco control activities. Currently, most TPEP program components are below the CDC guidelines, especially when adjusting for inflation. Given that sufficient funds are not being appropriated to support the necessary programming and other efforts to erode TPEP funding continue, the TPEP program cannot be expected to have the impacts on tobacco use that would be possible with adequate funding. To the extent that additional funding is provided for other programming, that additional funding should count toward compliance with the CDC guidelines.

- **Reevaluate funded programs that are not within the scope of tobacco prevention and cessation programming, as defined by the CDC guidelines, for their value in contributing to reduction of smoking and tobacco-related disease.** (continuation of a recommendation in the previous evaluation report.)

We continue to recommend that programs that are not likely to have an impact on tobacco use (Breastcare, Trails for Life, UAPB Addiction Studies program, Act 1220, and the non-tobacco-related components of Healthy Arkansas) be supported with other funds. While these programs are potentially valuable, using tobacco funds to support them weakens the anti-tobacco effort.

- **Change the process TPEP must use to budget its funds to be in line with the other Tobacco Settlement programs.** (Continuation of a recommendation in the previous evaluation report.)

Because the legislature funded an Arkansas Rainy Day Fund by shifting the first year of funds out of the Tobacco Prevention and Cessation Program account, budgeting is more complicated for TPEP than for the other programs receiving Tobacco Settlement funding.[2] As a result of this shift in funds, TPEP had to borrow funds to support its tobacco prevention and cessation activities, which then are repaid in the next cycle of Tobacco Settlement funding. Therefore, TPEP has held significant amount of funds in reserve to guard against having insufficient funds to meet all of its financial demands. While this money can be rolled over, this situation delays TPEP's ability to use funding, to weakening its impacts on smoking behaviors.

- **Provide technical assistance in evaluation.** (Continuation of a recommendation in the previous evaluation report.)

Coalition grantees have demonstrated that they still do not fully understand the codes used in the Web-based reporting system. Thus, more concentrated and repeated training and

---

[2] The purpose of the Rainy Day Fund was to make funds available to assist the state Medicaid program in maintaining its established levels of service in the event that the current revenue forecast is not collected.

technical assistance is needed to assist the coalitions in accurately using this system. One of the duties for TPEP's new evaluator, when hired, could include training and technical assistance in local evaluation.

- **Evaluate the statewide media campaign in the next year both in terms of output (PSAs and community events) and focus, given that a statewide workplace smoking ban went into effect in July 2006.** (New recommendation.)

The output of the campaign has declined somewhat over the last two years, and this campaign needs to be evaluated for the next round of media. Also, the media campaign has focused a great deal on the dangers of secondhand smoke, providing strong support for the statewide ban. Given that a ban has now been passed, the media campaign should begin to pursue other goals (e.g., prevention in youth and compliance with the ban).

- **Adopt a formal quality management process and committee within TPEP, accompanied by reporting of results to the TPEP Advisory Committee.** (New recommendation.)

Although TPEP does an excellent job in building evaluation into all its program components, it could improve the synthesis and analysis of evaluation data. A standing quality management committee, in which staff present and discuss data from all the programs, could help make such a process routine. In addition, reporting quality improvement and monitoring activities to the advisory committee would ensure that this issue is given high priority, and it also would enable staff to learn from the perspectives of its advisory committee members. For example, the school and community coalition grantees are all assessed by TPEP through a site visit and use of a structured protocol and submit quarterly and final reports. The results of these evaluations should be synthesized and assessed across all the school and community coalition grantees, with discussion at meetings of the Quality Management Committee as well as the TPEP Advisory Committee. This ongoing process could help TPEP strengthen current programs, plan future RFPs, and guide training and technical assistance efforts. RAND staff has already discussed possible formats and procedures that could be used in this regard.

- **Strengthen communication between TPEP staff and the TPEP Advisory Committee.** (New recommendation.)

TPEP meets quarterly with the advisory committee and presents useful information for advisory committee members to consider. However, the advisory committee has a great deal of expertise that is not being fully utilized. For example, in addition to presenting reports that summarize performance across all the programs (as discussed in the previous recommendation), TPEP could present barriers and challenges it is experiencing and engage the TPEP Advisory Committee members to help them address those challenges. Advisory committee members could also be better used to educate state legislators about the benefits of the TPEP program, helping to preserve the MSA funding.

APPENDIX TO CHAPTER 3

Community Prevention Programs that Reduce Youth Tobacco Use

Indicator: Number of community-level community changes initiated, especially newly enacted secondhand smoke policies.

Table 3.A1
Community Changes for Tobacco Prevention

Six—month Time Period	Number of Community Changes[a]
Jan-Jun 2002	NA
Jul-Dec 2002	2
Jan-Jun 2003	15
Jul-Dec 2003	3
Jan-Jun 2004	13
Jul-Dec 2004	35
Jan-Jun 2005	39
Jul-Dec 2005	63

SOURCE: Reports from participating educational cooperatives.

a. Community changes are new or modified programs, policies, or practices in the community facilitated by the initiative that reduce risk factors for tobacco use and subsequent tobacco-related illness and death (e.g., a "no smoking" policy).

The key indicator for this aspect of the tobacco control strategy is the number of permanent effects the Arkansas Department of Health (ADH) coalitions have had in their communities. In 2004, the coalitions' efforts have led eighteen restaurants, seven workplaces, five medical facilities, a ballpark, a library, two large festivals, and all county-owned buildings in Johnson County to go smoke-free. Other changes caused by coalition efforts included new cessation activities and decreased tobacco advertising. As shown in Table 3.A1, there was a sharp increase in community changes during July through December 2004, and again in July through December 2005. In 2005, two new city ordinances were passed (Pine Bluff, Fairfield Bay), cessation referral networks were established, schools adopted stronger anti-tobacco policies, and several restaurants and multisite hospital systems went smoke-free.

Local School Education and Prevention Programs in K–12 that Include School Nurses When Appropriate

Indicator: Percentage of CDC-recommended approaches put in place in each participating educational cooperative.

Table 3.A2

Implementation of the CDC-Recommended Approaches for Tobacco Prevention Education by ADH Educational Cooperatives, December 2005

Educational Co-ops	Recommended CDC Approaches Implemented by Programs						
	1	2	3	4	5	6	7
AR River Ed	Full	Full	Full	Full	Full	Full	Full
Central Region	Full	Full	Full	Full	?	?	Full
Crowley's Ridge	Partial	Partial	None	None	?	?	Full
Dawson	Partial	Full	Partial	Full	Full	Full	Full
DeQueen-Mena	Full	Full	Full	Full	Full	Full	Full
Northeast AR	Partial	Full	Full	Partial	Full	?	Full
NW AR	Full	Full	Full	Full	Full	Full	Full
OUR Harrison	Full	Full	Full	Full	Partial	Full	Full
South Central	Full	Full	Full	Full	Full	Full	Full
Southeast AR	Partial	Full	Full	Full	?	?	Full
SW AR	Partial	Full	Partial	Full	Full	Full	Full
Wilbur Mills	Full	Full	Full	Full	?	?	Full
Number of co-ops with missing information	0	0	0	0	4	4	0
Percentage of co-ops in full compliance with guidelines[a]	58	92	75	83	58	58	100
Compliance from previous report (in percent)	50	93	54	67	77	64	10

NOTE: Numbers 1 through 7 refer to the set of best practice guidelines listed in the text. The *average* compliance across approaches is 75 percent, compared to 72 percent in last year's report. A question mark (?) Indicates there was insufficient information to assess implementation status.

a. Missing data were treated as an indication of non compliance.

Successful prevention education programs focus on helping youth to identify reasons not to use tobacco, to understand how tobacco use could affect them in their everyday lives and social relationships, to understand the benefits of not using, to believe that they can successfully resist pro-tobacco pressure, and to understand that most people do not use tobacco. Based on published evidence on school programs for tobacco prevention education, the CDC developed the following set of best practices guidelines specifically designed for schools (CDC, 1994):

1. Develop and enforce a school policy on tobacco use.

47

2. Provide instruction about the short- and long-term negative physiologic and social consequences of tobacco use, social influences on tobacco use, peer norms regarding tobacco use, and refusal skills.

3. Provide tobacco-use prevention education in kindergarten through grade; this instruction should be especially intensive in junior high or middle school and should be reinforced in high school.

4. Provide program-specific training for teachers.

5. Involve parents or families in support of school-based programs to prevent tobacco use.

6. Support cessation efforts among students and all school staff who use tobacco.

7. Assess the tobacco-use prevention program at regular intervals.

To develop documentation on the extent to which the school programs funded by the ADH were adhering to the CDC guidelines, RAND and the ADH worked together to develop reporting forms and a monitoring system that tracks adherence in all educational co-ops across Arkansas. The public health nurses and school personnel completed these evaluation forms for January through December 2005.

Data on compliance with the CDC guidelines are shown in Table 3.A2. In general, the level of compliance as reported by the cooperatives changed little from the last report (75 percent vs. 72 percent). The degree to which parents were involved and cessation was promoted declined somewhat. Some of the educational cooperatives did not report on their compliance with the CDC guidelines. For those that did report, the compliance percentages varied across the guidelines. Four cooperatives were in full compliance with all CDC guidelines (compared to three in the previous report).

All cooperatives had a school policy, although the degree of enforcement varied greatly. The most common mechanism to deliver the anti-smoking policy to students is the student handbook. Most cooperatives have either implemented or purchased evidence-based anti-tobacco curricula, in at least some grades K–12. These materials address the necessary knowledge, attitudes, and skills needed to prevent tobacco use, as recommended by the CDC. Cooperatives that received a "partial" rating did so because their curriculum was not yet being implemented or was not being implemented in all grades as recommended by the CDC. In addition, most cooperatives have provided training to the teachers responsible for implementing the prevention curriculum, and a majority of them have involved community stakeholders and support cessation. The weakest areas across the all the guidelines and cooperatives are the school policies and the involvement of parents in promotion of cessation. Furthermore, the large differences in compliance across the seven approaches—from 58 percent on three (numbers 1, 5, and 6) to almost complete adherence on two (numbers 2 and 7), and the relatively large improvements on two (numbers 3 and 4) and decline on one (number 5) pose questions. What are the reasons for these differences? Why are schools successful on some, and are there lessons to be learned from them to apply to the others? Further information should be gathered on these matters.

Enforcement of Youth Tobacco Control Laws

Indicator: Number of stores checked by the Tobacco Control Board for compliance with rules not to sell tobacco products to minors.

Table 3.A3
Compliance Checks of Stores by the Arkansas Tobacco Control Board

Six–Month Time Period	Number of Checks by the ATCB	Percentage Found in Violation
Jul–Dec 2002	1,138	24.1
Jan–Jun 2003	945	17.8
Jul–Dec 2003	4,147	16.5
Jan–Jun 2004	3,878	11.8
Jul–Dec 2004	3,661	10.7
Jan–Jun 2005	4,385	8.0
Jul–Dec 2005	2,312	6.5

The enforcement arm of the ADH tobacco prevention and cessation strategy is the ATCB checks of stores regarding sales of tobacco products to youth. Enforcement of under-18 laws to restrict purchase of tobacco products by youth is an important part of a comprehensive strategy to reduce young people's use of tobacco. To be most effective, however, minors' access restrictions need to be combined with merchant education and a comprehensive tobacco control program that reduces the availability of social sources and limits the appeal of tobacco products.

The number of checks performed by the ATCB is reported in Table 3.A3. The ATCB remained generally consistent in the number of store checks it performed in 2004 but declined in 2005—according to what was agreed to in the ATCB contract—in order to allow ATCB officers to conduct more merchant education. The average violation rates for 2004 and 2005 continue to drop and are below 20 percent, which is the benchmark used by Synar. Because the goal of these checks is to target stores suspected to be in violation, we would expect to see higher violation rates than those obtained in the Synar data. Synar found a violation rate in 2004 of 16.6 percent, which declined to 4.2 percent in 2005.[3] Therefore, the ratio of ATCB rates to Synar rates increased from 2003 to 2004, which probably indicates better targeting of noncompliant merchants in the ATCB checks.

---

[3] The Synar data were collected in the summers of 2003 and 2004 and published in reports dated the following years.

Tobacco Cessation Programs

Indicator: Number of smokers enrolled in the Cessation Network program.

Indicator: Number of smokers enrolled in the Quitline.

Table 3.A4
Enrollments and Quit Rates for ADH Tobacco Cessation Programs

Time Period	Quitline				Cessation Network		
	Contractor	Enrolled	Three Months[a] Quit Rate at (in percent)	Six Months[a] Quit Rate at (in percent)	Contractor	Enrolled	Total Quit after Three months[a] (in percent)
Jan–Jun 2003	Mayo	1,402	19.8	None eligible[b]	AFMC	785	None eligible[b]
Jul–Dec 2003	Mayo	421	18.1	20.3%	AFMC	878	20.0
Jan–Jun 2004	Mayo	329	30.0	22.6%	AFMC	761	18.7
Jul–Dec 2004	Mayo	581	27.0	17.1%	AFMC	696	21.8
Jan–Jun 2005	Mayo	749	25.9	21.9%	AFMC	560[c]	21.8
Jul–Dec 2005[d]	College of Public Health	1351	17.9	None eligible[b]	College of Public Health	236	26.1

SOURCE: Quarterly reports from the Mayo Clinic program and from the AFMC program.

a. This rate reflects only those confirmed to have quit of those enrolled, the most conservative depiction.

b. Participants were not eligible for their follow-up assessment at the time

c. January 1, 2005-March 31, 2005 only.

d. Starting July 2005, the College of Public Health took over the contract for the Quitline and the Cessation Network.

The CDC best practices guidelines (CDC, 1999b) stress cessation as a critical component of their recommended tobacco control strategy. While preventive interventions are most important to keep youth from ever using tobacco products, cessation services are needed to address the health needs of current tobacco users. These types of services greatly reduce the risk of premature death due to tobacco use (US DHHS, 1990).

Table 3.A4 shows the three- and six-month quit rate by each semiannual period for both the Mayo and AFMC programs. According to Table 3.A4, the Quitline has been yielding good cessation results, higher than what has been previously been reported in the literature for proactive quitlines. Even among those who have not quit using tobacco, Mayo has been able to document that a significant portion of this group is using tobacco less (39 percent at three months and 35 percent at six months for all of 2004). In July 2005, COPH took over the contract for both the Quitline and Cessation Network.[4] The new Quitline has enrolled a large number of persons and obtained good quit rates. Again, 17.9 percent is in the range of what can be expected for this type of program. The 17.9 percent rate reflects only those confirmed to have quit of those enrolled (i.e., whether they completed treatment or not), the most conservative depiction. The rate for those who completed treatment is much higher, 34.3 percent, suggesting the benefit of receiving the full treatment package. Alternatively, the benefit of completing the treatment might be a function of the motivation of the completer; such people could have been more likely to quit with any treatment, or perhaps even with no treatment.

The Cessation Network, first run by AFMC and then by COPH (since July 2005), has also yielded high quit rates. The overall 19 to 21 percent quit rates demonstrated by AFMC are excellent, given the typically low quit rates for even the best smoking cessation programs. For example, results from several studies (Fiore et al., 2000) show that quit rates for nicotine replacement and other drug therapies alone range between 18 to 36 percent and that behavioral interventions range from about 11 to 27 percent. It has also been established that higher quit rates are often achieved when individuals receive more treatment sessions for more minutes or when multiple formats are used at once (e.g., nicotine replacement with a behavioral intervention). The 26.1 percent rate demonstrated by the COPH Cessation Network is superior. The enrollment numbers declined somewhat since COPH took over for AFMC because of issues involved in starting new sites.

Several factors should be noted when interpreting these quit rates. First, at the time of measurement, not all those enrolled during each particular time period were eligible for their three- and six-month follow-up assessments, so the denominators are only those for whom three or six months have passed since discharge. Second, the programs were not able to contact about 20 to 33 percent of discharged participants to assess their quit status. In particular, the Mayo, AFMC, and COPH programs served individuals who are low-income, have a low educational level, and are highly transient. Finally, it can be difficult to compare quit rates achieved by the university-based cessation studies mentioned above with treatment in community settings because the latter programs almost always have fewer resources.

For Table 3.A4, enrollees who could not be contacted were considered not to have quit, and rates were calculated by dividing the number contacted who reported they quit by the total number enrolled. Thus, the actual quit rates may be higher than what TPEP has been able to document. For example, the Mayo Clinic program quit rates for the subset of enrollees who were successfully contacted were about 50 percent at three months and 48 percent at six months for all of 2004.

_____

[4] All of TPEP's major contracts must be approved by the Peer Review Legislative Committee, responsible for monitoring contracts between state agencies. The legislative review process of TPEP's Mayo contract resulted in Mayo losing its (then) contract. Apparently, a legislator called the Quitline and was told he would have to wait two weeks for services. That violates the Quitline contract. TPEP followed up and found that Mayo had a staff shortage and had trouble responding to huge increases from the states it was servicing. Both these developments eroded upper level management support for Mayo at TPEP. TPEP transferred the Quitline from Mayo to COPH as of July 28, 2005.

Tobacco-Related Disease Prevention Programs

Indicator: Number of miles of hiking trails constructed in the Trails for Life program.

Tobacco use increases the risk for a number of diseases that need to be treated and prevented even in the face of lessening tobacco use. Therefore, the CDC recommends addressing tobacco use in the larger context of these diseases, attempting to link tobacco control activities to those taken to prevent tobacco-related diseases such as cancer, cardiovascular disease, asthma, oral cancers, and stroke (CDC, 1999a). The Trails for Life grant program, which provides funding to construct walking trails, can be a part of this comprehensive strategy.

On August 11, 2004, it was announced that 18 sites received funding to build a trail. All either have been completed or are near completion, for a total of almost 7.5 miles of trail. In 2005, another seven trail grants were awarded, of which six are completed or near completion, for another 1.5 miles of trail. While these amounts of trail are miniscule by almost any standard, they can be viewed as a first step to getting Arkansans out of their automobiles and on their feet. However, information on how much these trails are used and by whom must be obtained in order to justify the Trails for Life program.

Comprehensive Public Awareness and Health Promotion Campaign

Indicator: Number of public service announcements and community events to support tobacco prevention and cessation activities.

Indicator: Percentage of media ad funds leveraged as donated funds from the media companies.

Indicator: Percentage of youth surveyed who recall the SOS media campaign.

Table 3.A5
Media and Community Events for Tobacco Prevention and Cessation

Six-Month Time Period	Community Events	PSAs/Media Coverage
Jan-Jun 2002	0	5
Jul-Dec 2002	8	630
Jan-Jun 2003	27	295
Jul-Dec 2003	30	114
Jan-Jun 2004	86	274
Jul-Dec 2004	23	58
Jan-Jun 2005	19	121
Jul-Dec 2005	10	35

Media campaigns have been documented to reduce smoking among current smokers and to prevent initiation among nonsmokers (Farrelly et al., 2005; Hamilton, 1972; Siegel and Biener, 2000). Such campaigns are even more effective when implemented along with other elements of a tobacco control strategy, such as the other components of the ADH Tobacco Prevention and Cessation Program. Guidance from the U.S. Department of Health and Human Services states that media campaigns need to have sufficient reach, frequency, and duration to be effective; that all media should be pretested with the target audience; and that effects of the media campaign should be continuously monitored (US DHHS, 2000).

Since its start, the SOS campaign run by ADH has maintained a steady presence in local communities and has placed hundreds of paid advertisements across the state. As shown in Table 3.A5, the community events increased slowly over time, peaking in the first half of 2004 and then declining. The PSAs and media spots built momentum more quickly, peaking in the second half of 2002. They declined substantially in the second half of 2004, increased in the first half of 2005, and then declined in the second half of 2005 to the lowest level since the start of the campaign.

Table 3.A6
Media Advertisement Costs Paid by the ADH and from Donated Funds

Six-Month Time Period	Campaign Paid by ADH	Donated	Leverage Ratio (donated/paid)[a]
Jul–Dec 2002	448,723	875,877	1.95
Jan–Jun 2003	371,434	1,000,619	2.69
Jul–Dec 2003	1,021,054	1,827,316	1.79
Jan–Jun 2004	1,378,946	884,574	0.64
Jul–Dec 2004	615,880	1,361,173	2.21
Jan–Jun 2005	748,857	1,189,130	1.58
Jul–Dec 2005	678,974	468,911	0.69

SOURCE: Cranford, Johnson, Robinson Woods reports.

a. This leveraged amount is actually an underestimate because much of the spending is "front-loaded" and should increase as the campaign progresses.

The SOS contractor has been successful in leveraging additional funding that has enabled it to provide additional media beyond what the ADH contract covered, as shown in Table 3.A6. This funding includes free print and TV advertisements and public relations coverage of ADH activities, sponsorships, and other partnerships that significantly enhanced the actual campaign budget. The amount of donated media has varied a great deal from a low of 0.64 times the amount of paid media to a high of 2.69 times the amount of paid media. In the last half of 2005, the figure of 0.69 may be an underestimate because the media contractor had still not received all its evaluation forms for sponsorship at the time this report was written.

Table 3.A7
Percentage of Survey Respondents Who Reported They Recalled the
SOS Media Campaign

Time period		General Teens	African American Teens	Adults
October–November 2002	Number surveyed	401	400	400
	Percentage recall	73	73	44
August 2003	Number surveyed	400	404	400
	Percentage recall	87	89	63
September 2004	Number surveyed	402	405	404
	Percentage recall	92	91	75
January 2006	Number surveyed	150	80	600
	Percentage recall	91	98	76

The SOS contractor hired a local survey research firm—Opinion Research Associates—to assess its media penetration over time using three representative statewide samples (about 400 teens, 400 African-American teens, and 400 adults obtained through random-digit sampling). As shown in Table 3.A7, recall of the SOS campaign was 73 percent for both all teens and African-American teens in November 2002. Recall increased to 87 percent of all teens and 89 percent for African-American teens in August 2003, and increased again to 91–92 percent in September 2004. However, the recall rates for each of the individual elements of the campaign were much lower (not shown in the table). Recall also increased among adults, from 44 percent in 2002, 63 percent in 2003, and 75 percent in 2004. In 2005, the SOS campaign recall remained at these levels. Unfortunately, recall rates have not been linked to the number of PSAs in any particular time period.

Minority Initiatives

Indicator: Percentage of graduates from UAPB Addiction Studies who obtain an addiction job within Arkansas after graduation.

Cigarette smoking is a major cause of disease and death for minorities, especially for African Americans (Chatila et al., 2004; US DHHS, 1998). Smoking prevalence increased in the 1990s among African-American and Hispanic youth. This reverses a trend of large declines during the 1970s and 1980s, especially among African-American youth, which may be due to tobacco industry marketing efforts targeted toward minority populations (Geobel, 1994; Ling and Glantz, 2002; Robinson, Barry, and Bloch, 1992; Robinson, Pertschuk, and Sutton, 1992; US DHHS, 1994, 1998, 2001; Yerger and Malone, 2002). At the same time, minority populations traditionally have less access to prevention and treatment services, and there is clear evidence that the disproportionate tobacco-related disease burden experienced by minority communities requires specific attention.

In spring 2004, the program graduated 15 students. In December, the program graduated an additional 6 students for a total of 21 graduates. Out of this group, 16 (76 percent) have obtained addiction-related jobs in Arkansas. In 2005, eight more students graduated, five of whom obtained addiction-related jobs in Arkansas (total of 21 out of 29, or 72 percent).

Chapter 4
College of Public Health

PROGRAM DESCRIPTION

Expectations Specified in the Initiated Act

The Initiated Act resulted in legislation that established and provided funding for the Arkansas School of Public Health (changed to the College of Public Health through Act 856 of 2003, and henceforth called COPH). According to the act,

> The Arkansas School of Public Health is hereby established as a part of the University of Arkansas for Medical Sciences for the purpose of conducting activities to improve the health and healthcare of the citizens of Arkansas. These activities should include, but not be limited to the following functions: faculty and course offerings in the core areas of public health including health policy and management, epidemiology, biostatistics, health economics, maternal and child health, environmental health, and health and services research; with courses offered both locally and statewide via a variety of distance learning mechanisms.

> It is intended that the Arkansas School of Public Health should serve as a resource for the General Assembly, the Governor, state agencies, and communities. Services provided by the Arkansas School of Public Health should include, but not be limited to the following: consultation and analysis, developing and disseminating programs, obtaining federal and philanthropic grants, conducting research, and other scholarly activities in support of improving the health and healthcare of the citizens of Arkansas.

Update on Program Activities

COPH of the UAMS was appropriated funds by the Arkansas General Assembly to begin operations July 1, 2001. As of January 2002, COPH began to offer a 42-hour Master of Public Health (MPH) program with a number of specializations available and an 18-hour Post-Baccalaureate Certificate program. In addition, as of summer 2003, the UAMS College of Medicine and COPH offered a combined MD/MPH degree program that permitted students to enroll concomitantly in both the College of Medicine and COPH and complete all requirements for both degrees in four years. Beginning in fall 2003, COPH students could pursue the Juris Doctor (JD) and the MPH degrees concurrently in the William H. Bowen School of Law at the University of Arkansas at Little Rock and COPH. As of January 2004, COPH added the Doctor of Public Health program (DrPH), and the combined PharmD/MPH program was offered with the UAMS College of Pharmacy beginning in fall 2005.

COPH is presently working toward reaccreditation. The Council on Education for Public Health (CEPH) has recently revised accreditation criteria that the college will be required to meet by December 2007. The most significant changes will require COPH to offer three doctoral programs (past requirement was one) with a minimum faculty requirement of five full-time equivalents (FTEs) for each doctoral program, and five FTEs, three of which must be individuals working full-time, for master's programs. COPH has progressed in the process of approving two new doctoral programs developed in August 2005. The PhD application in Health Systems Research was considered by the Arkansas Department of Higher Education in its meeting at the end of April 2006, and the PhD in Health Promotion and Prevention Research was considered in August, 2006. The self-study was delivered to CEPH in May, 2006, and the accreditation site visit results will be available in early 2007.

COPH created the Office of Community-Based Public Health (OCBPH) as a part of the dean's office in 2003. COPH has three community liaisons who primarily establish collaborative partnerships with four community-based organizations in the state. As of 2005, COPH established a memorandum of agreement with La Casa to further mutual goals emanating from community-based projects, set parameters on how they will work together, and outline policies regarding publications and research.

COPH has engaged in a number of activities that have supported the general assembly over the past four years. During 2005, COPH faculty and staff worked frequently with the Senate and House interim committees on public health of the Arkansas General Assembly. One highlight was a presentation to the House Public Health, Welfare, and Labor Committee regarding baseline data compiled to evaluate the impact of Act 1220 of 2003, which was funded by a Robert Wood Johnson Foundation grant. In addition, COPH was awarded a contract from TPEP to operate its Tobacco Cessation Network beginning in July 2005. In June 2005, COPH was directed by a legislative committee of the Arkansas General Assembly to submit a proposal to TPEP to operate the Arkansas Quitline contract, which had been administered by an out-of-state provider. This proposal also was funded.

PROGRESS TOWARD ACHIEVING FIVE-YEAR AND SHORT-TERM GOALS

All program goals were established as part of the Arkansas Tobacco Settlement Evaluation activities in spring 2005 and were first specified in the 2005 RAND report (Farley et al., 2005b).

Goal 1: Establish doctoral programs in three areas by 2007–2008.

Progress on Goal 1: ON SCHEDULE. In response to the changes in the CEPH accreditation criteria, which require accredited schools of public health to offer at least three doctoral programs, COPH developed two new PhD programs, for which it is in the process of seeking final approval from the Arkansas Department of Higher Education. One of the programs is a PhD in health systems research, coadministered by the UAMS Graduate School and COPH's Department of Health Policy and Management. The other is a PhD in health promotion and prevention research, coadministered by the UAMS Graduate School and COPH's Department of Health Behavior and Health Education. Students enrolled in these programs in August 2006.

Goal 2: Establish staffing of a minimum of five faculty for each of the three doctoral programs.

Progress on Goal 2: ON SCHEDULE. COPH has established the five full-time faculty positions needed to satisfy CEPH's requirements for all three doctoral programs. However, as noted in the review of the new doctoral programs by the Arkansas Department of Higher Education, an additional health economist faculty member is needed to support the

PhD program in health systems research. In addition, a faculty member in the Department of Health Behavior and Health Education has been recruited away from UAMS, so an additional faculty member will be required to support the new PhD program in health promotion and prevention research. Recruitments will need to be initiated to fill these positions.

Goal 3: Increase distance-accessible education.

Progress on Goal 3: ON SCHEDULE. Currently, COPH has three classes available on the Web, with several additional courses in development for Web-based delivery in the coming academic year. In addition, COPH provides multiple classes that take place over three weekends per semester, minimizing the number of times students must drive to Little Rock to attend class but still maintaining opportunities for student group interaction and in-person faculty mentoring. COPH has recently begun planning with the Department of Health and Human Services Division of Health to use its renovated auditorium to teach distance-accessible classes, which will include video. COPH's hope is to increase the number of students, the number of classes, and the modes of delivery. We encourage COPH to set a target for next year for the number of classes that it would like to offer on the Web and through weekend courses.

Goal 4: Increase outside grant funding for research by 20 percent above 2004–2005.

Progress on Goal 4: AHEAD OF SCHEDULE. Figure 4.1 depicts active funding as of June for 2002–2005. The data show that COPH has increased funding from $2,146,126 in June 2004 to $3,466,777 in June 2005, an increase of 61 percent.

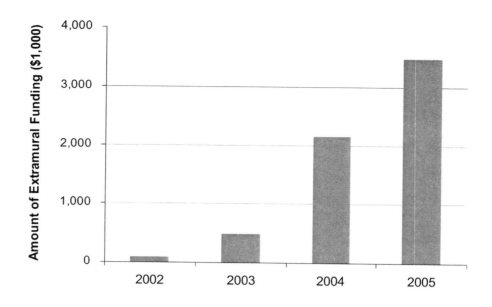

Figure 4.1—External Grant Funding for COPH, June 2002–2005

PERFORMANCE ON PROCESS INDICATORS

Four indicators were chosen to represent the overall progress in implementing the COPH program. These indicators track progress on fulfilling the mandates in the act for the program to (1) increase the number of communities in which citizens receive public health training, (2) obtain federal and philanthropic funding, (3) conduct research, and (4) serve as a resource to the general assembly, the governor, state agencies, and communities.

This section briefly highlights performance on some indicators. Further description of these indicators is provided in the appendix at the end of this chapter. Since its inception, COPH continues to be successful in recruiting a diverse student body, which is representative of the diverse population in the state of Arkansas. Overall, COPH has had 50 students graduate, and 90 percent of these graduates are currently employed in Arkansas in a public health–related field. The number of publications has steadily increased since 2001 and is up to 78 for FY2005. COPH continues to conduct legislative briefings and was involved in several special projects in 2005. These projects include speaking in support of a smoking ordinance that would ban smoking in restaurants and public buildings (enacted into law April 2006), having faculty volunteer at schools, and bringing members of the Arkansas General Assembly to view the workings of the contracted tobacco-use cessation programs operated by COPH faculty and staff.

PERFORMANCE ON MANAGEMENT INTEGRITY CRITERIA

Types and Performance of Governing and Advisory Boards

COPH is overseen by the Board of Trustees of the University of Arkansas (UA) system. COPH reports directly, through the dean, to the UAMS chancellor. The chancellor, in turn, reports to the UA president. The UA system is governed by the UA Board of Trustees. COPH is not at liberty to develop an independent governing board.

The UA Board of Trustees consists of ten members—each appointed by the governor to ten-year terms. The UA Board of Trustees meets at least quarterly but often more frequently. In 2006, its regularly scheduled meetings were held in January, March, May, July, September, and November.

RAND staff asked COPH leadership to rate the level of involvement by the UA Board of Trustees in three categories of COPH management functions: oversight, monitoring program performance, and providing interface with communities. RAND staff then confirmed those ratings with interviews and document reviews. These ratings are shown in Table 4.1. Given that COPH is far down in the hierarchy of the UA system, the low degree of direct oversight exercised by the board of trustees is neither surprising nor disturbing.

Table 4.1
Governance Oversight of the College of Public Health by the University of Arkansas Board of Trustees

Management Functions	Rating[a]
Oversight	
Goals and planning	1
Priorities	2
Budget	2
Quality management	1
Monitoring Program Performance	
Progress toward goals	1
Spending	2
Quality performance	1
Providing Interface with Communities	
Community needs	1
Community interactions	1
Fund-raising	1

a. Definitions of ratings: 1 = not involved, 2 = minimally involved,
3 = not intense involvement, 4 = fully considers, 5 = directive.

Quality Improvement Process

In this section, we review the comprehensiveness of COPH's quality improvement process—defined as a written process used to continually improve program performance over time. Broadly, this involves collecting various types of performance data, analyzing them, formulating improvement plans based on the analysis, and performing monitoring and feedback on progress.

COPH has a number of processes in place by which it tracks its own activities and seeks to continually improve program performance. The college's formal quality management process has been in place since COPH was established in 2001. The Dean's Executive Committee (DEC) and, ultimately, the dean, are the entities within COPH responsible for quality management.

The DEC advises the dean on all matters that it considers significantly related to the efficient and effective administration of the college programs. Membership on the DEC is defined in the college's governance document, which was approved by the college's faculty. The dean serves as permanent chair of the DEC, with the COPH associate dean for public health practice as vice chair. The chairs of all departments, associate dean for public health practice, associate dean for academic affairs, and designated college-wide center directors serve as members of this committee. All assistant deans and the college's administrator are ex officio members without vote and are excused from executive sessions.

Other standing and ad hoc committees are also charged with quality management responsibilities (but not program management). The following standing committees meet on an ongoing basis, have a specific area of responsibility, and offer recommendations to the DEC and the dean for final action: Committee on Academic Standards; Faculty Appointment, Promotion and Tenure Committee; Research Committee; Continuing Education Committee; Minority Recruitment and Retention Committee; Student Admission Committee; Student Council; Honor Council; and Appeals Committee.

The CEPH accreditation process provides an additional, national process through which COPH engages in self-study, site visit evaluations, and review by CEPH's board of councilors. This process and the evaluation of the college's performance are based on nationally derived criteria. The independent evaluation conducted by RAND also acts as a quality management tool.

Overall, COPH is doing well on aspects of quality management and has acted to make improvements through its quality management process. For example, when COPH was originally organized and the MPH program approved and implemented, plans for students' preceptorship and integrative projects were only briefly described. During COPH planning retreats, and later in the work of an ad hoc committee, plans were refined and approved by the Academic Standards Committee, DEC, and the dean. Over time, the policy and guidelines for students have been further developed and refined, addressing a variety of issues, including grading policies.

In addition, during COPH's retreat in October 2002, research infrastructure was a topic considered by the faculty. An ad hoc committee of faculty was then formed and charged by the faculty and dean with investigating and prioritizing the development of different components of infrastructure identified during the retreat (including costs). Formal and informal input was solicited from faculty by the committee, and a final report was developed and presented to the dean, DEC, and faculty. This report identified high-, medium-, and low-priority needs.

Financial Management Process

COPH uses the UAMS accounting system, called Systems Applications Processes (SAP), to report spending to the state for the Tobacco Settlement program. This system is operated by

Enterprise IT, a centralized UAMS unit. The COPH administrator and selected members of the staff have access to the system to enter transactions and retrieve data. There is no additional, local automated system at COPH.

The UAMS chancellor informs the board of trustees on all relevant financial matters, and provides any information requested or pertinent to management and accounting practices. The COPH has established separate accounts for its key program components on the UAMS system. The state system is called the Arkansas Administrative Statewide Information System (AASIS) and is a SAP program, as is the separate UAMS system. COPH maintains detailed information on research projects and other administrative information necessary for effective operations. All personnel who perform the COPH financial management and accounting functions have the required qualifications.

Contract Management

COPH does not contract with other organizations to perform any of the program activities supported by the Tobacco Settlement funding. Agreements or contracts are formed mainly to create collaborative relationships or to establish academic sites for students to complete graduation requirements. For example, the La Casa memorandum of agreement establishes the COPH relationship with this community partner and sets out the UAMS process of documenting research and other activities. The Joint Oversight Committee agreement designates membership, outlines the purpose of the group, and specifies the focus areas of the group. COPH has signed agreements with more than 30 agencies and organizations that are willing to follow the guidelines to allow students to complete their integration or preceptorship projects with them.

ANALYSIS OF SPENDING TRENDS

Act 1576 of 2001, HB 1717 of 2003, and HB 1553 of 2005 appropriated funds to COPH for the first three biennium periods of the Tobacco Settlement Fund Allocation. Table 4.2 summarizes these appropriations by fiscal year.[5] It is important to note, however, that the appropriation represents the maximum leveling that can be received and that actual funding to COPH is fixed at 5 percent of the total funds received annually in Arkansas from the Master Settlement Agreement. The college has always received less than the appropriated amount of funding.

We continue our detailed review of COPH's expenditures of Tobacco Settlement funds by adding the spending from January 2005 through December 2005. The spending totals for January to June 2004 are included as the third and fourth quarters of fiscal year 2005. This completes the total spending for FY2005. The spending totals for July to December 2005 are the first two quarters of FY2006. Since spending data do not exist yet for the last half of FY2006, it is not possible to fully analyze spending in FY2006 or for the third biennium.

---

[5] The appropriated amounts in Table 4.2 come directly from Act 1576, HB 1717, and HB 1553; however, COPH actually received less than the full amount appropriated in these bills.

Table 4.2

Tobacco Settlement Funds Appropriated to the College of Public Health, by Fiscal Year

Item	Second Biennium		Third Biennium	
	2004	2005	2006	2007
(1) Regular salaries	$2,500,613	$2,500,613	$2,468,592	$2,468,592
(2) Personal service matching	484,316	484,316	596,229	596,229
(3) Maintenance and operations				
(A) Operations	196,784	196,784	233,610	233,610
(B) Travel	40,000	40,000	55,787	55,787
(C) Professional fees	100,000	100,000	76,708	76,708
(D) Capacity outlay	165,000	165,000	55,787	55,787
(E) Data processing	0	0	0	0
Annual total	$3,486,713	$3,486,713	$3,486,713	$3,486,713
Biennium total	$6,973,426		$6,973,426	

Table 4.3 presents the total Tobacco Settlement funds received and spent by COPH during this period. In all four full fiscal years, COPH received less actual funding than was appropriated. Continuing the trend from prior years, COPH received $1,000,210 less than the appropriated amount for FY2005 and expects to receive $978,706 less than the appropriated amount for FY2006. COPH expenditures in FY2005 decreased approximately $25,000 from FY2004. However, COPH also spent $330,586 more than it received in FY2005. COPH reported that its total budget consists not only of tobacco funds but also annual cost-of-living adjustments, 30 percent of tuition obtained within the college's programs, 30 percent of indirect costs generated by COPH faculty, and additional state funds available to the chancellor. These combined sources of funds are what are budgeted annually to cover the college's expenses in addition to grant and contract direct costs. Tobacco funds were fully expended during FY2005, and the additional expenditures were covered by other sources, including carry-forward tobacco funds from FY2004 and the other sources of state funds included in the college's overall annual budget. Spending during the first half of FY2006 is lower than that from FY2005, but similar to the spending in the first half of FY2004. As of December 31, 2005, COPH had spent about 47 percent of the FY2006 funds expected to be received.

Table 4.3

Tobacco Settlement Funds Received and Spent by COPH, by Fiscal Year

Item	2003 Received[a]	2003 Spent	2004 Received	2004 Spent	2005 Received	2005 Spent[b]	2006 Received	2006 Spent[c]
(1) Regular salaries		$2,130,281	$2,133,695	$2,041,404	$1,798,000	$2,034,480	$1,881,415	$864,689
(2) Personal service matching		445,223	484,316	404,707	431,520	420,242	387,138	174,862
(3) Maintenance and operations								
(A) Operations		140,336	196,784	247,057	96,983	272,109	200,000	115,856
(B) Travel		24,907	40,000	33,024	40,000	41,228	20,000	16,385
(C) Professional fees		0	100,000	78,500	90,000	29,978	0	0
(D) Capacity outlay		288,418	100,000	37,224	30,000	19,052	19,454	4,962
(E) Data processing		0	0	0	0	0	0	0
Annual total	$3,219,800	$3,029,165	$3,054,795	$2,841,916	$2,486,503	$2,817,089	$2,508,007	$1,176,754

a. Data for received amounts for individual categories were unavailable in 2003.

b. Overspending in FY2005 was covered by leftover funds from FY2004.

c. Amounts spent in the first half of fiscal year through December 31, 2005.

Figure 4.2 highlights quarterly trends in COPH spending through the first two quarters of FY2006. COPH monthly expenditures for regular salaries, personal service matching, and maintenance and operations increased steadily from inception through FY2003, reflecting the initial growth while getting the COPH programming into place. Spending levels declined in the first quarter of FY2004, before steadily increasing through the rest of FY2004 and then leveling off in the first two quarters of FY2005. The maintenance and operations (M&O) expenditures in the fourth quarter of FY2005 appear to be zero. COPH spent approximately $119,000 on M&O during this quarter, but these expenditures were covered with funds from other budgeted state sources. Because Figure 4.2 reflects only Tobacco Settlement Fund spending by COPH, it does not include these expenditures. Spending through the first two quarters of FY2006 is below FY2005 levels, but it is similar to the spending in the first two quarters of FY2004. The jump in maintenance and operations at the end of FY2003 occurred when COPH moved into its new building.

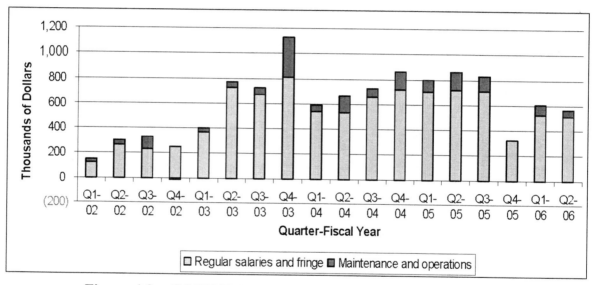

**Figure 4.2—COPH Tobacco Settlement Funding Spending by
Quarter in Fiscal Years**

COPH has five streams of funding: Tobacco Settlement; 30 percent of tuition and 30 percent of indirect costs credited to COPH; state funds from other sources allocated by the chancellor to the college to develop its programs; philanthropy; and direct costs from grants and contracts. Figure 4.3 presents the percentage shares, by fiscal year, of the total COPH expenditures funded by these five funding categories. With each fiscal year, COPH has increased funding from sources other than the Tobacco Settlement funds. Currently, more than half of the total COPH funding comes from grants and contracts obtained by the COPH faculty.

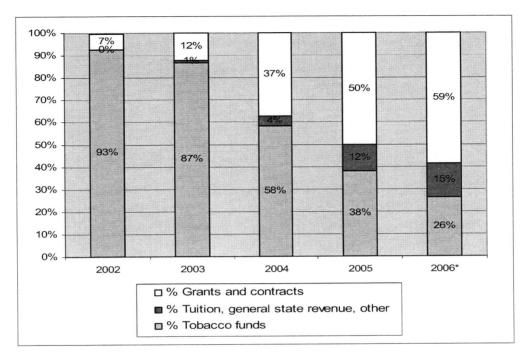

Figure 4.3—Percentage of Spending from Tobacco Settlement Funds and Other Funds, by Fiscal Year

RESPONSES TO EVALUATION RECOMMENDATIONS

Recommendation 1: COPH should continue to hire more faculty, particularly diverse faculty (2004 and 2005).

> *Program Response:* COPH remains committed to maintaining a diverse faculty. In 2005, COPH hired eleven new full-time faculty, two of whom are from ethnic minority groups. To date, seven of the forty full-time faculty members (18 percent) are from ethnic minority groups.

Recommendation 2: COPH needs to provide evaluation expertise to its community partners to assess the impact of the work they are doing in the community (2004).

> *Program Response:* The Office of Community-Based Public Health (OCBPH) is involved in many different activities that address this need. OCBPH has four formally recognized community partners: (1) Boys, Girls, and Adults Community Development Center in Marvel, (2) Walnut Street Works in Helena/West Helena, (3) We Care in Pulaski County, and (4) La Casa in Pulaski County. The director of OCBPH is working with other staff and faculty to assist the Tri-Country Rural Health Network, which includes Walnut Street Works, in evaluating its Community Connector Program. COPH staff oversee the analysis of data from a community tobacco-usage survey conducted by We Care as part of its tobacco prevention grant program. OCPBH has been asked to assist the U.S. Department of Agriculture Delta Nutrition Intervention Research Initiative in providing training to its Arkansas community partners in community-based participatory research. This project will directly benefit the Boys, Girls, and Adults

Community Development Center in Marvel; and lessons learned will be shared with the other three COPH community partners.

Recommendation 3: COPH should maintain the discount for ADH employees (2004).

> *Program Response:* COPH advised RAND and the Tobacco Settlement Commission in 2004 that COPH has no direct control over this recommendation. This decision must be agreed to by the UA Board of Trustees, the president of the UA system, and the chancellor of UAMS. The 70 percent discount was discontinued in 2005; however, even without the discount, more than 10 percent of the COPH student body continues to come from the Department of Health employee pool.

Recommendation 4: COPH should provide scholarships and discounts for distance-learning students (2004).

Recommendation 5: COPH should provide assistantships to students to help support the cost of obtaining a degree (2004).

> *Program Response:* COPH has no direct control over appropriations and cannot guarantee allocation of additional funds to COPH for scholarships and assistantships. More than 90 percent of the COPH students are part-time, nontraditional students who are working at a full-time job as they pursue their degrees. Nonetheless, a number of students are being supported as research assistants with extramural funding. A system has also been established in the Office of Student Services to compile student funding opportunities from outside the college and distribute this information to students. In addition, the Department of Environmental and Occupational Health has been able to secure contributions to establish tuition scholarships for students pursuing specialized MPH degrees in the department. In consultation with the family of the late Dr. Fay Boozman, the College of Public Health has also established the Fay W. Boozman Public Health and Community Service Scholarship fund to help support a deserving MPH student each year.

Recommendation 6: COPH should increase grant funding and leverage funding from other sources (2005).

> *Program Response:* As of 2005, COPH had more than 50 active grants totaling more than $5.3 million for the current fiscal year. COPH has significantly increased grant funding in a very short time.

Recommendation 7: COPH should develop curricula for the new doctoral programs (2005).

Recommendation 8: COPH should develop the two new doctoral programs that will be required to maintain accreditation and recruit students into these programs (2005).

> *Program Response:* Two new doctoral programs were developed in August 2005, one in health systems research (HSR) and the other in health promotion and prevention research (HPPR). The board of trustees approved these courses in January 2006. The Arkansas Department of Higher Education (ADHE) met in April and gave final approval to the HSR application. The ADHE considered the HPPR application at its August 2006 meeting. Once programs are approved by the ADHE, COPH will be able to advertise the programs and recruit students. Students are expected to enroll in these programs in January or August 2007.

RECOMMENDATIONS FOR PROGRAM IMPROVEMENT

COPH has excelled over the past four years in teaching, research, obtaining funding, and serving as an Arkansas-based resource to the public, communities, and state agencies. It has many difficult challenges ahead, however, of which its leadership is well aware. The most important of these challenges arises from the change in national accreditation criteria for schools of public health.

- **COPH should continue in its efforts to meet the new accreditation requirements by December 2007, to expand full-time faculty for doctoral and master's programs and recruit students for the new doctoral programs, and to obtain funding to support the additional salaries.**

This change requires that COPH have faculty and students in place for all three doctoral programs and the master's programs by December 2007. In specific terms, each of the three doctoral programs must have five full-time faculty, and an additional five FTEs (of whom three must be full-time faculty members) are required to staff the master's programs. Just finding the new faculty and recruiting adequate numbers of students would be challenge enough, but, especially given the anticipated decrease in Tobacco Settlement funding (the extent of this decrease is uncertain), the college faces the major burden of finding money to pay for this growth. RAND therefore recommends not only that COPH continue in its efforts to reach these difficult goals in the upcoming year, but also that ATSC, UAMS and, if necessary, the Arkansas legislature support this valuable state asset.

APPENDIX TO CHAPTER 4

Performance on Process Indicators through 2005

Four indicators were chosen to represent the overall progress in implementing the COPH program. These indicators track progress on fulfilling the mandates in the act for the program to (1) increase the number of communities in which citizens receive public health training, (2) obtain federal and philanthropic funding, (3) conduct research, and (4) serve as a resource to the general assembly, the governor, state agencies, and communities. An endpoint indicator is that COPH should receive accreditation from CEPH by May 2004, which is discussed above.

Increase the number of communities in which citizens receive public health training.

Indicator: Percentage of all enrolled students who originate from each of the AHEC regions.

The enrollment goal was to ensure that COPH attracted students for public health training from a broad geographic range of communities and counties across the state. COPH has undertaken numerous activities to recruit a wide range of students, including providing information online, at relevant conferences, college fairs, and town hall meetings, in brochures, and via a toll-free number. COPH presents information to high school students, offers nondegree classes, and collaborates with other universities in the state. From 2002 to 2005, it also offered a 70 percent tuition discount to full-time employees for ADH, Department of Environmental Quality (DEQ), and Arkansas Minority Health Commission (AMHC) employees. This discount is no longer being offered.

Table 4.A1 and Figure 4.A1 show the distribution of students by region of origin (birthplace). COPH has had students from many different regions attend its program. Because these percentages are based on a student's birthplace, there appears to be a large proportion of foreign and out-of-state students; however, all students seeking degrees in the program are current Arkansas.

Table 4.A1

Distribution of Students by Region of Origin

Region	Spring 2002	Summer 2002	Fall 2002–03	Spring 2003	Summer 2003	Fall 2003–04	Spring 2004	Fall 2004–05	Spring 2005	Summer 2005	Fall 2005–06
Number enrolled	43	15	93	119	86	177	190	181	179	60	219
Central	49.0%	58.8%	28.0%	32.7%	23.3%	28.0%	28.0%	28.0%	30.0%	40.0%	34.0%
South Central	13.7	11.8	12.9	14.3	25.6	16.0	17.0	14.0	11.0	8.0	12.0
North Central	2.4	0.0	3.2	5.0	5.8	7.0	7.0	9.0	8.0	3.0	9.0
Northeast	9.4	11.8	8.6	3.4	5.8	7.0	7.0	7.0	6.0	2.0	5.0
Northwest	4.6	0.0	4.3	3.4	5.8	5.0	5.0	4.0	5.0	3.0	4.0
Southwest	0.0	0.0	4.3	7.6	3.5	3.0	4.0	3.0	3.0	3.0	4.0
South	2.4	0.0	3.2	3.4	5.8	5.0	4.0	4.0	3.0	7.0	4.0
Delta	2.4	0.0	4.3	4.2	1.2	3.0	3.0	3.0	3.0	3.0	4.0
Out of state	13.7	17.6	20.4	19.3	17.4	18.0	16.0	19.0	21.0	18.0	17.0
Foreign	2.4	0.0	10.8	6.7	5.8	8.0	9.0	9.0	10.0	13.0	7.0

SOURCE: College of Public Health

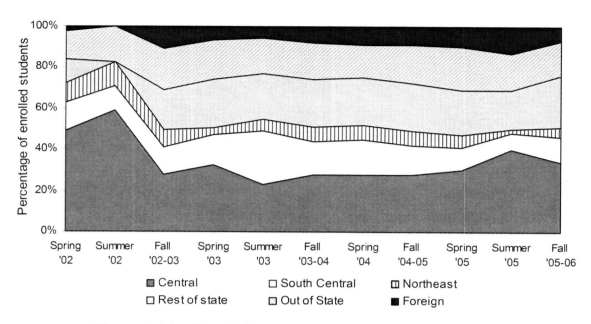

Figure 4.A1—Trends in Enrollment Distribution by Region

Indicator: Percentage of graduates pursuing employment in a public health–related field.

The first student graduated in December 2003. As of December 2005, 45 out of 50 (90 percent) graduates are employed in a public health–related field.

Indicator: Percentage of all enrolled students who are African American, Latino, or Asian American.

Table 4.A2 and Figure 4.A2 show the percentage of COPH students enrolled by race/ethnicity and compare the percentages to the state of Arkansas. COPH has been quite successful in recruiting African Americans and Asian Americans well above their representation in the Arkansas population, although the ratio of African American to white students appears to have dropped in the past couple of years.

Table 4.A2
Distribution of COPH Students by Race or Ethnicity

	White	Black	Asian, other	Latino	Native American
Arkansas Students Enrolled by Quarter (in percent)					
State population	79	16	1	3	1
Spring 2002	50	41	7	2	0
Summer 2002	47	47	6	0	0
Fall 2002–2003	59	34	5	2	0
Spring 2003	57	36	5	2	0
Summer 2003	52	41	6	1	0
Fall 2003–2004	60	32	7	1	1
Spring 2004	60	31	7	1	1
Fall 2004–2005	64	27	7	1	1
Spring 2005	64	26	8	1	1
Summer 2005	63	28	7	2	0
Fall 2005–2006	66	25	6	1	0

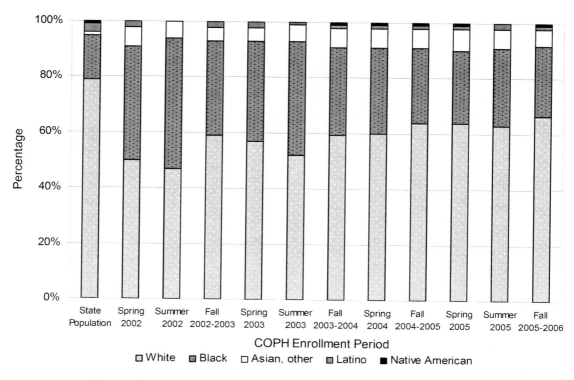

Figure 4.A2—Student Distribution by Race or Ethnicity

Obtain federal and philanthropic funding.

Indicator: Number of grants submitted for funding by all COPH faculty.

Indicator: Amount of grant funds awarded for all COPH faculty.

This goal was to have faculty in COPH pursue funding opportunities to bring new research to the college. Table 4.A3 shows the number of grants submitted each six-month period from the second half of 2001 through December 2005. In addition, it indicates how many of these grants were successfully funded and which grants are still pending as of December 2005. Table 4.A4 shows the funding amounts that COPH has received in total and for research for new awards at the time awarded. The two tables indicate that COPH has been very successful in receiving funding. Virtually all of the funding obtained has been for the conduct of research. In January through June 2005, COPH received two very large grants/contracts; one grant in the amount of $1,118,963 (Act 1220 evaluation) and one contract in the amount of $1,972,618 (Tobacco Cessation Network). This explains why the COPH funding decreased in the following funding period.

Table 4.A3
Grants Submitted by COPH Faculty

Six-month Period	Number Submitted	Number Funded	Number Pending
Jul-Dec 2001	2	2	0
Jan-Jun 2002	1	1	0
Jul-Dec 2002	11	11	0
Jan-Jun 2003	7	6	0
Jul-Dec 2003	8	6	2
Jan-Jun 2004	22	17	7
Jul-Dec 2004	24	21	0
Jan-Jun 2005	31	18	4
Jul-Dec 2005	27	20	5

Table 4.A4
New Grant Amounts Funded for COPH Faculty

Six–Month Period	Total Amount Funded	Amount Funded for Research
Jul–Dec 2001	$ 79,342	$ 70,325
Jan–Jun 2002	1,097,414	1,097,414
Jul–Dec 2002	803,835	803,835
Jan–Jun 2003	1,045,450	1,045,450
Jul–Dec 2003	858,090	858,090
Jan–Jun 2004	1,710,549	1,522,370
Jul–Dec 2004	1,280,921	1,176,172
Jan–Jun 2005	4,362,106	4,134,916
Jul–Dec 2005	2,187,244	1,870,264

Conduct research.

Indicator: Number of peer-reviewed papers by all faculty accepted for publication.

Indicator: Number of ongoing research projects conducted by all faculty.

The successful conduct of research was measured by documenting the number of research projects conducted by the COPH faculty and the number of peer-reviewed publications generated from their research. Tables 4.A5 and 4.A6 show that COPH has increased both the number of publications and research projects each year. COPH went from three ongoing research projects in 2002 to twenty in 2003, and publications nearly tripled during that time.

Table 4.A5
Papers Published by COPH Faculty

Year	Number of Publications	Number per FTE
2001	0	0
2002	12	.80
2003	32	1.20
2004	43	1.30
2005	78	1.79

Table 4.A6
Ongoing Research Projects by COPH Faculty

Six–Month Period	Ongoing Research Projects
Jan–Jun 2002	3
Jul–Dec 2002	12
Jan–Jun 2003	19
Jul–Dec 2003	20
Jan–Jun 2004	21
Jul–Dec 2004	35
Jan–Jun 2005	29[a]
Jul–Dec 2005	34[a]

a. The actual list has more projects; however, a portion of these projects are technical service agreements or do not involve research.

Serve as a [policy and advisory] resource to the general assembly, the governor, state agencies, and communities.

Indicator: Number of service activities to the state.

COPH has engaged in a number of activities that have supported the general assembly, state agencies, and organizations in the community. Table 4.A7 and Figure 4.A3 indicate that COPH has substantially increased its service since its inception in 2001, moving from 16 to 103 talks and lectures per six-month period. COPH also conducted several legislative briefings and special projects during this period.

Table 4.A7
Service Activities to the State by COPH Faculty

Six-Month Period	Talks and Lectures	Legislative Briefings	Special Projects
Jul-Dec 2001	16	6	12
Jan-Jun 2002	25	6	4
Jul-Dec 2002	59	3	4
Jan-Jun 2003	85	4	6
Jul-Dec 2003	103	4	4
Jan-Jun 2004	118	13	12
Jul-Dec 2004	47	13	9
Jan-Jun 2005	Agreed to count annually	13	3
Jul-Dec 2005	83[a]	15	8

a. This number does not accurately reflect the number of public talks and lectures because several faculty who normally have talks or lectures to report did not report this period.

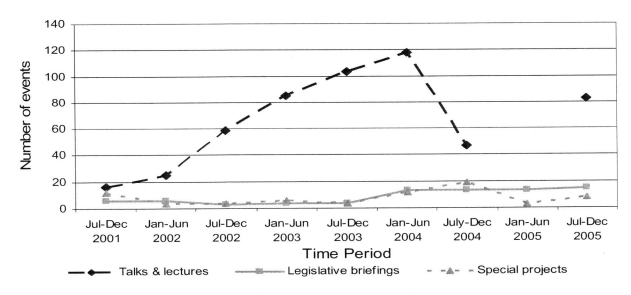

* Agreed to count annually (Talks and lectures)

** This number does not accurately reflect the number of public talks/lecture as several faculty who normally have talks/lectures to report did not report this period.

Figure 4.A3—Service Activity Trends

Chapter 5
Delta AHEC

PROGRAM DESCRIPTION

The Initiated Act designates the Delta Area Health Education Center (Delta AHEC) as one of the Targeted State Needs programs, and it provides for funding to UAMS to create the Delta AHEC. The act states that

the new AHEC shall be operated in the same fashion as other facilities in the UAMS AHEC program including training students in the field of medicine, nursing, pharmacy and various allied health professions, and offering medical residents specializing in family practice. The training shall emphasize primary care, covering general health education and basic medical care for the whole family.

The act specifies the following goals for the Delta AHEC:

- Short-term goal: "Increase the number of communities and clients served through expanded AHEC/DHEC offices."

- Long-term goal: "Increase the access to a primary care provider in underserved communities."

The intent was that these offices would serve the seven counties that comprise the Delta region: Chicot, Crittenden, Desha, Lee, Monroe, Phillips, and St. Francis. The Delta AHEC was designed to take over some of the activities formerly provided by the Delta Health Education Center (DHEC), which the state of Arkansas started in the 1970s based on the national Health Education Center model. In the 1990s DHEC started to receive funds from the federal Health Resources and Services Administration (HRSA) as a Health Education and Training Center (HETC). This money was earmarked to support public health activities. With the new influx of funds from the Tobacco Settlement Proceeds Act in 2001, half the HRSA funds provided to DHEC were diverted to southwest Arkansas to serve the expanding Hispanic population in Sevier, Howard, and Hemstead counties.

Since our last report, the Delta AHEC received notification that the HETC funding was removed from the federal budget. Beginning September 1, 2006, HRSA will no longer provide HETC funding, which accounts for approximately $175,000 to Arkansas. This funding loss will affect a variety of programs, including the Medical Application of Science for Health (MASH), continuing education, health career recruitment, and minority-based outreach programs. The sizeable deficit in funding will also seriously affect educational programming. At the time of this report, alternative funding resources were being explored, such as Delta Bridge and local and regional foundations.

The Delta AHEC maintained its professional health education opportunities in the Delta region in 2005. However, the UAMS Department of Family and Preventive Medicine changed its criteria so community size limits were no longer operational for senior medical students completing four-week elective primary care preceptorships. This change enabled students to remain in Little Rock for that experience, which seriously reduced the number of rotations in the Delta.

During early 2005, the program was assigned new AHEC evaluators who are working on establishment of goals and objectives for each of the program activities that the Delta AHEC provides. Evaluation has led to improvements in program participation tracking, which is discussed later in this chapter. Over the course of 2005, the Delta AHEC planned and oversaw the building of its new facility in Helena. In addition, the collaboration with other health care providers in the area has improved, specifically with the Helena Regional Hospital.

PROGRESS TOWARD ACHIEVING FIVE-YEAR AND SHORT-TERM GOALS

All program goals were established as part of the Arkansas Tobacco Settlement Evaluation activities in spring 2005. The goals and progress are specified below.

Goal 1: Expand consumer health education activities that address the region's health problems.

    a. Operate programs out of the new Delta AHEC building by spring 2006.

    b. Expand consumer health education services 20 percent by 2010.

Progress on Goal 1:

    a. ON SCHEDULE. The Delta AHEC has moved to the new facility and has opened its doors for classroom-based activities. Its physical fitness center is still under construction but the walking track is available for use.

    b. ON SCHEDULE. Despite budget cuts, the Delta AHEC reports that programming has increased due to their new 31,000-square-foot facility. The wellness center is more than five times the size of its previous facility. Increased programming includes a weight watchers' group and a lupus support group.

Goal 2: Improve program evaluation activities.

    a. Automate data collection and analyses by spring 2007.

    b. Conduct annual program improvement processes, including monitoring programs for culturally appropriate content, through 2010.

Progress on Goal 2:

    a. AHEAD OF SCHEDULE. Automated data collection for health education has begun, and the program is working on getting its clinical activities automated. Data analyses have yet to be initiated.

    b. ON SCHEDULE. The Delta AHEC engages in a semiannual strategic planning process called SWOT (strengths, weaknesses, opportunities, and threats). For this process, staff from the Delta AHEC brainstorm as a group on the Delta AHEC's particular strengths and weaknesses. This analysis is used to plan for the coming year's activities. In addition, the UAMS AHEC director, Dr. Cranford, spends two days with staff every year to discuss concerns of the Delta AHEC, staff perceptions about the executive director and activities, and plans for future activities. Dr. Cranford incorporates the SWOT process into the overall goal-making process for the UAMS programs.

Goal 3: Implement a marketing program for the Delta AHEC.

a. By spring 2006, establish a marketing committee, identify a staff person to implement and support the program, develop strategies to recruit health professional students, engage and educate health care professionals, and promote consumer health education activities.

b. Implement and maintain marketing program and annual fundraising events through 2010.

Progress on Goal 3:

a. ON SCHEDULE. The program has redesigned its approach to meeting this goal. Instead of creating a marketing committee, it has hired a part-time consultant to engage in fundraising events and public relations. The Delta AHEC health professional recruiter left the program, and with the budget cuts, the program cannot replace this position. Instead it is partnering with a local hospital to help recruit health professionals to the area.

b. ON SCHEDULE. During the fourth quarter of 2005, the marketing consultant and advisory board members engaged in planning the grand opening activities for the wellness center, which included representation from local, state, and national leaders. Activities to increase funds to the Delta include opportunities to sponsor a room in the new facility or membership at the wellness center.

Goal 4: Become a provider of continuing education for nursing by spring 2010.

a. By spring 2006, identify program staff and complete a needs assessment (i.e., location, method of delivery, job role, educational background).

b. Complete accreditation process and system for processing paperwork by 2007.

c. Introduce course offerings in 2007 and maintain through 2010.

Progress on Goal 4:

a. BEHIND SCHEDULE. The Delta AHEC has assigned the duties to reach this goal to its associate director, who has assessed the cost of offering a program supported by the Delta AHEC. In the past, the Delta AHEC has partnered with local hospitals to purchase a program offered by the UAMS Rural Hospital Programs. However, this program has not been well attended by local nurses. Instead, the associate director has learned that many nurses are accessing free continuing education opportunities available on the Internet. However, not all nurses have access to the Internet, and the Delta AHEC is considering offering Internet access in its facilities rather than becoming an accredited continuing education provider. The associate director is working on a needs assessment of nurses at the Helena Regional Medical Center to determine how they are currently meeting their continuing education requirements and how the Delta AHEC can assist them.

b. NOT INITIATED. It is unclear whether the Delta AHEC will continue to pursue the goal of becoming an accredited provider of continuing nursing education. It may be more feasible for it to offer access to continuing education through the Internet at its facilities. The Delta AHEC is conducting a needs assessment of the local nurses to help determine how it will increase access to continuing education in the region.

c. NOT INITIATED. See above response.

PERFORMANCE ON PROCESS INDICATORS

As noted in previous reports, three indicators were developed to track progress of the Delta AHEC activities: (1) increasing the number of communities and clients served through the Delta AHEC; (2) providing training in the health care professions, emphasizing primary care; and (3) increasing access to primary care providers in the Delta. In general, the number of community members served by the Delta continues to grow. Sixteen out of the 21 community consumer-oriented programs showed an increase in the number of encounters over the past year as compared to 2004. The number of training encounters for health care students and personnel has been sustained, with a high rate of participation among African Americans. The Delta AHEC continues to struggle to provide the same access to a primary care provider as other AHECs do, given that it lacks the infrastructure to support such programming (i.e., physician family residency training program). Detailed information on trends for the process indicators is provided in the appendix to this chapter.

PERFORMANCE ON MANAGEMENT INTEGRITY CRITERIA

Types and Performance of Governing and Advisory Boards

The University of Arkansas system is governed by its board of trustees, appointed by the governor to ten-year terms. The Delta AHEC is subsumed under this existing governance structure and is not at liberty to develop an independent governing board. The

UA Board of Trustees, which consists of ten members, meets at least quarterly but often more frequently. In 2006, its regularly scheduled meetings were held in January, March, May, July, September, and November.

The Delta AHEC has two advisory boards. The Regional Programs Advisory Council consults on various aspects of planning and implementation for the AHEC program from a statewide perspective. An internal advisory council also offers valuable input from various departments within the institution.

While much of the direction for AHECs is derived from the larger UAMS system, the Delta AHEC has formed both consumer and advisory boards, which meet quarterly. Governance, leadership, and strategic direction are provided using a committee approach; five committees were designed to accomplish the many advisory tasks needed by the Delta AHEC: Adolescent Health; Wellness Programs; Community Outreach; Chronic Disease; and the Center on Aging. Board members assigned to each division have contributed to formulation of and prioritization of objectives for each area of focus.

Board representation includes minorities and representatives from the AMHC, UAMS COPH, and ADH. Board members meet quarterly to identify essential services needed in the region and reflect depth, diversity, and a balanced representation of stakeholders. Members are as follows:

UAMS Regional Programs Advisory Council
- Robert Atkinson, administrator, Jefferson Regional Medical Center, Pine Bluff
- Gary Bebow, administrator, White River Medical Center, Batesville
- Jerry Bookout, state senator, Jonesboro
- Melanie Campbell, director, Boston Mountain Rural Health Center, Marshall
- Jo E. Carson, attorney at law, Fort Smith
- Susan Hanrahan, PhD, dean, College of Nursing and Health Professions, Arkansas State University, Jonesboro
- Ed Henley, PhD, Bruce Drugs, Inc., Smackover
- Ross Hooper, CEO, Crittenden Memorial Hospital, West Memphis
- John Lipton, Warren
- Mitch Llewellyn, Thompson and Llewellyn, Fort Smith
- Buddy McMahon, Fort Smith
- Blanche Moore, Little Rock
- Ken Tillman, rural health director, Arkansas Farm Bureau Federation, Little Rock
- Dick Trammel, executive vice president, First National Bank & Trust Company, Rogers
- P. Vasudevan, MD, Helena
- Fred Vorsanger, Fayetteville

- Jess Walt, President, First National Bank of Altheimer, Altheimer

UAMS Internal Advisory Council

- John I. Blohm, vice chancellor for development and alumni affairs
- Stephanie Gardner, PharmD, dean, College of Pharmacy
- Geoffrey Goldsmith, MD, chair, Department of Family and Community Medicine
- Melony Goodhand, vice chancellor for fiscal affairs and CFO
- Linda C. Hodges, EdD, RN, dean, College of Nursing
- Larry Milne, PhD, vice chancellor for academic affairs and sponsored research
- Dick Pierson, vice chancellor for clinical programs
- E. Albert Reece, MD, PhD, dean, College of Medicine
- Ronald Winters, PhD, dean, College of Health Related Professions

The ratings in Table 5.1 indicate the Delta AHEC board's involvement with different program aspects on the part of the UA Board of Trustees as well as the Delta AHEC's advisory councils. The UA Board of Trustees primarily oversees the financial performance (i.e., budget and spending levels) of the Delta AHEC as part of its review of all the AHECs in Arkansas. The board of trustees provides little oversight in other aspects of governing, such as goals and planning, priorities, quality management, performance, and interface with communities. The AHECs also are governed by two advisory councils that oversee all of the AHECs, a statewide regional programs advisory council and a regional UAMS internal advisory council that consists solely of UAMS-affiliated members. The regional programs (external) advisory council meets twice a year, and the different AHECs across the state take turns presenting to it. The Delta AHEC board is made up of chairs of the board of trustees and/or a representative from each of the seven AHECs and representatives from statewide partners, such as the Farm Bureau and Community Health Centers. Their role is advisory in status, so changes in program goals and financials are minimal. The UAMS Regional Programs Advisory Council plays a significant role in setting priorities and providing input from the community. A fundraising subcommittee has been convened by the regional advisory council to address this specific activity. The UAMS Internal Advisory Council meets infrequently. It is made up of deans and department heads of UAMS. Its role is to deal more with the student rotations and issues that relate to UAMS.

Table 5.1
Performance of the Governing Board and Medical Advisory Board on Dimensions of Board Oversight for the Delta AHEC, Scale of 1 to 5

Management Functions	UA Board of Trustees	Advisory Councils	
		Regional Programs and Internal	Consumers
Oversight			
Goals and planning	1	2	4
Priorities	1	3	4
Budget	3	2	3
Quality management	1	3	4
Monitoring program performance			
Progress toward goals	1	3	3
Spending	3	2	2
Quality performance	1	2	2
Providing interface with communities			
Community needs	1	4	4
Community interactions	1	2	4
Fund-raising	1	4	4

NOTE: Definitions of ratings: 1 = not involved, 2 = minimally involved, 3 = not intense involvement, 4 = fully considers, 5 = directive

Quality Improvement Process

Table 5.2 presents the ratings for the Delta AHEC on different aspects of quality management. The Delta AHEC director meets with the staff every other month to review monthly reports and discuss program improvement. The director does not report having any formal written quality improvement process for the organization as a whole. However, in late 2005 and early 2006, staff planned for programs in the new facility, including the development of policy and procedures notebooks for the Diabetes Clinic, cardiopulmonary resuscitation (CPR) training programs, Kids for Health, adolescent health programs, physical fitness center, and new center space. The Diabetes Clinic, which is certified by the American Diabetes Association (ADA), uses a specific quality improvement process that is outlined by the American Association of Diabetes Educators (2005). Evaluation activities are improving with the development of an online tracking system (see progress under goal 2 above and recommendation 5 below for more details on this process).

Table 5.2
Ratings of the Delta AHEC on Quality Management Activities

	Not Applicable	Needs Improvement	Does Satisfactorily
1. Specifies criteria for quality performance			X
2. Collects information on technical quality measures			X
3. Collects information on consumers' experience with service			X
4. Collects data on program enrollments, demographic characteristics of enrollees, service encounters			X
5. Has quantified quality measures for technical aspects of service		X	
6. Has quantified measures of consumers' experience with service			X
7. Has quantified measures on program enrollments, demographic characteristics of enrollees, service encounters that may be compared to targets			X
8. Analyzes technical quality data to identify potential quality deficiencies		X	
9. Analyzes consumer experience data to identify potential quality deficiencies		X	
10. Analyzes measures on program enrollments, etc. to identify potential quality deficiencies		X	
11. Formulates quality recommendations that are addressed to who needs to take action		X	
12. Reports results of quality analyses to executive management/boards		X	
13. Reports results of quality analyses to relevant committees		X	
14. Disseminates quality recommendations to the public ("report cards")	X		

The Delta AHEC collects data on enrollment in programming. Some, but not all, programs have instituted satisfaction and outcome data collection and analyses. The Delta AHEC is working on improving data collection and analyses through a Web-based system. Other improvements that have been made in the past two years include expanding programming to meet demand by opening the new wellness center, transitioning smoking cessation interventions to more evidence-based methods (i.e., from group to one-on-one counseling), and instituting a consumer satisfaction evaluation component to the inpatient diabetes education program provided at the Regional Helena Medical Center. The Delta AHEC continues to work on improving its evaluation activities to meet its goals and RAND recommendation 5.

Financial Management Process

The Delta AHEC uses the Systems Applications Processes (SAP) to report spending for the Tobacco Settlement program to the state. The Delta AHEC does not have a local automated system. The board of trustees, the Delta AHEC's governing board, uses the SAP information to oversee program spending. All personnel who perform the Delta AHEC program's financial management and accounting functions have the required qualifications.

Contract Management

The Delta AHEC contracts to Crittenden Memorial Hospital (CMH) to provide services to the northern part of its mandated service delivery region.

Performance Specifications. The contract specifies that CMH will provide the services of a director, librarian, and youth coordinator, who will plan, implement, and evaluate programs that reflect the goal of area specific recruitment and retention of health care professionals, professional support and education of health professionals, and public health education in Crittenden and St. Francis counties.

Financial Reporting. Program spending is reported yearly to the Delta AHEC. The director of the AHEC assesses comparisons to actual program activity.

Quality Performance and Reporting. The CMH staff reports to the director of the Delta AHEC, as do other Delta AHEC program staff. The number of programs delivered, number of participants, and other evaluation data are collected. As noted under progress of goal 2, staff are now using an automated database to enter program performance information into a system that the executive director may use to review program activity.

Payment Structure. The contract specifies $200,000 for FY2005–2006. Payments are made yearly and are not tied to performance.

ANALYSIS OF SPENDING TRENDS

Act 1580 of 2001, HB 1717 of 2003, and HB 1553 of 2005 appropriated funds for the Delta AHEC for the first three biennium periods of the Tobacco Settlement Fund Allocation. Table 5.3 details the appropriations by fiscal year.

The following analysis updates the Delta AHEC expenditures with spending from January 2005 through December 2005. Because December 2005 is in the middle of the first year of the third biennium, no year totals for FY2006 are presented, and it is not possible to fully detail expenditures in the third biennium.

Table 5.4 presents the total annual Tobacco Settlement funds spent by the Delta AHEC through December 2005. The Delta AHEC spent less than its total appropriation budget in FY2005, but it did spend slightly more than the appropriated amount in one category while spending less in other categories. For FY2005, the Delta AHEC underspent its funds in regular salaries, operating expenses, professional fees, travel, and capacity outlay and overspent its funds in personal service matching.

Figure 5.1 highlights quarterly cross-sections of Delta AHEC spending from FY2002 through the first two quarters of FY2005. After peaking in the fourth quarter of FY2003, monthly M&O expenditures dropped markedly in early FY2004. Spending in this area increased somewhat through the remainder of FY2004 before dropping again in the early quarters of FY2005. The fourth quarter of FY2005 saw a large jump in expenditures, due mostly to increases in M&O expenditures. Salary and fringe spending in the first half of FY2006 remained at levels similar to previous quarters, while maintenance and operations costs were lower than in many of the previous quarters.

Monthly expenditures for regular salaries and personal service matching also peaked in the fourth quarter of FY2003 and then dropped in the first quarter of FY2004. Spending in these areas increased through the rest of FY2004 before stabilizing in the early part of FY2005.

The Delta AHEC has three funding streams: Tobacco Settlement funds, grants and donations, and general state funds. Figure 5.2 shows the percentage of Delta AHEC spending attributed to each of these sources from FY2002 through the first half of FY2006. Tobacco Settlement funds account for the largest amount of spending, representing 55 to 70 percent of the AHEC's overall spending. The Delta AHEC continues to use these funds to leverage funding from grants and donations. The percentage of the Delta AHEC's spending from grants and donations declined from a high of 39 percent in FY2003 to 25 percent in FY2005. General state funding ranges between 1 and 7 percent each year. Through the first half of FY2006, Tobacco Settlement funds accounted for 72 percent of the spending, while grants and donations accounted for 27 percent.

Table 5.3
Tobacco Settlement Funds Appropriated to the Delta AHEC, by Fiscal Year

Item	Second Biennium		Third Biennium	
	2004	2005	2006	2007
(1) Regular salaries	$1,347,405	$1,195,000	$1,201,754	$1,201,754
(2) Personal service matching	245,270	280,000	271,964	271,964
(3) Maintenance and operations				
(A) Operations	340,800	539,475	820,540	820,540
(B) Travel	41,000	25,000	9,298	9,298
(C) Professional fees	0	85,000	0	0
(D) Capacity outlay	350,000	200,000	20,920	20,920
(E) Data processing	0	0	0	0
Annual total	$2,324,475	$2,324,475	$2,324,476	$2,324,476
Biennium total	$4,648,950		$4,648,952	

Table 5.4
Tobacco Settlement Funds Spent by the Delta AHEC, by Fiscal Year

Item	2003	2004	2005	2006[a]
(1) Regular salaries	$1,057,681	$1,132,323	$1,118,850	$520,723
(2) Personal service matching	228,551	250,530	280,010	130,259
(3) Maintenance and operations				
(A) Operations	390,060	415,422	383,178	51,403
(B) Travel	62,629	26,589	9,706	0
(C) Professional fees	-7,086	7,700	0	0
(D) Capacity outlay	439,488	12,326	124,365	0
(E) Data processing	0	0	0	0
Annual total	$2,171,323	$1,844,890	$1,916,109	$702,385

a. Funds spent for the first half of the fiscal year through December 31, 2005.

89

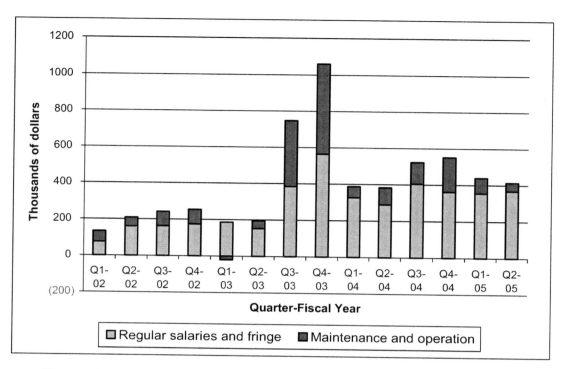

Figure 5.1—Delta AHEC Tobacco Settlement Fund Spending, by Quarter of Fiscal Years

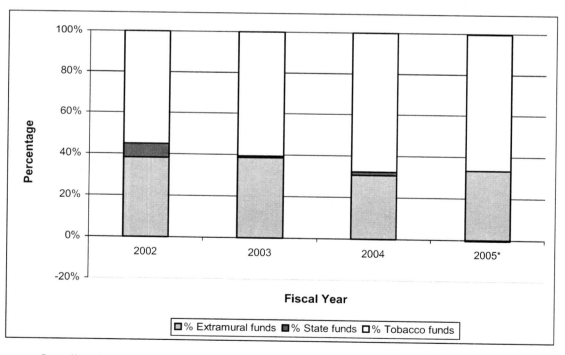

a. Spending through December 31, 2005.

Figure 5.2—Percentage of Delta AHEC Budget from Tobacco Settlement Funds, by Fiscal Year

RESPONSES TO EVALUATION RECOMMENDATIONS

Recommendation 1: Build additional program capacity so that needed health education programming for the community can continue to be expanded.

> *Program Response:* In collaboration with the Helena Health Foundation, a $4 million wellness center was built to serve the entire seven-county area. The 31,000-square-foot facility—complete with a medical library, auditorium, classrooms, and walking track and gymnasium—has replaced the 4,500-square-foot building that previously housed the Delta AHEC. The new facility will allow the Delta AHEC to increase its capacity to conduct consumer health education programming as well as health professional education. As of spring 2006, the center was open and offering classroom-based education. The new physical fitness center is still under construction, but the walking track and auditorium are complete.

Recommendation 2: Expand collaboration efforts to reach disenfranchised populations.

> *Program Response:* The Delta AHEC partnered with the Minority Health Initiative to continue its Eating and Moving for Life program in Phillips County churches. Delta AHEC has assumed the salary and expenses for this program and has contracted with the local office of the Arkansas Cooperative Extension Service for implementation of the program in African-American churches. In addition, the Delta AHEC continues to work with other tobacco-funded programs. In November, the Arkansas Department of Health/College of Public Health tobacco cessation program placed a tobacco interventionist at the Delta AHEC. The Phillips County Delta Bridge Project has received more than $8 million in support from the Walton Foundation, in collaboration with Southern Financial Partners, a part of Southern Bancorporation. The Delta AHEC director is chairing the Health Goal Team. During two years of strategic planning, six health care goals were developed and approved.

In the fourth quarter, the Delta AHEC submitted two requests for funding to the Delta Bridge Project. In partnership with Crittenden Memorial Hospital, the Delta AHEC received funds from the Arkansas Department of Health to implement a worksite wellness program designed to improve quality of care. Curriculum objectives are to (1) increase awareness of the signs and symptoms of heart disease and stroke, (2) encourage the appropriate use of 911, (3) improve management of blood pressure, diabetes, and cholesterol, and (4) decrease the use of tobacco products. Activities include training industry employees in CPR and first aid, presenting the American Heart Association's "Taking Hypertension to Heart," and making a blood pressure monitor available onsite at a wellness station for employees to monitor blood pressure on a regular basis. Employees will receive glucose and cholesterol screenings and nutrition counseling, and the Finally Free from Tobacco model will be implemented to assist employees in tobacco cessation.

The Delta AHEC also partners with the Delta Area Center of Aging (CoA) by providing office space for CoA staff. A new CoA regional facility was opened in West Memphis in August 2005. The facility will provide an array of much-needed services for the seniors in the Arkansas Delta region, and it provides Delta seniors access to quality health care within a 50-mile radius of their homes. A $200,000 grant from the Assisi Foundation in Memphis helped to renovate the clinic space. The new CoA facility is the result of a unique partnership among the Donald W. Reynolds Institute on Aging at UAMS, the UAMS Delta AHEC, and Crittenden Memorial Hospital in West Memphis.

A culturally competent breast and cervical health program, designed for African-American and medically underserved women, was implemented in collaboration with local hospitals, Cancer Control Outreach Center's cancer councils, and other cancer control organizations. Breast and cervical health education as well as cervical cancer and mammography screenings were provided using mobile and modular mammography units in counties that had limited or no access to certified mammography facilities. Additionally, the collaborating organizations increased participation in health fairs to provide a variety of health screenings and information about other diseases in addition to breast and cervical cancer. People attending these events are becoming aware of the benefits of early detection and the importance of a healthy lifestyle.

Recommendation 3: Consider new methods to increase funding for and access to community health education services.

Program Response: Individuals and businesses are sponsoring dedicated spaces in the new building. These sponsorships will help reduce the building debt and thereby reduce monthly expenses. As noted above, the Delta AHEC continues to collaborate with other organizations to build opportunities for funding and increase access to health education and health care. The Delta AHEC continues to maintain external grant funding (i.e., $33,000 for teen pregnancy prevention from the Arkansas Department of Health; $40,000 from the National Institute of Occupational Safety and Health (NIOSH)). A $13,000 grant from the Komen Foundation for breast cancer ended in March 2006.

Recommendation 4: As additional health education programs are developed, focus on programs that have demonstrated effectiveness.

Program Response: As mentioned previously, the Delta AHEC has expanded its ADA-certified diabetes management program to serve newly diagnosed diabetics at Helena Regional Hospital. The Delta AHEC reported that it is building upon the AHA "Heart and Soul" programming offered in Phillips county churches by picking up the Eating and Moving for Life program, after it was determined to be feasible by the Arkansas Minority Health Commission.

Recommendation 5: Increase resources to conduct program assessment activities.

Program Response: A new Delta AHEC educational database has been developed and implemented through the UAMS Regional Programs office. Working closely with the AHEC associate director and AHEC central database manager, security, data quality, and effective reporting systems were designed for Web-based data entry. Delta AHEC personnel were trained to enter public education programs online and to use a new scannable form for program evaluation. Phase II of the project will incorporate clinical data.

Recommendation 6: Use the next appropriations cycle to adjust the distribution of the budget line items so that the appropriation better represents the Delta AHEC program spending needs.

> *Program Response:* This has been achieved; the appropriation for 2005 was amended by Act 1320. Personal service matching was the only category that exceeded appropriations (by $10).

Recommendation 7: Continue to engage and educate local physicians.

> *Program Response:* The new chief of staff at Helena Hospital is very supportive of the Delta AHEC. He visits weekly to discuss issues with the staff and services on the community advisory board for the AHEC. Physicians have access to continuing education through the compressed video offered at the Delta AHEC. In 2006, seven physicians utilized these services. A referral system has been designed so that physicians may send inpatients or outpatients to the Delta AHEC for smoking cessation, diabetes self-management, parenting, and breast-feeding classes. The Delta AHEC is averaging more than 50 referrals each month.

RECOMMENDATIONS FOR PROGRAM IMPROVEMENT

Recommendation 1: Continue to increase resources to conduct program evaluation activities.

The Delta AHEC uses the SWOT process in strategic planning and program meetings. These meetings are based on staff input. Data gathered from clients should also be presented, reviewed, and incorporated into the semiannual program planning process. Decisions for future programming should be based in part on client-level data, such as participation, satisfaction, and self-reported changes in knowledge, attitudes, and/or behaviors. As new programs and processes are established, the Delta AHEC will want to incorporate evaluation into its strategic planning activities. For example, the referral system for physicians should include a mechanism for both physicians and clients to provide feedback on how the system is working. This information should be reviewed as part of the strategic planning sessions. In addition, an automated database has now been set up to track program activities. Although data are now being entered into the database, the Delta AHEC and its evaluators still need to develop reporting functions so that the data being entered into the system can be accessed and used for strategic planning purposes.

Recommendation 2: Use performance and quality management processes.

In order to reach the Delta AHEC goals, the executive director should engage in goal setting with staff and manage staff based on those goals. For example, the director may want to institute monthly reporting from staff that includes an assessment of how well the staff is reaching their goals. Although the director meets with staff monthly to discuss performance issues, the meetings may consist of a more formalized process where program performance is compared to goals. As the Delta AHEC continues to expand its activities, it will become more important to structure regular feedback around program goals and formalize the quality management process. Performance management processes should also be put into place for any contracts, so that payments are tied to activities related to the AHEC goals. Strategies to improve staff and contract performance should be outlined as part of a quality management plan.

APPENDIX TO CHAPTER 5

Performance on Process Indicators through December 2005

Increase the number of communities and clients served through the expanded AHEC/DHEC offices.

Indicator: Session encounter rates per 1,000 residents, by residents in the Delta region participating in the AHEC health education and promotion programs, by type of program (note new census estimates were used).

Table 5.A1
Session Encounter Rates per 1,000 Delta Residents for Delta AHEC Programs

	July 01–Dec 01	Jan 02–June 02	July 02–Dec 02	Jan 03–June 03	July 03–Dec 03	Jan 04–June 04	July 04–Dec 04	Jan 05–June 05	July 05–Dec 05
Asthma Education	0.96	2.35	4.33	0.73	0.84	0.05	0.00	0.00	1.03
CPR for Consumers	0.15	0.18	0.35	2.17	3.21	2.00	1.53	1.86	1.71
Exercise Programs -Aerobics/Tai Chi	0.99	2.27	4.95	4.55	8.67	23.96	20.93	27.86	23.96
Geriatric Education Support Groups	0.41	0.49	0.62	3.38	5.92	2.85	8.24	12.06	10.63
Health Screenings	0.69	1.20	1.78	15.80	15.77	10.48	19.58	14.40	16.45
Kids for Health[a]	0.00	4.09	2.48	2.50	4.50	8.70	39.34	8.25	26.63
MASH	0.08	0.14	0.23	0.13	0.0	0.18	<0.01	0.38	0.10
Medical Library Services/Consumers	0.13	0.15	0.21	4.73	1.99	3.59	0.80	1.11	7.11
Sickle Cell Project	0.19	0.50	0.85	4.68	3.23	2.14	4.64	1.76	2.38
Teen Pregnancy Program	0.17	1.98	2.87	9.68	10.30	5.16	2.85	8.03	5.64
Tobacco Prevention and Cessation Program	2.86	4.22	5.32	1.68	17.06	9.13	28.37	30.60	28.88
CHAMPS	NA	0.05	0.09	0.03	0.06	0.09	0.00	0.11	0.13
How Healthy Is Your Faculty?	NA	1.56	2.32	4.53	4.34	2.30	0.00	0.53	1.58
How Healthy Is Your Industry?	NA	0.25	0.50	0.78	0.83	1.24	8.05	12.32	1.25
Mentoring Program for Minority/Disadvantaged Youth	NA	0.06	0.09	0.84	0.32	0.74	6.23	0.48	0.17
Diabetes Education	NA	NA	NA	0.61	0.92	1.34	6.35	3.63	4.08
Prescription Assistance	NA	NA	NA	NA	NA	NA	0.97	2.26	1.95
Prenatal/Healthy and Teen Parenting	NA	NA	NA	NA	NA	NA	4.60	9.43	4.97
STI Education	NA	NA	NA	NA	NA	NA	0.26	0.71	0.00
Comprehensive Health Education (CHE) for Adolescents	NA	NA	NA	NA	NA	NA	1.25	32.16	6.46

96

Table 5.A1—Continued

	July 01–Dec 01	Jan 02–June 02	July 02–Dec 02	Jan 03–June 03	July 03–Dec 03	Jan 04–June 04	July 04–Dec 04	Jan 05–June 05	July 05–Dec 05
Substance Abuse Prevention	NA	NA	NA	NA	NA	NA	1.60	0.28	2.07
Total Encounter Rates	6.65	19.50	27.00	56.82	77.97	73.95	146.94	123.36	131.73

NOTE: NA indicates data not available.

a. The rates for Kids for Health are number of participants per 1,000 Delta residents, rather than number of encounters.

97

Table 5.A2
Session Encounter Rates for Delta AHEC Programs by Race,
July 2004 through December 2005

Delta AHEC Program	July 04–Dec 04		Jan 05–June 05		July 05–Dec 05	
	African American	Hispanic	African American	Hispanic	African American	Hispanic
Asthma Education	0.00	0.00	0.00	0.00	1.57	0.00
CPR for Consumers	1.83	0.00	2.44	0.00	1.67	0.00
Exercise Programs–Aerobics/Tai Chi	10.29	0.00	9.59	0.46	8.79	0.00
Geriatric Education Support Groups	9.30	3.33	9.46	24.36	13.36	0.46
Health Screenings	21.68	5.71	14.44	2.09	19.98	4.87
Kids for Health	65.73	12.86	9.82	5.80	35.12	3.02
MASH	0.01	0.00	0.30	0.00	0.04	0.0
Medical Library Services/Consumers	0.42	0.71	2.29	0.23	10.54	0.23
Sickle Cell Project	7.75	0.00	3.43	0.00	4.60	0.00
Teen Pregnancy Program	4.98	0.95	15.02	0.00	10.81	0.00
Tobacco Prevention and Cessation Program	37.42	2.14	45.21	14.85	29.50	9.74
CHAMPS	0.00	0.00	0.06	0.00	0.06	0.00
How Healthy Is Your Faculty?	0.00	0.00	0.64	0.00	1.91	0.70
How Healthy Is Your Industry?	9.32	0.00	13.95	0.00	1.46	0.00
Mentoring Program for Minority/Disadvantaged Youth	9.64	0.00	0.93	0.00	0.10	0.00
Diabetes Education	7.53	0.24	3.12	0.00	4.64	1.16
Prescription Assistance	1.08	0.00	2.92	0.00	1.62	0.0
Prenatal/Healthy and Teen Parenting	8.96	0.00	15.00	0.00	7.23	1.86
STI Education	0.51	0.00	0.98	0.00	0.00	0.00
Comprehensive Health Education (CHE) for Adolescents	2.04	1.90	47.34	40.37	8.32	0.00

Table 5.A2—Continued

Delta AHEC Program	July 04–Dec 04		Jan 05–June 05		July 05–Dec 05	
	African American	Hispanic	African American	Hispanic	African American	Hispanic
Substance Abuse Prevention	2.91	0.71	0.00	0.00	3.72	0.00
Total encounter rates	185.92	25.95	130.70	47.80	144.16	20.19

The new AHEC shall be operated in the same fashion as the other facilities in the UAMS AHEC program, including training for students in the fields of medicine, nursing, pharmacy, and various allied health professions, and offering medical residents a specialization in family practice. The training shall emphasize primary care, covering general health education and basic medical care for the whole family.

Indicator: Number of primary care and family practice training session encounters for students and health care personnel in the fields of medicine, nursing, pharmacy, and allied health professions and number of students supported by the AHEC.

Table 5.A3
Delta AHEC Training Encounters for Health Care Students and Personnel and Number of Nursing Students Supported by the AHEC

	July 01–Dec 01	Jan 02–June 02	July 02–Dec 02	Jan 03–June 03	July 03–Dec 03	Jan 04–June 04	July 04–Dec 04	Jan 05–June 05	July 05–Dec 05
Continuing Medical Education	74	126	177	477	1,342	1,471	713	693	482
CPR for Health Professionals	23	21	43	49	43	55	165	109	201
Medical Library Services/Professionals	42	49	77	314	412	865	337	1,443	424
Total Session Encounters	139	196	297	840	1,797	2,391	1,215	2,245	1,107
Nursing Education Program (number of students)									
BSN and MSN	2	3	4	10	12	12	15	18	13
LPN Program	NA	NA	NA	23	13	11	0	0	0
CNA Program	NA	NA	NA	23	25	7	328	315	168
Total Students Participating	2	3	4	56	50	30	343	333	181

NOTE: NA indicates not applicable

Table 5.A4
Percentage of Delta AHEC Training Encounters for African-American and Hispanic Students, July 2004 Through December 2005

	July 04–Dec 04			Jan 05–Jun 05			July 05–Dec 05		
	Number of Encounters	Percentage African-American	Percentage Hispanic	Number of Encounters	Percentage African-American	Percentage Hispanic	Number of Encounters	Percentage African-American	Percentage Hispanic
Continuing Medical Education	713	NA	NA	693	20.8	2.31	482	36.3	0.0
CPR for Health Professionals	165	46.7	0.0	109	15.6	0.00	201	44.3	1.49
Medical Library Services/Professionals	337	49.9	1.8	1,443	30.3	0.07	424	35.1	0.0
Total session encounters	1,215	NA	NA	2,245	26.7	0.75	1,107	37.3	0.28
Nursing Education Program (students)									
BSN and MSN	15	46.7	6.7	18	27.8	5.56	13	15.4	0.0
LPN Program	0			0	0.0	0.0	0	0.0	0.0
CNA Program	328	68.3	0.0	315	82.9	0.0	168	93.4	0.0
Total Students Participating	343	67.4	0.2	333	79.9	0.3	181	87.9	0.0

NOTE: NA means not applicable.

Increase access to a primary care provider in underserved communities.

Indicator: Number of new primary care providers recruited to serve the Delta region, including physicians, nurse practitioners, nurses, medical students, pharmacists/students, and allied health professions.

Table 5.A5

Primary Care Providers Recruited by the Delta AHEC

	July 01–Dec 01	Jan 02–Jun 02	July 02–Dec 02	Jan 03–Jun 03	July 03–Dec 03	Jan 04–Jun 04	July 05–Dec 04	Jan 05–Jun 05	July 05–Dec 05
Recruitment for									
Allied health professionals	NA	3	4	0	0	0	0	5	0
Nurses	NA	12	16	3	0	4	24	3	1
Pharmacists	NA	0	0	0	0	0	0	0	0
Recruitment for physicians									
MATCH	NA	0	5	0	0	1	0	2	0
Preceptorships	NA	2	3	3	10	20	4	1	0
Rural loans	NA	0	0	0	4	0	0	0	0
Senior rotations	NA	1	2	5	6	15	5	112	4
Residents in OB/gynecology rotations	NA	2	2	2	10	5	1	0	0
Total providers recruited	NA	20	32	13	30	45	34	123	5
Telemedicine encounters	NA	NA	NA	NA	NA	48	5	23	13

Table 5.A6
Percentage of Primary Care Providers Recruited by the Delta AHEC Who Were African-American or Hispanic, July 2004 Through December 2005

	July 04–Dec 04			Jan 05–Jun 05			July 05–Dec 05		
	Number of Providers Recruited	Percentage African-American	Percentage Hispanic	Number of Providers Recruited	Percentage African-American	Percentage Hispanic	Number of Providers Recruited	Percentage African-American	Percentage Hispanic
Recruitment for									
Allied health professionals	0	0.0	0.0	5	20.0	0.0	0	0.0	0.0
Nurses	24	20.8	4.2	3	66.7	0.0	1	0.0	0.0
Pharmacists	0	0.0	0.0	0	0.0	0.0	0	0.0	0.0
Recruitment for physicians									
MATCH	0	0.0	0.0	2	0.0	0.0	0	0.0	0.0
Preceptorships	4	25.0	0.0	1	100.0	0.0	0	0.0	0.0
Rural loans	0	0.0	0.0	0	0.0	0.0	0	0.0	0.0
Senior rotations	5	60.0	0.0	112	14.29	0.0	4	25.0	0.0
Residents in obstetrics/gynecology rotations	1	0.0	0.0	0	0.0	0.0	0	0.0	0.0
Total number of providers recruited	34	26.5	2.9	123	16.2	0.0	5	20.0	0.0
Telemedicine encounters by video	5	60.0	0.0	23	8.7	0.0	13	NA	NA

Chapter 6
Arkansas Aging Initiative

PROGRAM DESCRIPTION

As defined in the Initiated Act, the goal of the Arkansas Aging Initiative (AAI) is to "establish healthcare programs statewide that offer interdisciplinary educational programs to better equip local health care professionals in preventive care, early diagnosis, and effective treatment for the elderly population and that provide access through satellite centers to dependable healthcare, education resource and support programs for the elderly" (Tobacco Settlement Proceeds Act of 2000).

The Arkansas Aging Initiative continues to expand activities through the seven Centers on Aging (COAs)[6] and four satellite centers across the state.[7] Details about progress made in each region are provided in the appendix at the end of this chapter. To meet the clinical goals established by the AAI leadership, a primary objective is to increase access to geriatric interdisciplinary care to within a 60 mile radius of all Arkansans. Each COA region is host to a Senior Health Clinic (SHC). In the next five years, the AAI plans to open a new COA and associated SHC in Hot Springs and establish an SHC in Mountain Home, which currently houses a satellite of the Schmieding Center in northwest Arkansas.

In the last year, the COAs provided more than 43,000 educational encounters for community provider, student, and paraprofessional populations—up 6 percent from 2004. Although the AAI has made a conscious decision not to bring programs out to each county, it has worked to ensure that almost everyone can have access to COA resources. Attendees at the various educational programs came from all but one of Arkansas' 75 counties. In addition, the SHCs provided more than 36,000 clinic encounters—up almost 22 percent from 2004.

Although educational programming in the COAs has continued to expand, recent changes to the federal budget will have a significant impact on the future of much of the education for health care professionals, students, and paraprofessionals. The Arkansas Geriatric Education Center (AGEC), which generates the professional education programs for the AAI, is a federally funded center housed at UAMS with the primary mission of improving health care for older adults in the state through education of health care professionals. Funding for the Geriatric Education Centers (GECs) has been cut out of the FY2007 federal budget, thus formally ending the program in June 2006. A no-cost extension will carry program activities through the summer but no later. AAI leadership has been actively working to convince legislators to reinstate the funding. However, even if federal funds are restored to GEC programs, every GEC program (50 in all) will have to reapply for these funds, which will result in a gap in educational programming. The AAI is currently pursuing other funding sources, including foundations and granting agencies, to fund some of the projects for which they would have used AGEC funds.

---

[6] The seven COAs are Springdale–Schmieding Center (Northwest COA), El Dorado–South Arkansas COA (SACOA), Texarkana Regional COA (TRCOA), Jonesboro–Northeast COA (NECOA), Pine Bluff–South Central COA (SCCOA), West Memphis–Delta COA, and Forth Smith COA.

[7] Three of the four satellite COAs are affiliated with the Schmieding Center (Bella Vista, Mountain Home, and Harrison), and the fourth is affiliated with the Delta COA (Helena).

PROGRESS TOWARD ACHIEVING FIVE-YEAR AND SHORT-TERM GOALS

Since its inception, the AAI has developed long-term goals to achieve its mission. The program recently completed the third year of a three-year plan. During summer 2005, the AAI leadership held a retreat with the COA directors and education directors to establish another plan with long-term goals for the program. The result was a five-year plan for FY2006 through FY2010 with the following six goals:

1. *Clinical Services:* Provide older adults with cost-efficient, age-appropriate, evidence-/consensus-based health care that promotes optimal quality of life.

2. *Education:* Be, in partnership with the AGEC, the premier provider of quality geriatric education for the state of Arkansas.

3. *Promotion:* Be the recognized leader in education, resource information, and clinical services for the aged.

4. *Policy:* Positively impact policies for the elderly population at the local, state, and national levels.

5. *Sustainability:* Have permanent funding sufficient to provide services and education to older adults and the health care providers who serve the geriatric population.

6. *Research:* Evaluate selected health, education, and cost outcomes for older adults who are provided services.

Given that a long-range plan was going to be developed shortly, we agreed last year to establish only short-term (one-year) goals for the AAI and revisit and establish a set of long-term goals for future reporting this year. Each of these goals is associated with a set of objectives, strategies to achieving those objectives, and stated deliverables or outcomes that will become the basis of the long-range goals to be selected for tracking in the future. These short-term goals are necessary to fulfill the AAI mission of improving access to high-quality interdisciplinary geriatric health care for older adults, educating professionals and older adults and their families about issues important to older populations, and influencing health and social policy. Of the four short-term goals established, three were accomplished and one was not, as detailed below.

Goal 1: By June 2006, the AAI will have an established strategic plan for implementation of at least one geriatric best practice guideline in at least three Senior Health Centers.

Progress on Goal 1: ACCOMPLISHED. A program has been developed around diabetes education based on best practice guidelines. A proposal was submitted to the Arkansas Biosciences Institute (ABI) that, if funded, will enable this program to be implemented in three COAs beginning July 1, 2006. The ABI should be making a funding decision in June. The three COAs that will first employ the best practice guideline are the Jonesboro and Texarkana COAs and the Reynolds Institute on Aging in Little Rock.

Goal 2: Each COA will offer at least eight opportunities for professional education as guided by the needs assessment and at least one program per county for older adults and their families in collaboration with community partners by June 2006.

    a. _Opportunities for professional education.

    b. Programs for older adults and their families.

<u>Progress on Goal 2:</u>

    a. ACCOMPLISHED. In 2005, the COAs provided more than 4,400 education encounters. All but two of the COAs provided at least eight opportunities for professional education (including health care professionals, paraprofessionals, and students of the health care professions). Bella Vista and Mountain Home provided a total of six educational encounters. Although they did not individually achieve this goal, they are satellite programs of the Schmieding Center; as a whole, this region achieved the goal.

    b. ON SCHEDULE. Given the challenges of reaching some of the counties in the state, the second part of this goal was modified so that at least one program is conducted in each county over a two-year period. Although programming was not located in every county, community members from all but four counties attended educational programs in the last year. The AAI does not have information readily available on where the programs actually took place. In the future, we may be able to better track this information with the development of the uniform database described below.

Goal 3: By June 2006, the AAI will have developed and implemented a uniform database for tracking participants in AAI educational encounters.

    <u>Progress on Goal 3:</u> ACCOMPLISHED. A Web-based database was established and is currently in use for tracking COA activities. The AAI can track educational encounters (both at COA and SHC), clinic visits, media outreach, health fair activities, scholarly work (presentations, journal publications, etc.), and financial data (donations, grants, etc.). The database is very flexible and capable of reporting the gender and race mix of education program attendees, the professional background of attendees for educational programs targeted at health care professionals, along with the more generic reports based on COA activities. Data on attendees can only be summarized at the COA level, so reports of the gender and race mix of attendees cannot be separated to show who is attending specific programs.

Goal 4: By June 2006, the AAI will work toward influencing health and social policy by compiling a list of grants, foundations, and independent organizations that provide research funding and will develop a database that will be updated periodically to keep this list current.

    <u>Progress on Goal 4:</u> PARTLY ACCOMPLISHED. AAI staff are still in the process of putting together a database of funding opportunities. Although they are actively working on the database, we must report this goal as only partly accomplished because the work was completed by June 2006.

PERFORMANCE ON PROCESS INDICATORS

    Below is a summary of the trends in each of the process indicators tracked over time for the Arkansas Aging Initiative (Table 6.1). Four process indicators were developed during this evaluation. Please see the appendix at the end of this chapter for data tables and more detailed descriptions of the progress on each of these indicators.

Table 6.1
Summary of Performance on Arkansas Aging Initiative Process Indicators

Indicator	Status
Educational encounter rate for seniors at each Senior Health Clinic	There is substantial variation in encounter rates across regions where an SHC is located. In general, rates are increasing over time
Number of encounters at classes offered for community members	The encounter counts are generally very erratic over time, although most COAs enjoyed increases in the number of community members attending AAI classes
Number of educational encounters for health care professionals participating in the Arkansas Geriatric Education Centers programs	AGEC activity has been inconsistent across COAs. This is due in part to the fact that while the AGEC activities are available across the state, COAs do not always host them in their regions. All but one of the COAs offered at least one course during 2005
Number of educational encounters at programs for students in health and social service disciplines	There is substantial variation across regions and over time in these encounters. Four COAs did not offer educational opportunities to students in 2005
Number of educational encounters for health professionals from regional sites participating in education through the Arkansas Geriatric Education Center	The AR-GEMS program is an educational program that is self-paced and requires a substantial amount of the student's time. As a result, few health care professionals avail themselves of this program
Number of educational encounters for active paraprofessionals and paraprofessional students	There is substantial variation across regions and over time in the number of educational encounters for paraprofessionals and paraprofessional students, with no ascertainable patterns in attendance. The Delta region and the Schmieding Center are the leaders in providing educational opportunities for paraprofessionals and paraprofessional students

PERFORMANCE ON MANAGEMENT INTEGRITY CRITERIA

Types and Performance of Governing and Advisory Boards

The AAI does not have a governing board but is advised by the Community Advisory Board (CAB) of the Reynolds Institute on Aging. The AAI is one of several programs run through the Reynolds Institute (which includes the Reynolds Department of Geriatrics and the Reynolds Center on Aging). The CAB supports and advises the Reynolds Institute on development and marketing activities, with a strong focus on fundraising for the Institute and not for specific programs under its umbrella.

The CAB is made up of 36 community members chosen by the Reynolds Institute Executive Committee and approved by the full board. Board members can serve up to three terms of three years each. The board meets four times a year.

RAND staff asked AAI leadership to rate the level of involvement by the Reynolds Institute Community Advisory Board in three categories of management functions: oversight, monitoring program performance, and providing interface with communities. RAND staff then confirmed those ratings with interviews and document reviews. These ratings are shown in Table 6.2.

Table 6.2
Performance of the AAI Community Advisory Board on Dimensions of Board Oversight Functions, Scales of 1 to 5

Management functions	Rating[a]
Oversight	
Goals and planning	2
Priorities	2
Budget	1
Quality management	1
Monitoring program performance	
Progress toward goals	3
Spending	1
Quality performance	1
Providing interface with communities	
Community needs	3
Community interactions	3
Fund-raising	4

a. Definitions of ratings: 1 = not involved, 2 = minimally involved, 3 = not intense involvement, 4 = fully considers, 5 = directive

The CAB is minimally involved in setting goals and supporting planning and priorities for the AAI. It provides no support to the development of the AAI budget or with quality management. Likewise, the CAB has no involvement with spending or quality performance for the AAI, although it does review progress toward goals. The CAB provides some insight into community needs and supports some community interactions. However, most of the CAB members come from central Arkansas, so they are not well positioned to provide outreach and support community interactions to the outlying regions of the state. Plans are beginning to be developed for the CAB to be more directly involved in fundraising. Recently, a subcommittee of the CAB was created to support the AAI specifically, and chairs of the regional Community Advisory Committees were invited to sit on the CAB subcommittee.

Financial Management Process

The AAI central leadership has fiduciary responsibility for each COA. A budget policy and procedure has been developed and is followed. In addition, the COA central leadership reviews each COA account is reviewed quarterly and discusses variances from budget with the regional COA leadership. The local AHEC serves in an administrative capacity, providing human resources functions such as managing payroll, ordering supplies, and paying vendors. Until recently, the AHECs were also responsible for financial reporting, but that job has now been assumed by the UAMS grant office.

Quality Management

The AAI does not have a formal quality management process in place. The AAI strategic plan provides direction to achieve the AAI goals. The AAI leadership tracks activities are tracked for each COA; each COA's activities are matched against the strategic plan, and the AAI leadership oversees progress toward the goals. Educational program curricula are also guided by the relevant evidence base. The AAI has initiated evaluation projects; however, these projects cannot be considered quality improvement (QI), as QI is, by definition, an ongoing, real-time assessment and improvement process. The evaluation projects have been one-time efforts over a specific period of time.

ANALYSIS OF SPENDING TRENDS

Funds were appropriated for the Arkansas Aging Initiative by Act 1575 of 2001, HB 1717 of 2003, and HB 1553 of 2005 for the first three bienniums of the Tobacco Settlement Fund Allocation. Table 6.3 details the appropriations by fiscal year.

Tables 6.4 and 6.5 present the total Tobacco Settlement funds received and spent by the AAI for the first two bienniums and the first half of the first year of the third biennium. The spending is reported by individual COA in Table 6.4 and by appropriation line item in Table 6.5. Each year, the AAI received less money than was specified in the appropriations. As shown in Table 6.4, for FY2005, the AAI received a total of $1,693,068, of which $1,395,242 was allocated to the regional COAs.

Table 6.3
Tobacco Settlement Funds Appropriated to Arkansas Aging Initiative, by Fiscal Year

Appropriation Item	First Biennium		Second Biennium		Third Biennium	
	2002	2003	2004	2005[a]	2006	2007
(1) Regular salaries	$491,040	$1,222,071	$1,278,528	$1,175,000	$1,345,756	$1,345,756
(2) Personal service matching	92,408	224,114	232,733	300,000	295,383	295,383
(3) Maintenance and operations						
(A) Operating expense	59,000	198,515	198,525	604,475	606,636	606,636
(B) Conferences and travel	25,000	56,500	56,500	20,000	51,134	51,134
(C) Professional fees	0	0	0	150,000	0	0
(D) Capacity outlay	201,552	558,200	558,200	75,000	25,567	25,567
(E) Data processing	0	0	0	0	0	0
Annual total	$869,000	$2,259,400	$2,324,476	$2,324,475	$2,324,476	$2,324,476
Biennium total	$3,128,400		$4,648,951		$4,648,952	

a. The Legislative Peer Review Committee adjusted the original FY2005 allocations to better meet program needs. These numbers reflect the re-allocated appropriation.

The available funding for COA management and operations is further reduced by the overhead paid by the COAs to the AHECs for their administrative role. The AAI was able to reduce the fee this year from 7.5 percent to just over 4 percent. This year, for the first time, the UAMS grant office had responsibility for preparing the financial statements for the UAMS tobacco-funded programs. It provided this service free of charge.

Table 6.4
Tobacco Settlement Funds Received and Spent by the Arkansas Aging Initiative, by Each Center on Aging

Center on Aging	Fiscal Year 2002		Fiscal Year 2003		Fiscal Year 2004		Fiscal Year 2005		Fiscal Year 2006	
	Received	Spent	Received	Spent	Received	Spent	Received	Spent	Received	Spent[a]
Central Admin.	$248,026	$233,839	$243,876	$424,175	$250,000	$259,448	$276,804	$267,349	$274,000	$115,555
Schmieding	15,000	24,136	243,876	212,912	250,000	229,838	209,000	229,162	196,100	93,542
SACOA	325,000	282,318	243,876	241,719	250,000	210,609	208,194	247,605	196,100	79,884
COA NE	75,000	74,944	243,876	243,780	250,000	250,001	202,640	202,639	138,750	79,431
TRCOA	75,000	74,997	243,876	243,876	250,000	204,982	209,000	254,018	196,100	99,566
Helena	30,000	24,072	243,876	130,242	125,000	112,556	152,644	165,088	196,100	66,398
SCCOA	NA	NA	243,876	259,066	250,000	243,933	208,990	215,067	196,100	74,722
Fort Smith	NA	NA	243,876	176,822	234,152	189,343	205,286	250,095	196,100	91,866
Evaluation	NA	NA	0	71,964	140,848	9,443	20,490	151,895	82,655	34,416
Annual total	$768,026	$714,306	$1,951,008	$2,004,553	$2,000,000	$1,710,153	$1,693,068	$1,982,918	$1,672,005	$735,381

a. Represents spending for the first half of the fiscal year (July–December 2005).

Table 6.5

Tobacco Settlement Funds Received and Spent by the Arkansas Aging Initiative by Appropriation Line Item

Appropriation Line Item	Fiscal Year 2002		Fiscal Year 2003		Fiscal Year 2004		Fiscal Year 2005		Fiscal Year 2006	
	Received	Spent	Received	Spent	Received	Spent	Received	Spent	Received	Spent[a]
Regular salaries, personal matching	$525,000	$517,196	$1,445,993	$1,323,226	$1,494,985	$1,362,046	$1,376,731	$1,425,301	$1,238,982	$616,789
Maintenance and Operations										
Operating expense	52,144	66,930	198,515	372,314	195,585	280,496	211,177	385,747	402,528	107,462
Conferences, travel	23,000	10,586	56,500	37,315	56,500	25,283	28,542	26,168	30,495	6,660
Professional fees	0	0	0	0	0	449	61,498	125,000	0	0
Capacity outlay	167,882	119,597	250,000	271,698	250,000	35,894	15,120	20,702	0	4,470
Data processing.	0	0	0	0	0	5,985	0	0	0	0
Annual total	$768,026	$714,306	$1,951,008	$2,004,553	$2,000,000	$1,710,153	$1,693,068	$1,982,918	$1,672,005	$735,381

NOTE: There are small differences between the "biennium differences" in Tables 6.A7 due to rounding.

a. Represents spending for the first half of the fiscal year (July–December 2005).

The issue of programming constraints created by the appropriation line item allocations was discussed in the 2004 evaluation report, which recommended that the appropriation for FY2005 be adjusted to ensure that the programs have funding allocations that support their programming needs. As a result, UAMS developed a proposal to make these adjustments for several programs, which was approved by the Legislative Peer Review Committee. The resulting adjustments to the AAI FY2005 appropriation are detailed in Table 6.6.

Table 6.6
Adjustments Made to the Line Items in the Arkansas Aging Initiative
FY2005 Appropriation

Arkansas Aging Initiative	Authorized Appropriation	Reallocated Appropriation
Salaries	$ 1,278,527	$ 1,175,000
Personal services match	232,733	300,000
Operating expenses	198,515	604,475
Travel and Conferences	56,500	20,000
Professional fees and services	0	150,000
Capital outlay	558,200	75,000
Total	$ 2,324,475	$ 2,324,475

Tobacco Settlement funds that were not spent in first year of the first biennium were carried over to the second year. These funds were reallocated by the central administration to the individual COAs after the Center on Aging directors and education directors prioritized a list of needs they had developed. During the first biennium, these leftover funds were used to purchase eight vans, one for each of the COAs, as well as to conduct a needs assessment and an evaluation of the AAI activities.

In the second biennium, funds were also carried over from the first to the second year. The carryover funds were reallocated to the individual COAs and to the evaluation. Of the $265,504 available, $135,000 was allocated to evaluation and the remaining $130,504 was primarily allocated to operating expenses for the COAs. The funds were particularly important for evaluation, as only 7 percent of the funds received for evaluation in FY2004 were spent in that year, and no funds were originally budgeted for this purpose for FY2005. The AAI has spent $267,718 from FY2003 through the first half of FY2006 to evaluate the program.

Total AAI spending in FY2005 increased 16 percent over FY2004. This includes a 60 percent increase in spending for M&O, largely due to $125,000 spent on professional fees for the evaluation. Excluding this expenditure, spending for M&O increased 25 percent over the prior year, while spending for salaries and benefits increased 4.6 percent. For the first half of FY2006, total spending is about 5 percent lower than it was in the first half of FY2005, excluding the $83,483 spent on professional fees for the evaluation in the first half of FY2005.

Figure 6.1 presents the AAI spending by quarter, broken down by two categories: salaries and fringe benefits, and operations and maintenance. It does not include spending for the evaluation. The appendix at the end of this chapter contains annual numbers for each individual COA, with more detailed reporting by appropriations category. While the quarterly expenditures varied across COAs and over time, there was a general upward trend in spending over the course of the first biennium, reflecting the growth in staff of the COAs through the third quarter of FY2003. We also see a large amount of capital spending in the fourth quarter of FY2003, which was when the vans were purchased for the COAs. The large increase in spending for M&O in the fourth quarter of FY2005 is a repetition of historically higher spending levels in the fourth quarter, with a contribution from the reallocation of the appropriation that made more funds available for operating expenses.

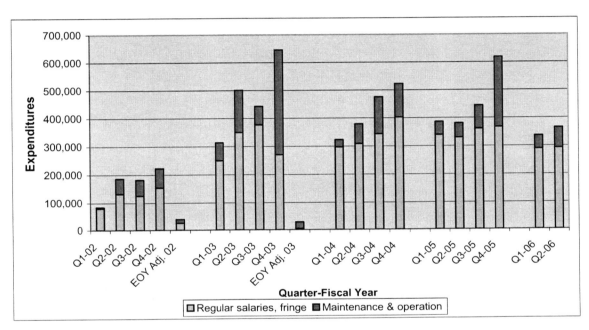

Figure 6.1—Quarterly Expenditures by the Aging Initiative

RESPONSES TO EVALUATION RECOMMENDATIONS

During the past year, the AAI has taken the following actions relevant to the recommendations made in the FY 2003 and FY2004 evaluation reports.

Recommendation 1: The central leadership at the Regional COA should put more emphasis on and create more opportunities for regions to collaborate and build on the successes of the local COAs.

> *Program Response:* The education directors and the COA directors meet in Little Rock with AAI leadership every other month to discuss progress and plan the future development of the Arkansas Aging Initiative. In March 2005, the education directors met for the first time prior to the meeting with AAI leadership to discuss ideas and collaborate on programming opportunities. They have subsequently met once face to face and also participated in a conference call. In addition, the AAI leadership has developed a new model for educational programming across regions. They will select a topic each year, and each region will create education modules and share them with the other regions. The topic for this year is dementia, selected as one of the priority conditions

reflecting both the priorities of the needs assessments conducted in each region and the health priorities of the state. Finally, Texarkana Regional COA (TRCOA), South Central COA (SCCOA), and South Arkansas COA (SACOA) are in developing a proposal to be submitted to the Blue Cross and You Foundation in June. This grant would fund a program to train and certify individuals in tai chi. They would subsequently teach tai chi to older adults in these regions.

In addition to the cross-COA collaborations described above, the COAs have engaged many of their local community partners in activities to further the mission of the AAI. Examples of the work the COAs do with other agencies and organizations in their local areas include the following:

- Family caregiver programs are being conducted with the local Area Agencies on Aging.

- The COAs are partnering with many community colleges and local universities for rotation of students in the health care professions and paraprofessions.

- All regions are involved in promoting and sponsorship of the Peer Education Program Promotes Independence (PEPPI).

- The Delta COA is working with the foster-grandparent program in Chicot County to develop grandparenting programs.

- The Delta COA and the South Central Center on Aging are partnering with the Alzheimer's Association to get HOPE for the Future in Monticello.

- The AAI leadership is developing plans for collaboration with the Minority Health Commission (MHC). No specific plans have been developed as yet, but they are in the process of identifying shared goals and developing a joint program. In the meantime, the Delta COA is working with the MHC on a hypertension program in Lee County.

- The AAI is collaborating with the College of Public Health to evaluate portions of the Arkansas Aging Initiative. They are currently engaged with Ty Borders at COPH to evaluate programs of the AAI; a proposal has been submitted to the ABI.

- All of the COAs are partnering with their local AHECs as well as local, state, and national initiatives to educate older adults regarding Medicare Part D coverage. Workshops are being held and seniors are being assisted in all parts of the state.

Recommendation 2: Given that many of the regions do not have co-located COAs and SHCs, the AAI might want to consider ways to reduce perceived barriers to services and resources.

Program Response: Since our last report, the South Arkansas COA in El Dorado expanded its Senior Health Clinic, and with the expanded space, the COA was able to move to the same floor as the SHC. The Delta COA in West Memphis had its grand opening in the summer of 2005, with the COA and the SHC located adjacent to each other at Crittenden Hospital. The COAs in Jonesboro and Texarkana are the only COAs not co-located with their SHCs. Although not co-located, the director of the SHC is also the education director for the COA in Jonesboro, so there are fewer perceived barriers in that region. The COA in Texarkana is located in Arkansas, while the SHC is located in Texas. Attempts to co-locate the two have been unsuccessful to date.

Recommendation 3: The AAI needs to make fundraising a higher priority across all regions.

Program Response: There are strong efforts to build Community Advisory Committees (CACs) in each region to provide local support for each COA and SHC and serve in a local fundraising capacity to ensure long-term sustainability of the COAs. The primary challenge faced by the COAs is that their staffs are trying to continue to grow programming in each region, leaving little time to build and nourish the CACs. The AAI secured the services of a consultant who has strong ties to many of the communities where COAs are located. The consultant is working with many of the regions to make sure that their legislators are aware of the work being done by the AAI and the COAs. In all but two regions, a chair and, in some regions, a vice chair have been named to head up the CACs; the Schmieding Center has not yet developed an advisory committee, and the Delta region just recently established its COA in West Memphis and is still building capacity. The goal is to have each committee operational by July 1, 2006 (although the Delta CAC may be delayed). Below is an update of the status for each CAC:

- COA-NE: Jonesboro has an operational committee with both the chair and vice chair in place. It meets on call. It will become more active when the director of development at St. Bernard's (the hospital that runs the SHC) is appointed and they begin a joint fundraising campaign.

- SACOA: El Dorado has one of the oldest established advisory committees, with a chair in place. It is staffed and functioning on a regular basis.

- SCCOA: Pine Bluff is in the process of forming a committee and has a chair in place. It has three standing members and a list of eight other people being interviewed and asking to serve on the committee.

- Delta COA: The COA celebrated its grand opening last summer and is still getting established. Plans are to begin the process of forming a committee in FY2007.

- TRCOA: A chair and vice chair have been appointed to the CAC in Texarkana. Members will subsequently be appointed.

- Fort Smith COA: A chair has been named for this CAC. The first meeting of this CAC took place in January 2006 and they have met one other time subsequently. The goal is to appoint a total of ten members to the CAC.

- Schmieding Center: The Schmieding Center at Springdale does not have an advisory committee at this time, but it does have the services of a part-time fundraiser furnished by UAMS. A strategic plan has been put into place to address the special needs of this region.

Individual COAs continue to leverage the Tobacco Settlement funds for programming, although the amounts raised to date have been quite small. For example, the COA in Bella Vista raised $6,400 between July and December 2005; $3,900 was contributed by the local Area Agency on Aging to fund family caregiver programs, and $2,500 was contributed by a pharmaceutical company for the Bella Vista Health Fair. Bella Vista has also received in-kind contributions from the United Way to cover rent and assistance with the development of a resource directory. Texarkana raised $1,050 from the pharmaceutical industry for community and health care professional education.

Recommendation 4: UAMS should consider centralizing responsibility for financial management and reporting to the Reynolds Institute on Aging.

Program Response: Currently, each COA has an AHEC partner that serves in an administrative capacity, paying salaries and other relevant expenses of the regional COA. This proposal to centralize financial management and reporting with the AAI leadership was brought to the UAMS chancellor last summer, but it was not approved. Previous concerns were that the AHECs had greater influence over the COA activities than was originally intended, but working relationships continue to improve. Although he rejected the proposal to centralize funds with the AAI, the UAMS chancellor directed that AHEC overhead be reduced from 7.5 percent to approximately 4 percent last summer. The UAMS Grants Office now has responsibility for preparing all the financial reports for all of the UAMS Tobacco Settlement–funded programs, in effect centralizing much of the financial reporting.

Recommendation 5: AAI leadership should work with each COA to improve the consistency in reporting on process indicators and other data needs.

Program Response: As reported above, one of the short-term goals of the AAI was to develop and implement a uniform database for tracking participants in AAI activities. This goal was achieved and the database is in use to gather data across all COAs. Although the database does not guarantee consistent reporting, it will strengthen the capacity for consistent reporting on process indicators and other measures across the region and over time. AAI leadership will need to conduct occasional checks of the data to ensure that they are accurate and consistently reported across COAs.

Recommendation 6: The AAI and the regional COAs should continue to emphasize outreach to the counties most distant from the COA facility location.

Program Response: With the growth in activity in each COA, more efforts have been made to reach the outlying counties in each region. Originally, the AAI aimed to provide programming in every county every year. In light of diminishing budgets and increasingly high cost of travel, the AAI leadership modified this goal to increase programming in each county, offering at least one program in each county every two years. In addition, some of the COAs are testing the possibility of collaborating with each other to reach counties that may not be in their own region but are geographically closer than is the COA in that county's region. It is believed that these plans will make better use of limited funds.

RECOMMENDATIONS FOR PROGRAM IMPROVEMENT

The AAI continues to make good progress in most areas of activity, including reaching out to communities and providing education to older adults, their families, and other community members, as well as to local health care providers. The AAI leadership and regional COA staff continue to turn limited funds into important resources for the state. There is still work to be done, however. Given the potential for a decrease in the Tobacco Settlement funds and other budget constraints, leveraging existing funds should become the priority for the AAI. In the past year, the AAI has invited evaluation from several sources, including the Lewin Group, the International Longevity Center (ILC), and the College of Public Health. We encourage these efforts and others that offer both formative and summative feedback to the AAI.

- **The AAI needs to make fundraising across all regions one of its highest priorities, identifying and pursuing funding opportunities through the state and federal governments, foundations, and the private sector.**

Although the AAI has undertaken several fundraising efforts to leverage the Tobacco Settlement funds it receives, it may still be some time before the CACs are capable of the level of fundraising necessary to guarantee the long-term sustainability of the local COAs. One method for leveraging these funds has been to engage the CAC in each region to develop and implement fundraising plans to support educational efforts and COA infrastructure. Most of the COAs have made substantial progress toward developing their CAC. In addition, the Reynolds Institute on Aging Community Advisory Board has established a subcommittee to provide guidance to the AAI and will include the leadership from local boards in some Reynolds Institute on Aging CAB meetings. The short-term goal to establish a database of funders was not achieved this year but should become a priority for this next year. More important, this work needs to be extended to developing fundable proposals.

In addition to the challenge to sustainability of the local COAs, the loss of funding to the Geriatric Education Center (GEC) is a major loss to the AAI. The national GEC was the primary engine behind the professional education programs offered through the COAs. Without these funds, the AAI will need to identify other funding sources immediately and for the long term to ensure that it stays true to its mission as stated in the act.

- **The AAI should ensure that each COA establishes and maintains a formal quality improvement process to monitor, assess, and improve performance, and it should establish a strategic plan for evaluation in which the AAI central office assesses COA performance on a periodic basis.**

While the AAI has the basis for performance standards defined (e.g., each COA's activities are matched against the strategic plan and the AAI leadership oversees the progress toward goals), the level of performance is not being addressed. This is the primary role of quality improvement. Systematic performance monitoring of the COAs is necessary and can be facilitated by the uniform database for tracking activities at the local level. Finally, quality improvement activities need to be put in place to make improvements in performance.

Evaluation is a cornerstone of program development and improvement. The FY2006–2010 strategic plan for the AAI includes a research and evaluation component. Some evaluation work is underway or at least in the proposal stage; projects include an evaluation of the financial viability of the SHCs and a proposal under consideration by the ABI to evaluate diabetes programs (in collaboration with faculty at the COPH). Among the objectives of this portion is to establish the Murphy Rural Aging Research Center to be located at the Reynolds Institute on Aging. Researchers at the center will conduct intramural and extramural research and serve as a resource for and conduct studies with the COAs. Before this center can be established, and in order to facilitate research once it is established, the AAI should begin to develop a strategic plan for evaluating the COAs and their activities.

Previous evaluation efforts have focused primarily on satisfaction with programs and have consistently reported high levels of satisfaction. Every other year a survey is mailed out to participants in professional education to gather information about satisfaction with programming and to serve as a needs assessment for future programming. While this survey consistently reports high satisfaction, the response rate has been at or below 15 percent, which is not sufficient to produce generalizable results. Future evaluation plans should include efforts at more strategic sampling efforts and move beyond studying satisfaction to systematically testing whether educational efforts lead to knowledge gained and behavior change.

- **The AAI should establish its long-range goals for tracking through the Arkansas Tobacco Settlement Evaluation.**

We agreed last year to establish only short-term (one-year) goals for the AAI and revisit and establish a set of long-term goals for future reporting this year. Each of the goals in the strategic plan described previously is associated with a set of objectives, strategies to achieving those objectives, and stated deliverables or outcomes. With support from RAND, the AAI should identify a set of five-year goals with measurable outcomes. Outcomes should be defined for the five-year period, and intermediate goals should also be established to measure progress toward the long-term goals.

APPENDIX TO CHAPTER 6

Update on Centers on Aging

All of the Centers on Aging (COAs) are now fully operational and providing educational opportunities to older adults, their families, other community members, and health professionals across the state. All but one of the COAs also has an associated Senior Health Center (SHC) providing geriatric health care services to older adults in those regions and supporting educational efforts in the community. Below is a description of the progress being made in each region to develop education programs and build geriatric health care capacity.

Schmieding Center (Northwest COA): The Schmieding Center and the satellite sites in Bella Vista, Harrison, and Mountain Home continue to grow, as measured by the number of community members attending educational sessions. The SHCs at Schmieding and Bella Vista also continue to provide education to patients at higher rates than any other SHCs. There was some concern that the hospital serving the northwest region would remove its support for the SHC in Bella Vista; however, it remains at the site and continues to serve patients. In Mountain Home, the director is a family practice physician who is currently considering entering a fellowship program for geriatrics. There is some hope that, with this director's interest and new leadership at the local hospital, an SHC may be located there. There are no immediate plans for an SHC in Harrison.

South Arkansas COA (SACOA): SACOA continues to develop good programs and expand its availability to outlying counties. The SHC is very successful in this region and, in the last year, the clinic expanded. In addition, the COA moved its education staff and resources to the same floor as the clinic, creating a more seamless entity. The demand for geriatric care in south Arkansas continues to increase, and the SHC is looking for another geriatrician to staff the clinic. Although SACOA continues to serve a large community base, it has decided to pull back some of its activities in outlying counties, as travel is difficult for staff and few people attend events.

Texarkana (TRCOA): The Texarkana COA has more than doubled its activities in the community in the last year. It has a strong director and has established itself as an excellent resource for educating not only the community but also students in the health professions. In the first half of 2005, the COA provided 60 training opportunities in the region, equaling 644 encounters. The COA is still challenged by the distance between it and the SHC in the region. The SHC is located on the Texas side of the state border, and it remains a lesser priority to the hospital that runs it.

COA-Northeast (COA-NE): COA-NE is currently the leader in creating educational opportunities for health care professionals in the region. It is also highly successful in creating educational opportunities for students in various health care professions. Although this region has been challenged in the past by several staffing changes, a new fellowship-trained physician has been hired to start in June 2006. The current COA director has been recruited away from the center but will remain until his replacement arrives. The COA is going to be moving to a new building with a better configuration to meet its needs and goals. In this new location, patients will walk through the COA to go to the clinic and thus will be exposed to the COA's educational resources. Co-locating the clinic and the educational component of the COA has made a significant difference in this region in terms of increasing access to services and support for community members.

Pine Bluff (SCCOA): The COA in Pine Bluff (South Central COA) continues to maintain a strong educational program. It is a leader in creating educational opportunities for paraprofessionals and student paraprofessionals. It also shows signs of improvement in bringing education to patients seen in the clinic. Although the SHC is a primary care clinic, it mainly serves as a referral site for patients. The plans to hire an outreach coordinator in Hot Springs to ease the burden on staff in Pine Bluff did not come to fruition; however, the Cello Foundation in Hot Springs has been working with the AAI leadership to develop the plans for a new COA to be located in Hot Springs. This new COA would absorb some of the counties currently served by Pine Bluff and Schmieding. There are some legal battles in the region that are halting plans to establish the COA, so it may be another year before this goal is attained.

Delta COA: The grand opening of the West Memphis site of the Delta COA occurred in August 2005. The COA received a $250,000 foundation grant to facilitate the startup of the center, and the staff there has developed plans for a house calls program and has submitted a proposal to this same foundation to support that program. The COA's new director recently completed a fellowship and has done an excellent job of bringing the staff together and creating a strong and cohesive team. The AAI leadership continues to work closely with the COA education director to increase her community outreach. The education director in West Memphis and the outreach coordinator in Helena (located at the Delta AHEC) have developed a good working relationship; however, the community does not distinguish between AHEC and COA activities in the region. Still, educational efforts focused on community members and paraprofessionals/student paraprofessionals are among the most successful in the state.

Ft. Smith (WCCOA): Since our last report, St. Edwards hospital has become a less active supporter of the COA and SHC in the region. Sparks Hospital continues to support the SHC, and the clinic's director (who also directs the COA) is a strong leader with geriatrics training. The clinic is trying to hire another geriatrician. The education director, who joined the COA since the last report, has developed very innovative materials; and the COA has developed a strong presence in the community, with almost 2,000 educational encounters with community members in the last year. Educational encounters with patients in the SHC continue to increase; currently, they average more than one educational encounter per patient encounter.

Performance on Process Indicators through December 2005

As discussed in previous reports, six indicators were selected to represent the overall progress of the Arkansas Aging Initiative. These indicators reflect the goal stated in the act to "increase the number of Arkansans participating in health improvement activities." The indicators reflect efforts to increase educational encounters (1) for seniors at each Senior Health Clinic, (2) at classes offered for community members, (3) for health care professionals participating in the Arkansas Geriatric Education Center programs, (4) at programs for students in health and social service disciplines, (5) for faculty from regional sites participating in postgraduate education through the Arkansas Geriatric Education Mentors and Scholars (AR-GEMS) program in the Arkansas Geriatric Education Center, and (6) for active paraprofessionals and paraprofessional students. A seventh one-time indicator was to complete community needs assessments to prioritize needs and activities of the COAs.

Increase the educational encounter rate for seniors at each Senior Health Center.

Indicator: Educational encounter rate for seniors at each Senior Health Center.

The goal of this indicator is to report individual educational encounters occurring in the SHCs. The SHC, one of two components of the COA, plays a critical role in the education mission by providing individual encounters as well as providing health and social services. Educational encounters can be provided to the patient by the physician, nurse, nutritionist, social worker, or COA staff. Table 6.A1 summarizes the educational encounter rate for seniors at each Senior Health Clinic. The numerator is the number of educational encounters provided in the COA, and the denominator is the number of patients seen in the SHC during the relevant six-month time period. We only report data beginning in 2004 because this indicator was established at the beginning of that year.

Table 6.A1
Educational Encounter Rates at Senior Health Clinics for Older Adults

	Jan–Jun 2004		Jul–Dec 2004		Jan–Jun 2005		Jul–Dec 2005	
	Encounters per Patient	Number of SHC Patients	Encounters per Patient	Number of SHC Patients	Encounters per Patient	Number of SHC Patients	Encounters per Patient	Number of SHC Patients
Schmieding COA	1.03	6,830	2.02	3,120	1.12	5,528	1.30	5,824
— Harrison	[a]	[a]	[a]	[a]	[a]	[a]	[a]	[a]
— Mountain Home	[a]	[a]	[a]	[a]	[a]	[a]	[a]	[a]
— Bella Vista	NA	NA	1.22	1,207	1.09	2,756	1.11	2,108
SACOA	0.48	2,840	0.45[b]	4,560	0.74	2231	NR	NR
Texarkana	NA	NA	NR	NR	NR	NR	NR	NR
COA—NE	0.09	2,200	0.79[b]	1,350	0.98	1,334	0.76	1,761
South Central COA	0.45	411	0.58	573	0.62	563	0.66	740
Delta COA—West Memphis	[a]	[a]	[a]	[a]	[a]	[a]	NR	NR
Delta COA—Helena	[a]	[a]	[a]	[a]	[a]	[a]	[a]	[a]
Fort Smith	0.00	798	1.01	1,614	NR	NR	1.06	1,243

NOTE: NA indicates data not tracked during this time. NR is data not reported.

a. The program was not in operation during this time period.

b. Based on five months of data.

There is substantial variation across regions in the rate of education encounters. The data reported in 2004 varied in part due to the process of developing a system for gathering data, varying data-collection start times by the COAs, and inconsistencies in the operating definition of an educational encounter. Each COA must rely on clinic staff to report these data. Inconsistencies in reporting are influenced by staff turnover (thus the need for continuous staff orientation), understanding of the importance of data collection, and overall hospital commitment to this task. The Schmieding Center has the highest educational encounter rate of all the centers (probably because it has three tobacco-funded satellites and adds the work of the Schmieding Center, which is paid for by a grant), although the rate declined substantially between the second period of 2004 and the first period of 2005. Despite an increase in the second period of 2005, the rate is still substantially lower than it was during the same period a year earlier. The educational encounter rate at the Schmieding Center exceeds that of any other center in part because it has a full-time social worker on staff providing education to patients—no other COA has that level of staffing. Bella Vista has consistently reported an educational encounter rate over 1.0, although even this center has experienced fluctuations in the rate. SACOA, SCCOA, and Fort Smith all experienced increases in their educational rates, although all three COAs report rates less than 1.0.

Increase the number of encounters at classes offered for community members.

Indicator: Number of encounters at classes offered for community members.

Table 6.A2 summarizes the educational encounters for each of the COAs for six-month time intervals over the past three years. Again, vagaries in data collection make interpretation inconclusive. The encounter counts are generally very erratic over time, although most COAs enjoyed increases in the number of community members attending AAI classes. Encounters at Harrison, Bella Vista, SACOA, and SCCOA were more erratic, with increases and decreases in encounter rates. Bella Vista hosted a large health fair during the second period of 2005, which explains the dramatic increase in this last period. In most COAs, staff increased course offerings, particularly education course offerings. Exercise classes are generally offered more than once a week, and attendees are counted each time they attend, which also explains general increases in the number of encounters over time.

Table 6.A2
Encounters at AAI Classes for Community Members

	Jan–Jun 2002	Jul–Dec 2002	Jan–Jun 2003	Jul–Dec 2003	Jan–Jun 2004	Jul–Dec 2004	Jan–Jun 2005	Jul–Dec 2005
Schmieding COA Springdale	NR	NR	NR	NR	535	739	1657	1431
— Harrison	a	379	547	429	691	284	436	230
— Mountain Home	a	a	a	a	113	399	640	1,770
— Bella Vista	a	a	538	324	1,276	1,226	1,119	2,948
SACOA	20	755	1,442	973	2,532	1,887	3280	2,466
Texarkana	a	296	780	630	1,318	1,463	3013	3,342
COA—NE	a	216	1,066	1,509	1,385	1,390	2404	1,687
South Central COA	a	a	338	1,182	3,012	1,990	3186	2,812
Delta COA—W. Memphis	a	a	260[b]	1,526[b]	3,767[b]	3,924[b]	1,319	1,526
Delta COA—Helena	a	a	b	b	b	b	2613	2,725
Fort Smith	a	a	b	563	205	699	731	1040

NOTE: NR is data not reported.

a. The program was not in operation during this time period.

b. The encounter counts for the Delta COA were reported as a combined count for the West Memphis and Helena campuses until CY2005.

Increase the number of educational encounters for health care professionals participating in the Arkansas Geriatric Education Center's programs.

Indicator: Number of educational encounters for health care professionals participating in the Arkansas Geriatric Education Center's programs.

Table 6.A3 presents counts of educational encounters for health care professionals participating in AGEC programs. The AGEC is funded by the Health Resources and Services Administration (HRSA) and is run jointly by the Reynolds Institute on Aging and the Veterans Healthcare System. The AGEC sponsors geriatric-focused conferences and videoconferences throughout the year. HRSA awarded the AAI director of education a supplemental grant to do a series of one-day conferences on mental health issues for the elderly at each COA site, which accounts for large encounter counts for the first period of 2004. AGEC activity has been inconsistent across COAs. This inconsistency is due in part to the fact that while the AGEC activities are available to the state, COAs do not always host them in their regions. Most of the COAs offered at least one course during 2005. Most AGEC offerings within the regions are videoconferences, which have been taped and can be taken out into the counties and regional COAs for outreach.

Table 6.A3
Encounters at Geriatric Education Center for Health Care Professionals

	Jan–Jun 2002	Jul–Dec 2002	Jan–Jun 2003	Jul–Dec 2003	Jan–Jun 2004	Jul–Dec 2004	Jan–Jun 2005	Jul–Dec 2005
Schmieding COA Springdale	NR	NR	NR	NR	101	0	3	9
– Harrison	a	0	0	0	0	0	8	0
– Mountain Home	a	a	a	a	16	0	0	19
– Bella Vista	a	a	27	0	0	0	0	0
SACOA	0	12	49	114	241	0	129	38
Texarkana	a	6	112	0	84	0	15	0
COA-NE	a	13	26	76	161	108	127	412
South Central COA	a	a	21	8	129	54	12	16
Delta COA – W. Memphis	a	a	0[b]	20[b]	65[b]	0[b]	23	17
Delta COA – Helena	a	a	b	b	b	b	3	2
Fort Smith	a	a	a	0	76	17	14	16

NOTE: NR is data not reported.

a. The program was not in operation during this time period.

b. The encounter counts for the Delta COA were reported as a combined count for the West Memphis and Helena campuses until CY2005.

Increase the number of educational encounters at programs for students in health and social service disciplines.

Indicator: Number of educational encounters at programs for students in health and social service disciplines.

Just as the COAs support educational opportunities for health care professionals, they also support educational activities for students in the health and social service disciplines. Training is provided to medical students, geriatric nurse practitioners, nurses, social workers, physical therapists, pharmacists, dieticians, and others. Table 6.A4 summarizes the educational encounters for students across the COAs. There is substantial variation across regions and over time in these encounters. For example, Texarkana had 644 student encounters in the first period of 2005 resulting from 60 course offerings, but only 6 encounters in the second period of 2005. Harrison was among the more consistent in terms of offering student educational encounters and had high numbers of encounters relative to other COAs; however it had no student encounters at all in 2005. Variation is due to differences in the opportunities for student education over time and across regions. Not all regions have the capacity to mentor students, due to lack of appropriate staff, lack of appropriate training opportunities, or other nearby programs training health and social service professionals.

Table 6.A4
Encounters at AAI Education for Health and Social Service Students

	Jan–Jun 2002	Jul–Dec 2002	Jan–Jun 2003	Jul–Dec 2003	Jan–Jun 2004	Jul–Dec 2004	Jan–Jun 2005	Jul–Dec 2005
Schmieding COA Springdale	NR	NR	NR	NR	40	0	2	2
— Harrison	a	0	0	19	177	74	0	0
— Mountain Home	a	a	a	a	0	0	0	6
— Bella Vista	a	a	0	0	0	0	0	0
SACOA	0	38	450	122	38	34	28	94
Texarkana	a	24	19	39	26	0	644	6
COA—NE	a	0	0	30	54	111	11	127
South Central COA	a	a	12	129	65	94	8	157
Delta COA—W. Memphis	a	a	0[b]	2[b]	2[b]	1[b]	0	0
Delta COA—Helena	a	a	b	b	b	b	15	17
Fort Smith	a	a	a	0	33	10	32	8

NOTE: NR is data not reported.

a. The program was not in operation during this time period.

b. The encounter counts for the Delta COA were reported as a combined count for the West Memphis and Helena campuses until CY2005.

Increase the number of encounters for health professionals from regional sites participating in education through the Arkansas Geriatric Education Mentors and Scholars (AR-GEMS) program in the Arkansas Geriatric Education Center.

Indicator: Number of educational encounters for health professionals from regional sites participating in education through the Arkansas Geriatric Education Center.

AR-GEMS is a continuing education program for health professionals who work with older adults and who want to improve the way they provide care. Previously, this program was described as postgraduate education targeted at regional faculty; however, it was not accurately reported. Rather, the AR-GEMS program is a 240-hour free training program primarily for nurses, pharmacists, and social workers. AR-GEMS program requirements include different educational activities using various modes of learning: videoconference, in-person workshops, self-instruction, and experiential practice in a geriatric setting with a mentor. These programs operate over an extended period of time, which explains the low numbers in Table 6.A5. Additionally, these courses are generally only offered once a year beginning in the summer. This program still has not grown despite the substantial emphasis by the Arkansas Aging Initiative on professional education.

Table 6.A5
Postgraduate Encounters at Geriatric Education Center for Regional Faculty

	Jan–Jun 2002	Jul–Dec 2002	Jan–Jun 2003	Jul–Dec 2003	Jan–Jun 2004	Jul–Dec 2004	Jan–Jun 2005	Jul–Dec 2005
Schmieding COA Springdale	NR	NR	NR	NR	0	0	1	0
— Harrison	a	0	0	0	0	0	0	0
— Mountain Home	a	a	a	a	0	0	NR	0
— Bella Vista	a	a	0	0	0	0	0	0
SACOA	0	1	0	0	0	0	NR	0
Texarkana	a	0	2	2	2	0	0	0
COA-NE	a	0	0	2	0	1	0	1
South Central COA	a	a	7	0	0	0	1	0
Delta COA—W. Memphis	a	a	0[b]	1[b]	1[b]	0[b]	0	NR
Delta COA—Helena	a	a	b	b	b	b	0	0
Fort Smith	a	a	a	0	0	0	2	0

NOTE: NR is data not reported.

a. The program was not in operation during this time period.

b. The encounter counts for the Delta COA were reported as a combined count for the West Memphis and Helena campuses until CY2005.

Increase the number of educational encounters for active paraprofessionals and paraprofessional students.

Indicator: Number of educational encounters for active paraprofessionals and paraprofessional students.

Table 6.A6 presents counts of educational encounters for paraprofessionals and paraprofessional students. A paraprofessional is an unlicensed individual who provides hands-on care to clients who need moderate to maximum assistance. This care is provided under the direction of a health care professional and may be delivered in the home, hospital, community-based program, or long-term care facility. There is substantial variation across regions in the number of educational encounters for paraprofessionals and paraprofessional students. The Delta region had the most educational encounters through the second period of 2004 (reflecting programs offered at both the West Memphis and Helena campuses of the COA), followed by the SCCOA. The Delta had fewer course offerings in the first period of 2005 and more encounters at the Helena site. However, the number of encounters increased to more than 400 in the second period of 2005. The Schmieding Center also has many course offerings for paraprofessionals and paraprofessional students. In 2005, the Delta COA offered 30 courses, compared to 21 in South Central and 43 at Schmieding. Texarkana and Fort Smith have not made the training of paraprofessionals a focus to date. Other regions currently may not be well equipped to support such educational encounters.

Table 6.A6
Educational Encounters for Paraprofessionals and Paraprofessional Students

	Jan–Jun 2002	Jul–Dec 2002	Jan–Jun 2003	Jul–Dec 2003	Jan–Jun 2004	Jul–Dec 2004	Jan–Jun 2005	Jul–Dec 2005
Schmieding COA Springdale	NR	NR	NR	NR	198	166	328	281
— Harrison	[a]	70	185	167	272	37	37	0
— Mountain Home	[a]	[a]	[a]	[a]	0	256	0	16
— Bella Vista	[a]	[a]	NA	33	12	89	24	17
SACOA	NA	NA	135	524	235	195	120	NR
Texarkana	[a]	NA	NA	NA	0	0	0	0
COA—NE	[a]	NA	NA	0	151	98	0	13
South Central COA	[a]	[a]	NA	156	474	499	373	467
Delta COA—W. Memphis	[a]	[a]	34[b]	211[b]	531[b]	769[b]	24	6
Delta COA—Helena	[a]	[a]	[b]	[b]	[b]	[b]	274	423
Fort Smith	[a]	[a]	[a]	57	5	0	0	0

NOTES: A paraprofessional is an unlicensed individual who provides "hands-on care" to clients who need moderate to maximum assistance. This care is provided under the direction of a health care professional and may be delivered in the home, hospital, community-based program, or long-term care facility.
NA indicates data were not collected for this indicator during this time period.
NR is data not reported.

a. The program was not in operation during this time period.

b. The encounter counts for the Delta COA were reported as a combined count for the West Memphis and Helena campuses until CY 2005.

Finally, Table 6.A7 shows expenditures for the AAI, by Center and Fiscal Year.

Table 6.A7
Expenditures of the Arkansas Aging Initiative, by Center and Fiscal Year

	FY2002	FY2003	FY2004	FY2005	FY2006[a]
Central Administration					
(1) Regular salaries	$192,238	$219,907	$195,717	$197,707	$81,400
(2) Personal service matching	37,935	47,227	40,250	46,568	16,958
(3) Maintenance and operation					
(A) Operating expense	-4,524	20,850	17,680	20,125	13,175
(B) Conference and travel	3,290	7,732	5,352	(551)	4,023
(C) Professional fees	0	0	449	0	0
(D) Capacity outlay	4,900	128,459	0	1,500	0
(E) Data processing	0	0	0	0	0
Schmieding					
(1) Regular salaries	17,291	132,984	149,427	159,824	72,913
(2) Personal service matching	3,345	30,491	36,989	41,822	19,387
(3) Maintenance and operation					
(A) Operating expense	3,500	44,680	38,057	11,754	1,242
(B) Conferences and travel	0	4,758	1,611	0	0
(C) Professional fees	0	0	0	0	0
(D) Capacity outlay	0	0	3,754	15,701	0
(E) Data processing	0	0	0	0	0
SACOA					
(1) Regular salaries	144,389	92,510	121,503	132,581	48,672
(2) Personal service matching	25,757	23,098	31,537	36,345	13,652
(3) Maintenance and operation					
(A) Operating expense	20,790	93,684	47,289	78,149	14,923
(B) Conference and travel	4,862	3,387	4,285	6,525	2,638
(C) Professional fees	0	0	0	0	0
(D) Capacity outlay	47,328	4,989	5,995	(5,995)	0
(E) Data processing	0	0	0	0	0
COA Northeast					
(1) Regular salaries/(2) Personal service	30,693	211,821	192,676	155,949	55,093
(3) Maintenance and operation					
(A) Operating expense	3,512	26,163	47,996	42,577	24,338
(B) Conference and travel	1,821	2,866	2,222	3,665	0
(C) Professional fees	0	0	0	0	0
(D) Capacity outlay	38,917	2,931	7,107	449	0
(E) Data processing	0	0	0	0	0
TRCOA					
(1) Regular salaries/(2) Personal service	29,226	169,136	168,398	174,536	82,466
(3) Maintenance and operation					

Table 6.A7—Continued

	FY2002	FY2003	FY2004	FY2005	FY2006[a]
TRCOA					
(A) Operating expense	11,465	53,353	33,898	71,737	17,100
(B) Conference and travel	613	13,891	2,686	4,833	0
(C) Professional fees	0	0	0	0	0
(D) Capacity outlay	33,693	7,496	0	2,912	0
(E) Data processing	0	0	0	0	0
Helena					
(1) Regular salaries	9,408	20,833	70,543	87,561	47,131
(2) Personal service matching	1,610	3,549	13,234	18,253	10,766
(3) Maintenance and operation					
(A) Operating expense	13,054	41,732	21,106	53,027	8,501
(B) Conference and travel	0	455	6,455	4,702	0
(C) Professional fees	0	0	0	0	0
(D) Capacity outlay	0	63,673	1,218	1,545	0
(E) Data processing	0	0	0	0	0
SCCOA					
(1) Regular salaries	0	138,168	152,639	148,798	58,079
(2) Personal service matching	0	27,982	30,841	30,216	11,305
(3) Maintenance and operation					
(A) Operating expense	0	44,083	53,183	24,906	5,338
(B) Conference and travel	0	1,790	1,384	3,227	0
(C) Professional fees	0	0	0	0	0
(D) Capacity outlay	0	42,740	5,886	7,921	0
(E) Data processing	0	0	0	0	0
Fort Smith					
(1) Regular salaries	0	106,589	122,449	135,161	52,239
(2) Personal service matching	0	23,372	26,400	31,261	12,311
(3) Maintenance and operation					
(A) Operating expense	0	25,450	21,287	83,427	22,846
(B) Conference and travel	0	0	1,288	3,577	0
(C) Professional fees	0	0	0	0	0
(D) Capacity outlay	0	21,411	11,934	(3,331)	4,470
(E) Data processing	0	0	5,985	0	0
Evaluation					
(1) Regular salaries		63,363	8,269	21,776	29,828
(2) Personal service matching		12,566	1,174	4,883	4,587

Table 6.A7—Continued

	FY2002	FY2003	FY2004	FY2005	FY2006[a]
(3) Maintenance and operation					
(A) Operating expense	0	303	0	46	0
(C) Professional fees	0	0	0	125,000	0
(D) Capacity outlay	0	0	0	0	0
(E) Data processing	0	0	0	0	0

a. Represents spending through December 31, 2005.

Chapter 7
Minority Health Initiative

PROGRAM DESCRIPTION

The Initiated Act mandates that the Minority Health Initiative (MHI) be implemented by the Arkansas Minority Health Commission (AMHC). The act specifies that the initiative (1) increase awareness of hypertension, strokes, and other disorders disproportionately critical to minorities by utilizing different approaches that include but are not limited to the following: advertisements, distributing educational materials, and providing medications for high-risk minority populations; (2) provide screening or access to screening for hypertension, strokes, and other disorders disproportionately critical to minorities (but also provide this service to any citizen within the state regardless of racial/ethnic group); (3) develop the following intervention strategies to decrease hypertension, strokes, and other disorders noted above, as well as associated complications: educational programs, modification of risk factors by smoking cessation programs, weight loss, promoting healthy lifestyles, treatment of hypertension with cost-effective, well-tolerated medications, and case management for patients in these programs; and (4) develop and maintain a database that will include biographical data, screening data, costs, and outcomes.

The act specifies the following short-term goals for the MHI: prioritize the list of health problems and planned intervention for minority population(s), and increase the number of Arkansans screened and treated for tobacco-related illnesses. The long-term goal for the MHI is to reduce death/disability due to tobacco-related illnesses of Arkansans.

In 2005, an amendment was passed to change the line item in the appropriations regarding funds for the provision of "drugs and medicine" to "screening, monitoring, treatment, and outreach" (SB 80).

PROGRESS TOWARD ACHIEVING FIVE-YEAR AND SHORT-TERM GOALS

Over the past year, the program claims significant improvements in its financial management activities by developing a local automated system. Performance standards for three of the MHI's contracts have been instituted. Progress on the process indicators is noted in the appendix at the end of this chapter.

Here, we consider the program goals established as part of the Arkansas Tobacco Settlement Evaluation activities in spring 2005 and first specified in the 2005 RAND report (Farley et al., 2005b).

Goal 1: Continue needs assessment activities to help inform health needs and policy recommendations for minority populations in Arkansas.

    a. Perform costs analyses for a comprehensive statewide health telephone survey by fall 2005; then identify stakeholders and potential funding sources by winter 2005/2006 and submit application for funding by the end of 2005.

    b. Conduct and analyze statewide comprehensive health telephone survey of Arkansans by fall 2009 with oversampling of minority subpopulations.

    c. Submit application for funding by the end of 2005.

d. Conduct and analyze statewide comprehensive health telephone survey.

Progress on Goal 1:

    a. ACCOMPLISHED. Quotes were obtained last year in the $250,000–$300,000 range for a survey using an existing protocol developed by the Commonwealth Fund (i.e., a minority health survey).

    b. ACCOMPLISHED. The MHI has identified stakeholders and continues to do so as it works to develop this project.

    c. NOT ACCOMPLISHED. Although applications were not submitted on time, one proposal has been submitted and another is planned: $200,000 was requested for first-year survey preparation in a proposal to the Robert Wood Johnson Foundation in March 2006 (which was subsequently not funded). Further funding for $275,000 in direct funds over two years is to be requested via a R21 proposal that was planned for submission in June 2006 in response to an NIH call for research on racial/ethnic discrimination in health care.

    d. REPORTED ON SCHEDULE. The MHI reports that it is still on target to implement a telephone survey by fall 2009. We did not obtain a time management plan for this effort that would confirm this report.

Goal 2: Increase awareness and education activities to reach Hispanic populations by including Spanish subtitles to all MH Today TV shows by spring 2007 and developing a cookbook and collaterals for Hispanic population by 2008.

Progress on Goal 2: REPORTED TO BE ON SCHEDULE. The executive director reports that the MHI challenged to find a vendor to create the subtitles of its programming but still believe that the spring 2007 deadline can be met. The MHI continues to plan development of a cookbook and collaterals for the Hispanic population by 2008. We did not obtain any evidence to confirm this report.

Goal 3: Expand current intervention activities.

    a. Increase enrollment in the CHC-based Hypertension Initiative by 5 percent annually within each participating county, based on the enrollment numbers at the end of FY2004.

    b. Expand Eating and Moving for Life Initiative to ten counties by 2010.

Progress on Goal 3:

    a. NOT ACCOMPLISHED. The AMHC reports that enrollment has declined at the three Community Health Centers that are contracted to provide hypertension services. (See the appendix at the end of this chapter for enrollment trends). The MHI notes that enrollment of participants into any treatment program may decrease over time, as the pool of more easily identified and enrolled persons becomes exhausted. In order to increase enrollment, the MHI plans to increase the number of entities conducting screenings and try to develop another site to offer treatment.

    b. NOT ACCOMPLISHED. The MHI initially expanded to Phillips County in early 2005 but then ended support for this expansion in fall 2005. The MHI reports no plans to expand the Eating and Moving for Life (EMFL) program, given current funding levels. It is considering a more cost-effective program that will meet the same goals of the EMFL Initiative. Along with the MHI-developed "Southern Ain't Fried Sundays" nutrition education program, MHI plans to support the American Cancer Society (ACS) Active for Life programming, which is a ten-week curriculum that promotes physical activity. For the ACS program, a train-the-trainer model is planned. The executive director reports that Ouachita County has agreed to pilot this program. Training planned to take place in June is being scheduled with representatives from churches in the county.

There is a reason why goal 3 might be given lower priority. The cost of these programs, both in and of themselves and in terms of opportunity costs for MHI, might lead to a decision to spend the money elsewhere. We address this issue in Chapter 12.

Goal 4: Increase external funding by the following:

a. 5 percent in spring 2006

b. 10 percent annually in following years (spring 2007–2010)

Progress on Goal 4:

a. ACCOMPLISHED. External funding was documented as $13,000 in 2005 and increased to $86,000 by spring 2006, an increase of more than 500 percent. External funding is shown in Table 7.1.

b. TO BE DETERMINED. With this positive start, the AMHC expects to be able to increase funding for MHI activities by 10 percent annually over the next four years.

Table 7.1
External Funding by Grant, Activity and Dollar Amount, Spring 2006

Funding Source	Activity	Amount
Private donations	Second annual Southern Ain't Fried Sundays events	$40,000
Abbott Renal Care	Lab testing for MESH study	25,000
ADH Cardiovascular Health Program	Training programs to improve blood pressure screening in children	13,000
Lilly Pharmaceuticals	Testing for MESH study	5,000
Jefferson Comprehensive Care System, Inc.	AIDS/HIV Awareness Program	3,000

PERFORMANCE ON PROCESS INDICATORS

As noted in previous reports, five indicators were developed to track progress of the MHI activities: tracking of MHI awareness activities, documentation of health screenings for minorities, screening and enrollment into the MHI-supported intervention activities, documentation of a prioritized list of health priorities, and a biographical database. Refer to the appendix to this chapter for tables with detailed trend information.

Some of the MHI activities initiated to date have continued to grow, while others have declined. Regarding MHI awareness efforts, the TV, radio, newspaper exposure, and collateral distribution decreased in 2005. However, telephone calls to the MHI were reported to have increased. The reporting of the visits to the Web site was changed in the last data reporting period (July–December 2005), so it is not possible to make comparisons to previous time periods.

In terms of health screenings, the number of health fairs that the MHI participated in (either through attendance or financial contribution) held steady over the past three years (35 or 36), as did the reported number of screenings up to June 2005. For July–December 2005, the reported number of screenings is low. The reason could be that temporary staffing shortfalls meant that the MHI was unable to attend some health fairs, and therefore has no reliable information about how many screenings took place at those events. In the future, screeners should be instructed to record—even in rudimentary fashion—each screening that takes place, and to provide this information to the MHI.

The number of participants in the two MHI health-related interventions (Hypertension Initiative and Eating and Moving for Life (EMFL)) has varied over time. For the Hypertension Initiative, in 2005, the number screened increased by 15 percent while the number treated decreased by 71 percent compared to 2004. For the EMFL Initiative, the number screened and enrolled increased in 2005 by 85 percent and 107 percent, respectively, compared to 2004.

For other indicators, the prioritized list of health needs among African Americans was completed and submitted in July 2004, although similar priorities have not been developed for other minorities. The biographical database for the Hypertension Initiative has not yet been completed for a variety of reasons that the AMHC claims is not related to its efforts.

PERFORMANCE ON MANAGEMENT INTEGRITY CRITERIA

Types and Performance of Governing and Advisory Boards

The MHI operates under the AMHC governing board. This board is made up of 12 members who serve at the will of the person or body that appointed them. Act 912 of 1991 stipulates that the board is to be made up of the following:

1. Four members of the general public to be appointed by the governor, with each of the four Arkansas congressional districts represented

2. Two members of the general public to be appointed by the president pro tempore of the Arkansas Senate

3. Two members of the general public to be appointed by the speaker of the Arkansas House of Representatives

4. The director of the Division of Alcohol and Drug Abuse Prevention of the Department of Human Services (now DHHS), or his or her designee

5. The director of the Division of Aging and Adult Services of the Department of Human Services (now DHHS), or designee

6. The director of the Department of Health (now DHHS), or designee

7. The director of the Division of Mental Health (now within DHHS), or designee

The current board of AMHC commissioners is as follows:

1. Larnell Davis (commission chairman), executive director of Jefferson County Comprehensive System, Inc., 4th district representative

2. Alvin Coleman, Jr. music teacher, 1st district representative

3. Vanessa Davis, assistant director, Division of Behavioral Health, DHHS, Division of Mental Health representative

4. Vivian Flowers, student in the Clinton School of Public Service, House representative

5. Joe Hill, Director for the Division of Alcohol and Drugs, Division of Behavioral Health, DHHS, Alcohol and Drug Abuse Prevention representative

6. Eddie Mae Martin, registered nurse for the Phillips County DHS, Division of Aging and Adult Services representative

7. Christine Patterson, director of the Office of Minority Health and Health Disparities, Division of Health, DHHS, Division of Health representative

8. Mary Powell, self-employed health care management consultant, 3rd district representative

9. Carmen Ramirez, PhD, nurse at the University of Arkansas for Medical Sciences, 2nd district representative

10. Willa Sanders, Assistant Dean for Governmental Relations and Special Projects, UAMS Faye W. Boozman College of Public Health, Senate representative

11. Dr. Theresa Travis, physician with Hospice Care, House representative

12. Josetta Wilkens, PhD, retired state legislator and retired university professor, Senate representative

The AMHC's governing board met three times in 2004. The location of the meeting is moved around the state in order to include input from different communities. The governing board has one subcommittee, the Planning and Review Subcommittee, that meets on an as-needed basis.

A Medical Advisory Board for the AMHC was created in 1999, consisting of health care providers who are appointed by invitation and serve at their own will. The board meets on an as-needed basis. The AMHC notes that the need for intensive review by the Medical Advisory Board has lessened from 2002 to present, and the current ratings are only for FY2004–2005.

Table 7.2 reports the ratings developed in the evaluation regarding the AMHC governing board's involvement with different program aspects of the AMHC governing board (MHI and others) and the Medical Advisory Board's involvement with the Hypertension Initiative.

Table 7.2
Performance of the AMHC Governing Board and Medical Advisory Board on Dimensions of Board Oversight for the Minority Health Initiative, Scales of 1 to 5

	AMHC Governing Board	Medical Advisory Board (Hypertension Initiative)
P-1: Goals and planning	5	2
P-2: Priorities	5	2
P-3: Budget	3	2
P-4: Quality management	3	2
M-1: Progress toward goals	5	2
M-2: Spending	5	1
M-3: Quality performance	5	2
C-1: Community needs	5	2
C-2: Community interactions	5	3
C-3: Fund-raising	4	1

NOTE: Definitions of ratings: 1 = not involved, 2 = minimally involved, 3 = not intense involvement, 4 = fully considers, 5 = directive

Quality Improvement Process

Currently, neither the AMHC as a whole nor the MHI has a formal written quality improvement process. The executive director meets with all staff on a weekly basis to collect information to address quality. The only MHI program for which a written quality improvement process is in place is the Hypertension Initiative. Staff reports that a written quality improvement process for the EMFL Initiative is underway.

Because no other unit within the MHI has any quality management system, Table 7.3 provides ratings of the different aspects of quality management only for the MHI Hypertension Initiative. This information highlights areas in which the initiative is performing satisfactorily and those in which it needs improvement. For example, the MHI collects technical information about the quality of its blood pressure screening efforts, but the quality management activities around the hypertension treatment activities need improvement. The MHI has collected information on consumer experience, but the response rates have been low (26 percent). Due to the small amount of information that has been collected, the MHI has not yet analyzed the technical quality data for treatment and consumer experiences.

Table 7.3
Ratings of the MHI Hypertension Initiative on Quality Management Activities

	Not Applicable	Needs Improvement	Does Satisfactorily
1. Specifies criteria for quality performance			X
2. Collects information on technical quality measures		X (treatment)	X (screening)
3. Collects information on consumers' experience with service		X	
4. Collects data on program enrollments, demographic characteristics of enrollees, service encounters		X	
5. Has quantified quality measures for technical aspects of service		X	
6. Has quantified measures of consumers' experience with service		X	
7. Has quantified measures on program enrollments, demographic characteristics of enrollees, service encounters that may be compared to targets			X
8. Analyzes technical quality data to identify potential quality deficiencies		X	
9. Analyzes consumer experience data to identify potential quality deficiencies		X	
10. Analyzes measures on program enrollments, etc. to identify potential quality deficiencies			X
11. Formulates quality recommendations that are addressed to who needs to take action			X
12. Reports results of quality analyses to executive management/boards			X
13. Reports results of quality analyses to relevant committees			X
14. Disseminates quality recommendations to the public ("report cards")	X		

Financial Management Process

The AMHC uses the AASIS (Arkansas Administrative Statewide Information System) to report spending to the state on the Tobacco Settlement funding. An administrative assistant enters invoices received for payment into the system using a standard template for payment. Then, the information is faxed to the service bureau to receive warrants. Assigned internal AMHC staff pick up the warrants and bring them back to the office to be photocopied and mailed out.

The AMHC also uses a local automated accounting system that is set up in Microsoft Excel. In summer 2005, a consultant was hired to develop the local system and to train staff in its use. AMHC staffs enter the data into the Excel program according to individual cost center codes and general ledger codes. Monthly reports provide the executive director with monthly spending information broken down by cost center and general categories. These reports are also shared with the governing board. The AMHC reported that all current financial personnel are qualified and trained to use the appropriate bookkeeping and accounting tools, but it is not clear that such qualification and training goes beyond data entry and printout.

Contract Management

The AMHC manages the following six contracts to meet the goals of the Initiated Act for the MHI. For each of these contracts, we report information about performance specifications, financial reporting, quality performance and reporting, and payment structure.

Community Health Centers of Arkansas, Inc. (CHCA). Contracted to oversee the implementation of the MHI Hypertension Initiative.

Performance Specifications. This contract has provisions that continuation is contingent upon the output or effects that the agency is expected to achieve. Each Community Health Center that is participating in the three targeted counties (Crittenden, Chicot, and Lee) is subject to review by AMHC program staff during regularly scheduled and unscheduled site visits, and is expected to comply with a set of performance standards and goals for the MHI Hypertension Initiative. These standards and goals include, but are not limited to, minimum number of community members screened, number of clients returning for visits, submission of billing records, tracking of average cost per visit, and average medicine cost per participant. If a participating Community Health Center in one of the targeted counties fails to consistently meet the performance standards, it is expected to submit an improvement plan to the AMHC. If performance does not improve or the AMHC does not believe that the improvement plan is adequate, then that CHC can be terminated from the program. To date, none of the CHCs has been terminated. One site was asked to submit an improvement plan.

Financial Reporting. This contract requires financial reporting. Comparisons to actual program activity are now beginning to be assessed, but we have not seen any analyses to date. The three CHCs report spending to the AMHC on a monthly basis.

Quality Performance and Reporting. For this contract, CHCA, Inc., is responsible for managing quality. CHCA is responsible for oversight of the CHCs through its multidisciplinary provider network. Each of the CHCs also a medical director who is responsible for day-to-day monitoring of clinical protocols and processes and clinical quality assurance. The medical director of the hypertension program, Dr. Camille Jones, participates in monthly calls with representatives of the three centers to assess and monitor quality of the blood pressure screening. Dr. Jones is responsible for overall technical oversight of the contract, including blood pressure measurement training and certification, and evaluating process outcomes such as numbers screened, referred, and treated.

Payment Structure. This is a fixed-price contract. The budget for this contract covers outreach, monitoring, screening, and visit costs (i.e., treatment).

University of Arkansas Cooperative Extension Program. Contracted to oversee the Eating and Moving for Life Initiative.

Performance Specifications. This contract has provisions that continuation is contingent upon output or effects that the agency is expected to achieve. The AMHC reported that each of the three targeted counties participating in EMFL (Sevier, Mississippi, Lee) is subject to review by AMHC program staff during regularly scheduled and unscheduled site visits and is expected to comply with a set of performance standards. These standards include, but are not limited to, a minimum number of community members enrolled and changes in weight, blood pressure, glucose, and cholesterol status. If a participating county fails to meet the performance standards for three months, it expected to submit an improvement plan to the AMHC. If the AMHC does not believe that the improvement plan is sufficient to cause a reasonable change in outcomes, the county can be terminated from the program. These performance standards went into effect as of July 2005. To date, none of the EMFL sites has been terminated or asked to submit an improvement plan.

Financial Reporting. Program spending is reported once a year to the AMHC. Comparisons to actual program activity are not assessed.

Quality Performance and Reporting. The cooperative extension's family and consumer sciences specialist, Ms. Easter Tucker, oversees quality at the three sites. Monthly reports are sent to the AMHC on the number screened and enrolled in the program.

Payment Structure. Payment per unit of service is not specified in this contract. The budget for this contract is for a total of approximately $174,000 per year to run the EMFL curriculum. Currently, the contracts are $39,000 for Sevier County to (minimally) to enroll 65 participants, $72,000 in Mississippi County to enroll 80 participants, and $59,000 in Lee County to enroll 80 participants. In sum, $174,000 is being paid to enroll 225 participants.

College of Public Health (Drs. Nash and Ochoa). Contracted to study health disparities among Arkansans.

Performance Specifications. The initial contract (July 2003–June 2004) specified that the services to be provided were to develop a strategic plan for the AMHC health disparities study, conduct focus groups, analyze secondary data, interpret state and national data, and facilitate collaboration between the AMHC and other health entities in order to recommend and implement short- and long-term solutions to reduce and eliminate racial and ethnic health disparities in Arkansas. The investigators were also charged to work with AMHC professional consultants to research grants and federal and state funding for the disparities project, submit progress reports, and create a final report upon completion of each phase of project. This scope of work was not changed when the contract was renewed in 2004 and 2005.

Financial Reporting. Program spending is reported monthly to the AMHC. Comparisons to actual program activity are not assessed.

Quality Performance and Reporting. The executive director and medical director interact regularly with the contractors to assess and monitor quality.

Payment Structure. The contract specifies 50 percent effort for Dr. Nash and 30 percent effort for Dr. Ochoa.

University of Arkansas for Medical Sciences, Division of Nephrology (Dr. Camille Jones and Patricia Minor). Contracted to work on the AMHC Hypertension Initiative.

Performance Specifications. This contract does not require payments contingent upon output or effects. The contract contains the following 25 tasks for the two staff persons (not specified by position):

1. Participate in the development and implementation of programs by performing needs assessments, doing social market research, and assisting in the development of intervention and evaluation programs.

2. Engage in problem solving and strategic planning for program initiatives.

3. Provide technical assistance in policy planning and the development, administration, and monitoring of health programs.

4. Provide day-to-day oversight of the conduct of interviews and other data collection activities for the examination survey.

5. Direct the administration of interventions to clients and develop and implement screening clinics for hypertension and other cardiovascular disease risk factors.

6. Review and maintain database of participant screening, treatment, and intervention records for the preparation of various required reports.

7. Serve as a liaison among participants, doctors, and other health professionals for designated activities related to the hypertension program, including the population-based examination survey and the school blood pressure surveillance project.

8. Confer with participants, families, students, and communities (via community groups and organizations, designated leaders, activists, and others) to identify and meet needs.

9. Present information and printed materials to community groups and organizations concerning available health services.

10. Select training materials and present in-service training on public health issues, including blood pressure measurement protocols.

11. Develop and instruct health education classes with emphasis on hypertension, diabetes and the metabolic syndrome, exercise and weight loss, and other behaviors and risk factors known to affect risk of cardiovascular disease.

12. Counsel participants and family members concerning general health assessment and risk factors related to hypertension and other cardiovascular disease risk factors.

13. Provide assistance to physicians in the collection of specimens.

14. Assign and coordinate work activities related to particular projects (e.g., examination survey) and monitor performance of staff participating in the project.

15. Provide comprehensive lifestyle modification instructions to patients and families and provide training in effective lifestyle modification educational techniques to local project coordinators.

16. Prepare and present reports and maintain records.

17. Review the goals, objectives, proposed strategies for continual implementation, required data collection, reporting requirements, time lines, manager/coordinator responsibilities, training curriculum, and other hypertension and stroke prevention and education program components. Provide recommendations to the AMHC for program modifications.

18. Review relevant data and statistics for targeted Arkansas counties.

19. Establish proposed protocols, indicators, data to be reported, and the time and format for reporting for the Hypertension Examination Survey.

20. Assist in the identification of indicators and data to be collected and in the development of the reporting format for that data. Assist in the compilation, aggregation, and analysis of data.

21. Attend, as determined necessary, program coordinators meetings regarding hypertension program projects.

22. Assist AMHC with training of additional staff for implementation of the Examination Survey.

23. Receive, review, and make recommendations about program data and information.

24. Attend MHI Medical Advisory Committee meetings.

25. Perform related responsibilities as required or assigned. To date, Dr. Jones has been involved with supervising and monitoring quality and effectiveness of the Hypertension Initiative, including the training and certification of blood pressure measurement at the three Community Health Centers. Dr. Jones is the principal investigator (PI) of the Marianna Examination Survey on Hypertension (MESH), with the UAMS College of Public Health investigators as co-principal investigators (PIs). She also is participating in the Arkansas Cardiovascular Health Survey (ARCHES) with the Arkansas Department of Health and the Children's Blood Pressure Screening Project.

Financial Reporting. Program spending is reported monthly to the AMHC. Comparisons to actual program activity are not assessed.

Quality Performance and Reporting. The executive director and commission members interact with and receive reports from contractor to assess and monitor quality.

Payment Structure. Payment per unit of service is not specified in this contract. The contract specifies 100 percent effort for both Dr. Camille Jones and Ms. Patricia Minor.

Department of Health, Department of Health and Human Services (Dr. Namvar Zoohori). Contracted to provide senior epidemiology consultation. Part of Dr. Zoohori's time is to participate in development and implementation of the ARCHES and MESH.

Performance Specifications. The initial contract (July 2004–June 2005) specified that Dr. Zoohori is to provide epidemiological and statistical expertise that will support the AMHC goals of ending health disparities in the state. The contract contained nine performance measures, including the design, planning, intervention, data collection, analyses, and evaluation of special initiatives and interventions including, but not limited to, a longitudinal community-based survey. He is also to participate in grant writing, assistance with program evaluation, data analyses, and interpretation of results. This scope of work was renewed in 2005.

Financial Reporting. Program spending is reported monthly to the AMHC. Comparisons to actual program activity are not assessed.

Quality Performance and Reporting. The executive director and medical director interact regularly with the contractor to assess and monitor quality.

Payment Structure. The contract specifies a lump sum payment of 25 percent full-time equivalent to Dr. Zoohori.

College of Public Health (Dr. LeaVonne Pulley and Dr. Zoran Bursac). Contracted to provide consultation in study design and analyses for the MESH.

Performance Specifications. This contract specifies that the College of Public Health is to provide technical assistance for the development and implementation of an examination survey (MESH) to be conducted in Marianna, Arkansas. This includes participation in meetings to plan survey and implementation, institutional review board materials, and supervisor and interviewer training (Dr. Pulley) as well as preparation of statistical analyses, consultation on study database, data analyses, and manuscript writing (Dr. Bursac). The goal of the study, which began in June 2005, is to further characterize the prevalence of diagnosed and undiagnosed hypertension, the proportion of persons with diagnosed hypertension who are receiving anti-hypertensive medications, and the proportion of persons with diagnosed hypertension whose blood pressure is controlled to goal levels.

Financial Reporting. Spending is reported monthly to the AMHC. Comparisons to actual program activity are not assessed.

Quality Performance and Reporting. The executive director and medical director interact regularly with the contractors to assess and monitor quality.

Payment Structure. The 2005 contract specified 10 percent effort for both Drs. Pulley and Bursac for six months (January–June 2005).

ANALYSIS OF SPENDING TRENDS

Act 1571 of 2001, SB 285 of 2003, and SB 80 of 2005 appropriated funds for the MHI for the first three biennium periods of the Tobacco Settlement Fund Allocation. Table 7.4 details the appropriations by fiscal year. The AMHC financial staff reported that the MHI received slightly less than the appropriated amount in FY2002, more than the appropriated amounts in FY2003 and FY2004, and less than the appropriated amount in FY2005 and FY2006.[8] The MHI was able to carry over unspent funds from FY2004 to FY2005.

---

[8] The AMHC financial staff reports receiving $801,187 in FY2002, $2,575,790 in FY2003, $2,129,100 in FY2004, $1,733,017 in FY2005, and $1,732,999 in FY2006.

Table 7.4
Tobacco Settlement Funds Appropriated to the Minority Health Initiative, by Fiscal Year

Item	First Biennium		Second Biennium		Third Biennium	
	2002	2003	2004	2005	2006	2007
(1) Regular salaries	$27,855	$132,482	$139,369	$143,132	$136,458	$140,568
(2) Personal service matching	10,844	38,203	41,482	42,149	49,030	49,927
(3) Maintenance and operations						
(A) Operations	200,000	425,000	425,000	425,000	374,873	374,873
(B) Travel	2,500	3,000	3,000	3,000	3,000	3,000
(C) Professional fees	358,077	739,508	739,508	739,508	739,508	739,508
(D) Capacity outlay	5,000	26,000	0	0	0	0
(E) Data processing	0	0	0	0	0	0
(4) Screening, monitoring, treating and Outreach[a]	304,224	997,907	663,646	663,646	663,646	663,646
Annual total	$908,500	$2,362,100	$2,012,005	$2,016,435	$1,966,515	$1,971,522
Biennium total	$3,270,600		$3,938,037		$4,028,440	

a. This line item was renamed in FY2005. It was formerly called "Drugs and Medicine."

The following analysis describes the expenditures of the MHI from January 2001 until December 2005. Because December 2005 is the middle of the first year of the third biennium, no year totals for FY2006 are presented.

Table 7.5 presents the total annual Tobacco Settlement funds spent by the MHI through the first half of FY2006. Although spending increased significantly in FY 2004—due primarily to a more than doubling of expenditures on professional fees—spending leveled off in FY2005. Expenditures for the first half of FY2006 are just slightly higher than they were in the first half of FY2005.

Table 7.5
Tobacco Settlement Funds Spent by the Minority Health Initiative, by Fiscal Year

Item	2002	2003	2004	2005	2006[a]
(1) Regular salaries	$17,175	$107,958	$128,441	$125,474	$73,204
(2) Personal service matching	13,185	35,028	43,504	47,637	23,044
(3) Maintenance and operations					
(A) Operations	68,366	191,419	279,304	659,611	169,542
(B) Travel	9,978	13,256	16,236	4,092	1,410
(C) Professional fees	180,070	641,555	1,302,009	632,584	186,176
(D) Capacity outlay	848	9,038	0	0	0
(E) Data processing	0	0	0	0	0
(4) Screening, monitoring, treating and outreach[b]	0	0	0	307,338	191,405
Annual total	$289,621	$998,255	$1,772,572	$1,777,005	$644,782

a. Amounts spent through December 31, 2005.

b. The AMHC financial staff did not break out drugs and medicine as a separate line item in its accounting system until FY2005. Funds for drugs and medicine appear under the professional fees and services line item until FY2005 when they were included in this line item. Other CHC costs for the Hypertension program and the MESH project costs are also included in this line item.

Figure 7.1 highlights the quarterly spending of the MHI for two categories: personal salaries and fringe benefits and maintenance and operations (M&O). The MHI had a very long start-up period. Spending for regular staff to manage the program was erratic until the end of FY2003. Spending on M&O grew in later quarters, but spending levels varied substantially from quarter to quarter.

The large swings in spending from one quarter to another are largely the result of changes in operating expenses and professional fees related to specific programs, and spending has historically accelerated in the last two quarters of the fiscal year. The substantial decrease in maintenance and operations spending, which includes professional fees, from the fourth quarter of 2004 and the first quarter of 2005 is due to the expiration of professional contracts with Collaborative Strategies and Advantage Communication at the end of the fiscal year. The large increase in spending on operations from the first quarter of 2005 to the second quarter of 2005 can be attributed to an increase in expenses related to the AIDS Awareness program and the "Southern Ain't Fried Sundays" nutrition education program.

Spending on professional fees represented 14 percent to 36 percent of total spending the last two quarters of FY2005 and the first two quarters of FY 2006. Table 7.6 documents spending for each professional contract for FY2004, FY2005, and the first half of FY2006. In FY2005, the AMHC began reporting spending under the Community Health Center contract under the line item of screening, monitoring, treating, and outreach rather than under professional fees. The difference between professional fees in Table 7.5 and the contract total in Table 7.6, minus the CHC spending, is noncontract spending. Examples of these expenses are design work, hosting for weekly shows, speaker and conference fees, consulting fees, moderating/hosting for quarterly health fairs, and radio personality fees.

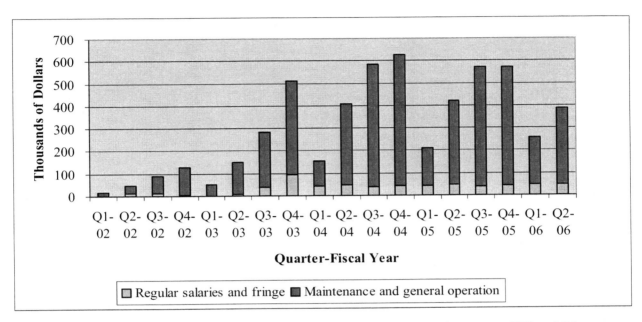

Figure 7.1—MHI Tobacco Settlement Fund Spending, by Quarter of Fiscal Years

Table 7.6
Minority Health Initiative Spending on Professional Contracts, by Fiscal Year

Contract	Contract Description	FY2004 Contract	FY2004 Spending	FY2005 Contract	FY2005 Spending	FY2006 Contract	FY2006 Spending[a]
Collaborative Strategies	Grant writer and professional development	$50,000	$58,820	$0	$0	$0	$0
UAMS College of Public Health	Health Disparities Study	104,187	149,932	104,187	79,447	81,910	15,265
Community Health Center of AR	Implementing of Hypertension Program	663,000	563,770	530,400	463,663	381,888	132,825
UAMS College of Medicine	Medical Director—Hypertension Program	192,500	128,935	192,500	185,196	271,250[b]	64,006
Univ of AR Coop. Ext. Service	Implementing Eating and Moving Program	156,453	105,392	156,453	156,452	174,667	48,526
Advantage Communications	Media and marketing facilitator	141,000	144,998	NA	0	NA	0
Arkansas Dept. of Health	Epidemiologic and statistical service	NA	NA	32,380	0	32,380	32,380
UAMS IT Dept.	Hypertension database	NA	NA	12,000	0	NA	NA
UAMS College of Medicine	Nurse for Hypertension projects	NA	NA	NA	23,310	[b]	[b]
COPH, DOH	MESH project	NA	NA	NA	NA	193,112	47,247
CWS	Grant writer	NA	NA	NA	NA	65,000	12,371
Total amount		$1,307,140	$1,151,347	$1,027,920	$908,068	$1,200,207	$352,620

a. Spending for the first half of FY2006 (July–Dec 2005).

b. In 2006, the contracts for the Medical Director and the Nurse for the Hypertension Program were combined.

Approximately 40 percent of the MHI's total spending in FY2005 was allocated to the Hypertension and EMFL initiatives. An analysis of spending for these two programs is presented in Table 7.7. The key figures presented are the average costs per enrollee for each of the two programs.

The costs of the Hypertension Initiative continue to be high (see Table 7.7). In our previous reports, we estimated the costs per enrollee based on the total dollars spent on the program and number of individuals that were enrolled for treatment at the participating Community Health Centers. Using this method, the costs were estimated at $1,684 per enrollee in FY2004 and $5,563 per case in FY2005. In FY2006, the costs appear lower ($3,109); however, the MHI pays out significantly more under its contracts in the second half of the fiscal year, and so comparisons to FY2006 may be misleading. For example, the MHI paid $0 under its contract with the Community Health Centers and with UAMS for the medical director in the first quarter of FY2006. As documented in previous reports, the costs per enrollee appear extraordinarily high given the costs associated with treating hypertension.

Table 7.7
Minority Health Initiative Spending on the Hypertension and Eating and Moving Programs, by Fiscal Year

	FY2004	FY2005	FY2006[a]
Hypertension Program			
Number of individuals screened	3,954	4110	2056
Number of individuals enrolled	373	100	53
Percentage of screened enrolled in program	9.4	2.4	2.6
Costs:			
Community Health Centers	$563,770	$463,663	$132,825
Medical Director (50 percent time/salary)	64,468	92,598	32,003
Total Hypertension costs	$628,238	$556,261	$164,828
Estimated cost per enrollee[b]	$1,684	$5,563	$3,109
Eating and Moving Program			
Number of individuals screened	244	415	365
Number of individuals enrolled	223	345	269
Percentage of screened enrolled in program	91	83	74
Costs:			
UA Cooperative Extension Service	$105,392	$156,452	$48,526
Total Eating and Moving costs	$110,892	$156,452	$48,526
Estimated cost per enrollee[b]	$473	$453	$180

a. Represents 1st half of FY 2006 (July-December 2005)

b. Represents Number of Enrollees divided by total costs

The MHI reports that estimating costs based on number enrolled for treatment is misleading, given the amended language to the act in FY2005 that the MHI provide "screening, monitoring, treating, and outreach" rather than just "drugs and medicine." Recall that in the 2004 RAND Biennial Report, we estimated that the MHI could treat approximately 750 people a year, given the funding appropriated for drugs and medication. In the first half of FY2006, the MHI was able for the first time to provide medication costs and information on clinic visits. Table 7.8 presents a summary of the medication costs and clinic visits. Over that six-month period, 107 patients were served. The average number of patient visits was fairly consistent at the three locations, ranging from 2.5 to 2.8. The AMHC financial staff reported that the wide variation in the medication cost per patient ($32 to $139) at the three sites is due to the fact that the CHCs use a sliding scale based on the patient's means to arrive at the patient charge. The remaining cost of the medications is billed to the MHI. However, even given this additional information, RAND is unable to determine how the money used for screening, monitoring, treating, and outreach is spent across these categories.

Table 7.8
Minority Health Initiative Hypertension Program Patients and Medication Costs, First Half of FY2006

CHCs	Medication Costs	Number of Patients Served	Medication Cost per Patient	Total Patient Visits	Average Number of Visits per Patient
East Arkansas	$2,890	47	$62	133	2.8
Lee County	832	26	32	70	2.6
Chicot County	4,730	34	139	87	2.5
Total	$8,452	107		290	

NOTE: First half of FY2006 is July–December 2005.

Taking the cost information into account with the other CHC billing information, medication costs accounted for 4.5 percent of the CHCs' billing for the program, patient visits accounted for 3.8 percent, and recruitment for 7.6 percent. Salaries and overhead constituted the remaining 84 percent. Information that delineates spending across the four activities—"screening, monitoring, treating, and outreach"—was not provided. The CHCs report the number of individuals screened that are enrolled is a small (1 percent). The majority of those who screen positive report having a primary care physician that they have seen in the past year. The AMHC reports that those individuals are counseled to visit their physician, given that their hypertension is uncontrolled. Hence, the majority of those being treated as part the Hypertension Initiative are walk-ins to the participating CHCs. It is not clear whether the walk-ins are the result of the outreach or other MHI or CHC activities.

Spending per enrollee for the Eating and Moving program decreased about 4 percent from FY2004 to FY2005. While the cost per enrollee appears to have decreased significantly in the first half of FY2006, spending under the UA Cooperative Extension Service contract has historically accelerated in the second half of the fiscal year, making comparisons difficult.

Although the AMHC has made some progress in its financial reporting systems and was able to provide us more detail than previously about the spending for the hypertension program, it remains difficult to obtain the information we require in a timely way.

RESPONSES TO EVALUATION RECOMMENDATIONS

Recommendation 1 *(*2004): Finalize the development of the prioritized list of health needs for minority populations, drawing upon available information from past research, best practices, and lessons learned from other communities working to reach similar goals.

> *Program Response:* The program reported that the prioritized list for health needs of African Americans was completed and submitted in July 2004. This information is available in the 2005 RAND report. However, similar lists of priorities for other minorities in the state have not yet been developed.

Recommendation 2 (2004): Improve the staff skills and capacity to carry out program activities funded by the Tobacco Settlement funds, and to provide more oversight of contractors performing duties related to Act funding.

> *Program Response:* The MHI claims that training to improve staff skills is an ongoing and continual process as new opportunities become available for training. The MHI provided a detailed list of training and staff development activities for each of the main staff members. These activities are mostly ones that would be associated with normal professional staff development. However, the recommended remedial training to improve skills and capacity was largely not accomplished. It remains true that the MHI cannot perform the necessary analyses to assess accomplishment of its own objectives.

Recommendations 3 and 4 (2004 and 2005): The AMHC should establish an effective financial accounting system and it should use that system to track actual expenditures, consistency of spending on each of the contracts relative to the contract terms, and how much of the Tobacco Settlement funding was returned.

> *Program Response:* The AMHC established a financial tracking system for local use to track actual expenditures, consistency of spending on each of the contracts relative to the contract terms, and how much of the Tobacco Settlement funding was returned in 2005 (see previous section titled "Financial Management Process"" for more information). All current and future AMHC financial staff have been or will be trained in this program. RAND's examination of this tracking system leads us to the conclusion that it is a good first step, but it does not provide ready information on the level of detail required.

Recommendations 5 (2004 and 2005) ***and 6*** (2005): Increase resources dedicated to monitoring the performance of programs and assessing the effects of the programs on desired outcomes. Increase oversight and program improvement for the Hypertension Initiative.

> *Program Response:* New performance standards have been developed and implemented in the EMFL to ensure program standards and consequences. Revised performance standards have been implemented, and increased oversight of the Community Health Centers has occurred with hiring of a CHCA liaison who can perform onsite visits on a regular basis for quality improvement. In addition, a monthly CHCA-led project coordinators meeting has been established.

Recommendation 7: (2005): Strengthen strategies to reach target populations (i.e., minority Arkansans).

> *Program Response:* This is an ongoing and continual process for AMHC through new and continuing collaborations with other agencies that reach out to the minority populations of Arkansas. Some examples include the following:
>
> - ***MESH.*** Involving collaborations with UAMS COPH, UAMS College of Medicine (COM), Arkansas Department of Health (DOH), Lee County Cooperative Clinic, Marianna Housing Authority, Marianna Water Authority, Marianna Mayors Office, Delta AHEC, Marianna Post Office, UAMS General Clinical Research Center (GCRC), Abbott Renal Care, legislators, and grassroots organizations.
>
> - ***ARCHES.*** Involving collaborations with DOH, UAMS COPH, and Abbott Renal Care.
>
> - ***Children's Blood Pressure Screening Pilot.*** Involving collaborations with Marianna School System (superintendent and school nurse), Children's Hospital Division of Nephrology (Dr. Ilyas and Dr. Wells), and volunteers, including EMTs, nurses, and high school students participating in a health careers program.

RECOMMENDATIONS FOR PROGRAM IMPROVEMENT

During the past two years, the MHI program has made considerable strides in accomplishing the mission given to it by the Initiating Act. There has been outreach to minority communities, and two health improvement initiatives are underway. In addition, the MHI has contracted with the College of Public Health and other UAMS units to provide needed expertise and assistance. Financial awareness has improved, and contracting is being reviewed. However, there continues to be serious concern over the oversight and management of MHI activities. The program's quality management processes only exist to a minor extent; they should be refined where they exist and formalized where they are only informal. Efforts should be made to complete tasks that are not completed and to achieve stated participation goals in outreach programs. Here, we present high-priority recommendations that can help the program continue along its path of improvement.

- **Improve the financial and quality management activities for all MHI activities.**

Most of the MHI activities continue to lack proper oversight and quality management. The program established financial and quality management processes for the Hypertension Initiative during FY2005 and the first half of 2006, but these processes require major improvements. For example, the amended Act language now specifies that a large proportion of the MHI funds go to "screening, monitoring, treating, and outreach" rather than "drugs and medicine." Although the MHI is now able to provide information on medication spending for the Hypertension Initiative, it cannot yet manage, monitor, or report spending according to the four activities specified in the amendment. Moreover, the contract with the entities responsible for carrying out these activities fails to specify that performance in line with these activities is required for payment. We repeat our recommendation of last year that the MHI needs to consider tying payments to clinics for the activities specified in the act.

Most MHI activities lack quality improvement and monitoring requirements. For example, the contract to provide the EMFL Initiative now has performance standards, but over the past two years, RAND has yet to be provided with evaluation data that demonstrates the program's effectiveness. Formal quality improvement exists only for the Hypertension Initiative, and that system requires improvement. Both of these issues were addressed in our 2004 report (Farley et al., 2005a) and again in last year's interim report (Farley et al., 2005b), and we consider that MHI is not been fully responsive to our previous recommendations. In addition to repeating those recommendations, this year we strongly recommend that the AMHC install a formal quality management process for its own central administration.

In addition, contractual language needs to be regularly reviewed. The MHI reported that tasks specified in the contract for the medical director and registered nurse for the Hypertension Initiative were out of date and did not specify which position would fulfill the tasks.

- **Improve the capacity for the program to carry out program activities funded by the act and performance-monitoring activities.**

In past reports, we have recommended that the program improve staff skills and capacity to carry out the activities funded by the act. This has not been done. The AMHC executive director reported that current limits on staffing as specified by state law restrict the number and salary level of its employees. The AMHC has responded by contracting with other state entities (UAMS, COPH) to assist it with carrying out the MHI activities funded by the act; however, it has yet to fulfill the need to monitor performance. The program needs to build capacity to monitor both its internally funded activities as well as the contracted workload—perhaps by contracting with a separate entity to fulfill this need or proposing to modify state law.

- **The MHI should continue its efforts to develop a database and design it in consideration of quality improvement processes.**

The act's mandate to create a biographical database that includes biographical data, screening data, costs, and outcome has yet to be implemented for any of the MHI activities. Such data is essential for an effective quality improvement process. For example, the MHI process (e.g., attendance, clinic visits) and outcome data (e.g., weight lost, blood pressure change) should be included in the database.

- **Continue to study racial and ethnic health disparities and prioritize needs.**

The MHI's involvement with other partners, such as the DHHS and the College of Public Health, to conduct research on these issues should continue. Updates to the prioritized list of needs should be provided in future years, with a focus on needs on other minority populations in the state, as new data becomes available.

- **Continue strategies to reach target populations (i.e., minority Arkansans) across the state.**

In our last report, we noted that in 2004, the MHI shifted a great deal of its efforts to Lee County. In our previous report, we indicated the number of African Americans in other counties around the state. Lee County and many of the Delta counties are among the poorest counties in the state, and are significantly medically underserved. Few telephone calls are being made directly to the MHI, although it appears that hits to its Web site have increased. As stated in our last report, staff may want to consider what part of the population their awareness efforts are reaching and if there are ways to increase health education dissemination. In 2005, the MHI reported efforts to increase health education dissemination through enhancement of the educational materials provided during the Hypertension Initiative outreach screenings. This is being done with the recognition that the majority of persons screened will say that they have a primary care provider, and will only get MHI-provided health information at the time of the screening. Our last report also sated that the number of health screens as a result of MHI planned events has not increased over time and remains low (around 2 per 1,000 minorities in 2005). We offered ways to increase screenings in our last report. We also noted that the prioritized list and future systematic needs assessment for other minority populations in the state—specifically Hispanics—is needed.

APPENDIX TO CHAPTER 7

Performance on Process Indicators through December 2005

Increase awareness of hypertension, strokes, and other disorders disproportionately critical to minorities by utilizing different approaches that include but are not limited to the following: advertisements, distribution of educational materials, and providing medications for high-risk minority populations

Indicator: Number of events to increase awareness, by type of effort.

Table 7.A1

Media Communication Events for the Minority Health Initiative

	Number of Events Carried Out								
	Jul–Dec 2001	Jan–Jun 2002	Jul–Dec 2002	Jan–Jun 2003	Jul–Dec 2003	Jan–Jun 2004	July–Dec 2004	Jan–Jun 2005	July–Dec 2005
1. Mass media placements									
— TV shows (30-min)	0	0	0	6	26	26	36	48	24
— TV ads (30-sec units)	0	0	0	0	373	600	7,130	720	0
— Radio ads (60-sec units)	0	0	280	1,780	1,660	1,176	600	0	0
— Radio ads (30-sec units)	0	0	0	0	0	0	0	16,380	21,840
— Newspaper ads	0	0	16	17	7	18	30	75	1
2. Website hits									
— Number of unique visitors	NA	NA	NA	325	1,038	1,368	1,323	1,534	5,253[b]
— Total number of hits	NA	NA	NA	14,305	37,873	57,388	66,053	122,224	314,213
— Average number of hits per visitor	NA	NA	NA	44	37	42	50	NA	NA
3. Direct calls to AMHC[a]	NA	NA	35	140	71	53	42	508	119
4. Materials distributed (collaterals, pamphlets, handouts[a])	0	110	226	4,668	9,076	11,021	8,864	10,132	4,937

NOTE: NA indicates data not available.

a. Increases in counts result partially from improvements in recordkeeping

b. For the July–Dec 2005 reporting period, number of visitors, not the number of unique visitors, was available.

Provide screening or access to screening for hypertension, strokes, and other disorders disproportionately critical to minorities, but also provide this service to any citizen within the state regardless of racial/ethnic group.

Indicator: Screening rate for minority Arkansans for disorders disproportionately critical to minorities at MHI-sponsored events and recorded in the MHI database (not including the Hypertension Initiative).

Table 7.A2
Number of Health Screening Opportunities by AMHC Involvement

	Jul–Nov 2001	Jan–Jun 2002	Jul–Dec 2002	Jan–Jun 2003	Jul–Dec 2003	Jan–Jun 2004	Jul–Dec 2004	Jan–Jun 2005	July–Dec 2005
AMHC public health forums	0	0	0	1	2	1	2	1	2
Health fair: AMHC-organized	0	0	0	2	9	5	2	7	0
Health fair: AMHC-assisted	0	7	4	11	11	14	11	9	17
Total health forums and fairs	0	7	4	14	22	20	15	17	19
Percentage of events held in Little Rock	0	17	100	57	55	60	67	59	68

Table 7.A3
Total Number of Screenings and Screening Rates, by Type of Screening

Health Condition	Minorities Screened in Each Six-Month Period								
	July–Dec 2001	Jan–Jun 2002[a]	July–Dec 2002	Jan–Jun 2003	July–Dec 2003	Jan–Jun 2004	July–Dec 2004	Jan–Jun 2005	July–Dec 2005
Number of screenings									
Cardiovascular[b]	0	885	425	431	1,404	1,648	1,011	1,201	278
Diabetes	0	435	79	276	482	661	557	484	165
Cancer[c]	0	112	0	119	45	115	180	75	11
Depression	0	0	60	40	0	10	0	0	0
HIV	0	255	0	82	0	50	90	255	0
Other[d]	0	0	65	69	0	175	30	295	0
Screening rate (per 1,000 minority individuals)									
Cardiovascular[b]	0.0	1.5	0.7	0.7	2.3	2.6	1.6	1.9	0.4
Diabetes	0.0	0.7	0.1	0.5	0.8	1.1	0.9	0.8	0.3
Cancer[c]	0.0	0.2	0.0	0.2	0.1	0.2	0.3	0.1	0.0
Depression	0.0	0.0	0.1	0.1	0.0	0.0	0.0	0.0	0.0
HIV	0.0	0.4	0.0	0.1	0.0	0.1	0.1	0.4	0.0
Other[d]	0.0	0.0	0.1	0.1	0.0	0.3	0.0	0.5	0.0

NOTE: Values presented in this table are estimates because they may include non minorities and may represent duplicated counts.

a. Rates are high in this period because many MHI screenings were at health fairs sponsored by other organizations; rates dropped in the next period after a major sponsor discontinued its fairs.

b. Cardiovascular includes screenings for blood pressure, cholesterol, and body mass index.

c. Cancer includes screenings for mammography/breast and prostate.

d. Other includes child ID, flu, and vision screenings.

Table 7.A4

Estimated Number of Minorities Screened and Screening Rates at MHI-Sponsored Events, by Type of Screening—Not Including Screenings as Part of the Hypertension Initiative

	Number of Minorities Screened								
	July–Dec 2001	Jan–Jun 2002	July–Dec 2002	Jan–Jun 2003	July–Dec 2003	Jan–Jun 2004	July–Dec 2004	Jan–Jun 2005	July–Dec 2005
Number of screenings									
Cardiovascular[a]	0	0	0	115	871	550	421	711	208
Diabetes	0	0	0	114	322	221	197	279	80
Cancer[b]	0	0	0	3	45	20	50	45	1
Depression	0	0	0	40	0	0	0	0	0
HIV	0	0	0	79	0	50	0	255	0
Other[d]	0	0	0	3	0	0	30	195	0
Screening rate (per 1,000)									
Cardiovascular[a]	0.0	0.0	0.0	0.2	1.4	0.9	0.7	1.1	0.3
Diabetes	0.0	0.0	0.0	0.2	0.5	0.4	0.3	0.4	0.1
Cancer[b]	0.0	0.0	0.0	0.0	0.1	0.0	0.1	0.1	0.0
Depression	0.0	0.0	0.0	0.1	0.0	0.0	0.0	0.0	0.0
HIV	0.0	0.0	0.0	0.1	0.0	0.1	0.0	0.4	0.0
Other[c]	0.0	0.0	0.0	0.0	0.0	0.0	0.0	0.3	0.0

NOTE: Values presented in this table are estimates because they may include non minorities and may represent duplicated counts.

a. Cardiovascular includes screenings for blood pressure, cholesterol, and body mass index

b. Cancer includes screenings for mammography/breast and prostate.

c. Other includes child ID, flu, and vision screenings.

Develop intervention strategies to decrease hypertension, strokes, and other disorders in Table 7.A4, as well as associated complications: educational programs, modification of risk factors by smoking cessation programs, weight loss, promoting healthy lifestyles, treatment of hypertension with cost-effective, well-tolerated medications, and case management for patients in these programs.

Indicator: Treatment program registration rates by minority Arkansans for disorders.

Table 7.A5
Number of Screened and Enrollment Rates for the MHI Hypertension and Eating and Moving Programs

	Jan–Jun 2003		Jul–Dec 2003		Jan–Jun 2004		Jul–Dec 2004		Jan–Jun 2005		Jul–Dec 2005	
	Number	Rate[a]	Number	Rate[a]	Number	Rate[a]	Number	Rate[a]	Number	Rate[a]	Number	Rate[a]
Hypertension												
Screenings	660	1.08	1,612	2.64	2,342	3.74	1,614	2.58	2,496	3.91	2,056	3.22
Enrollments	94	0.15	271	0.44	102	0.16	59	0.09	41	0.06	53	0.08
Eating and Moving												
Screenings	58	0.09	118	0.19	126	0.20	192	0.31	223	0.35	365	0.57
Enrollments	58	0.09	108	0.18	115	0.18	122	0.19	223	0.35	269	0.42

a. Screening and enrollment rates are the numbers screened or enrolled per 1,000 minority individuals in the state. The rates displayed in this table have changed from previous reports given the access to new census estimates.

Chapter 8
Arkansas Biosciences Institute

PROGRAM DESCRIPTION

The Initiated Act of 2000 provides that 22.8 percent of the Tobacco Settlement Program Fund be used to support bioscience and tobacco-related research. The act provided funding to establish the Arkansas Biosciences Institute (ABI).

The act structured ABI to foster the conduct of research through its member institutions—the University of Arkansas for Medical Sciences (UAMS), University of Arkansas, Division of Agriculture (UA-Ag), University of Arkansas, Fayetteville (UAF), Arkansas Sate University (ASU), and Arkansas Children's Hospital (ACH). Separate Tobacco Settlement funds were appropriated to each of these five institutions. The act charged ABI to encourage and foster the conduct of research and pursue the following purposes:

1. Conduct agricultural research with medical implications.

2. Conduct bioengineering research focused on the expansion of genetic knowledge and new potential applications in the agricultural-medical fields.

3. Conduct tobacco-related research that focuses on the identification and applications of behavioral, diagnostic, and therapeutic research addressing the high level of tobacco-related illnesses in the state of Arkansas.

4. Conduct nutrition and other research focusing on prevention or treatment of cancer, congenital or hereditary conditions, or other related conditions.

5. Conduct other research identified by the primary educational and research institutions involved in ABI that is reasonably related, or complementary to, research identified in points 1-4.

The ABI Board, which oversees ABI, was created to "provide overall coordination of the program, develop procedures for recruitment and supervision of member institution research review panels, provide for systematic dissemination of research results to the public and the health care community, develop policies and procedures to facilitate the translation of research results into commercial alternate technological and other applications wherever appropriate and consistent with state and federal law, and transmit....a report to the general assembly and the governor."

UPDATE ON PROGRAM ACTIVITIES

Since its inception, ABI has leveraged tobacco funding to attract extramural funding, worked collaboratively among the five different institutions, brought in new faculty, and disseminated its research findings to the community. During FY2004–2005, ABI institutions brought in almost $3 for every ABI dollar received. Extramural funding has increased from approximately $12 million across the five institutions in 2002 to approximately $34 million in FY2005. In addition, the number of extramural projects on which the institutions collaborated has increased. ABI had 50 collaborative publications for FY2003–2004 and 65 collaborative publications for FY2004–2005. The number of independent publications increased from 128 in FY2003–2004 to 225 in FY2004–2005. ABI also significantly increased its media contacts and press releases from 16 total newspaper articles, conferences, and press releases in 2004 to 83 in 2005, indicating that it is working hard on publicizing its research and mission. Of note, publications, seminars, media contacts, and press release numbers were all recalculated this year to ensure that the activities are only counted one time within and across institutions. This information is detailed further in the appendix to this chapter, where revised criteria for this indicator are summarized.

PROGRESS TOWARD ACHIEVING FIVE-YEAR AND SHORT-TERM GOALS

In 2005, RAND staff met with ABI leadership to specify long-term programmatic goals that define the program's vision for its future scope of activities. Three long-term goals were identified, and the ABI progress in achieving these goals is presented here.

Goal 1: Maintain at least the current level of total grant funding (as of FY2005).

Progress on Goal 1: ACCOMPLISHED. The amount of extramural funding received by ABI scientists during FY2005 exceeded funding received in FY2004 by approximately $7 million. The ratio of extramural funding to ABI monies remained fairly steady at 2.9:1 in FY2004 and 3.1:1 in FY2005.

Goal 2: Increase applied research that will have community impacts and increase collaboration with local businesses.

Progress on Goal 2: ON SCHEDULE. Researchers at UAMS, UAF, and ASU have applied for and received some funding through SBIR (small business innovation research) and STTR (small business technology transfer) grant mechanisms to support new developments and to involve the community. For example, a biotech company was started and received funding to develop a new therapy to treat drug addiction. At ASU, several companies have also been developed, including BioStrategies and LC, Nature West Company, and Hyphenated Solutions. In addition, ASU is renting ABI space to Radiance Technologies, which is working with ABI researchers on detection technologies (funded by the U.S. Department of Defense). ABI also supported a one-day technology and business workshop in Jonesboro.

Goal 3: Bring ABI scientific and research capabilities to pilot or community-based programs.

Progress on Goal 3: ON SCHEDULE. ASU is involved in several community outreach programs that are supported by ABI. ASU has a student science project in which students come to ASU to work with ABI researchers in their labs for the summer. In addition, Arkansas has a state undergraduate research fellowship (SURF) that allows undergraduates to conduct in-depth research projects. At UAF, for example, 14 students work on ABI-related research. In addition, ACH is developing a summer research program intended to encourage promising young scientists to choose a career in research. ACH researchers are also exploring the role of home characteristics and environmental factors, including exposure to environmental tobacco smoke, on asthma morbidity in a predominately low-income, African-American population in the rural Delta region of Arkansas. Families participating in the asthma study receive tailored education materials that will allow them to better manage the disease. They will also receive free an asthma assessment and allergy skin testing—services that are not readily available to this medically underserved population.

PERFORMANCE ON PROCESS INDICATORS

As discussed in previous reports, three indicators were selected to represent the overall progress of the ABI program. These indicators track progress on fulfilling the mandates in the act for the program to (1) develop targeted research programs in each of the five areas specified by the act, (2) encourage and foster the conduct of research through the five member institutions, and (3) provide for systematic dissemination of research results to the public and the health care community so these findings may be applied to planning, implementation, and evaluation of any other programs of this state.

This section briefly highlights performance on some indicators. Further description on these indicators is provided in the appendix to this chapter. Overall, ABI continues to collaborate on projects among the five institutions, with an average of 28 percent of extramural funding for collaborative research projects. The ratio of extramural funding to ABI monies has also remained steady, averaging approximately $2 to $3 for every dollar received. Of note, ABI's total publications (collaborative and independent) have increased substantially from 81 in FY2002–2003 to 290 in FY2004–2005. In addition, the in-person media contacts increased from 13 in FY2003–2004 to 70 in FY2004–2005, indicating that it is working hard on publicizing the research and mission of ABI to the community.

PERFORMANCE ON MANAGEMENT INTEGRITY CRITERIA

Types and Performance of Governing and Advisory Boards

Governing Board. ABI is governed by a board whose composition was specified in the Initiated Act of 2000, consisting of the following:

- President of the University of Arkansas
- President of ASU
- Chancellor of UAMS
- Chancellor of UAF
- UA vice president for agriculture
- President of the Arkansas Science and Technology Authority
- Director of the National Center for Toxicological Research
- President of ACH

- Two individuals possessing recognized scientific, academic, or business qualifications appointed by the governor. (Dr. George Blevins, coordinator of minority initiative grants, UA at Pine Bluff; and Mr. Kurt Knickrehm, vice president, Rebsamen Insurance, Little Rock)

- Director of ABI (Dr. Lawrence Cornett, professor of physiology and biophysics, UAMS)

The members appointed by the governor serve four-year terms. The director of ABI is appointed by the president of the University of Arkansas system, in consultation with the president of ASU and the president of Arkansas Children's Hospital, and with the advice and recommendation of the board. The director is an employee of the University of Arkansas and is responsible for recommending policies and procedures to the board. There is no term limit for the director. The board meets quarterly.

Advisory Boards. ABI has three different advisory boards: the Scientific Coordinating Committee, the Science Advisory Committee, and the Industry Advisory Committee.

Members of the Scientific Coordinating Committee represent the five member institutions and work with the ABI director to help facilitate ABI-related research projects. There are seven members on the Scientific Coordinating Committee—one appointed by the ABI board member representing each of the five institutions, plus representatives from the National Center for Toxicological Research and the Arkansas Cancer Research Center. There are no set terms for membership. The Scientific Coordinating Committee meets as needed throughout the year. Members of this committee are as follows:

- Dr. Don Bobbitt, dean, J. William Fulbright College of Arts and Sciences, University of Arkansas,

- Dr. Carole Cramer, executive director, ASU Biosciences Institute, Arkansas State University

- Dr. Richard Jacobs, president, Arkansas Children's Hospital Research Institute, Arkansas Children's Hospital

- Dr. Fred Kadlubar, director, Division of Molecular Epidemiology, National Center for Toxicological Research

- (Vacant) Arkansas Cancer Research Center, University of Arkansas for Medical Sciences

- Dr. Greg Weidemann, associate vice president, Division of Agriculture, University of Arkansas, Fayetteville

- Dr. Charles Winter, associate dean for research, College of Medicine, University of Arkansas for Medical Sciences

The Science Advisory Committee is composed of five knowledgeable people in the science fields. They are appointed to four-year terms by the ABI board. The Science Advisory Committee meets annually, usually in conjunction with the ABI Fall Research Symposium. Members of this committee are as follows:

- Dr. James Giovannoni, research molecular biologist, Cornell University

- Dr. Mary Good, dean, University of Arkansas at Little Rock

- Dr. Rowena Matthews, professor of biological chemistry, University of Michigan

- Dr. John Peters, director of Nutrition Science Institute, Proctor & Gamble

- Dr. Roberto Romero, chief of perinatology research branch, Wayne State University School of Medicine

The Industry Advisory Committee is composed of five knowledgeable people in industries related to ABI research. They were appointed by the ABI board to four-year terms. The Industry Advisory Committee meets annually, usually in conjunction with the ABI Fall Research Symposium. Members of this committee are as follows:

- Dr. Edwin Anderson, coordinator for laboratory automation group, Pioneer Hi-Bred International

- Dr. R. Barry Holtz, president and CEO, InterveXion Therapeutics

- Dr. Richard Roop, senior vice president for science and regulatory affairs, Tyson Foods, Inc.

- Dr. Kathy Brittain White, president, Rural Sourcing, Inc.

- One vacancy

Board Involvement in Program Oversight. Ratings of the performance of the ABI governing board and advisory boards in oversight of the ABI activities are presented in Table 8.1. As can the ratings show, the ABI board is very involved with goals and planning, being briefed on the progress toward these goals, determining priorities, and managing the quality and performance of ABI. By contrast, ABI's advisory boards are not intensely involved with many ABI activities. Because they function as advisory boards, they do not need to be so closely involved in all of the different functions of ABI.

Table 8.1
**Performance of the ABI Governing Board and Advisory Committees on Dimensions
of Board Oversight Functions, Scales of 1 to 5**

Management Functions	Governing Board	Scientific Coordinating Committee	Scientific Advisory Committee	Industry Advisory Committee
Oversight				
Goals and planning	5	3	3	3
Priorities	5	3	3	3
Budget	3	3	1	1
Quality management	5	3	1	1
Monitoring program performance				
Progress toward goals	5	3	3	3
Spending	3	3	1	1
Quality performance	5	3	3	3
Providing interface with communities				
Community needs	3	3	2	2
Community interactions	3	3	2	2
Fund-raising	1	1	1	1

NOTE: Definitions of ratings: 1 = not involved, 2 = minimally involved, 3 = not intense involvement, 4 = fully considers, 5 = directive.

Quality Improvement Process

Table 8.2 provides ratings for the ABI on different aspects of quality management. The ABI governing board performs both program and quality management oversight. Part of the quality management process involves reporting for the RAND evaluation and also completing an annual report to the governor and the legislature.

Table 8.2

Ratings of the Arkansas Biosciences Institute on Quality Management Activities

	Not Applicable	Needs Improvement	Does Satisfactorily
1. Specifies criteria for quality performance	X		
2. Collects information on technical quality measures			X
3. Collects information on consumers' experience with service	X		
4. Collects data on program enrollments, demographic characteristics of enrollees, service encounters	X		
5. Has quantified quality measures for technical aspects of service		X	
6. Has quantified measures of consumers' experience with service	X		
7. Has quantified measures on program enrollments, demographic characteristics of enrollees, service encounters that may be compared to targets	X		
8. Analyzes technical quality data to identify potential quality deficiencies		X	
9. Analyzes consumer experience data to identify potential quality deficiencies	X		
10. Analyzes measures on program enrollments, etc. to identify potential quality deficiencies	X		
11. Formulates quality recommendations that are addressed to who needs to take action		X	
12. Reports results of quality analyses to executive management/boards			X
13. Reports results of quality analyses to relevant committees			X
14. Disseminates quality recommendations to the public ("report cards")			X

As noted in table 8.2, ABI is doing well on most aspects of quality management. It needs improvement in three somewhat overlapping areas: quantifying quality measures for technical aspects of service, analyzing technical quality data to identify potential quality deficiencies, and formulating quality recommendations that are addressed to those who need to take action. Although the ABI governing board is responsible for overall quality management as it relates to ABI research, it is difficult for a single oversight group to effectively manage the complex research because ABI's participating institutions are funded and operate separately. Thus, measuring and quantifying ABI research is done at the institutional level, as is development of recommended actions in response to performance that is below expectations. These findings are then reported to the ABI board. This two-tiered quality management system, although not ideal, is mandated by the organizational structure.

ABI has taken actions to improve the quality of its program. For example, in order to stimulate collaborative research among ABI scientists located on different campuses, the ABI board requested that the ABI director use administrative funds to support mini-symposia focused on scientific topics that would draw ABI researchers of varying scientific backgrounds. A prototype conference was held at UAMS (March 22–23, 2006) on heavy-metal toxicity. Scientists from UAMS and ASU met with an international expert in heavy metals. From the conference, it is anticipated that new collaborative teams will form, and ultimately grant applications will be submitted to support novel approaches to studying metal toxicity in humans. In addition, ABI has encouraged ABI-funded researchers who talk to the press or media about their research to mention ABI in order to publicize the institute and its mission. This has resulted in an increase of in-person media contacts that mention ABI from 13 to 70 within one year.

Financial Management Process

The Initiating Act provides that each of the five member institutions directly receives Tobacco Settlement funds. ABI as an institution therefore has no control over this funding, and each member institution has its own accounting system for expenditures and reporting. All personnel at all institutions who perform the ABI program's financial management and accounting functions have the required qualifications.

Contract Management

ABI does not contract with other organizations to perform program activities supported by the Tobacco Settlement funding. ABI has oversight of the five member institutions: UAMS, UAF, UA-Ag, ACH, and ASU. ABI keeps track of grants, publications, collaborative projects, and other measures as part of the evaluation. ABI monitors performance, takes any corrective actions needed, and regularly reports on the performance of the institutions as part of the RAND evaluation and its annual report to the governor.

ANALYSIS OF SPENDING TRENDS

Table 8.3 details the appropriations by institution and fiscal year. Funds were appropriated for the individual institutions making up the ABI by Acts 1569 (ASU), 1577 (UAMS and ACH), 1578 (UAF), and 1579 (UA-Ag) of 2001; Acts 1056, 1320, and 376 of 2003; and Acts 425, 1402, and 1403 of 2005 for the first three bienniums of the Tobacco Settlement Proceeds Act. Continuing trends from prior years, ABI received less money than the amount appropriated in FY2005 and in FY2006, since appropriations represent not the actual dollars received but the maximum that may be expended by category as revenues are received.

Table 8.4 presents the total Tobacco Settlement funds received and spent by ABI from July 1, 2004, through the first two quarters of FY2006. Note that only half a year of spending is presented for FY2006, the first year of the third biennium. This spending analysis provides only information for the total expenditures, since providing amounts spent in different categories would have unduly burdened the institutions without adding value to the evaluation. A percentage of the funds received by each institution supports the central ABI central administration, totaling $250,000 each year.

Table 8.3
Tobacco Settlement Funds Appropriated to ABI Institutions, by Fiscal Year

Appropriation Item	Second Biennium		Third Biennium	
	2004	2005	2006	2007
Arkansas State University				
(1) Regular salaries	$2,317,370	$2,317,370	$2,023,228	$2,230,616
(2) Extra help			51,000	51,000
(3) Personal service matching	626,197	626,197	611,035	673,341
(4) Maintenance and operations				
(A) Operating expenses	824,771	824,771	1,209,939	1,140,245
(B) Conferences and travel	137,970	137,970	100,000	100,000
(C) Professional fees	391,004	391,004	0	0
(D) Capacity outlay	617,890	617,890	920,000	720,000
(E) Data processing	0	0	0	0
Annual total	$4,915,202	$4,915,202	$4,915,202	$4,915,202
Biennium total	$9,830,404		$9,830,404	
UA for Medical Sciences				
(1) Regular salaries	$1,926,987	$1,926,987	$1,801,863	$1,801,863
(2) Personal service matching	350,773	350,773	414,552	414,552
(3) Maintenance and operations				
(A) Operating expenses	524,144	524,144	796,267	796,267
(B) Conferences and travel	60,000	60,000	57,463	57,463
(C) Professional fees	300,000	300,000	16,418	16,418
(D) Capacity outlay	1,000,000	1,000,000	1,017,908	1,017,908
(E) Data processing	0	0	0	0
(4) Arkansas Children's Hospital	1,994,772	1,994,772	2,052,205	2,052,205
Annual total	$6,156,676	$6,156,676	$6,156,676	$6,156,676
Biennium total	$12,313,352		$12,313,352	
University of Arkansas Fayetteville				
(1) Regular salaries	$586,622	$586,622	$586,622	$586,622
(2) Extra help	0	0	0	0
(3) Personal service matching	132,987	132,987	132,987	132,987
(4) Maintenance and operations				
(A) Operating expenses	586,622	586,622	586,622	586,622
(B) Conferences and travel	0	0	0	0
(C) Professional fees	0	0	0	0
(D) Capacity outlay	1,040,259	1,040,259	1,040,259	1,040,259

Table 8.3—Continued

Appropriation Item	Second Biennium		Third Biennium	
	2004	2005	2006	2007
(E) Data processing	0	0	0	0
Annual total	$2,346,490	$2,346,490	$2,346,490	$2,346,490
Biennium total	$4,692,980		$4,692,980	
UA Division of Agriculture				
(1) Regular salaries	$1,316,855	$1,358,521	$1,358,521	$1,358,521
(2) Personal service matching	304,635	312,969	347,969	347,969
(3) Maintenance and operations				
(A) Operating expenses	375,000	375,000	375,000	375,000
(B) Conferences and travel	50,000	50,000	15,000	15,000
(C) Professional fees	0	0	0	0
(D) Capacity outlay	300,000	250,000	250,000	250,000
(E) Data processing	0	0	0	0
Annual total	$2,346,490	$2,346,490	$2,346,490	$2,346,490
Biennium total	$4,692,980		$4,692,980	
ABI annual total	$15,764,858	$15,764,858	$15,764,858	$15,764,858
ABI biennium total	$31,529,716		$31,529,716	

Table 8.4
Tobacco Settlement Funds Received and Spent by the Arkansas Biosciences Institute, by Fiscal Year

Institution	2004		2005		Biennium Difference	2006 (July–Dec)[a]	
	Received	Spent	Received	Spent		Received	Spent
ASU	$3,852,488	$2,728,273	$3,616,124	$3,089,744	$1,650,595	$976,599	$975,596
UAMS	3,319,412	1,875,428	3,041,360	4,485,344	0	945,954	1,154,128
ACHRI	1,798,006	774,264	1,463,517	1,206,439	1,280,820	647,336	534,841
UAF	2,055,818	820,828	1,673,368	2,644,296	264,062	267,123	267,123
UA-Ag	2,055,818	1,943,079	1,673,368	1,786,107	0	843,914	759,332
Total	$13,081,542	$8,141,872	$11,467,737	$13,211,930	$3,195,477	$3,680,926	$3,691,020
ABI Central[b]	$250,000	$196,001	$250,000	$302,245	$1,754	$250,000	$101,378

a. Only the first two quarters of FY2006 are represented in these data.

b. This amount is included in the expenditures of the individual institutions and therefore is not included in the annual total.

Table 8.4 also shows the amount of funds received and spent by each ABI institution for the past two and a half years. Funds that were received in FY2004, the first half of the biennium, could be held over for spending in FY2005, the second half of the biennium. The table shows that more than $3 million was received but not spent in the most recently completed biennium. UA-Ag, UAMS, and ABI spent the highest percentage of their biennium funds: 100 percent, 100 percent, and 99.6 percent, respectively. The Arkansas Children's Hospital, ASU, and UAF spent 61 percent, 78 percent, and 93 percent, respectively. In the first half of FY2006, the institutions have been more aggressive in their spending.

Table 8.5 presents the percentage of Tobacco Settlement funds spent on research grants to faculty members for each institution. There are two categories of expenditure. The first category includes expenditures made through peer-reviewed proposal and grant mechanisms that directly support a specific research project. These expenditures are reported in Table 8.5. The remaining funds are spent on infrastructure to support research. These expenditures may include purchase of equipment or new technology used in research, support for new researchers, salaries not included in grants, and other related investments toward building the research programs. This infrastructure may be used to support later Tobacco Settlement grant-funded projects, of the type reported in Table 8.5, or as leverage for obtaining other external funds for projects. The ABI institutions varied in the extent of their existing research infrastructure at the onset of the Tobacco Settlement. Therefore, some institutions were initially required to spend more on building their infrastructure base than on grants. It is expected that institutions will spend less on infrastructure over time and shift funding towards project grants.

Table 8.5
Semi-annual Expenditures on Research Grants by ABI Institution

	FY2002		FY2003		FY2004		FY2005		FY2006[a]
	First Half	Second Half	First Half	Second Half	First Half	Second Half	First Half	Second Half	First Half
ASU									
Research grant amount	0	0	0	$1,292,484	$533,963	$533,988	$847,415	$683,982	$204,785
Number of projects	0	0	0	10	10	10	10	38	7
Percentage spent on research grants	0	0	0	72	55	30	87[b]	32	21
Percentage spent on research infrastructure	100	100	100	28	45	70	13	68	79
UAMS									
Research grant amount	$29,703	$329,890	$723,524	$3,039,439	$624,492	$1,093,453	$1,152,934	$2,413,948	$1,140,256
Number of projects	4	12	19	49	13	36	61	78	70
Percentage spent on research grants	39	86	c	c	87	88	95	74[d]	99
Percentage spent on research infrastructure	61	14	c	c	13	12	5	26	1
ACHRI									
Research grant amount	NA	$263,826	$149,410	$1,239,630	$246,974	$224,113	$480,737	$449,765	$420,110
Number of projects	NA	3	5	9	6	12	10	13	16
Percentage spent on research grants	NA	67	61	70	71	52	77	77	79
Percentage spent on research infrastructure	NA	33	39	30	29	48	28	23	21
UAF									
Research grant amount	e	e	e	e	e	$482,013	$972,633	$1,461,022	$227,055
Number of projects	e	e	e	e	e	14	21	21	15
Percentage spent on research grants	e	e	e	e	e	81	85	85	85

Table 8.5—Continued

| | FY2002 | | FY2003 | | FY2004 | | FY2005 | | FY2006[a] |
	First Half	Second Half	First Half	Second Half	First Half	Second Half	First Half	Second Half	First Half
Percentage spent on research infrastructure	e	e	e	e	e	19	1	3	15
UA-Ag									
Research grant amount	0	0	$55,707	$415,273	$184,674	$550,391	$254,562	$382,090	$199,567
Number of projects	0	0	7	10	15	15	14	14	10
Percentage spent on research grants	0	0	6	36	26	45	29	42	26
Percentage spent on research infrastructure	100	100	94	64	74	55	71	58	74

NOTES: Grant expenditures are shown in semi annual periods representing Quarters First Half and Quarters Second Half of the fiscal year. NA indicates no expenditures were made during this time period, on research projects or otherwise. Zero indicates there was spending on salaries and infrastructure but not on specific research projects.

a. Data were available only through the first two quarters of FY2006.

b. A difference in ASU's reported FY2005 First Half expenditures for the 2005 RAND report and the 2006 report has produced this apparent sudden increase in research grant expenditures. This percentage is expected to drop twenty to fifty percentage points when corrected data are obtained.

c. UAMS changed accounting systems during the year, and most non research entries were made in June 2003, making it impossible to determine the percentage of funds spent on research projects.

d. A change in the reported total expenditures for FY2005 led to this apparent decrease in UAMS research grant expenditures. It is expected that updated grant expenditure data will correct this percentage to more than 90 percent.

e. University of Arkansas, Fayetteville, did not separate out the expenditures on research projects until January 2004. Thus, they did not have data to report prior to that date in this table.

While the institutions varied in how rapidly they established their grants programs, by the end of FY2004 all of them had started funding research grants. Semiannual expenditures on grants varied across institution and over time. From FY2005 through the first half of FY2006, the semiannual percentage of total Tobacco Settlement spending on research grants ranged from 26 percent to more than 99 percent. During this period, UAMS consistently spent a higher percentage on research grants than any other institution. The Arkansas Children's Hospital and the UAF also spent a high percentage of their funds on research grants: 77 to 79 percent and 85 to 97 percent, respectively. The UA-Ag and Arkansas State University both spent relatively low percentages of their tobacco funds on research grants: 26 to 42 percent and 21 to 87 percent, respectively. This is to be expected as less established research institutions, such as ASU, may need to spend more on infrastructure initially compared with more established institutions, such as UAMS.

RESPONSES TO EVALUATION RECOMMENDATIONS

Recommendation 1 (2004 and 2005): ABI should work to better publicize the ABI initiatives to the state of Arkansas and nationally.

> *Program Response*: ABI support has generated many research publications, and these publications continue to increase each year. ABI-supported researchers continue to increase their number of media contacts (newspaper articles, press releases, and news conferences). The substantial increase in media contacts from 2004 to 2005 (13 to 70) indicates that ABI is working hard to publicize its mission and research to the community.

Recommendation 2 (2004): ABI should begin to collaborate with the surrounding community.

> *Program Response*: ABI-supported scientists are providing information and opportunities for Arkansas students and the community to participate in its research. Some institutions, such as ASU, have a summer science program for students that is supported by ABI. ACH is also developing a summer research program for students. These programs are intended to encourage promising young scientists to choose a career in research.

At ASU, Dr. Carole Cramer presents information to middle schools and high schools, civic clubs, and businesses about ABI and opportunities for people to become involved in ABI-related research. ASU has also established several formal educational outreach programs to include the community in ABI-related research, including bringing high school and middle school students on tours of the ABI labs, where they extract DNA from strawberries, learn about genetics, and tour the greenhouse building to get exposure to plant- and medical-based research. This brings about 100 students per month to the ASU campus. Within ASU, ABI has also partnered with a crime scene investigator program to bring high school students into a one-week camp where they investigate a crime, including collecting and analyzing evidence. ABI's role has been to help with the DNA forensic technologies.

In addition, UAF held a conference, the Arkansas IDeA Network of Biomedical Research Excellence (Arkansas INBRE) that included 350 students and many faculty. UAF brought in guest speakers, held poster sessions, and conducted faculty presentations. Prizes were awarded to undergraduates for the top three posters in biosciences, physics and chemistry, and biochemistry.

Recommendation 3 (2004): Strategies should be identified to increase the collaborative process among the five institutions .

> *Program Response*: ABI has been working hard to increase collaborations among the five institutions, as evidenced on many levels, including the increase in collaborative publications, their ability to recruit experienced scientists, and their work on proposals. For example, some of the ABI institutions have core facilities that are utilized among all the institutions and help increase collaborations between institutions and also help with recruitment. Specifically, at UAF, there is Center for Protein Structure and Function, and at UAMS there is a Microarray Facility and a Proteomics Facility. Part of the recruitment tool for scientists at different institutions is to showcase these facilities and to emphasize that they are available for all ABI researchers. In addition, inter-institutional collaborations have focused on preparing a proposal to build a national laboratory for bio- and agro-terrorism at the Pine Bluff Arsenal. There are also plans for inter-institutional collaboration for the next Experimental Program to Stimulate Competitive Research (EPSCoR) proposal.
>
> Finally, as noted earlier in the report, to stimulate collaborative research between ABI scientists located on different campuses, the ABI board requested that the ABI director use administrative funds to support mini-symposia focused on a scientific topic that would draw ABI researchers of varying scientific backgrounds. A prototype conference was held at UAMS (March 22–23, 2006) on heavy-metal toxicity.

Recommendation 4 (2004): ABI should begin to examine outcomes of its program.

> *Program Response*: ABI is starting to assess its "people" impact. Specifically, it is apparent that ABI yields benefits for more than just the areas surrounding the campuses. The students who are part of ABI research and attend the universities can have an impact on other areas inside and outside of the state. Thus, in addition to the information collected on extramural funding, publications, and media contacts, ABI has started to collect information on students associated with ABI-supported research projects, to begin to examine where the students go when they have completed their degrees. For example, ABI would like to begin to assess how many students stay in Arkansas and in what areas of the state they choose to live.

Recommendation 5 (2005): ABI should begin to examine the short-term impact of its research on the broader Arkansas community.

> *Program Response*: ABI has begun to work more in the surrounding community. For example, ASU conducted a business-related workshop for the community that provided information on how to develop a business plan for starting a technology-based business. In addition, as stated earlier, some institutions have a summer program for students to encourage them to become interested in research. Investigators may also help a middle school or high school student complete a science project for school. ABI-supported researchers also continue community outreach, including presenting to civic groups and serving as judges for school science competitions.

RECOMMENDATIONS FOR PROGRAM IMPROVEMENT

ABI has worked hard to address previous recommendations and to achieve the goals that it set over the last year. The organization has continued to produce publications and work collaboratively across institutions. Inter-institutional collaboration is key to increasing research productivity. The facilities that are available, such as the Microarray Facility at UAMS, are very important from both a recruitment standpoint and for increasing collaborative work among the different institutions. ABI has also improved in the last year in several other areas, including publicizing its research and mission and beginning to work with the surrounding community. The work that ABI is doing in the community is significant, as creating strong ties with businesses and schools can provide future opportunities for collaboration and increased applications from prospective students who become interested in science through the ABI school-based programs.

- **Because the tobacco funding is not assured and has decreased each funding period, ABI should be prepared to accommodate potentially severe cuts in funding. For example, it needs to ensure that the new faculty it hires are not supported solely by tobacco money. ABI needs to continue to obtain grant funding at a level that can support the infrastructure that has been established at the different universities.**

The success of ABI in obtaining extramural funding to leverage the Tobacco Settlement funding is mitigating, in part, the potential threat of decreased tobacco settlement money in the future. However, the Tobacco Settlement funding provides numerous opportunities for researchers at the five institutions to conduct pilot work and collaborate and to provide infrastructure, such as equipment—all of which may then lead to more extramural funding. Thus, ABI must begin to assess how it can continue to fund these types of activities so that research productivity can increase even as tobacco dollars decrease over time.

APPENDIX TO CHAPTER 8

Performance on Process Indicators

As discussed in previous reports, three indicators were selected to represent the overall progress of the ABI program. These indicators track progress on fulfilling the mandates in the act for the program to (1) develop targeted research programs in each of the five areas specified by the act, (2) encourage and foster the conduct of research through the five member institutions, and (3) provide for systematic dissemination of research results to the public and the health care community so these findings may be applied to planning, implementation, and evaluation of any other programs of this state.

Indicator: Number and amount of funding for ABI-supported research projects, by institution and category of research as specified in the Initiated Act.

The goal of this indicator was to ensure that ABI conducted research in areas that were relevant to the problems occurring in the state of Arkansas due to tobacco-related diseases. The data in Table 8.A1 show the number of projects in each of the research areas for each institution and the total amount of funding for each project. Total funding is the sum of ABI-allocated monies and extramural funding. As expected, certain institutions focus on particular areas of research. For example, a good deal of research at UA-Ag focuses on agricultural research with medical implications (research category 1).

	July 2001–June 2002		July 2002–June 2003		July 2003–June 2004		July 2004–June 2005	
	Number of Projects	Total Funding	Number of Projects	Total Funding	Number of Projects	Total Funding	Number of Projects	Total Funding
Category 1								
ACH	0	$ 0	0	$ 0	0	$ 0	0	$ 0
ASU	0	0	0	0	4	164,357	16	1,284,585
UA-Ag	2	3,163,121	3	3,051,057	17	1,971,638	15	3,214,412
UAMS	0	0	0	0	0	0	0	0
UAF	2	5,629,645	7	4,195,755	12	6,174,018	16	4,564,881
ABI total	4	8,792,766	10	7,246,812	33	8,310,013	47	9,063,878
Category 2								
ACH	0	0	0	0	0	0	0	0
ASU	0	0	0	0	3	606,302	2	100,000
UA-Ag	0	0	1	166,308	2	405,241	2	375,360
UAMS	0	0	0	0	0	0	0	0
UAF	0	0	1	120,000	1	76,000	1	239,775
ABI total	0	0	2	286,308	6	1,087,543	5	715,135
Category 3								
ACH	0	0	0	0	0	0	2	498,925
ASU	1	643,013	5	1,756,342	8	2,101,483	21	901,607
UA-Ag	0	0	1	136,483	1	120,709	1	115,567
UAMS	17	2,992,748	41	7,804,005	23	5,511,850	45	17,943,403
UAF	0	0	1	291,000	0	0	1	25,000
ABI total	18	3,635,761	48	9,987,830	32	7,734,042	70	19,484,502
Category 4								
ACH	1	307,015	2	4,465,862	5	3,127,589	3	2,368,262
ASU	0	0	1	125,105	0	0	0	0
UA-Ag	0	0	0	0	0	0	0	0
UAMS	0	0	0	0	22	5,889,784	20	4,633,910

Table 8.A1—Continued

	July 2001–June 2002		July 2002–June 2003		July 2003–June 2004		July 2004–June 2005	
	Number of Projects	Total Funding	Number of Projects	Total Funding	Number of Projects	Total Funding	Number of Projects	Total Funding
UAF	0	0	2	795,916	0	0	1	340,200
ABI total	1	307,015	5	5,386,883	27	9,017,373	24	7,342,372
Category 5								
ACH	2	570,540	5	1,724,778	6	3,072,743	7	2,622,256
ASU	0	0	3	264,279	3	912,696	4	132,669
UA-Ag	0	0	0	0	0	0	0	0
UAMS	5	3,809,576	5	5,725,284	7	7,460,421	10	4,532,011
UAF	0	0	0	0	1	1,131,531	2	683,029
ABI total	7	$4,380,116	13	$7,714,341	17	$12,577,391	23	7,969,965

NOTE: Research categories are the following:

1. To conduct agricultural research with medical implications.

2. To conduct bioengineering research focused on the expansion of genetic knowledge and new potential applications in the agricultural-medical fields.

3. To conduct tobacco-related research that focuses on the identification and applications of behavioral, diagnostic, and therapeutic research addressing the high level of tobacco-related illnesses in the State of Arkansas.

4. To conduct nutritional and other research focusing on prevention or treatment of cancer, congenital or hereditary conditions or other related conditions.

5. To conduct other research identified by the primary educational and research institutions involved in ABI.

Indicator: Number of collaborative ABI research projects that involve researchers at more than one participating institution.

The five institutions that make up ABI have worked collaboratively on many different projects, as shown in Tables 8.A2 and 8.A3. The data in Table 8.A2 highlight that collaborative projects across institutions doubled from 2002 to 2003 and remained fairly steady during the past two fiscal years and through December 2005. The data in Table 8.A2 also demonstrate how the collaborative process provides support to each university as newer, less established research institutions, such as ASU, are able to lead projects and partner with more established institutions, such as UAMS. Table 8.A3 indicates that the percentage of collaborative extramural projects decreased from 26.8 percent in 2003–2004 to 15 percent in 2004–2005. From July 2005 to December 2005, however, the percentage increased again to 28.3 percent.

Table 8.A2
Collaborative Research Projects by ABI Institutions

Sponsoring Institution	Collaborative Projects Led by Institution	ABI Institutions Collaborating on Projects					Other Collaborators
		ACH	ASU	UA-Ag	UAMS	UAF	
July 2001–June 2002							
ACH	2				2		1
ASU	1				1		0
UA-Ag	1	1			1		1
UAMS	1	1					0
UAF	1				1		0
Total ABI-funded	6	2	0	0	5	0	2
July 2002–June 2003							
ACH	2				2	1	1
ASU	4	1			3		0
UA-Ag	3	1			3		1
UAMS	1	1					0
UAF	3			2	2		2
Total ABI funded	13	3	0	2	10	1	4
July 2003–June 2004							
ACH	3				3	1	1
ASU	5	2			5		2
UA-Ag	7	3			5		0
UAMS	1	1					0
UAF	4			1	4		2
Total ABI funded	20	6	0	1	17	1	5
July 2004–June 2005							
ACH	7				7	1	0
ASU	6			1	5		0
UA-Ag	6	3			4		0
UAMS	4	2				2	0
UAF	1				1		0
Total ABI funded	24	5	0	1	17	3	0

Table 8.A2—Continued

Sponsoring Institution	Collaborative Projects Led by Institution	ABI Institutions Collaborating on Projects					
		ACH	ASU	UA-Ag	UAMS	UAF	Other Collaborators
July 2005–Dec. 2005							
ACH	10				10	1	0
ASU	4			1	3		3
UA-Ag	4	1			3		0
UAMS	5	1	1			3	0
UAF	0				0		0
Total ABI funded	23	2	1	1	16	4	3

Table 8.A3

Portions of ABI and Extramural Funding Being Used for Collaborative Research Projects

	Percentage of Research Funding by Institution					Percentage of Total ABI Funding
	ACH	ASU	UA-Ag	UAMS	UAF	
July 2001–June 2002						
Funds from ABI	81.3	100.0	95.4	1.9	96.0	49.4
Extramural funds	100.0	100.0	100.0	0.0	80.4	55.3
July 2002–June 2003						
Funds from ABI	16.5	72.6	84.4	1.5	14.6	31.8
Extramural funds	10.7	96.1	100.0	1.7	19.1	17.5
July 2003– June 2004						
Funds from ABI	73.6	38.5	35.1	2.2	21.9	29.5
Extramural funds	62.0	64.7	46.1	1.2	53.7	26.8
July 2004–June 2005						
Funds from ABI	92.6	14.0	30.7	4.9	12.7	21.1
Extramural funds	79.9	70.3	31.7	0.3	12.4	15.0
July 2005–Dec. 2005						
Funds from ABI	86.9	8.9	23.2	11.8	0	19.4
Extramural funds	60.4	27.1	0	35.7	0	28.3

Indicator: Total dollar amount of ABI grant funding awarded for faculty research, total and by institution.

The data in Table 8.A4 and Figure 8.A1 indicate that each of the five institutions has continued to be successful in leveraging funds to support research. ABI indicated in its annual report that the five institutions brought in more than $2 for every ABI dollar received in fiscal year 2003–2004. In 2004–2005, the ratio of extramural funding to ABI funding was 3.1. The greatest leveraging was achieved by UAMS, UAF, and ASU.

185

Table 8.A4
Amounts of Funding Awarded for ABI Faculty Research

	ACH	ASU	UA-Ag	UAMS	UAF	ABI Total
July 2001–June 2002						
ABI funding	$535,100	$518,337	$750,000	$2,152,569	$520,855	$4,476,861
Total funding	$877,555	$643,013	$3,163,121	$6,802,324	$5,629,645	$17,115,658
Ratio of extramural to ABI	0.6	0.2	3.2	2.2	9.8	2.8
July 2002–June 2003						
ABI funding	$1,489,823	$1,316,671	$1,943,581	$3,632,974	$1,354,600	$9,737,649
Total funding	6,190,640	2,145,726	3,353,848	13,565,289	5,402,671	30,658,174
Ratio of extramural to ABI	3.2	0.6	0.7	2.7	3	2.1
July 2003–June 2004						
ABI funding	$1,495,240	$2,158,636	$1,897,962	$3,147,700	$1,312,963	$10,012,500
Total funding	6,200,332	3,784,838	2,548,396	18,862,055	7,381,549	38,777,170
Ratio of extramural to ABI	3.1	0.8	0.3	5.0	4.6	2.9
July 2004–June 2005						
ABI funding	$1,180,257	$2,148,743	$1,678,851	$4,422,353	$1,540,000	$10,970,204
Total funding	5,489,443	2,418,861	3,705,337	27,812,768	5,852,885	45,279,294
Ratio of extramural to ABI	3.6	.12	1.2	5.3	2.8	3.1
July 2005–December 2005						
ABI Funding	$574,553	$865,686	$758,304	$2,056,589	$872,624	$5,127,756
Total Funding	1,759,404	3,244,728	966,467	9,684,511	3,882,236	19,537,346
Ratio of extramural to ABI	2.1	2.8	.27	3.7	3.4	2.8

NOTE: Total funding is the sum of ABI funding and related extramural funding from other sources.

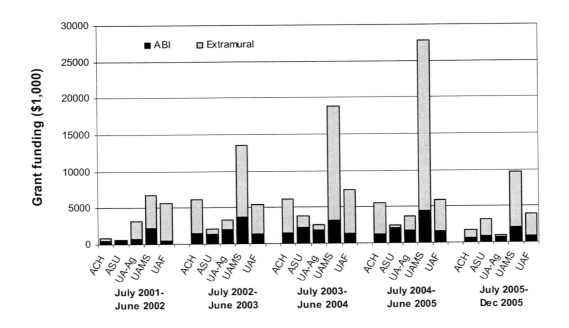

NOTE: Last period is only six months, while other periods are full years.

Figure 8.A1—ABI and Extramural Funding for ABI Faculty Research

Indicator: Number of each type of service and promotional activities conducted by ABI researchers both inside and outside of the university community.

Before the RAND evaluation began, ABI did not collect information from researchers on their service activities. Since that time, it has collected this information annually. Of note, the criteria for reporting these activities were recently updated to ensure that data were not counted more than once within and between universities. Because of these criteria, the counts have changed, and so these numbers reflect the most accurate counts of these activities. The criteria for counting the activities below are the following:

1. *Overarching Rule.* Activities should be counted only once—that is, publications, patents, grants, seminars, newspaper articles, etc., should be counted only for the first person listed.

    Example: If a newspaper article is about three different researchers, it can only be counted once for one person. In the aggregate counts, it does not matter which researcher it counts.

    Example: If people collaborate on a journal article, that article should only be counted for the first author.

2. *Publications.* In order to be counted as a published article for ABI, the article must meet the following criteria:

Be the direct result of ABI-supported research.

Be published or in press in a peer-reviewed journal. Be counted as a publication for the **first** author of that publication and should therefore be listed only once. If the research is ABI funded and for some reason the first author is **not** ABI funded, then the article should be counted for the first author listed who is ABI funded.

Can only be counted at one university, preferably the one at which the first author did most of the work on the research (in case a researcher has an appointment at more than one university).

The following publications are **not** to be counted as published articles:

1. Papers that are in preparation or submitted to a journal for review
2. A book chapter

3. *ABI Collaborative Publications.*

The CVs must match the count on the spreadsheet. If someone has three publications on the CV and one is counted as a collaborative and two are independent, then this must be how it is written on the CV (versus having all three listed under a generic heading "publications").

ABI-collaborative publications must be counted as a publication for the **first** author of that publication and should therefore be listed only once. If the research is ABI funded and for some reason the first author is **not** ABI funded, then the article should be counted for the first author listed who is ABI funded.

The data in Table 8.A5 indicate that ABI has generated numerous publications and has also worked to present information to the community through lectures and seminars, in-person media contacts, and press releases. Publications and seminars and lectures increased. In addition, media contacts increased from 13 in FY2003–2004 to 70 in FY2004–2005. Press releases also increased during this time from 3 to 13.

Table 8.A5
Service and Promotional Activity Encounters by ABI Research

	ACH	ASU	UA-Ag	UAMS	UAF	ABI Total
July 2001–June 2002						
[Data not available]	NA	NA	NA	NA	NA	NA
July 200–June 2003						
Publications	13	3	11	38	16	81
Lectures and Seminars	3	0	3	6	5	17
In-person media contacts	2	3	8	4	2	19
Press releases	0	0	0	5	5	10
July 2003–June 2004						
Publications	29	24	15	53	24	145
Lectures and Seminars	12	12	15	9	7	55
In-person media contacts	1	6	5	0	1	13
Press releases	0	1	1	0	1	3
July 2004–June 2005						
Publications	77	25	31	87	70	290
Lectures and Seminars	7	9	5	25	6	52
In-person media contacts	24	26	5	12	3	70
Press releases	4	2	2	3	2	13

NOTE: NA indicates not available. In-person media contacts include newspaper articles and conferences. Publications for 2003–2005 include both independent and collaborative publications.

Chapter 9
Medicaid Expansion Programs

PROGRAM DESCRIPTION

As defined in the Initiated Act, the goal of the Medicaid Expansion Programs is to "expand access to healthcare through targeted Medicaid expansions, thereby improving the health of eligible Arkansans." Four programs were implemented through the act: (1) expanded Medicaid coverage and benefits to pregnant women; (2) expanded inpatient and outpatient hospital reimbursements and benefits to adults ages 19 to 64; (3) expanded non-institutional coverage and benefits to Medicare beneficiaries age 65 and over; and (4) the creation and provision of a limited benefits package to adults ages 19 to 64.

The most notable achievement for the Medicaid Expansion Programs since the last report is the approval by the Centers for Medicare and Medicaid Services (CMS) of a limited benefits package for adults ages 19 to 64. Previously called the AR-Adults program, this new program is now called the Arkansas Safety Net Benefit (ASNB) program. The Department of Health and Human Services (DHHS) will begin to enroll potential beneficiaries in the program by January 2007, through an intermediary. DHHS is in the process of developing the request for proposals to be disseminated to insurance companies to generate bids for the selection of the program intermediary. More details about the ASNB program can be found below.

From January 2005 to December 2005, the Pregnant Women's Expansion program and the AR-Seniors program continued to grow steadily. Enrollment for the Pregnant Women's Expansion program increased by 42.9 percent, which far exceeds the 4 to 7 percent annual growth in the general Medicaid program. AR-Seniors enrollment increased by 8.7 percent in the last year as well. It is expected that the AR-Seniors program will grow substantially in the coming year; DHHS recently decided to expand the AR-Seniors program by increasing the financial eligibility criteria from 80 percent of the federal poverty level (FPL) to 100 percent of the FPL. DHHS estimates that this change could potentially double the size of the enrolled population to approximately 10,000–12,000 individuals. The implementation date for this expansion has not yet been determined. The number of Medicaid recipients ages 19 to 64 benefiting from the expanded hospital reimbursements declined in this last year by 30 percent from the second period of 2004.

At the end of August, Hurricane Katrina drove thousands of Mississippi and Louisiana residents from their homes. Approximately 200,000 evacuees from these states, as well as from Texas as a result of Hurricane Rita, put a strain on Arkansas' resources (staff, time, and financial). The impact of the hurricanes was felt for some time; management, data management staff, and county operations staff who are usually responsible for supporting enrollment and eligibility checks were directed to support the needs of the evacuees. As much as 75 percent of the DHHS Medicaid workforce was directed to hurricane relief. By December, 10–15 percent of the workforce was still attending to the needs of evacuees and the fallout from the disasters. The diversion of DHHS staff to respond to these disasters contributed to delays in executing many of the plans for education and outreach to those currently enrolled in the Medicaid Expansion Programs as well as potential enrollees.

PROGRESS TOWARD ACHIEVING TWO-YEAR AND SHORT-TERM GOALS

Given that the Medicaid budget is subject to regular and unanticipated changes, it is difficult for DHHS to plan beyond the next budget cycle. As a result, two-year goals were established for the Medicaid program, rather five-year goals.

In a previous report, we detailed the findings from a set of focus groups we conducted with enrollees of the AR-Seniors program and the Pregnant Women's Expansion (Farley et al., 2005a). We learned from these focus groups that there was some confusion about what services they were eligible to receive as a result of their enrollment in Medicaid. Two of the goals established last year (goals 1 and 2) were derived from this concern that individuals enrolled in either of these programs were not using services at the same rate as others, due in part to a lack of knowledge about eligibility.

Another concern was that enrollment into these expansion programs was below where estimates suggest they should be. Goals 3 and 4 were established in response to this concern. To achieve these goals, DHHS was going to engage in more outreach efforts to potential enrollees and providers to inform them of available coverage and services. Below is an update on progress toward these goals.

Goal 1: Beneficiaries currently enrolled in the AR-Seniors program will utilize services at the same or higher levels as the average dually-eligible beneficiary not enrolled in the AR-Seniors program.

Progress on Goal 1: CANNOT YET DETERMINE. To achieve this goal, DHHS planned to conduct educational outreach efforts for current enrollees, the newly enrolled, and potential enrollees for the AR-Seniors program. A previous educational outreach effort was deployed among currently enrolled AR-Seniors beneficiaries in the fall of 2004. However, no educational efforts were conducted during the last year. Based on preliminary analyses, AR-Seniors enrollees appear to be using services at lower rates than other dually eligible individuals. However, these analyses are limited by several issues, discussed in detail below. It is our intention to repeat these analyses, with the goal of addressing the limitations and presenting these analyses again, in next year's report.

To evaluate progress toward this goal, we evaluated service utilization data for individuals enrolled in AR-Seniors during calendar year (CY) 2005 compared to dually eligible older adults (both Medicare and Medicaid eligible) who were automatically enrolled due to Supplemental Security Income (SSI) eligibility (referred to below as the control group). We compared average monthly utilization over the calendar year, measured as the percentage of enrollees who used at least one service during the month.

Some measurement issues make it difficult to attribute any differences in utilization between these groups to poor knowledge about services or providers available. First, these analyses do not control for any differences in case mix between the two groups. Additionally, those in the control group may have been enrolled longer and have had enough time to identify the appropriate provider networks, thus also potentially explaining the differences in utilization. SSI beneficiaries become eligible for this benefit if they are low income and either over 65 or under 65 and blind or have a disability.

192

Many SSI beneficiaries "age into" Medicare, meaning they were previously disabled or blind, and were enrolled in SSI and Medicaid eligible for a length of time before they reached age eligibility for Medicare enrollment. The AR-Seniors enrollees, by definition, have higher incomes than do those enrolled in Medicaid owing to SSI eligibility. These considerations are indicative of a control group that may be sicker on average than the AR-Seniors group, thus explaining the higher rates of utilization.

On average, 63.6 percent of AR-Seniors enrollees used at least one service as compared to 75.9 percent among those in the control group. Figure 9.1 presents the average monthly utilization over time. The trend lines over the calendar year are fairly flat, suggesting that the differences in utilization are stable.

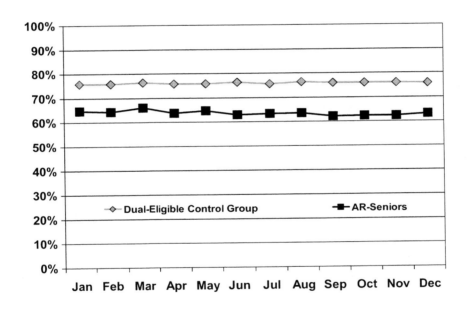

Figure 9.1—Percentage of Enrollees in the AR-Seniors Program Who Used at Least One Service, by Month, CY2005

Goal 2: Beneficiaries currently enrolled in the Pregnant Women's Expansion program will utilize services at the same or higher levels as the average pregnant Medicaid beneficiary not enrolled in the Pregnant Women's Expansion program.

Progress on Goal 2: ON SCHEDULE. To achieve this goal, DHHS planned to conduct educational outreach efforts for current enrollees, the newly enrolled, and potential enrollees for the Pregnant Women's Expansion program. However, no educational efforts were conducted during the last year. Service utilization for the women enrolled in the Pregnant Women's Expansion was similar to that of pregnant women enrolled in traditional Medicaid. Progress toward this goal was favorable even without outreach efforts.

We evaluated service utilization over CY2005 for pregnant women enrolled in Medicaid through the Pregnant Women's Expansion program as compared to utilization for pregnant women enrolled in Medicaid whose income was below 133 percent of the FPL (referred to below as the control group). We compared average utilization over time, measured as the percentage of enrollees who used at least one service during the month.

Measurement issues make it difficult to attribute any differences in utilization between these groups to poor knowledge about services or providers available. Differences observed may be the result of differences in case mix. Those in the lower income group may be more likely to have a high-risk pregnancy that requires more medical attention. Additionally, given that women enrolled through the expansion program have higher incomes, they may be more likely to pay out of pocket for certain items such as prenatal vitamins—thus explaining differences in utilization. Pregnant women enrolled through traditional Medicaid are, by definition, lower income than those enrolled through the expanded coverage. They may also have been enrolled in Medicaid for a longer period, reflecting greater need over an extended period of time.

On average, the utilization rate for women enrolled through the Pregnant Women's Expansion program was 57.2 percent, as compared to 62.2 percent for the control group. Figure 9.2 presents average monthly utilization for each group over time. Between January and July of 2005, utilization rates appear fairly steady, with a 4–5 percent difference between the two groups. However, these trend lines appear closer together and almost identical beginning in August through the remainder of the year, although no statistical tests were performed to determine if the differences are statistically significant.

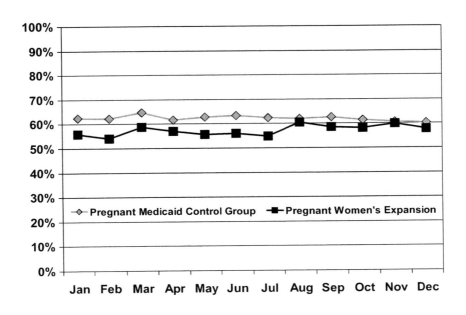

Figure 9.2—Percentage of Enrollees in Expanded Medicaid Pregnancy Benefits Who Used at Least One Service, by Month, CY2005

Goal 3: Enrollment in the AR-Seniors program will increase by 10 percent in CY2005.

Progress on Goal 3: NOT ACCOMPLISHED. The goal was to increase enrollment for the AR-Seniors program by 10 percent in CY2005. However, enrollment increased by only 7.3 percent during that time period. The slower than expected growth is partially attributable to the lack of any formal outreach programs for the AR-Seniors initiative during the year. Outreach efforts were not pursued in part due to the unknown impact of the Medicare Part D Prescription Drug plan and the approval of the waiver by CMS on the state budget.

Those who might be eligible for the AR-Seniors program might not be easily identified. Seniors must first enroll as Qualified Medicare Beneficiaries (QMBs) to be picked up for AR-Seniors. QMB status is available to all Medicare beneficiaries with income at or below 100 percent of the FPL. A QMB whose income dips below 80 percent, is automatically enrolled in the AR-Seniors program. Even an individual who is income-eligible for the AR-Seniors program will not be enrolled unless designated as a QMB. Current plans to increase income eligibility for the AR-Seniors program to 100 percent of the FPL will likely increase enrollment. With identical criteria for QMB and AR-Seniors eligibility, outreach efforts for each program can also be streamlined.

195

Goal 4: Enrollment in the Pregnant Women's Expansion program will increase by 15 percent.

Progress on Goal 4: ACCOMPLISHED AND EXCEEDED. The state has far exceeded the goal of increasing enrollment for the Pregnant Women's Expansion program by 15 percent. This program increased its enrollment from 1,957 enrollees as of December 2004 to 2,797 enrollees as of December 2005 (42.9 percent increase).

Despite no outreach efforts during the last year, the Pregnant Women's Expansion program realized a substantial increase in enrollment. This may be attributable in part to the merging of the Department of Health with the Department of Human Services into one agency (DHHS). The health services staff often has direct contact with pregnant women and may be able to better inform them about available services and direct them to the human services staff for enrollment. In some locations, a Division of County Operations worker is stationed in a local health unit to assist with Medicaid applications. In addition, there has been an effort to inform physicians of the availability of the program. However, economic factors outside the control of DHHS may have increased the number of women eligible for Medicaid, also explaining the large increase in enrollment. More than half of all births in Arkansas are paid for by Medicaid, and the Medicaid program continues to grow at a steady rate each year.

PERFORMANCE ON PROCESS INDICATORS

Table 9.1 summarizes the trends in each of the process indicators tracked over time for the Medicaid Expansion Programs. Four process indicators were developed during this evaluation. Please see the appendix at the end of this chapter for data tables and more detailed descriptions of the progress made on each of these indicators.

Table 9.1
Summary of Process Indicators for Performance on Medicaid Expansion Programs

Indicator	Status
Percentage of pregnant women with income between 133 percent and 200 percent of the federal poverty level (FLP) participating in Medicaid	Enrollment has increased substantially over the last year (42.9 percent), and by the second period of 2005 had reached 71.7 percent of expected enrollment.
Number of eligible Medicaid recipients using expanded inpatient reimbursements	Use of expanded inpatient reimbursements has decreased in each of the last two periods examined (CY2005). Tertiary hospitals are the primary beneficiaries of this expansion program, while the majority of hospital care takes place in smaller community hospitals.
Percentage of eligible persons age 65+ with income ≤80 percent of FPL using expanded coverage (AR-Seniors)	Enrollment has increased by 8.7 percent over CY2005 and has now exceeded the expected enrollment of 5,000 potentially eligible individuals by almost 3 percent (5,147 enrollees).
Percentage of adults eligible as AR-Adults participating in Medicaid expansion with limited benefits package	The Arkansas Safety Net Benefit Program was recently approved by CMS and is expected to be implemented by the end of CY2006.
Ratio of total spending to Tobacco Settlement funds allocated for the expanded Medicaid programs	Tobacco Settlement funds continue to be leveraged at similar levels as previously reported, and the program appears to be adequately funded.

PERFORMANCE ON MANAGEMENT INTEGRITY CRITERIA

The following is a summary of the RAND survey of management integrity for the Medicaid Expansion Programs. Given that much of the governance, finances, accounting, and contracting/oversight for the Medicaid Expansion Programs is predetermined, this chapter focuses only on Medicaid's quality improvement processes.

The Arkansas DHHS does not have a unique quality management process in place for eligibility determination, enrollment, or claims payment of the Medicaid Expansion Programs. All Medicaid eligibility categories are subject to the same timeliness and accuracy standards as determined by second-party reviews and supervisory reviews of casework. Similarly, all Medicaid claims are processed through the state's fiscal intermediary. The quality control procedures and claim processing accuracy requirements are printed in the state Medicaid plan. All of these quality management processes have been in place for more than 30 years.

There is no separate committee responsible for quality management in DHHS. The Division of County Operations (DCO) is responsible for the timeliness and accuracy of application processing and eligibility determination. The Division of Medical Services (DMS) is responsible for the timeliness, accuracy, and appropriateness of claims payments. Managers and supervisors at all levels of both divisions have some degree of responsibility for quality management. DCO staff responsible for quality management includes casework supervisors, local county administrators, area managers, and the assistant director for field operations.

As shown in Table 9.2, the Medicaid Expansion Programs satisfactorily perform eight out of fourteen components of the quality management process we defined. Six of the fourteen quality management processes require improvement.

Table 9.2
Ratings of the Medicaid Expansion Programs on Quality Management Activities

	Needs Improvement	Does Satisfactorily
1. Specifies criteria for quality performance		X
2. Collects information on technical quality measures		X
3. Collects information on consumers' experience with service	X	
4. Collects data on program enrollments, demographic characteristics of enrollees, service encounters		X
5. Has quantified quality measures for technical aspects of service		X
6. Has quantified measures of consumers' experience with service	X	
7. Has quantified measures on program enrollments, demographic characteristics of enrollees, service encounters that may be compared to targets		X
8. Analyzes technical quality data to identify potential quality deficiencies	X	
9. Analyzes consumer experience data to identify potential quality deficiencies	X	
10. Analyzes measures on program enrollments, etc., to identify potential quality deficiencies		X
11. Formulates quality recommendations that are addressed to who needs to take action		X
12. Reports results of quality analyses to executive management and boards		X
13. Reports results of quality analyses to relevant committees	X	
14. Disseminates quality recommendations to the public ("report cards")	X	

Over the last two years, there has been a greater focus on outreach and claims utilization analysis. For the AR-Seniors program, notices were sent to all program participants in fall 2004 reminding them that they have access to the full range of Medicaid benefits (excluding long-term care). As a result of this effort, there has been an increase in claims payments for this group.

ANALYSIS OF SPENDING TRENDS

Act 1574 of 2001, HB 1377 of 2003, and HB 2088 of 2005 appropriated funds for the Medicaid Expansion Programs for the first three biennium periods of the Tobacco Settlement Fund Allocation. Table 9.3 details the appropriations by fiscal year. Separate appropriations were made for three components of Medicaid operations—county operations (where enrollments are managed), Medicaid services (administration of health care benefits), and medical services (expenses for health care services delivered to recipients). The appropriation amounts reported include the federal matching dollars for the Medicaid program.[9]

As illustrated in Table 9.3, the FY2006 budget increased the line item for hospital and medical services by approximately $50 million over previous years' spending. These additional funds were appropriated as a cushion for emergency purposes, but they are not expected to be used. The prescription drug spending may exceed the $5 million budgeted for that line item in part because the state has been covering prescription drug costs for Medicaid enrollees during the transition to the Medicare Part D Prescription Drug program. If the state exceeds this appropriated amount, it can transfer funds from the hospital and medical services budget line to cover the shortfall. With the approval of the Arkansas Safety Net Benefit program, there is concern that the funds allocated to purchase data processing may not be sufficient.

The next analysis describes the expenditures for the Medicaid Expansion Programs from July 2001 until December 2005, including spending of both the Tobacco Settlement funding and the matching federal funds. Because December 2005 is the middle of the first year of the third biennium, no year totals for FY2005 are presented and it is not possible to fully detail expenditures in the third biennium.

Table 9.4 presents the total annual funds spent by the Medicaid Expansion Programs during this period. The original act creating the Medicaid Expansion Programs called for four different expansion programs; however, as described above, the AR-Adults program had not been approved as of the first half of FY2006. Therefore, it is not surprising that the Medicaid program did not spend the full amount it was appropriated in the first and second biennium and continued to underspend relative to the appropriation in FY2005 and the first two quarters of FY2006.

Due to the large difference between appropriated funds and expenditures, unspent Medicaid Expansion funds in FY2003 were put into a Rainy Day Trust Fund (Act 2002 [Ex. Sess.], No. 2, § 11) to be used during periods of budget shortfall for the general Medicaid

---

[9] The funds appropriated in the appropriations legislation included both the state and federal amounts to be spent on the Medicaid program. The Medicaid program staff reported that it was not possible for them to disaggregate the federal matching dollars from Tobacco Settlement funds, so they provided us with the total numbers.

program. This fund was used only in FY2003, when $17,733,032 in Tobacco Settlement funds were used for general Medicaid expenditures.

The additional staff and overhead required for the Medicaid Expansion Programs is minimal compared to the medical services expenses; and very little has been spent on regular salaries, fringe benefits, and M&O. Funds for medical services, in particular prescription drugs, were underspent, in large part because the AR-Adults program had not been implemented. In FY2005, both county operations and Medicaid services spent only 34 percent of the amount appropriated for each function.

Table 9.3

Appropriations for the Medicaid Expansion Programs: Sum of Tobacco Settlement Funds and Federal Matching Funds, by Fiscal Year

Item	First Biennium		Second Biennium		Third Biennium	
	2002	2003	2004	2005	2006	2007
Section 3: County operations						
(1) Regular salaries	$316,040	$1,242,171	$1,389,539	$1,427,057	$1,494,764	$1,540,391
(2) Personal service matching	91,652	360,230	466,522	473,403	536,538	545,531
(3) Maintenance and general operation						
(A) Operating expenses	197,974	195,795	195,795	195,795	195,795	195,795
(B) Conference and travel	0	0	0	0	0	0
(C) Professional fees	0	0	0	0	0	0
(D) Capacity outlay	69,300	0	0	0	0	0
(E) Data processing	0	0	0	0	0	0
(4) Data processing purchase	1,000,000	50,000	50,000	50,000	50,000	50,000
Section 4: Medicaid program management						
(1) Regular salaries	65,361	67,061	72,539	74,497	76,007	78,286
(2) Personal service matching	18,955	19,448	20,024	20,383	22,661	23,110
(3) Maintenance and general operation						
(A) Operating expenses	15,973	15,973	15,973	15,973	15,973	15,973
(B) Conferences and travel	2,000	2,000	2,000	2,000	2,000	2,000
(C) Professional fees	0	0	0	0	0	0
(D) Capacity outlay	9,000	0	0	0	0	0

Table 9.3—Continued

| Item | First Biennium | | Second Biennium | | Third Biennium | |
	2002	2003	2004	2005	2006	2007
(E) Data processing	0	0	0	0	0	0
Section 5: Medical services						
(1) Prescription drugs		7,769,669	29,063,678	29,063,678	29,063,678	5,000,000	5,000,000
(2) Hospital and medical services		23,432,208	46,765,542	46,765,542	46,765,542	100,428,742	45,428,742
Annual total	$32,988,132	$77,781,898	$78,041,612	$78,088,328	$106,722,480	$52,879,828
Biennium total	$110,770,030		$156,129,940		$159,602,308	

202

Table 9.4
Spending by the Medicaid Expansion Programs: Sum of Tobacco Settlement Funds and Federal Matching Funds, by Fiscal Year

Item	2002	2003[a]	2004	2005	2006[b]
Section 3: County operations					
(1) Regular salaries	$ 0	$ 230,661	$ 435,996	$440,236	$245,440
(2) Personal service matching	0	229,605	295,259	284,699	164,257
(3) Maintenance and general operation					
(A) Operating expenses	0	11,127	3,256	4,258	1,819
(B) Conferences and travel	0	0	0	0	0
(C) Professional fees	0	0	0	0	0
(D) Capacity outlay	0	0	0	0	0
(E) Data processing	0	0	0	0	0
(4) Data processing purchase	0	0	11,094	9,811	4,596
County total	$ 0	$471,393	$745,605	$739,004	$416,112
Section 4: Medicaid Program Management					
(1) Regular salaries	28,001	45,752	48,178	25,176	15,183
(2) Personal service matching	4,858	8,434	12,635	11,622	6,961
(3) Maintenance and general operation					
(A) Operating expenses	0	0	4,298	3,168	1,698
(B) Conferences and travel	0	0	0	0	0
(C) Professional fees	0	0	0	0	0
(D) Capacity outlay	0	0	0	0	0
(E) Data processing	0	0	0	0	0
Medicaid program total	$32,858	$54,186	$65,111	$39,966	$23,842

Table 9.4—Continued

Item	2002	2003[a]	2004	2005	2006[b]
Section 5: Medical Services					
(1) Prescription drugs	22,881	936,436	3,610,946	5,355,719	3,352,559
(2) Hospital and medical services	4,651,310	11,673,385	11,317,329	13,707,834	7,247,241
Medical services total	$4,651,310	$12,609,821	$14,928,275	$19,063,553	$10,599,800
Rainy Day Trust Fund[a]	0	17,733,032	0	0	0
Annual total	$4,707,049	$30,868,432	$15,738,991	$19,842,523	$11,039,754

a. Acts 2002 (Ex. Sess.), No. 2, § 11.

b. Amounts spent through December 31, 2005.

Total spending for the Medicaid Expansion Programs has grown steadily. In FY2005 total spending grew 27 percent over the prior year, and spending for FY2006 is running slightly ahead of FY2005. The increase is due to increased expenditures for medical services, as spending for both county operations and Medicaid services decreased. The nearly 28 percent increase in spending for medical services in FY2005 is attributable to increases of 48 percent for prescription drugs and 21 percent for hospital and medical services.

Figure 9.3 highlights the quarterly spending of the Medicaid Expansion Programs for the three major categories outlined in the appropriation: county operations, Medicaid services, and medical services. Spending for all three categories has increased with time, though not at a steady rate. Spending for operations for Medicaid program management is so small that it is barely visible on the figure. Expenditures for medical services for FY2005, first quarter and second quarter, have been adjusted downward since our prior report due to the mistaken drawing of some Tobacco Settlement funds to pay Children's Health Insurance Program (CHIP) claims. A total of $5,276,131 was overdrawn from the first quarter of FY2005 through the first quarter of FY2006. This is being corrected by not drawing any Tobacco Settlement funds for medical services until the difference is made up.

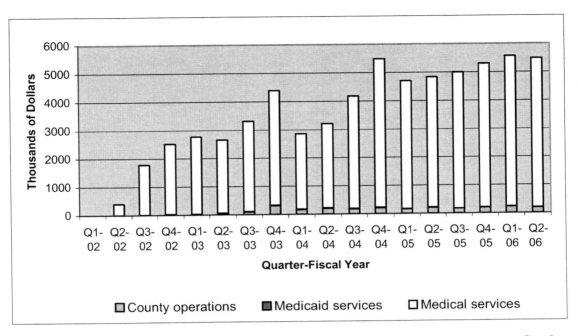

Figure 9.3—Medicaid Expansion Programs: Spending by the Sum of Tobacco Settlement Funds and Federal Matching Funds, by Program Office, by Quarter of Fiscal Years

Figure 9.4 shows the spending of the three operational Medicaid Expansion Programs from their inception in the second quarter of FY2002 through the second quarter of FY2006. The inpatient hospital program was the first program to begin spending Tobacco Settlement and matching federal funds in November 2001 (second quarter of FY2002). Spending for this program fluctuates from quarter to quarter and from year to year. Spending increased about 9 percent over the prior year in FY2005 but is still below the FY2003 level. The Pregnant Women's Expansion program began in November 2001 (second quarter of FY2002); however, expenditures lagged behind the beginning of the program due to global fee billings after delivery of the baby. After two quarters of startup, spending grew nearly 30 percent from FY2003 to FY2005. In the first half of FY2006, spending is slightly behind the first half of FY2005. The AR-Seniors program began in November 2002 (second quarter of FY2003), and spending has increased steadily from that point. Spending in FY2005 increased nearly 60 percent over the prior year. Note that expenditures on AR-Seniors increased, even though Figure 9.1 shows the same percentage of enrollees use at least one service. This increase in expenditures reflects both an increase in enrollment and an increase in intensity of use.

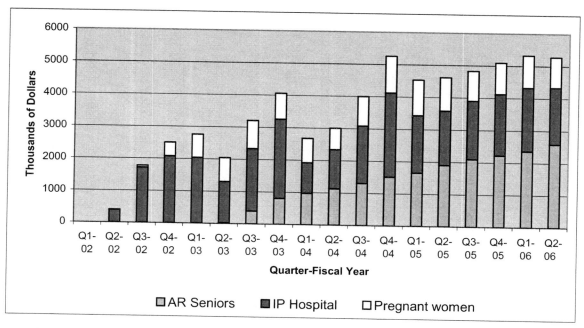

Figure 9.4—Spending by the Medicaid Expansion Programs: Sum of Tobacco Settlement Funds and Federal Matching Funds, by Program, by Quarter of Fiscal Years

RESPONSES TO EVALUATION RECOMMENDATIONS

During the past year, the Medicaid Expansion Programs have taken the following actions relevant to the recommendations made in the FY2003 and FY2004 evaluation reports.

Recommendation 1: The Medicaid Expansion Programs should continue to educate newly enrolled and current enrollees in the Pregnant Women's Expansion and the AR-Seniors programs regarding the services they are eligible to receive under their respective programs.

Program Response: Prior to the implementation of the Medicare Part D Pharmacy program and the approval of the waiver, DHHS was unsure of the impact that these programs would have on the Medicaid budget and the Tobacco Settlement–funded programs specifically. Now that Part D has been implemented and the waiver has been approved, DHHS has a better feel for their respective impacts on the budget and program policies. DHHS is preparing transmittals to be sent to health care providers to educate them about the Tobacco Settlement–funded programs and will notify relevant providers about the expansion of the AR-Seniors program. It is currently reviewing the FY2007 budget proposal and will consider increasing spending on education and outreach activities for AR-Seniors enrollees as well as Pregnant Women's Expansion program enrollees.

Recommendation 2: The Medicaid Expansion Programs should find alternate uses for allocated funds currently unspent.

Program Response: As mentioned previously, after working with CMS for several years, the state has received approval for a waiver to expand services to the 19- to 64-year-old population. A large share of the previously unspent funds were allocated to this program. With the CMS approval of the ASNB program, the state can now begin using these funds. In addition, DHHS has decided to expand AR-Seniors coverage from 80 to 100 percent of the FPL. This expansion will also utilize previously unspent funds.

Recommendation 3: Dedicate some of the Tobacco Settlement funds for Medicaid program administration to support outreach and education of beneficiaries in the expanded Medicaid programs.

Program Response: In November 2004, the Department of Human Services (DHS, now part of DHHS) sent a mailing to all AR-Seniors beneficiaries explaining to them what services they were eligible to receive. The mailing consisted of a one-page notice in large font with a copy of an Arkansas Medicaid Program card on it. Services and benefits— including prescription drug benefits, personal care services, eye exams, and coverage of Medicare deductibles, coinsurance, and premiums—were explicitly listed on the notice. This type of message was sent only once and only to AR-Seniors beneficiaries. Rather than send a similar notice to women enrolled in the Pregnant Women's Expansion program, brochures were distributed to appropriate providers in the state to make this information available to their patients. DHHS has indicated that the budget line item for outreach and client education activities in the FY2007 budget is currently under consideration for an increase to accommodate future education efforts.

Recommendation 4: Medicaid staff should continue to work with CMS to develop an acceptable waiver to provide a limited benefit package to the eligible 19- to 64-year-old population.

Program Response: As described above, CMS recently approved the waiver submitted by DHHS to develop a limited benefit package for 19- to 64-year-olds (entitled the Arkansas Safety Net Benefit program). Approval of the program was enabled in part by the inclusion of additional state funds from other Tobacco Settlement programs, including the Minority Health Initiative and the Tobacco Prevention and Cessation Program, under an umbrella program entitled the Health and Wellness Benefit Program. All Medicaid beneficiaries will benefit from a statewide wellness program in addition to the limited benefit package for 19- to 64-year-olds.

The ASNB program will offer a limited benefits package to employees ages 19 to 64 with income at or below 200 percent of the FPL working in firms with fewer than 500 employees. The benefit package will include a maximum of seven inpatient days per year, including acute hospital care and inpatient surgery; two outpatient hospital visits per year including outpatient surgery and emergency room visits; up to six outpatient physician visits per year; laboratory and x-ray services associated with a physician visit, inpatient admission, or outpatient service; and up to two prescriptions per month using a formulary established by the insurance company.

Employers are eligible to participate in the program and make these benefits available to their employees if they had not offered group health insurance in the previous 12 months. The total premium for the benefit package will be $100 per member per month. Employers will be required to cover all eligible individuals in their employment and will pay $15 per member per month, which will go into general revenues. The remainder of the premium ($85) will be split between state funds and a federal match. The state funds will come from the Tobacco Settlement and State Children's Health Insurance Plan (SCHIP) funds. The federal match is 73 percent, so the federal contribution will be approximately $62 and the state contribution will be approximately $23 per member per month. SCHIP funds will cover eligible individuals who are parents of SCHIP-enrolled children, and the Tobacco Settlement funds will cover eligible individuals without children (see Figure 9.5 for a depiction of the cost sharing for premiums).

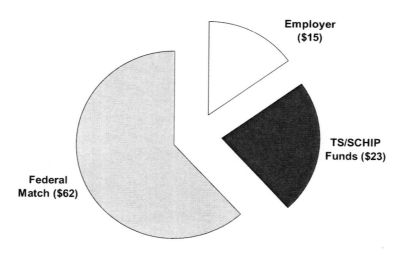

Figure 9.5—Relative Premium Share for the Arkansas Safety Net Benefit Program

The program will be implemented in two phases; in Phase I, the state expects to enroll 15,000 individuals who meet eligibility criteria. In Phase II, the state expects to enroll an additional 35,000 individuals. In Phase II, depending on how enrollment proceeds, the state may allow self-employed individuals to participate. The agency is currently developing the design of the program and the implementation plan. One or more private insurance companies will act as intermediaries and enroll employers and employees in the program. The state will not be directly involved in selling the insurance product to employers.

An RFP will be issued to identify the insurance contractor that will operate as the intermediary and administer the program. DHHS expects to have a contract in place with one or more intermediary by late summer, and the agency will then present the contract to the legislature prior to the contract's activation. Implementation of the program is tentatively scheduled for fall 2006 with the enrollment of employers, and the first beneficiaries will be enrolled by January 2007.

RECOMMENDATIONS FOR PROGRAM IMPROVEMENT

While the Medicaid programs show positive growth in most cases, there is still a substantial need for more education and outreach so the general population can be reached and informed about the available programs. In addition, DHHS needs to do more to educate enrolled populations, particularly those enrolled in the AR-Seniors program, to ensure that they understand their health care benefits under this coverage. The limited benefit package of the Arkansas Safety Net Benefit program was finally approved by CMS this year and will be implemented by the end of CY2006. We will need to confer with DHHS staff in the coming year to consider appropriate process indicators for measuring progress in the implementation of the program. Below are two recommendations that come out of our most recent evaluation process.

- **The Medicaid Expansion Programs should allocate funds to educate newly enrolled and current enrollees on a regular basis in the Pregnant Women's Expansion program and in the AR-Seniors program regarding the services they are eligible to receive under their respective programs.**

Based on feedback from the RAND evaluation, the DHS (now part of DHHS) distributed a packet of information to AR-Seniors enrollees in the fall of 2004 regarding the services they are eligible for under the program. However, this effort has not been repeated, nor have funds been set aside specifically for this effort. Women enrolled in the Pregnant Women's Expansion program have not received any educational materials. DHHS should create an ongoing consumer education campaign that will provide information to current and new enrollees at least once a year. Providers who have been seeing the same patient for an extended period may not be aware that that patient's insurance status has changed, and the patient may not know to inform the provider of that fact. Especially for AR-Seniors enrollees, the educational message should encourage them to always present their insurance cards to their providers, even those they have been seeing for a long time. This will ensure that those who are newly eligible for Medicaid benefits will have services appropriately billed to the insurer and reduce the chances that services are paid out of pocket unnecessarily.

- **The Medicaid Expansion Programs should initiate an outreach campaign to inform both potential enrollees and providers about the availability of the Medicaid Expansion Programs.**

Enrollment trends for the Pregnant Women's Expansion program have exceeded expectations but still lag behind projections developed by DHHS. More troubling is that income-eligible elderly individuals are overlooked for enrollment in the AR-Seniors program because they are not applying for Qualified Medicare Beneficiary status. DHHS should consider allocating resources to an outreach campaign that educates older adults and women of childbearing age, as well as their providers, about the availability of these programs and the eligibility criteria. Partnering with the Centers on Aging around the state (also funded by Tobacco Settlement funds), the Area Agencies on Aging (AAAs), the state quality improvement organization (QIO), and other relevant organizations can be an effective strategy for getting the word out about available programs in an efficient way. In addition, more resources should be allocated to educating providers about the availability of both of these programs on a regular basis (annually or biannually).

APPENDIX TO CHAPTER 9

Performance on Process Indicators through December 2005

As discussed in previous reports, five indicators were selected that represent the overall progress of the Medicaid Expansion Programs. These indicators reflect the goal stated in the act to "expand access to healthcare through targeted Medicaid expansions thereby improving the health of eligible Arkansans." The indicators reflect efforts to: (1) provide access to Medicaid services for pregnant women with income between 133 percent and 200 percent of the FPL, (2) expand Medicaid-reimbursed hospital care and reduce cost sharing for hospital stays of Medicaid beneficiaries ages 19 to 64, (3) expand Medicaid benefits to Medicare beneficiaries deemed eligible for Qualified Medicare Beneficiary status and with incomes below 80 percent of the FPL, (4) establish a new benefit to increase access to a limited package of Medicaid-funded services for indigent adults, and (5) leverage Tobacco Settlement funds allocated to the Medicaid Expansion Programs.

Provide access to Medicaid services for pregnant women with income between 133 percent and 200 percent of the federal poverty level.

Indicator: Percentage of pregnant women with income between 133 percent and 200 percent of the federal poverty level participating in Medicaid.

Table 9.A1 presents the enrollment activity for the Pregnant Women's Expansion program, both as the count of women enrolled in each period and the proportion of estimated eligible women. The denominator used in establishing the proportion was based on Department of Health 2002 estimates of potentially eligible individuals. In total, 7,800 women were estimated to be eligible in 2002, and we divided this amount by two to reflect the six-month time periods used for evaluation. The Department of Health (now DHHS) previously argued that the number of women between 133 percent and 200 percent of the federal poverty level might be lower than the estimated 7,800 because more of the women in the higher income group will have personal or third-party resources to cover their pregnancy. However, more than half of all births (55 percent) in Arkansas are covered by Medicaid, and the growth in Medicaid enrollment averages 4 to 7 percent annually. Therefore, this estimate may no longer be as conservative as previously thought. A new estimate of the potentially eligible population should be calculated in light of more recent trends.

There have been steady increases in enrollment for the pregnant women's Medicaid Expansion Programs over time. Although there was a dip in enrollment in the first period of 2004, enrollment continued to increase in each of the following three periods.

Table 9.A1
Use of Expanded Pregnancy Medicaid Benefits by Eligible Women

Six-Month Period	Enrollees in Pregnancy Benefits	
	Number	Percentage[a]
Jul–Dec 2001	266	6.8
Jan–Jun 2002	1,148	29.4
Jul–Dec 2002	1,705	43.7
Jan–Jun 2003	1,997	51.2
Jul–Dec 2003	2,081	53.4
Jan–Jun 2004	1,829	46.9
Jul–Dec 2004	1,957	50.2
Jan–Jun 2005	2,310	59.2
Jul–Dec 2005	2,797	71.7

a. The denominator used was 3,900 potential eligibles, based on a 2002 estimate established by the Department of Health of 7,800 potential eligibles annually, which was divided by 2 to reflect the six-month time periods used for the evaluation.

Expand Medicaid-reimbursed hospital care and reduce cost sharing for hospital stays of Medicaid beneficiaries ages 19 to 64.

Indicator: Number of eligible Medicaid recipients using expanded inpatient reimbursements.

Table 9.A2 presents the number of eligible adult Medicaid recipients using expanded hospital reimbursements. It includes use of either reduced co-payments or expanded hospital days covered per year from 20 to 24 days. The program experienced a steep decline in utilization between the first and second periods of 2003, and the slight increase in the second period of 2004 was only temporary; decreases in the number of individuals benefiting from the expanded reimbursements were observed for both periods of 2005. According the DHHS staff, hospital lengths of stay have not shifted considerably; however, few people are in the hospital long enough to benefit from the expanded reimbursements. The expanded benefit generally benefits tertiary hospitals the most, and there are fewer such hospitals relative to smaller community hospitals.

Table 9.A2
Medicaid Enrollees Using Expanded Inpatient Benefits

Six-Month Period	Number of Beneficiaries[a]
Jul–Dec 2001	2,448
Jan–Jun 2002	22,933
Jul–Dec 2002	26,305
Jan–Jun 2003	29,077
Jul–Dec 2003	21,303
Jan–Jun 2004	21,732
Jul–Dec 2004	24,961
Jan–Jun 2005	22,815
Jul–Dec 2005	19,203

a. The eligible population is Medicaid recipients between the ages of 19 and 64.

Expand Medicaid benefits to Medicare beneficiaries deemed eligible for Qualified Medicare Beneficiary status and with incomes at or below 80 percent of the FPL.

Indicator: Percentage of eligible persons ages 65 and over with income at or below 80 percent of FPL using expanded coverage (AR-Seniors).

Table 9.A3 presents summary information on enrollment of Medicare beneficiaries who have been deemed eligible for the AR-Seniors program. To be eligible, an individual must first apply to be a QMB. Once that individual's income falls to 80 percent of the FPL or lower, he or she becomes eligible for the AR-Seniors program and can receive the full array of Medicaid benefits. Table 9.A3 present the counts of individuals enrolled in each period as well as the proportion of all potentially eligible who are actually enrolled. It presents the proportions with two different denominators. The first denominator is based on Medicaid estimates of the eligible QMB population (approximately 5,000 enrollees). Based on this denominator, the AR-Seniors program is over capacity. Current enrollment is more than 5,000 enrollees, exceeding previous enrollment estimates. The second denominator comes from the Arkansas census data, Medicaid and SSI enrollments. We estimate that in 2005, there were just over 56,000 adults ages 65 and older whose income was at or below 80 percent of the FPL. We subtract from that those who were already eligible for Medicaid because of SSI eligibility and those already in an institution with incomes up to 300 percent of the SSI limit (these two populations are not eligible for AR-Seniors). The resulting denominator is 29,832 seniors who could be potentially eligible for the AR-Seniors program. Based on this denominator, the program is at just over 17 percent capacity. Overall, there has been a steady increase in enrollment for the AR-Seniors program.

Table 9.A3
Eligible Elderly Persons Using Expanded Medicaid Coverage

Six-Month Period	Participants in Expanded Coverage for Seniors		
	Number	Percentage of Eligible QMBs[a]	Percentage of Total Eligibles in AR[b]
Jul–Dec 2001	0	0	0
Jan–Jun 2002	0	0	0
Jul–Dec 2002	1,567	31.1	5.3
Jan–Jun 2003	3,795	75.9	12.7
Jul–Dec 2003	4,040	80.8	13.5
Jan–Jun 2004	4,120	82.4	13.8
Jul–Dec 2004	4,734	94.7	15.9
Jan–Jun 2005	4,946	98.9	16.6
Jul–Dec 2005	5,147	102.0	17.3

a. Denominator estimated by the Arkansas Medicaid program based on number of individuals in Arkansas enrolled as Qualified Medicare Beneficiaries (QMB) (5,000 enrollees).

b. Denominator obtained from the Arkansas census data in the PUMS one percent file (56,089 potentially eligible based on 2005 estimates), SSI enrollment, and Medicaid files. We subtracted from the census estimates that portion of the aged population (65+) already on SSI as of December 2005 (10,048 individuals) as they are eligible for Medicaid through normal channels. We also subtracted from this estimate the number of aged beneficiaries in a long-term care institution with incomes up to 300 percent of the SSI limit as of December 2005 (16,209). The resulting denominator is 29,832. Please note: all percentages have been recalculated and will differ from earlier reports.

Establish a new benefit to increase access to a limited package of Medicaid-funded services for indigent adults.

Indicator: Percentage of adults eligible as AR-Adults participating in Medicaid expansion with limited benefits package.

The Arkansas Safety Net Benefit program was just recently approved by CMS. The program is expected to begin enrolling beneficiaries in January 2007. Data for this program may not be available until the second period of 2007.

Leverage Tobacco Settlement funds allocated to the Medicaid Expansion Programs.

Indicator: Ratio of total spending to Tobacco Settlement funds allocated for the expanded Medicaid programs.

Part of the design of the Medicaid program is to match the state investment in Medicaid services to federal dollars. The federal match for Medicaid health care service costs has been $3 dollars for every state dollar spent (although as noted below, this will change in the second year of the next biennium). The match for program administration costs is one federal dollar for every state dollar. Therefore, by the basic program terms, the Tobacco Settlement funds applied to the Medicaid expansion are leveraging external dollars substantially.

Despite previous concerns about the implications of state education funding issues for the state budget, the Medicaid program appears to be adequately funded.

A source of concern for the Medicaid budget comes from (1) reductions in the Federal Financial Participation (FFP) rate and (2) proposals by the president and Congress to make reductions in the Medicaid program to control spending. The FFP has been reduced due to the loss of an enhanced matching level made available to states for several quarters and the recalculation of the state's rate based on our per capita income. The state is closely monitoring the potential impact of any program reductions by Congress as they attempt to balance the federal budget. Currently, for every dollar Arkansas allocates to Medicaid health care services, the federal government pays out $3. The future match rate was lowered to 73.77 percent in FFY2006 and will be lowered to 73.37 percent in FFY2007.

Chapter 10
Evaluation of Smoking-Related Outcomes

An important part of any evaluation is examining the extent to which the programs being evaluated are having affecting the outcomes of interest. The types of outcomes might range from attitudes and behaviors of the targeted population to the clinical health of those being served. Because the seven programs supported by the Tobacco Settlement funds are extremely diverse, the outcomes of interest vary widely.

Our evaluation of the effect of the funded programs on the well-being of the people of Arkansas is divided into two parts. This chapter presents our findings regarding the effect of the programs on smoking prevalence and on other behaviors related to smoking. Chapter 11 reports our evaluation of the effect of programs on non-smoking outcomes. Refer to Appendix B for detailed information about our outcome evaluation methods.

HIGHLIGHTS OF FINDINGS ON SMOKING OUTCOMES

Our analysis of smoking behavior in Arkansas provides evidence of the continued effectiveness of the Tobacco Settlement programs on smoking outcomes, especially for the most vulnerable populations, such as young people and pregnant women. Our main findings regarding smoking outcomes are summarized as follows:

- Smoking has decreased substantially among middle school and high school students since programming began, as found in the analysis by the Arkansas Division of Health (ADH) of data from the Youth Tobacco Survey (YTS).

- Tobacco Settlement programming has reduced smoking among young people compared with what would be expected based on pre-program trends.

    o Young adults ages 18 to 25 are smoking less than previously.

    o Pregnant teenagers are smoking less than previously.

    o Pregnant women ages 20 to 29 are smoking less than previously.

- The dramatic improvement in compliance with laws prohibiting sales of tobacco products to minors has continued and has been verified by federal auditors.

- The adult smoking prevalence declined in 2005, following a slight increase in 2004, but we cannot yet confirm that this recent decline is a real effect. The decline is not statistically significant from either Arkansas' previous trend in smoking rate or from what would have occurred if Arkansas had followed the rate of smoking reduction of other states that implemented successful comprehensive smoking control programs.

- Our analysis of the variation in smoking by county does not provide evidence that people who live in areas where ADH focused its TPEP activity are less likely to smoke. However, ADH has recently directed its attention to regional variations in smoking, which is a necessary first step to reducing geographic disparities.

- There have been declines in the prevalence of a variety of diseases that are affected by smoking and by secondhand smoke. The evidence is strongest in the cases of strokes and acute myocardial infarctions (heart attacks).

As in past years, our analysis of smoking rates for young adults, pregnant adults, and pregnant teenagers shows conclusively that these groups are smoking less than would be expected if there had been a continuation of the trends in rates that preceded the Tobacco Settlement programming. This year's report provides additional evidence from a new data source of decreased smoking among both middle school students and high school students. Reductions in smoking among young people are particularly advantageous because as this population ages, these reductions will provide health dividends to the state for years to come. This optimistic conclusion is based on the assumption that young people will not initiate or resume smoking when they are older; such an assumption is supported by the evidence.

In previous reports, we stated that the earliest we would expect to see definitive evidence of reduced smoking in the adult population is in 2005 data (i.e., in time for this report). This expectation was based on the experience of four other states in which reduced adult smoking rates were observed within three years of the full implementation of a comprehensive smoking control initiative (US DHHS, 2000). We did not observe definitive evidence of reduced adult smoking, which we think may be due in part to two reasons:

- The four states in which such evidence was observed within three years had much larger populations—ranging from approximately twice as large to more than ten times as large as that of Arkansas. The sample size of the principal survey that is used for estimating smoking rates is proportional to the each state's population. Larger sample sizes make it much more likely that an actual decrease in smoking rates will be observed in survey estimates.

- Two of the states implemented bans on smoking in public places as early components of their comprehensive smoking control programs. The lack of such a policy during the early stages may have limited the impact of Arkansas' program, reducing the size of the decrease in adult smoking prevalence. Now that such a policy has been adopted, we expect to see accelerated reductions in adult smoking in the future. This expectation follows evidence from many places where smoking control policies were introduced (Tobacco Advisory Group of the Royal College of Physicians, 2005).

OUTCOME ANALYSIS APPROACH

This chapter documents the cumulative effect of the smoking control policies and programs since the initiation of the Tobacco Settlement programs. The effects addressed here are changes in overall smoking behavior across the state's population, which are influenced collectively by the actions taken by various programs to affect this outcome, including tobacco taxes, smoke-free environment laws, and the Tobacco Settlement programs, in addition to possible other unidentified factors.

Our approach is guided by the conceptual model presented in Figure 10.1, which defines a continuum over time of outcomes that should occur in response to educational and treatment interventions to reduce smoking rates. According to this model, the first outcome we would expect to observe is a decline in self-reported smoking, which then should be validated by a decline in sales of tobacco products. As smoking rates decrease, we then should see reductions in short-term health effects of smoking, such as low birth weight infants or hospital stays due to asthma exacerbations. Effects on longer term health status will occur later, for example, in reduced incidence of cancer, emphysema, or heart disease.

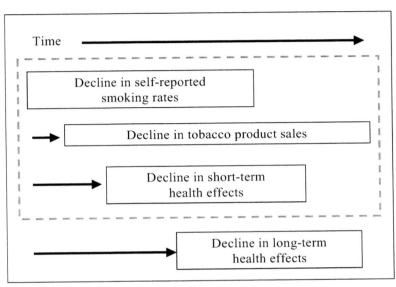

Figure 10.1—Conceptual Model of Behavioral Responses for Smoking Cessation

Assessment of program impacts requires the ability to connect the effort undertaken by a program to the expected outcome in a way that takes into account other factors that influence the outcome. If this is not done, changes in an outcome could be attributed incorrectly to a program's interventions when in fact the changes were due to other factors. Examples of other factors include the following:

- Broader (nationwide or regional) trends that are independent of local program efforts

- Continuation of trends that pre-date the program and reflect effects of earlier actions or interventions

- Changes in the demographic composition of the population

- Efforts by other related programs

Assessment also requires that findings be presented with an indication of their statistical precision. Whenever survey data are collected and analyzed, it is important to report not only the size of the effect, but also the degree of certainty. The degree of certainty can be reported as a margin of error (+/- so many percent), as a confidence interval (the narrower the interval, the more precise the estimate), or as a significance level on a hypothesis test (whether or not the finding is reliable or could occur by chance). Without this information, the reader does not know whether an apparent impact reflects changes in the underlying behavior or merely variability in the data or model.

Our analysis focuses on smoking outcome measures for the entire target population rather than for program participants alone. For example, we measure changes in smoking rates for all adults in Arkansas rather than for a group that participated in a particular education or cessation program. In many cases the target population is restricted to a particular demographic group (e.g., youth) or a specific geographic region (e.g., the Delta), but in all cases we measure outcomes for that entire target population, and not for a specific group of program participants.

There are several reasons for this approach. First, some components, such as smoking control measures, media campaigns, and other educational outreach efforts, do not have participants per se but are targeted at everyone in a particular population. In such cases, the entire target population must be the focus of the analysis. Second, some program components, either alone or in combination with other program components that have similar goals, are large enough that an impact should be measurable at a population level. In such a case, it is important to demonstrate that the program affects a broad segment of the population. Third, many programs have an impact that extends beyond the immediate participants. For example, programs that attempt to change the behavior of program participants through education can affect the behavior and health outcomes of other people who are in contact with the immediate participants. Finally, and perhaps most important from an evaluation standpoint, it is very difficult to distinguish between pre-program tendencies and the impact of the program under study if only outcomes for program participants are considered. The people who participate in a specific program frequently are the most motivated individuals in the population, and many would improve their outcomes even without participating in the program.

Only through comparison to a control group or through careful statistical modeling is it possible to determine whether the outcomes for a group of program participants are due to the program or simply reflect a high level of motivation on the part of program enrollees. However, in this case, creating a randomized control group is neither cost-effective nor politically feasible. Collecting voluminous background information on participants to use in statistical modeling is also expensive and intrusive. Therefore, we focus our outcomes evaluation on programs that we judge to be sufficiently large to have a measurable impact on an identifiable target population and for which we have population outcome measures. In adopting this approach, we acknowledge that we may not be able to detect small effects on the participants, but we gain the ability to measure better the more general effects that are the ultimate objective of the programs.

CHAPTER ORGANIZATION

This chapter is organized in a very similar fashion to the evaluation chapter in our past reports on smoking outcomes. However, with every year the amount of data increases, allowing us to extend our analyses and in some cases detect significant changes in trends. In the remainder of the chapter, we present the following information:

Adult Smoking. As we have for the last two years, we analyze trends in the percentage of adults in Arkansas who smoke and trends in cigarette sales.

Youth Smoking. We update our analysis of smoking by pregnant teenagers and by young adults, as well as our analysis of illegal sales of cigarettes to minors. We also review the analysis by ADH of the smoking behavior of middle school and high school students made possible by a new wave of data from the Youth Tobacco Survey.

Cigarette Sales. We update our analysis of the sales of cigarettes in Arkansas. However, a very large cigarette excise tax increase in Oklahoma at the beginning of 2006 has given rise to increased cross-border sales, making any interpretation of this analysis more problematic than in past years.

Geographic Analysis. We update our analysis of the distribution of Division of Health tobacco control spending and activities among Arkansas counties and the relationship with county-specific smoking trends.

Smoking-related Health Indicators. We update our analysis from the 2004 report on the incidence of smoking-related health conditions.

Several analyses were included in past reports that are not repeated in this year's report. The Arkansas Adult Tobacco Survey (AATS) and the Youth Risk Behavior Surveillance System (YRBSS) are biennial surveys for which new data were not available. Comparisons for adult smoking in surrounding states from the Behavioral Risk Factor Surveillance System (BRFSS) are omitted because the national data set has not yet been released. Likewise, the CDC has not released data for tax rates in surrounding states. We expect future reports to update these analyses as data become available. Finally, we discontinued our analysis of the relationship between the prevalence of Tobacco Control Board inspections in each county and change in smoking rates. Tobacco Control Board inspections are now covering virtually all cigarette vendors, so there is no meaningful variation to analyze.

STATEWIDE TRENDS IN SMOKING BEHAVIORS

In this section, we examine statewide trends in smoking behaviors and assess the extent to which there have been any changes in those trends since the inception of the programs supported by the Tobacco Settlement funds. Because the Tobacco Settlement programs are still relatively new, we focus our analysis on the earliest outcomes that are expected to be observed, as portrayed in Figure 10.1. These include self-reported smoking rates by adults and youth, sales of cigarette products, and compliance rates with prohibitions on sales of tobacco products to youth.

The most common measure of smoking behavior is the prevalence of adult smoking as measured by the BRFSS. The BRFSS is an annual telephone survey of randomly selected adults throughout the country that is coordinated by the U.S. Department of Health and Human Services CDC. The precision of the information available from this survey depends on the number of people surveyed. The sample size in Arkansas has risen from fewer than 2,000 in 1995 to more than 5,000 in 2005, so precision has increased over time, as reflected by the narrower confidence intervals in recent years.

Percentage of Adults Who Smoke

Key Finding: The adult smoking rate has fallen, but not by enough that we can definitely conclude that Arkansas is on a new trend of accelerated decreases in smoking rates that has been observed in other states with similar comprehensive tobacco control programs.

Figure 10.2 depicts the estimated percentages of adults in Arkansas who reported they smoked, for each year from 1996 through 2005, based on the BRFSS survey data. These rates are the percentage of adult Arkansans who reported that they smoke "every day" or "some days" in response to the survey question, "Do you now smoke cigarettes every day, some days, or not at all?" We also report the upper and lower limits of the 95 percent confidence intervals for these estimates.[10] As the graph illustrates, the prevalence of smoking has moved up and down within a narrow range over these years, with little downward trend. As shown by the confidence intervals, estimates from year to year are not so different that they fall outside of the confidence intervals of previous years' estimates. Therefore, differences are likely due to random fluctuation caused by the manner in which people were sampled rather than real changes in the percentages of the population who smoke.

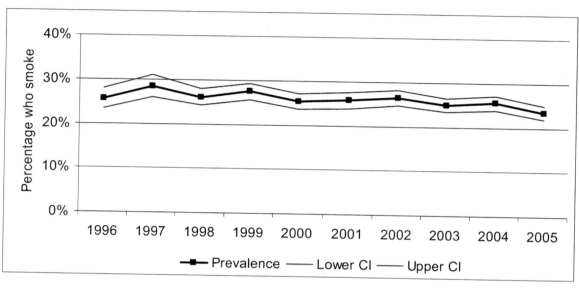

SOURCE: RAND analysis of Behavioral Risk Factor Surveillance System micro data files.
NOTES: Rates are not adjusted for changes in demographic characteristics. CI is confidence interval.

Figure 10.2—Percentage of Adults Ages 18 and Over in Arkansas Who Smoke, 1996 Through 2005

One goal of the outcome evaluation is to answer the question, "How do changes in smoking rates since the beginning of Tobacco Settlement programming compare to what would have happened to smoking rates if these programs had not been established?" Appendix B describes the estimation methods employed. The results of this analysis are presented in Figure 10.3.

We also include a hypothetical trend that indicates what the predicted smoking rates would be if Arkansas' anti-smoking programs and policies were as successful as those in California, one of the most successful statewide tobacco control programs in the United States to date. California experienced a 0.9 percent per year acceleration in its downward smoking trend

---

[10] These confidence intervals define a range within which estimated values would fall 95 percent of the time for survey samples if the survey were repeated over and over again—that is, where there is 95 percent confidence that the true value lies within that range. Estimates with wider confidence intervals must be interpreted with caution because apparent differences in values might not be statistically significant. Note that with increasing sample size over time, the confidence interval narrows, reflecting more reliable estimates.

during the first ten years of its program (California Department of Health Services, 2006). We include this line to predict the impact that could be expected in Arkansas from a successful program. The impact would be very small in the first few years, but the cumulative effect would cut smoking rates by almost one-third after ten years.

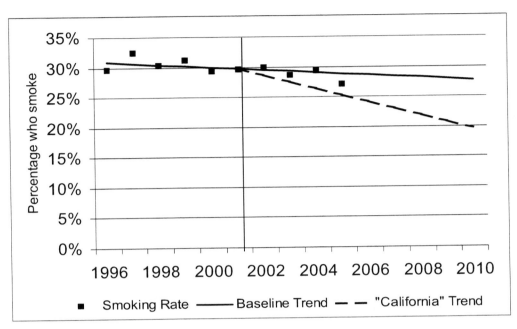

SOURCE: RAND analysis of Behavioral Risk Factor Surveillance System micro data files.

Figure 10.3—Percentage of Adults Ages 18 and Over in Arkansas Who Smoke, Adjusted for Changes in Survey Sample Demographic Characteristics

As time passes, the addition of more data points will better enable us to determine whether Arkansas is deviating from the baseline trend—the greater the deviation, the sooner we will be able to determine that the gains are tangible. Similarly, with more data points, we can determine whether any gains are different from the California trend of a highly successful program. In 2003, the adjusted smoking rate was between the baseline and the California trend, but in 2004, the data were back at baseline. Then in 2005, the adjusted smoking rate was between the two lines. Looking at all of this information, we are unable to conclude that Arkansas is following one trend as opposed to the other; Arkansas could be still at baseline, following the California trend, or somewhere in between. Given that Arkansas has only been incrementally implementing its smoking control program, the in-between hypothesis seems to be the most reasonable; as measures such as the just-passed Clean Indoor Air Act start to have effects, evidence from other places predicts that we should see greater deviations from baseline.

Amount of Cigarette Consumption per Adult Arkansan

Key Finding: Cigarette sales reverted to the trend that had begun before the recent tax increases and the start of the Tobacco Settlement programs, reversing the beginnings of the

221

shift to lower sales. This reversion likely reflects increased purchases from residents of Oklahoma due to the recent large cigarette tax increase in that state.

The amount of cigarettes consumed can be measured in two ways. Information on cigarette tax receipts can be used to estimate cigarette sales and consumption rates. We used the total state adult population as the denominator for the consumption rate, which we measured as the population over age 15. Second, people can be asked how much they smoke using surveys such as the AATS and BRFSS. However, the BRFSS stopped asking this question in 2000, and the AATS is repeated only every other year. Therefore, the only new information at this time comes from cigarette tax receipts.

The use of tax receipts to calculate cigarette consumption is complicated by sales to residents from neighboring states as well as by variation in tax rates along state borders. Since the Arkansas tax increase in 2003, it had a substantially higher tax rate than all of its neighbors, until Oklahoma raised its tax in 2005 from 23 cents per pack to $1.03 per pack.

Oklahoma's tax increase disrupted this analysis in two ways. First, prior to Oklahoma's tax increase, cigarette sales by Arkansas vendors adjacent to the Oklahoma border were taxed below the 59-cent rate levied in the interior of Arkansas. This border tax variance is granted in Arkansas to vendors near any state with a lower tax rate in order to discourage Arkansas residents from crossing to another state to make their purchases. Our calculation of cigarette sales from cigarette tax receipts assumed that all cigarette packs were taxed at the 59-cent rate and did not account for this tax variance. When the Oklahoma tax rate was increased, the variance was removed and more vendors paid the full 59-cent rate. Even if there had been no change in cigarette sales, this increase in the tax rate for those vendors would have increased tax revenues for the state and led us to calculate higher cigarette sales.

Second, the increase in the Oklahoma tax creates an incentive for Oklahoma residents to buy their cigarettes in Arkansas, leading to a further increase in Arkansas tax revenues (Oklahoma does not have a border tax variance). Together, these two effects would lead to an increased estimate of cigarette consumption in Arkansas even if Arkansans were not buying any more cigarettes.

Figure 10.4 shows the estimated cigarette sales in Arkansas throughout this period. The average amount of cigarette consumption per capita has been declining since 1998. The individual points on the graph are the cigarette sales per capita for each month. The vertical lines on the graph identify the three dates that state excise tax increases went into effect. The first two of these increases were in Arkansas, the third was in Oklahoma. Using these cigarette consumption data points for the pre-tax increase period of January 1998 through June 2001, we estimated a baseline trend line of cigarette consumption per capita. This trend line, when projected into the future, is an estimate of what cigarette consumption would have been in subsequent years if the baseline trends had continued without the introduction of tax changes or tobacco prevention and cessation interventions.

The trend line, which is the declining straight line on the graph, represents an average 3 percent decline in cigarette consumption per capita each year. Taxes increased from 31.5 cents per pack to 34 cents per pack in July 2001 and to 59 cents per pack in June 2003. Consumption data are the points plotted on the graph for each month. As can be seen by comparing the points of actual data to the trend line, our analysis did not find any change in the trend as the tobacco prevention and cessation activities began in 2002. The trend remained nearly constant overall, despite some short-term increases in sales just before (and subsequent short-term decline in sales immediately following) the enactment of higher taxes in 2001 and again in 2003.

In previous reports, we noted that following the June 2003 tax increase, many of the monthly sales fell below the projected trend, but this downward deviation was not sufficiently large to indicate a significant change in the trend. However, sales have reverted to the baseline trend following the tax increase in Oklahoma. As explained above, this increase could reflect changes in tax rates for Arkansas vendors on the Oklahoma border and increased sales to Oklahoma residents rather than any change in purchasing or consumption behavior by Arkansans.

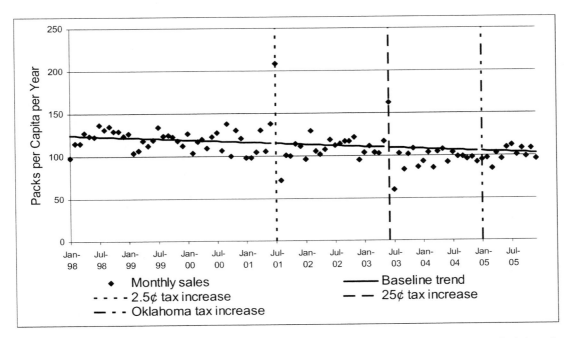

SOURCE: RAND analysis of monthly tax receipts (provided by Office of Excise Tax Administration, Arkansas Department of Finance) and population estimates from the U.S. Census Bureau.

NOTES: Monthly figures are multiplied by 12 to correspond to an annual purchase rate. The Oklahoma tax increase was 80 cents per pack.

Figure 10.4—Number of Packs of Cigarettes Sold per Arkansan, Age 15 and Older, 1998–2005

Percentage of Pregnant Women Who Smoke

Key Finding: In 2005, the percentage of pregnant women who reported smoking continued to be less than expected from baseline trends of smoking prevalence.

The subpopulation of pregnant women is of interest for evaluation purposes because smoking poses great medical risks during pregnancy, especially to the fetus. Furthermore, good data are available to analyze smoking patterns because every woman who delivers a child is asked whether she smoked during the pregnancy. Since pregnant women are exposed to many of the same programming influences as the general population (e.g., education, media campaigns), the information collected about their behavior can be used to provide insights on smoking outcomes that are unobtainable from the more limited data on the general population. However, one must be cautious about generalizing too readily from the population of pregnant women to the general population.

Figure 10.5 shows for each year from 1995 through 2005 the percentage of pregnant women who smoked during pregnancy, based on information reported on the application for a birth certificate. The annual rates show a slight downward trend from the mid-1990s through 2005. These numbers do not contain sampling error because they are the actual prevalence rates for everyone in this group. Therefore, no confidence intervals are needed to indicate the precision of the information, as would be necessary if the data had come from a random sample.

As discussed above for the prevalence of adult smokers, observed changes over time in the percentage of pregnant women who smoke could be explained simply by changes in their demographics, rather than by changes in smoking behaviors. Therefore, we estimated a baseline trend in smoking prevalence before the Tobacco Settlement programs began, adjusting for changes in demographics. This trend line is extended through the later period to provide an estimate of what the smoking rate would have been if that trend had continued.

Figure 10.6 presents the adjusted prevalence rates and the estimated baseline trend, which indicates that smoking prevalence among pregnant women has been decreasing, albeit very slowly. Over the six-year baseline period, the smoking rate among pregnant women decreased by 1 percentage point—a small but statistically significant decline. Comparing this trend (indicated by the trend line in the figure) to prevalence rates (indicated by the points in the figure) during the period that Tobacco Settlement programs were in operation, we find that smoking by pregnant women was virtually identical to the expected rate in 2002 and slightly below the expected rates in 2003, 2004, and 2005. These lower rates are slightly more than 1 percentage point below the trend and are themselves statistically significant.

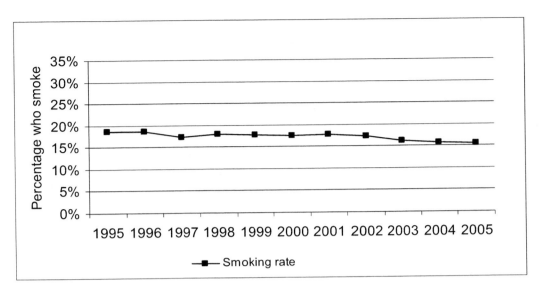

SOURCE: RAND analysis of birth certificate micro data files.

Figure 10.5—Percentage of Pregnant Women in Arkansas Who Smoke, 1995 Through 2005

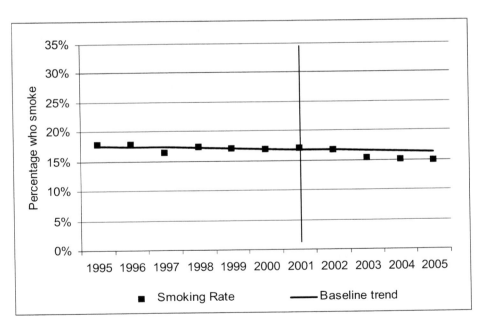

SOURCE: RAND analysis of birth certificate micro data files.

Figure 10.6—Smoking Prevalence of Pregnant Women in Arkansas, Adjusted for Demographic Changes, 1995 Through 2005

Percentage of Young People Who Smoke

Key Finding: The percentage of smokers among young people has declined below the baseline trend since the Tobacco Settlement programs have been in operation. This is true for all four categories of young people for whom we have data: youth (middle and high school students), pregnant teenagers (ages 14 to 19), young adults (ages 18 to 25), and pregnant young women (ages 20 to 29).

A newly available data set, the 2005 wave of the YTS, makes it possible to examine the change in smoking rates among youth since the onset of Tobacco Settlement programming. As shown in the first two rows of Table 10.1, smoking rates for middle and high school students have dropped dramatically since 2000.

These decreases are similar to the decrease that we have calculated for pregnant teenagers during the same interval. The decrease is greater for younger students. The decreases are smaller for the older segments of the young population, such as adults ages 18 to 25 and young pregnant women ages 20 to 29.

Table 10.1
Decreases in Smoking Prevalence Among Young People

Population	2000 Rate	2005 Rate	Percentage of Decrease
Middle school students[a]	15.8	9.3	41.1
High school students[a]	35.8	26.3	26.5
Pregnant teenagers (14–19)[b]	21.5	16.1	25.1
Young adults (18–25)[c]	31.2	28.9	7.4
Young pregnant women (20–29)[b]	15.9	15.2	4.7

NOTE: The estimated decrease is significant at the 5 percent level for all populations.

a. DHHS Division of Health calculations based on YTS.

b. RAND calculations based on Birth Certificates, adjusted for change in population demographics.

c. RAND calculations based on BRFSS, adjusted for change in population demographics.

In Figures 10.7 and 10.8 we present, as we have in past years, the changes in smoking among pregnant teenagers and young adults. When looking at these figures, readers should keep in mind that the decreases reported in Table 10.1 are likely to understatement the impact of the program because they do not take into account pre-program smoking trends. As shown in both figures, smoking was increasing for both young populations and pregnant women in their 20s before the initiation of Tobacco Settlement programming. If these trends had continued, the 2005 rate would have been higher than the 2000 rate. Therefore, the impact of the program is larger than the difference reported in Table 10.1. We only have one year of data prior to program initiation for middle school and high school students, so we cannot estimate a baseline trend. However, given the similarity in subsequent changes, it is likely that student smoking was also increasing prior to Tobacco Settlement programming.

In our first Biennial Report (Farley et al. 2005a), we provided information from the biennial YRBSS. This information included data from the 2003 wave of that survey, which showed decreases in youth smoking. As noted at the time, the 2003 data had not been approved by the CDC because of a very low response rate. The 2005 wave of this survey was not available in time to be included in this year's report, although we understand that it had an adequate response rate and will be a good source for information about youth smoking. We will include an analysis of this important survey in the next evaluation report.

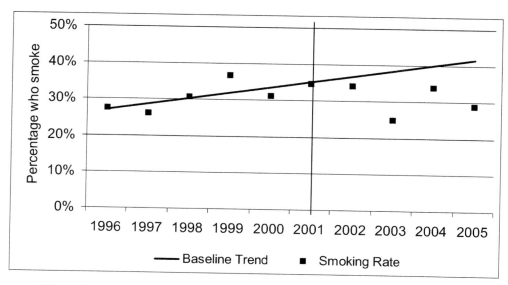

SOURCE: RAND analysis of Behavioral Risk Factor Surveillance System micro data files.

Figure 10.7—Prevalence of Young Adults in Arkansas Who Smoke, Adjusted for Demographic Changes, Ages 18 Through 25, 1996 Through 2005

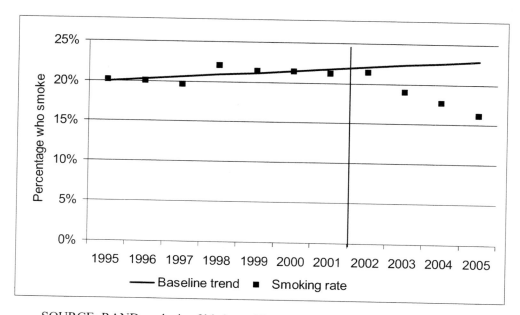

SOURCE: RAND analysis of birth certificate micro data files

Figure 10.8—Prevalence of Pregnant Teens in Arkansas Who Smoke, Adjusted for Demographic Changes, Ages 14 Through 19, 1995 Through 2005

Enforcement of Laws Forbidding Sales of Tobacco Products to Minors

Key Finding: Rates of violation of laws forbidding sales to minors have continued to decline following the dramatic decline reported last year.

Another measure of the effectiveness of educational and outreach efforts by the Tobacco Settlement programs is the trend in compliance with laws that forbid the sale of tobacco products to minors. The Synar data record the compliance of merchants as measured by inspections carried out by undercover underage purchasers. These inspections are carried out at randomly selected stores, with the goal of providing an unbiased estimate of the compliance rate among merchants within the state. Figure 10.9 provides the violation rate from federal fiscal year (FFY) 1997 through FFY2006.[11]

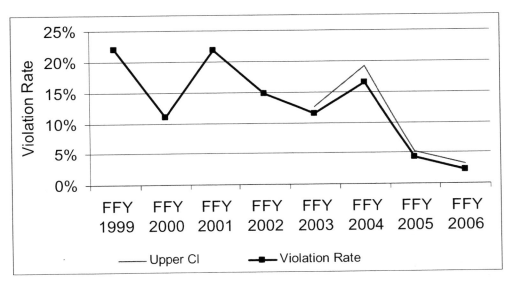

SOURCES: US Department of Health and Human Services, Substance Abuse and Mental Health Services Administration (SAMHSA) and Arkansas Annual Synar Reports for FFY 2003, 2004, 2005, and 2006 (Center for Substance Abuse Prevention, no date-a, no date-b, no date-c, no date-d).

NOTES: Inspections occur during the summer of the preceding calendar year. For example, FFY 2004 violation rate is calculated from inspections primarily conducted during May and June, 2003. Only upper CIs are provided in the published reports.

Figure 10.9—Compliance Rates for Not Selling Tobacco Products to Minors, FFY 1997 through FFY 2006

---

[11] The state reports its Synar data to the federal government by federal fiscal years. Therefore, we also use federal fiscal year (October–September) in presenting results of our analyses of the Synar data; all other analyses are reported by Arkansas fiscal year (July–June).

The results of the Synar inspections have produced violation rates that vary widely from year to year. Some of these variations are due to changes in methods used to perform the inspections and process the resulting data. Figure 10.9 shows a dramatic drop in the violation rate from over 15 percent in FFY2004 to under 5 percent in FFY2005 and FFY2006. The data collection and analysis methods remained virtually unchanged over this three-year span, allowing us to conclude that this drop represents a real decrease in the violation rate. This finding was verified by auditors from the U.S. Substance Abuse and Mental Health Services Administration (SAMHSA), who visited the Division of Health after the recent measures were released (Senner, personal communication, 2006. This finding thus represents a significant change in outcome from what we reported in 2004 (Farley et al., 2005a), which concluded that much of the variation in earlier years appeared to be due to changes in data-collection methods. In summary, earlier, it was difficult to determine whether there had been changes in compliance with the law; the latest evidence shows that changes have occurred.

GEOGRAPHIC ANALYSES FOR TPEP OUTCOMES

Key Finding: TPEP activity has been distributed throughout the state, with some areas receiving substantially more services than others. At this point, there is no evidence that areas with greater TPEP activity are experiencing greater decreases in smoking than areas with less TPEP activity.

Previous analyses examined trends in overall smoking rates across the state for various population groups and tested whether changes in rates of tobacco use are associated with the introduction of the programs supported by the Tobacco Settlement funds. In this section, we examine whether geographic variations in smoking trends and other outcomes are related to geographical patterns of the interventions implemented by TPEP. Due to the short amount of time since the introduction of the Tobacco Settlement funding, we do not expect to find large effects. However, this analysis is tailored to finding local program impacts that might be masked in the statewide data.

Using programming information provided by TPEP, along with data on smoking behaviors from the BRFSS and birth certificates, we examined county-level associations between levels of program effort and changes in smoking for county residents. In addition to the county-level analysis, we aggregated programming efforts to the regional level, using the familiar Area Health Education Center (AHEC) regions of the state, which are listed in Table 10.2. Regional variation in spending is described in Figure 10.10. We do this analysis to capture any impact of programming activities beyond the borders of the county in which an activity is centered. The data and methods are described in Appendix B.

We begin by estimating baseline smoking trends at the county level and the extent to which TPEP targeted its tobacco prevention and cessation activities to counties with high or increasing smoking baseline rates. We then examine whether there is a change in county-level smoking trends after TPEP programming begins, and whether the change in the trend is related to the amount of programming activity. We test the hypothesis that counties with more programming activity will have greater reductions in smoking rates.

It would be good to have additional measures of programming, such as the quality of local programming and the unique challenges faced at the county and regional level. Likewise, it would be useful to have measures of other outcomes, such as attitudes toward smoking.

230

Unfortunately, such data are not available at this time. Although these additional data would provide more detailed information on the mechanisms through which the programming produces reductions in smoking, the analysis we present is adequate to determine whether there is a relationship between resources and the ultimate outcome of smoking. To better understand the underlying mechanisms, these results should be interpreted in the context of the process evaluation information about the program activities presented in Chapter 3.

We estimated a separate outcome trend for each county, based on the level of programming. Since displaying the results of all 75 Arkansas counties would be unwieldy, we predicted outcome trends for representative counties at two different levels of program activity, those with high and low spending on tobacco prevention and cessation interventions. Below, we discuss all of the analyses but provide graphical results only for those relationships that are statistically significant.

Table 10.2
Arkansas Counties by AHEC Region

Region 1 Delta	Region 2 Pine Bluff	Region 3 S. Arkansas	Region 4 Southwest
Chicot	Arkansas	Ashley	Clark
Crittenden	Cleveland	Bradley	Hempstead
Desha	Drew	Calhoun	Howard
Lee	Garland	Columbia	Lafayette
Monroe	Grant	Dallas	Little River
Phillips	Hot Spring	Ouachita	Miller
St. Francis	Jefferson	Union	Nevada
	Lincoln		Pike
	Lonoke		Sevier
	Prairie		
	Saline		

Region 5 Fort Smith	Region 6 Northwest	Region 7 Northeast	Region 8 Pulaski
Conway	Baxter	Clay	Pulaski
Crawford	Benton	Cleburne	
Faulkner	Boone	Craighead	
Franklin	Carroll	Cross	
Johnson	Izard	Fulton	
Logan	Madison	Greene	
Montgomery	Marion	Independence	
Perry	Newton	Jackson	
Polk	Searcy	Lawrence	
Pope	Stone	Mississippi	
Scott	Washington	Poinsett	
Sebastian		Randolph	
Van Buren		Sharp	
Yell		White	
		Woodruff	

Community Grants, School Grants, and Sponsorship Funding

Figure 10.10 presents the regional distribution of combined cumulative annual TPEP per capita spending of the community, school, and sponsorship programs from January 2001 through June 2006. We reported last year that spending through June 2005 varied considerably across the regions. This pattern continues with per capita expenditures in the southwest region approximately twice as high as in the Delta, Pulaski, Pine Bluff, or northeast regions. Examination of the latest increment, represented by the uppermost portion of the bars in Figure 10.10, suggests that funding increased in the Delta and decreased in Fort Smith, to bring these two regions closer to the state average. The southwest, however, continues to receive funds larger than their population share, while the northeast continues to receive a disproportionately small share of the funding. Analysis at the county level demonstrates that the variation among counties also continues to be large.

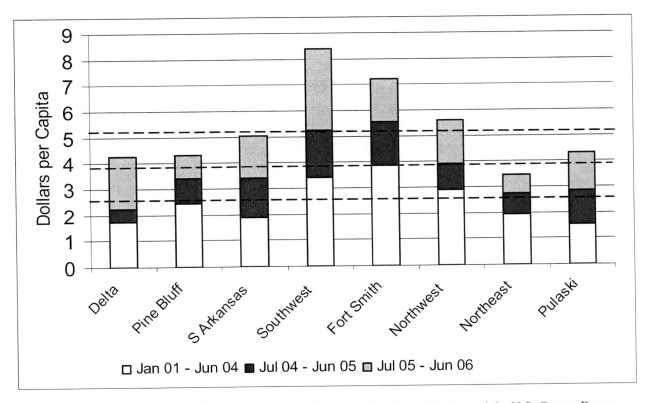

SOURCE: RAND analysis of data provided by the Arkansas Division of Health and the U.S. Census Bureau.

NOTE: The three dashed lines show average per capita spending of $2.58 from January 2001–June 2004, of $3.75 from January 2001–June 2005, and of $5.23 from January 2001–June 2006.

Figure 10.10—Cumulative Spending per Capita for the ADH Tobacco Prevention and Education Program Community Grants, School Grants, and Sponsorship Awards, January 2001–June 2006

As we noted in previous reports, this variation in program spending does not appear to be related to the need for smoking programs. Figure 10.11 updates a figure that was presented in our first report in 2004. It shows that counties with declining smoking rates for pregnant women prior to Tobacco Settlement programming received more funding than counties with flat smoking rates. TPEP has recently produced an analysis of county smoking rates (Baroud, no date). They provide further evidence that funding is not going to areas of need. Northeast and the Delta have among the highest smoking rates but receive little funding.

Figure 10.11 also demonstrates that higher funding in some counties does not appear to lead to greater decreases in smoking. Among pregnant women, counties with lower funding had a steeper drop in their smoking rates. This difference in smoking trends by funding level was statistically significant. This is not to suggest that lower funding produces better results; rather, it may be that areas with low funding could use more resources to take advantage of additional opportunities to reduce smoking.

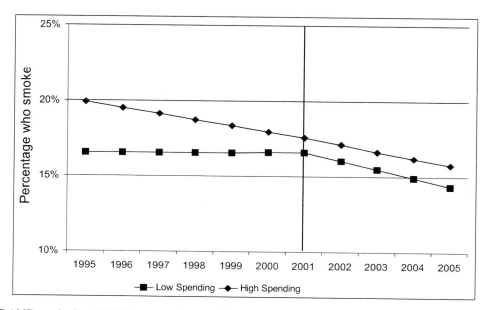

Source: RAND analysis of TPEP per capita spending (2001-2006) and birth certificate data (1995-2005)

Note: High spending county: spending for the (population weighted) 90th percentile. Low spending county: Spending for the (population weighted) 10th percentile.

Figure 10.11—Smoking Trends Among Pregnant Women by County Funding Levels for Tobacco Prevention and Cessation

Arkansas Foundation for Medical Care (AFMC) Clinics

Prior to the reassignment of cessation program funding to the College of Public Health, 15 counties in the state had AFMC cessation programs. We examined the BRFSS and birth certificate data to determine whether there were decreases in the percentage of smokers among residents of these counties following the initiation of the Tobacco Settlement programs. We excluded Pulaski County because the AFMC programs are all located outside of this densely populated county. Neither the BRFSS nor the birth certificate data showed any significant relationship between smoking trends and the presence of AFMC clinics. This finding suggests that these clinics were not reaching a large enough portion of the population to create change at the community level.

ANALYSIS OF SMOKING OUTCOMES IN THE DELTA REGION

Key Finding: There continues to be some weak evidence that smoking among pregnant women in the Delta is above baseline, and smoking among the general population in the Delta is below baseline. Both of these trends should be monitored in years to come.

This outcomes analysis examines trends in smoking behavior for the Delta region, with the goal of assessing whether the combined efforts of several tobacco control programs in this region are affecting smoking behaviors. Although several funded programs are serving the Delta region, the Delta AHEC is the key funded program serving the area. As detailed in Chapter 5, the Delta AHEC provides numerous health education and outreach programs, including smoking cessation programs. Several other Tobacco Settlement programs also serve the Delta region, including the MHI, the TPEP, and the AAI. Therefore, the results of some of our analyses reflect the combined effect of multiple program interventions in this region. We interpret each set of results carefully to ensure that any effects observed are attributed correctly to the program or programs with the most relevant programming.

We tested for deviations from baseline trends in smoking rates, using the BRFSS data for the general adult population, examining the patterns for both the entire population and the youngest adult cohort (ages 18 to 25 years). We performed analyses at both the region and the county level. Because much of the Delta AHEC programming occurs in its centers in Helena, West Memphis, and Lake Village, we also examined whether the three counties in which these centers are located have changes in their trends that differ from the rest of the region. We did not detect any systematic differences among the counties within the Delta, suggesting that any impact that the Delta AHEC programs might be having cannot be measured at the county level.

For all adult smoking rates, we reported in 2004 that trends in smoking rates in the Delta region are very different from the state-level trends, and that smoking rates were declining after start of the Tobacco Settlement programs. In reaching that conclusion, we had assumed that the program effect could be measured as early as 2001. We have since realized that because the Tobacco Settlement programs were not operating at full capacity until early 2002, the earliest that smoking rates are likely to be affected by these programs would be in 2002. The smoking trends in the Delta showed that baseline smoking rates were increasing in the late 1990s and that smoking rates then leveled off or declined after 1999. With the start of full operation of the Tobacco Settlement programs not happening until 2002, we found different baseline trends, and 2001 reductions in smoking would be due to pre-program influences. There is weak evidence that the 2004 and 2005 adult smoking rates are below the baseline trend, but the statistical evidence is not sufficiently strong to conclude that the Tobacco Settlement programs are as yet having a demonstrable effect on adult smoking rates. This incipient trend is promising, and it should be monitored in years to come.

Our analysis of the smoking rates for pregnant women in the Delta also differs from last year. Last year, we found a surprising increase in smoking rates among pregnant women in the Delta. The uptick of almost 5 percentage points was statistically significant. This year, smoking rates for pregnant women again are above the baseline trend, but not nearly as much. This pattern also should be monitored in years to come.

SHORT-TERM HEALTH OUTCOMES

Key Finding: For health conditions that are related to smoking, incidence rates for strokes and heart attacks are significantly reduced since the start of the Tobacco Settlement funding, and trends for pneumonia and asthma show weak evidence of improvement.

The above analysis indicates that the Tobacco Settlement programs are having an impact on vulnerable populations, such as young people and pregnant women. Another vulnerable population consists of people with health conditions that make smoking especially detrimental to their well-being. Although we do not observe reduced smoking among the adult population in general, it is possible that reductions in smoking by people with serious health conditions have led to healthier outcomes among this group. It is also possible that reductions in secondhand smoke brought about by attitude and policy changes have had positive health benefits.

Unfortunately, due to sample size and content limitations, we cannot use the BRFSS or other survey data to examine changes in smoking among people with serious health conditions. However, as we did in our 2004 report, we can examine the number of negative events associated with health conditions that are affected by smoking in the short run. We used the medical literature to guide our selection of conditions.

Some measures of health will respond to decreases in smoking only after a long time. For example, high rates of cancer and emphysema are the result of many years of high smoking rates and will show substantial decreases only after smoking rates have been reduced for many years. Other conditions, however, respond more quickly to changes in smoking behavior.

In consultation with health researchers and in our review of the literature, we identified five health measures that we expect to respond very quickly to reductions in smoking. In 2004, we provided baseline trends for these measures and recommended that they be followed for at least the next ten years. They can be used to confirm imprecise survey-based estimates of smoking reduction and to document the positive benefits from tobacco prevention and cessation programming.

The first of the five measures is the rate of low-birth weight births—the number of births weighing less than 2,500 grams per 100 total births. As reported in a study by Lightwood, Phibbs, and Glantz, maternal smoking contributes to approximately one-quarter of all low weight births (Lightwood, Phibbs, and Glantz, 1999). Reductions in maternal smoking can have an immediate impact on the number of low-weight births. The remaining four measures are based on hospital discharge records. In another article, Lightwood and Glantz document the dramatic drop in the relative risk for strokes and heart attacks (acute myocardial infarctions, or AMI) during the first four years following smoking cessation (Lightwood and Glantz, 1997). The two remaining measures are for pulmonary conditions. Nuorti et al. (2000) find that smoking is the strongest independent risk factor for pneumonia. Asthma has been shown to be aggravated in smokers and by secondhand smoke in nonsmokers (Floreani, 1999). In each of these cases, the literature demonstrates that reducing the prevalence of smoking will lead to rapid decreases in the negative health condition.

Figure 10.12 presents the annual values for each of these measures as well as baseline trends estimated from 1998 through 2001 and an estimated change in trend starting in 2002. The trends in hospitalizations for stroke, AMI, and asthma are showing downward changes in recent years, with the change for stroke and AMI being statistically significant. The rates of low birth weight babies and hospitalizations for pneumonia have not turned down following the initiation of Tobacco Settlement programming.

Of course, all these conditions are influenced by other factors as well. While promising, the downward changes in trend should not be considered as definitive evidence of an impact of Tobacco Settlement programming. In future work, we will use multivariate analysis to explicitly control for other factors that could be affecting the trends to better isolate the effect of the Tobacco Settlement. It would also be useful to compare the trend changes in Arkansas with those in surrounding states, where unmeasured factors are likely to be exerting similar influences, but such an analysis requires resources beyond those available at this time.

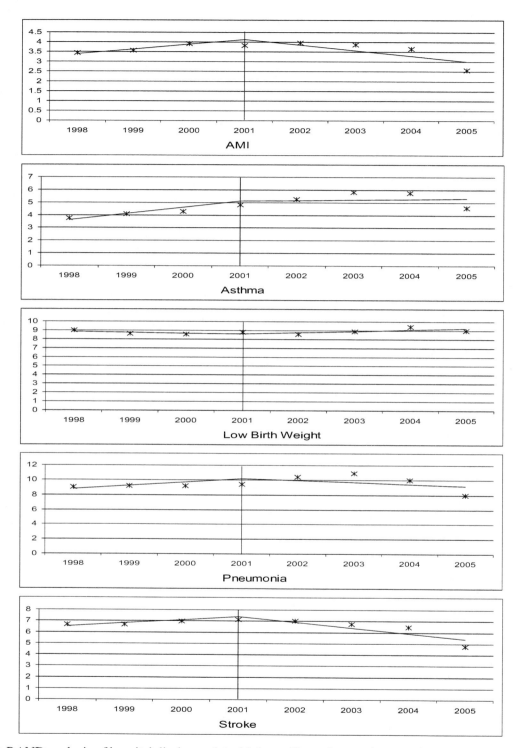

SOURCE: RAND analysis of hospital discharge data, birth certificate data, and census data.

NOTE: The marks for AMI, asthma, pneumonia, and stroke show the number of hospital discharges in each year per 1,000 people in Arkansas for the diagnosis. The marks for low birth weight show the number of low-birth-weight births in each year per 100 total births in Arkansas. The baseline trend lines for each condition are estimated from the first four years of data (1998–2001). The change in trend is statistically significant for AMI and stroke.

Figure 10.12—Short-Term Health Indicators, Baseline Trends, and Early Deviations

DISCUSSION

With another year of experience and data for the tobacco control activities supported by the Tobacco Settlement funds, we are finding conclusive evidence of decreases in smoking among young people, especially young pregnant women. We also find much lower violations of laws prohibiting cigarette sales to minors. Our analysis of short-term health outcomes provides promising evidence of improvements for people with smoking-related health conditions. Results remain mixed, however, with no conclusive evidence yet available for many of the measures, including smoking incidence among middle-aged and older adults. We expect that, with continued support of the statewide tobacco control activities as well as additional reinforcement through the just-passed Clean Indoor Air Act, additional progress can be made toward achieving the goal of healthy Arkansans.

Chapter 11
Evaluation of Nonsmoking Outcomes

This chapter presents a variety of outcome measures for the programs receiving Tobacco Settlement funding. Five programs involve delivery of health-related services. Two of them—the Tobacco Prevention and Education Program and the Medicaid Expansion Programs—operate at the state level, so their outcomes are measured at the state level. The remaining three programs—the Delta AHEC, Minority Health Initiative, and Arkansas Aging Initiative—provide services at the local or regional level. Therefore, outcome evaluations for these programs require analysis of primary data gathered on the experience of their participants as well as analysis of secondary administrative and survey data that describe the behaviors and health status of their entire target populations.

Two of the Tobacco Settlement programs—the College of Public Health and the Arkansas Biosciences Institute—are academic initiatives for which impacts on the health of Arkansans will occur either indirectly or in the future. Thus, our evaluation of their effects will focus on intermediate outcomes that are stepping stones to that ultimate goal.

Impacts of the TPEP program are smoking outcomes that are addressed in Chapter 10. This chapter provides our outcomes analysis for each of the other six programs. In last year's report, we presented plans for many new measures for these six programs. Initial results are available for most of these measures and are presented below.

We also report on the efforts of the service-providing programs to collect and analyze outcomes data on their participants. All of the programs have plans for such analysis, but none is making adequate progress. By this time, all of the service-delivery programs should have an evaluation apparatus in use for tracking their outcomes. We report on the steps each of these programs has taken to collect data on program participants, to design evaluations, and to report their findings.

OUTCOMES FOR THE DELTA AHEC

Key Findings: The Delta AHEC has made progress on the collection of participant data, including satisfaction and health outcomes information. However, progress has been slow on the management and analysis of these data. We encourage the program to direct additional resources toward assuring that data are collected and stored in a manner that lends itself to analyses that can be used to monitor program progress and evaluate participant outcomes.

Tobacco settlement funding to the Delta AHEC supports many health education and training programs. Its most advanced health care intervention is the diabetes clinic and education program in Helena. In addition, it runs a wide variety of health education programs for community members and continuing education programs for health professionals.

When we began our outcomes evaluation in 2004, we examined the effect of Delta AHEC programming on teen pregnancy and on prenatal care. Although the tobacco settlement resources the Delta AHEC devotes to programs affecting these outcomes are relatively small, we chose to examine these outcomes because we believed it was possible that the programs might have an effect fairly quickly and because we were able to get good outcomes data. We did not find an effect on these outcomes in either 2004 or 2005. We do not update this analysis in this year's report, because continuing to analyze these outcomes places too much emphasis on a relatively small portion of the Delta AHEC's programming effort.

In last year's report, we described plans for a new outcomes evaluation based on participant data that the Delta AHEC was planning to collect. The Delta AHEC reports that progress have been very slow on implementing these plans, due to loss of key staff and the demands placed on staff for completing and moving into their new building.

The data collection for the community education program is under way as a part of the statewide AHEC system. The statewide system has been modified to incorporate community education participation and satisfaction data for the Delta AHEC; other AHECs focus almost exclusively on continuing education for health care professionals. Although this system is now actively accepting data from the AHECs, no reports or analyses are available from the Delta AHEC at this time.

Progress on collecting clinical data from participants in the Helena diabetes program has been disappointing. Although the program has been certified by the American Diabetes Association (ADA), the original database only allowed for up to one year of information on participants. This posed a serious constraint for the program because many participants continue with the program beyond one year. Therefore, the program switched to a new database that allowed it to record and retain data for a longer period. Unfortunately, the new system has not been fully used owing to staff turnover. Although some data have been entered, no reports have been generated. The staff is attempting to remedy this problem in time for the application for renewed ADA certification later this summer.

By not having access to the participant data for its clinical and education programs, the Delta AHEC is missing important opportunities to monitor its progress and to demonstrate its successes to potential participants and regulatory bodies. The program needs to direct additional resources toward developing a database and acquiring expertise to assist with outcome analysis.

OUTCOMES FOR THE MINORITY HEALTH INITIATIVE

Key Findings: MHI has data on outcomes for two out of three counties for its Hypertension Initiative program participants, but no data for its Eating and Moving for Life program. RAND analysis demonstrates a possible effect of the hypertension program on blood pressure. MHI should improve its data collection in both programs and improve its data analysis capabilities.

The two main community interventions of the Minority Health Initiative are the Eating and Moving for Life program and the Hypertension program. Both programs are designed to improve the health status of Arkansans with respect to health conditions that are particularly prevalent in minority communities. We did not assess outcomes for MHI in our 2004 report because we were focusing at that time on state-level outcomes. In 2005, we reported on plans for data collection and analysis for both of these interventions. The hypertension program has produced useful participant data in two of the three counties in which it operates. Below, we review the data, provide some analysis, and suggest ways for MHI to expand upon this effort.

Participant Data Collection and Analysis

The Minority Health Initiative is currently moving into the second version of participant data collection protocols in both the Eating and Moving and Hypertension Initiative programs. In the following sections, we discuss the existing data-collection efforts, MHI's plans for improvement, and our suggested analyses. (See Chapter 7 for details on the programs.)

Hypertension and Stroke Prevention and Education

The hypertension program (as it is most commonly called) operates through Community Health Centers (CHC) in Lee, Chicot, and Crittenden counties. The program provides screening for hypertension and enrolls hypertensive individuals who do not have other resources for appropriate health care. It provides case management and medication for enrollees. Hypertension stages for these individuals are defined by the American Heart Association, as shown in Table 11.1.

Table 11.1
Blood Pressure Categories Recommended by the American Heart Association

Blood Pressure Category	Systolic Pressure (mm Hg)		Diastolic Pressure (mm HG)
Normal	Less than 120	and	Less than 80
Prehypertension	120-139	or	80–89
High:			
Stage 1	140-159	or	90–99
Stage 2	160 or higher	or	100 or higher

MHI has required data collection by local program administrators since the initiation of the program. MHI provided spreadsheet templates and instructions for data entry to local staff. However, data were collected inconsistently, so they could not be processed in a standardized way. MHI attributed this situation to changes in program personnel and periodic changes made to the data-collection forms. The MHI epidemiologist reformatted the data for two of the counties, resulting in information that RAND used to produce the following analysis of the outcomes of participants in the West Memphis and Lee programs.

Based on data received in March and April of this year, the two programs had enrolled a total of 585 participants between March 2003 and October 2005. Table 11.2 shows how many of them were at various stages of hypertension upon their first visit and the percentage who returned for more than one visit. For participants with hypertension, the return rates were correlated with severity. Later, we note that improvement was also correlated with severity.

Table 11.2
Participants in MHI Hypertension Program in West Memphis and Lee Counties, March 2003—October 2005

| | Hypertension Stage at First Visit | | | | | |
	Normal	Pre-hypertensive	High (Stage 1)	High (Stage 2)	Missing	Total
Total enrollment	27	95	169	287	7	585
Percent age who returned for at least one follow up visit	59	44	51	60	43	55

SOURCE: RAND analysis of data provided by MHI.

Table 11.3 provides information on changes in the blood pressure categories for enrollees from their entry to their last recorded visit. It shows that over two-thirds of enrollees who began the program in the worst category improved at least one category by their last recorded visit. Almost half of the participants in the second-to-worst category improved at least one category by their last visit. In additional analysis (not shown), we found that longer participation led to greater improvements in blood pressure.

Table 11.3
Changes in Blood Pressure for Hypertension Program Enrollees, by Hypertension Category

| | Hypertension Stage at Start of Enrollment | | |
	Pre-hypertensive	High (Stage 1)	High (Stage 2)
Number of patients	42	86	173
Percentage who:			
Got better	12	42	71
Stayed the same	57	34	29
Got worse	31	24	a

SOURCE: RAND analysis of data provided by MHI

NOTES: Contains all MHI Hypertension and Stroke Prevention and Education enrollees who participated for at least two visits. Blood pressure categories are defined in Table 11.1.

a. indicates that no one in this category could get worse because Stage 2 is the worst category.

We reported last year that MHI is in the final stages of testing a new data system for the hypertension program. The data system is being developed by the UAMS information technology department and is currently being tested by the CHC program coordinators. It is Web-based, with all data being stored centrally on a UAMS server. The data will be entered through structured templates by program staff after each encounter and will contain subject demographics, personal history, family history, and risk factors as well as tracking visits, medications, and test results for participants. We were told last year that the system was expected to be fully implemented during the summer of 2005. The data system is still not ready, but MHI staff remains optimistic that it will be ready shortly. We believe that such a system would bring opportunities for oversight and evaluation, but are concerned about the ongoing delay. We also suggest that greater effort be made to collect information on participants who do not return for second visits, in order to understand the barriers to continued participation.

Eating and Moving for Life

The second major program operated by MHI is the Eating and Moving for Life program. We were not able to obtain any data for participants in this program. MHI needs to improve its data-collection efforts and work with local experts to analyze outcomes for this program in accordance with our recommendations from last year.

Over Both Programs

In last year's report, we outlined a series of data analyses that we thought would be useful for understanding the progress of MHI's programs and participants. Our analysis of the hypertension program data demonstrates that such analysis is possible given current data. We recommend that MHI work closely with local experts, perhaps from the College of Public Health, to analyze participant data so as to understand what gains have been made and what challenges remain.

OUTCOMES FOR THE ARKANSAS AGING INITIATIVE

Key Findings: There is some evidence that the Centers on Aging (COAs) have reinforced the decline in avoidable hospitalizations in the counties where they are located. AAI data collection and analysis initiatives are making some progress toward providing useful evaluation of their programs.

As described in Chapter 6, the AAI is charged with providing the elderly with community-based education and support through its regional centers. In addition, these centers have enabled the establishment of affiliated senior health care clinics, so they have increased access to health care for the elderly. Finally, the centers offer educational programs to health care professionals treating the elderly. The outcome measures for the AAI are selected to assess its effects on these missions.

Update on Outcomes for Avoidable Hospitalizations

In the 2004 Biennial Report, we used data on inpatient stays to estimate baseline trends for avoidable hospitalization rates among elders for the counties containing the COA facilities. In its seminal study on access to health care in America, the Institute of Medicine (1993) argued that timely and appropriate outpatient care would reduce the likelihood of hospitalizations for ambulatory care–sensitive conditions. Since that study, measures of the rates of avoidable hospitalizations have been used in many analyses to demonstrate the effect of changing the availability and quality of primary care on subsequent health outcomes (Bindman et al., 2003).

We employed the definition of avoidable hospitalizations developed by McCall et al. (2001) to study the incidence of avoidable hospitalizations in Medicare+Choice–managed care plans. From a review of the literature, they identified 15 ambulatory care– sensitive conditions and performed a clinical review of those conditions to determine if they would apply to an elderly population. They developed three groups of avoidable hospitalizations: chronic, acute, and preventable. The conditions used to define avoidable hospitalizations are presented in Table 11.4.

A hospital stay was deemed avoidable if a code for one of these diagnoses was listed on the discharge abstract as the primary diagnosis for that stay. For each beneficiary, the total number of avoidable hospitalizations for chronic, acute, and preventive conditions was obtained from the hospital discharge file. We identified the population ages 65 and older who had one or more avoidable hospitalizations in each year from 1998 through 2005.

Table 11.4
Avoidable Hospitalization Conditions

Chronic Conditions	Preventable Conditions	Acute Conditions
Asthma/COPD	Malnutrition	Cellulitis
Seizure Disorder	Influenza	Dehydration
CHF		Gastric or duodenal ulcer
Diabetes		Urinary tract infection
Hypertension		Bacterial pneumonia
		Severe ENT infection
		Hypoglycemia
		Hypokalemia

We performed our baseline analysis of avoidable hospitalization rates in anticipation that these trends will be altered in future years by education activities and increased access to quality primary care brought about by AAI programming. In our benchmark analysis, we found that even prior to the opening of the COAs, the counties in which these facilities were located had lower rates of avoidable hospitalizations for acute and preventative conditions than the remainder of the state, but that rates were increasing everywhere.

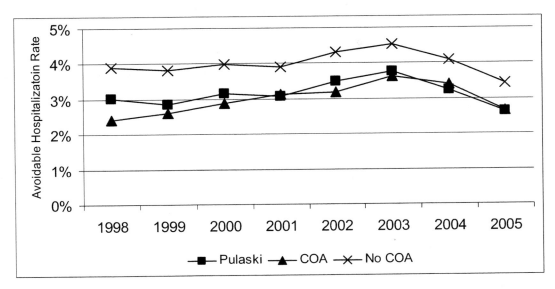

Figure 11.1—Fraction of Elderly with at Least One Avoidable Hospitalization for Preventable and Acute Conditions, Comparison of Counties

Our analysis of more recent data presented in Figure 11.1 indicates that avoidable hospitalizations for the elderly have been declining recently across the state. Prior to 2003, the trend upward had been steeper for counties with COAs than for counties without COAs. Therefore, the similar downward trend since 2003 represents a larger deviation from baseline for the counties with COAs. Although this finding is consistent with a positive impact of the COAs, this difference is not statistically significant. We will continue to monitor these trends as more data accumulate.

Aging Initiative Analysis of Outcomes

Last year, we reported that the AAI was making great strides in collecting and analyzing participant data and in designing additional studies with collaborators. These advances continue, albeit with delays that are typical in a program that is growing and learning. The AAI developed and implemented a database in which all COAs record counts and basic demographic characteristics of participants in all educational events. Although no outcome information is recorded in this database, the systematic information on participants will enable other data (e.g., BRFSS, hospital claims) to be used to investigate population outcomes in areas with substantial programming activity.

In June 2005, an evaluation of AAI by the Lewin Group was released (Lewin Group, 2005). This evaluation included anecdotal satisfaction measures based on focus groups of consumers and providers in five of the COAs. The evaluation found that consumers were very satisfied with both clinic services and educational programming. The provider focus groups were less conclusive, in part because it is difficult to determine whether the programming has had a real impact on provider practices and in part because of limited participation by physicians in the focus groups. Although the positive findings about consumer satisfaction are not necessarily representative of all AAI consumers, the details in the Lewin report provide some insight into successful AAI activities.

In order to get more representative information about consumer satisfaction, a researcher affiliated with COPH undertook a survey of elders participating in AAI education programs using an innovative instrument designed to reach a population in which many people have limited literacy. The survey indicated overwhelming satisfaction with the education programs. However, the instrument was too "blunt" to provide much useful information for improving the programming. The AAI plans to build on this experience to do additional survey work with the goal of implementing survey instruments that permit respondents to make finer distinctions among program attributes.

The AAI also plans to conduct a large survey of health professionals who attended educational programming. Funding limitations caused a planned survey of 3,700 health professionals to be delayed from last year to this coming year. In conversations with AAI leadership, we have expressed concerns about low response rates in previous surveys and about the difficulty of gleaning useful information when a single survey instrument is administered to individuals with diverse professional backgrounds who attend a wide variety of educational programming. We look forward to reviewing the results of the planned survey in next year's report.

In an ingenious move to examine outcomes among program participants, researchers affiliated with the AAI and COPH revised and greatly improved a proposal to study diabetic care and outcomes in three senior clinics associated with the AAI. The study will compare outcomes for elders in the interdisciplinary geriatric care settings associated with the COAs to outcomes for elders in traditional primary care clinics. This study is an example of the type of rigorous evaluation that all the service-providing programs should be undertaking. This proposal has been submitted to ABI and a decision regarding funding is pending.

OUTCOMES FOR THE MEDICAID EXPANSION PROGRAMS

Because the Medicaid Expansion Programs provide additional Medicaid benefits to eligible beneficiaries across the state, our outcome analysis examines potential program effects statewide. In the 2004 evaluation report, we reported results for effects of each of the three operational expansion programs—benefits for pregnant women, hospital benefits, and AR-Seniors. In this section, we update our findings.

Expanded Benefits for Pregnant Women

Key Findings: We continue to find that the expansion of benefits for pregnant women has led to increased prenatal care. We find NO evidence that the expansion has reduced smoking among pregnant women or increased birth weights of their babies.

One component of the Medicaid expansion provides benefits to pregnant women whose income is between 133 percent and 200 percent of the federal poverty level. We examine the extent to which this benefit led to better prenatal care for pregnant women in Arkansas. This analysis supplements the spending analysis for the Medicaid expansion presented in Chapter 9. The spending analysis demonstrates the extent to which pregnant women used the new benefit.

The analysis presented here examines whether the benefit led to additional care rather than to a shift to Medicaid from other payment sources.

For information on prenatal visit utilization, we use the number of prenatal visits reported on birth certificates. Adequate prenatal care was defined as having at least ten prenatal care visits during the pregnancy.

The birth certificate data do not contain information on Medicaid status, so we used county-level data on poverty status as a proxy for concentrations of Medicaid recipients. (There also were no county-level data on the percentage of the population receiving the expanded Medicaid for pregnant women.) The U.S. Census Bureau provides estimates of the percentage of the counties' population in each of several categories defined by the ratio of income to the poverty level. Using the categories that are most closely aligned with the benefit change, we calculated the percentage of the population in each county with income between 125 percent and 200 percent of the federal poverty level. We then examined whether there were increases in the percentage of women who had adequate prenatal care, and whether any increases were positively related to the percentage of the county population in this poverty category.

The analysis used data for all pregnant women in all counties in the state, and trends for the baseline and program periods were estimated. Then trends were projected for representative counties at the 10th and 90th percentiles of poverty levels for the county distribution, which are shown in Figure 11.2. The 10th percentile represents a county with 13.9 percent of people in the poverty range targeted by the Medicaid expansion, and the 90th percentile represents a county with 20.7 percent of people in that range.

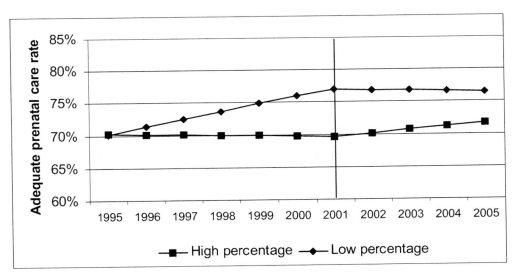

SOURCE: RAND analysis of birth certificate data and U.S. Census Bureau data.

Figure 11.2—Use of Adequate Prenatal Care Visits, for Counties with High and Low Percentages of People Eligible for Expanded Medicaid Benefits, Adjusted for Age, Sex, and Race, 1995 Through 2005

In a finding similar to those of 2004 and 2005, we found that after the Medicaid expansion was introduced, rates of women receiving adequate prenatal care increased in counties with higher percentages of people in the defined poverty category. During the baseline period (2001 and earlier, represented by the vertical line in the figure), the percentages of pregnant women receiving adequate prenatal care decreased over time in counties with higher percentages of people in the defined poverty range. At the same time, the percentages receiving adequate prenatal care increased over time in counties with lower percentages of people in the poverty range. When the Tobacco Settlement programs started, the trends reversed, and since 2001, prenatal care has increased in counties with more women in the targeted poverty range. The most recent data from 2005 show that this trend is continuing, and this finding remains statistically significant.

We used a similar method to determine whether pregnant women's smoking rates or newborn birth weights improved in counties with more pregnant women eligible for the expanded Medicaid benefit. We found no evidence of either effect, suggesting that additional steps should be taken to strengthen the impact of prenatal care on pregnant women's behavior and birth outcomes.

Expanded Medicaid Hospital Benefit

Key Findings: We find some evidence that one component of the expanded hospital benefit is associated with increased access to hospital care for conditions requiring very short stays. The other component, which reimburses for hospital days 21 through 24, appears to be reducing the amount of unreimbursed care rather than increasing the amount of care.

The expansion of the hospital benefit in November 2001 increased the amount that Medicaid could compensate hospitals by reducing the co-payment for the first hospital day of the benefit year from 22 percent to 10 percent and extending the maximum number of reimbursable inpatient days per year from 20 to 24 days. The impact on health outcomes for Arkansans from this benefit is difficult to predict or measure. Charges that are not reimbursed by Medicaid are the responsibility of the patient, but in practice, hospitals collect a very small fraction of these unreimbursed charges from patients.

If hospitals, doctors, and patients took the amount of Medicaid coverage into account when deciding among health care options, it is possible that the expanded payment could lead to more days of hospital care. Alternatively, the benefit expansion could lead to a decrease in out-of-pocket payments by Medicaid recipients or a decrease in the amount of unreimbursed care provided by hospitals, without having any significant impact on days of hospitalization. In this analysis, we work with state hospital discharge data to examine whether the benefit expansion had a direct impact on number of days of hospitalization for Medicaid recipients.

Our hypothesis is that if the reduction in the Medicaid co-payment is having an effect, it will occur primarily as an increase in the number of short hospital stays. If a condition is serious enough to merit a long hospital stay, it is unlikely to be influenced by a relatively small change in the cost of the first day of hospitalization. To test this hypothesis, we examined the distribution of cumulative hospital days for all patients for whom Medicaid is the primary payer for at least one hospital stay, to assess whether there has been an increase in the fraction of Medicaid hospital stays of very short duration. The Medicaid trends were compared to the trend for patients who have not received Medicaid.

Figure 11.3 presents information about short hospital stays for Medicaid patients relative to other patients. Prior to the reduction of the first day co-pay at the end of 2001, we see that the proportion of one-day stays is decreasing and two-day stays are increasing for Medicaid patients. After the reduction in co-pay, there was no further decrease in the proportion of one-day stays. This finding is consistent with what would be expected if patients, doctors, and hospitals were responsive to the higher payments for the first day and increased admissions for conditions requiring a very short stay.

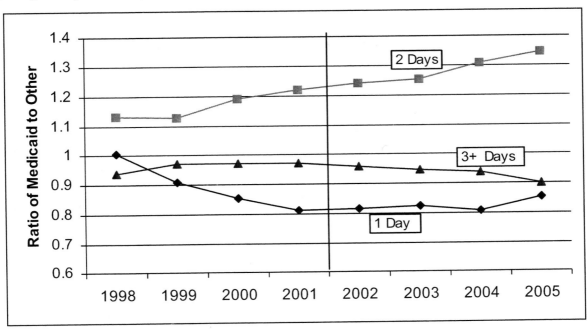

SOURCE: RAND analysis of Arkansas inpatient hospital discharge records.

Figure 11.3—Ratio of Medicaid to Other Hospital Stays by Length of Stay for Stays of Six Days or Less

To examine the effect of extending hospital benefits from 20 to 24 days per year, we looked at the number of inpatient days for people who had at least 19 days of hospitalization. We examined whether the increased benefit increased the proportion of these people who had between 21 and 24 days of total hospitalization.

Figure 11.4 presents information on long hospital stays for Medicaid recipients relative to others. There is no evidence that stays between 21 and 24 days are becoming more common for Medicaid recipients. Indeed, the opposite of the expected effect is seen. Non-Medicaid patients rather than Medicaid patients have an increased tendency to use days 21 through 24 of hospitalization. Therefore, we conclude that the extended coverage is not increasing the amount of hospitalization for the very ill.

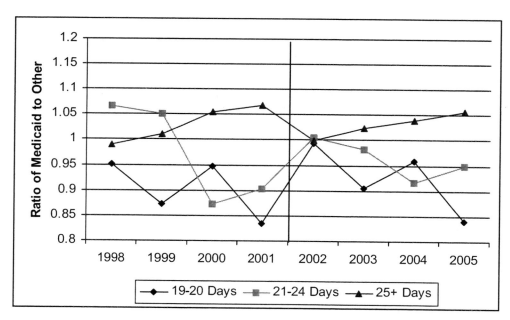

SOURCE: RAND analysis of Arkansas inpatient hospital discharge records.

Figure 11.4—Ratio of Medicaid to Other Hospital Stays by Length of Stays for Stays of 19 Days or More

These analyses lead us to conclude that the expansion of Medicaid hospital payments appears to have had a minor effect on the number of persons receiving hospital care for conditions requiring a very short stay. The lack of impact on long stays suggests that the benefit expansion is offsetting some previously unreimbursed costs for hospitals for patients who stay in the hospital longer than 20 days.

Medicaid AR-Seniors

Key Findings: There is weak evidence that the AR-Seniors program has accelerated the decline in avoidable hospitalizations among the elderly. We will monitor this incipient trend in future years.

In October 2002, tobacco funds were used to extend Medicaid benefits to people ages 65 and older who had incomes below 75 percent of the federal poverty level.[12] Increased access to quality medical care is expected to improve the health status of elderly Arkansans. Among the many consequences of poor access to primary care services is an increased likelihood of avoidable hospitalizations. In its seminal study on access to health care in America, the Institute of Medicine (1993) argued that timely and appropriate outpatient care would reduce the likelihood of hospitalizations for ambulatory care–sensitive conditions (see Table 11.4).

We examine here whether the number of avoidable hospitalizations is affected by the implementation of the AR-Seniors benefit. A greater decline in avoidable hospitalizations in

---

[12] The income limit for the AR-Seniors program subsequently was increased to 80 percent of the federal poverty level, which went into effect on January 1, 2003.

locations with more eligible seniors would be evidence that the benefit was contributing to improved health outcomes. We perform a county-level analysis that estimates the baseline trend in avoidable hospitalizations among the elderly and examines whether there is a deviation from the trend that is related to the percentage of county residents with income less than 75 percent of the poverty level.

Figure 11.5 graphs the estimated baseline trends in avoidable hospitalizations for the older population in representative counties with high and low rates of poverty, where a high-poverty county has 14.8 percent of the population with income below 75 percent of the federal poverty level (90th percentile) and a low-poverty county has 6.5 percent of the population with income below 75 percent of the federal poverty level (10th percentile). In addition, our estimates of the trend in avoidable hospitalization rates following implementation of the AR-Seniors benefit for those representative counties are shown on the graph. These results are for avoidable hospitalizations due to preventable or acute conditions.

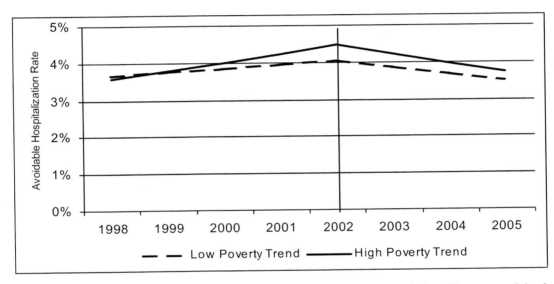

NOTE: High Poverty County: 14.8 percent of the population has income below 75 percent of the federal poverty level (90th percentile, population weighted). Low Poverty County: 6.5 percent of the population has income below 75 percent of the federal poverty level (10th percentile, population weighted).

Figure 11.5—Percentage of Elderly with at Least One Avoidable Hospitalization for Preventable and Acute Conditions, by Counties with High and Low Poverty Rates

Before the AR-Seniors benefit started at the end of 2002 (noted by the vertical line in Figure 11.3), avoidable hospitalizations were increasing in high-poverty counties and were relatively constant in low-poverty counties. Following the implementation of the benefit expansion, the rates turned down in all counties. The reduction in the high-poverty trend was somewhat greater, although the difference among counties due to their amount of poverty is not statistically significant. We obtained similar results for avoidable hospitalizations from chronic conditions. This analysis will be continued as more years of data are collected.

APPROACH FOR ASSESSING OUTCOMES FOR ACADEMIC PROGRAMS

Two of the programs supported by the Arkansas Tobacco Settlement funds—the College of Public Health (COPH) and the Arkansas Biosciences Institute (ABI)—are academic programs that are helping to build the health infrastructure in the state. Although these programs are expected to have large effects on the health of Arkansans, the effects are expected to be very long term ones, requiring many years before the programs' research, service, and training activities have measurable effects on health status. Therefore, our outcome evaluation is focusing on tracking the quality of their research, as measured by its impacts on the relevant scientific fields, and assessing how well the programs disseminate knowledge to the scientific community and targeted populations around the state.

We base our evaluation on a framework developed by our RAND colleagues for the evaluation of likely payoff from research investments (Wooding, 2004). The returns from research fall into the following categories:

1. Knowledge production

2. Research targeting and capacity building

3. Informing policy and product development

4. Health and health sector benefits

5. Wider economic benefits

We propose to measure knowledge production by using Journal Impact Factors to provide an approximate measure of the likely impact of research publications on furthering their specific areas of knowledge. We measure research targeting and capacity building by verifying that areas of research are consistent with intent of the act and by recording the communities from which students come and where they go. We measure the last three types of benefits by undertaking a qualitative review of selected projects to provide independent verification that they are likely to lead to payoffs of these types.

As described in last year's report, we are introducing two new measures for these programs. The first is an analysis of each institution's research publications, which is intended to track the quality of their research output. A crucial step in leveraging quality research is publishing findings in recognized scientific journals that are judged by scientific peers to be an indicator of quality research, which is worthy of building on and funding. We expect each institution to place more of publications in more prestigious scholarly journals with each passing year.

The second measure is an in-depth review of two exemplary projects from ABI and two from COPH—projects that they judge to be among their most promising work. This review of their prized work is intended as an independent verification of whether they are indeed producing work at the highest levels. High-quality research is likely to eventually produce a positive impact on the health of Arkansans because it is likely to generate new scientific discoveries, new clinical techniques, and new methods for translating these discoveries into quality health care. Furthermore, high-quality research will draw attention to the state that can be used to bring in additional research funds from national sources, as well as commercial activities that can lead to more jobs, better opportunities, and higher incomes.

Journal Impact Factor Analysis

Measuring the knowledge production of funded research requires making predictions about the extent to which a current research project will become the building block for future clinical and policy changes that will improve the health of Arkansans. Using Journal Impact Factors (JIFs) allows us to leverage the scientific reviews made by scholarly journals. JIFs measure the rate at which scholars have cited a journal's recent articles. A high citation rate indicates that scholars have judged the journal's articles to be of high scientific quality and therefore worth referencing in their own work. The JIF for a journal tends to be relatively stable over time because high-quality journals receive more submissions from which the editors and peer reviewers can select the best scientific work. If an ABI or COPH study is accepted in a high-JIF journal, that indicates that it has been judged to be of high scientific quality and likely to have an impact on the field. Therefore, we summarize the JIFs for journals in which ABI and COPH studies are published to track the likely impact of the research. Although the JIF is not a perfect measure of scientific quality, it has many advantages, including providing timely information and being low cost.

The Institute for Scientific Information (ISI), the producer of JIFs, assigns every journal that it rates to one or more subject categories, such as infectious diseases or health policy and services. Our quality measures are based on the ranking of journals within their subject categories. The citation rates measured by the JIFs differ dramatically among subjects because styles of scholarly writing and citation behavioral norms differ across subjects. However, JIFs provide a useful ranking of journals *within* a subject, so we can base our measures on whether funded research leads to publications in the top five or top ten journals in its subject.

Note that not all publications are in journals that are included in the ISI's citation index. Journals and other publication venues that do not receive JIF ratings tend to be non–peer reviewed, of minimal circulation, or rarely cited by other scientific journals. While publications in non-JIF rated venues can contribute to the research process, research published in ranked journals is likely to have a greater eventual effect on the well-being of Arkansans. Therefore, we define the following four quality levels of publications:

1. Publications in journals ranked in the top five by subject
2. Publications in journals ranked between top five and top ten by subject
3. Publications in journals ranked below top ten by subject
4. Publications in journals or other venues not ranked by ISI

As the quality of research produced by the funded programs increases over time, we expect an increase in the number of publications in top-five and top-ten journals.

Exemplary Project Review

To complement the quantitative analysis of publications, we undertook a review of two projects identified by COPH and two by ABI as exemplary of their contribution to improving the health of Arkansans, either now or in the future. We include this component in the outcomes evaluation in recognition that quantitative measures often miss some of the truly important aspects of an organization's work. Furthermore, the greatest impact of any institution may be better represented by the "home runs" hit by the stars of the organization than by the average performance that is usually the subject of quantitative analysis.

We first developed a set of criteria by which the exemplary projects would be reviewed. These criteria differed slightly between COPH and ABI, given the different missions and goals of the two institutions. Each criteria set referred to the goals set forth in the Initiated Act for the program as well as the mission statement and other materials developed by the programs to refine their approaches to fulfilling these goals. The criteria also referred to the five "returns from research" categories outlined above. In the case of COPH, the criteria also drew upon the literature regarding evaluation of community-based participatory research (CBPR), the type of research that COPH is emphasizing in its program.

In the next step, each of the institutions nominated four projects for consideration by RAND. They were instructed to choose projects that they thought would rank highly based on the criteria. COPH, was told that two should be CBPR projects. The institutions submitted brief descriptions of the nominated projects to RAND. From these projects, the RAND project team chose two from each institution that we believed would demonstrate the breadth of the institutions' activities.

For each of the selected projects, the two institutions submitted packets to RAND that included detailed project descriptions and a variety of documents that the projects had produced, including proposals, working papers, reports, and published articles. The packets also included lists of potential reviewers.

Two experts reviewed each project. A RAND researcher who was familiar with the project's subject matter did one of them. These reviewers were not members of RAND's Arkansas Tobacco Settlement Evaluation team, but were chosen specifically because of their subject matter expertise. The RAND reviewers also suggested reviewers from outside of RAND to perform the second review for each project. The RAND task leader then sought out an acceptable external reviewer, beginning with experts suggested by RAND's reviewers. In only one case was the external reviewer someone who had been suggested by the Arkansas project staff rather than by the RAND reviewer. The reviews are summarized below.

OUTCOMES FOR COLLEGE OF PUBLIC HEALTH

Key Findings: COPH's number of high-quality scholarly publications have increased substantially. Independent reviews of two of their leading projects confirm that COPH is making major contributions toward the health of Arkansans.

COPH is a new unit within the University of Arkansas for Medical Sciences, created with Tobacco Settlement funds. Like most academic units, it has the triple mission of providing education, research, and service. Its leadership and faculty take pride in the community-oriented way in which they work toward all three components of the COPH mission. By engaging in community-based participatory research, they are using a research method that is recognized to create academic-community partnerships—thereby improving outcomes and reducing disparities in the process of creating knowledge (National Center for Biotechnology Information, 2004). However, community-based research leads to a diversity of activities that makes it especially challenging to define specific direct measures of the effect of COPH's work. Therefore, relying on peer-review methods embodied in the Journal Impact Factors and the review of exemplary projects is particularly necessary.

Journal Impact Factors

Table 11.5 provides our analysis of the JIF of COPH publications for 2004 and 2005. It shows that COPH increased the number of publications that it placed in journals ranked among the top five in their subject areas. The number of publications in journals ranked between six and ten remained constant, while the overall number of publications in journals of any rank approximately doubled. This suggests that COPH is not only producing more publications, but that it is producing higher quality publications.

Table 11.5
Journal Impact Factor Rankings for COPH Publications

Ranking	2004	2005
Top five	7	12
Six through ten	5	5
Ranked below ten	12	31
Not ranked	10	21
Total	34	69

NOTE: Ranks based on highest within-subject ranking of Journal Impact Factor for each published (including accepted and in-press) article.

Qualitative Analysis of Exemplary Projects

The two projects that were chosen from the four nominated by COPH are (1) an evaluation of the implementation of Act 1220 on childhood obesity and (2) a CBPR project intended to link disabled people with the resources to help them continue to reside in the community. Both projects aim at contributing toward the long-range goal of elevating the overall ranking of the health status of Arkansas, as set forth in the Initiated Act.

The Act 1220 evaluation project was reviewed by an economist from RAND and a professor in the Department of Policy Analysis and Management the Cornell University College of Human Ecology. Both of these reviewers found the evaluation of Act 1220 to be of "high quality" and of "impressive comprehensiveness." One reviewer stated, "This is a model evaluation." The other noted, "Findings from this research will add greatly to the body of knowledge in the field of childhood obesity and will help identify effective policies and strategies to combat this important health concern." It was pointed out that a successful evaluation could help refine the ability of policies to improve the health of Arkansans.

The CBPR project was reviewed by a health services researcher from RAND and a physician from the UCLA School of Public Health. The first reviewer found that the CBPR project linking individuals to home care services was "a well-functioning and much-needed collaborative venture on the parts of seasoned and committed investigators. The project objectives are consistent with the COPH mission and the program focus described." The second reviewer noted that the project "offers great cost reduction in the delivery of long-term care services" and encouraged the researchers to continue their analysis to demonstrate these savings more formally. While both reviewers emphasized the challenges inherent in CBPR, especially the difficulty of fully engaging community members as research partners, they both documented extensive ways in which the project was a successful collaboration.

This initial round of exemplary project review has complemented the quantitative analysis of the COPH publication Journal Impact Factors by demonstrating that at least two of COPH's projects score highly when reviewed by independent reviewers according to criteria closely aligned with the goals set forth by the Initiated Act. Although it would be useful to review many more projects, resources are insufficient to provide such in-depth reviews for more than a few each year.

OUTCOMES FOR THE ARKANSAS BIOSCIENCES INSTITUTE

Key Findings: ABI's publication of research findings in top-quality scholarly journals has increased dramatically over the past three years. Its research is being disseminated in top journals in a wide variety of scientific subjects. Independent reviews of two recommended projects provide detailed verification that the top ABI projects are making major contributions in their field.

The primary purpose of ABI is to "encourage and foster the conduct of research" in accordance with a set of purposes outlined in Chapter 8 that relate to health and tobacco use. As part of a diversified portfolio of Tobacco Settlement activities, this program will take the longest time to realize its full benefits. However, the benefits could be quite large. Successful research activities can change the possibilities for health care and can create new economic activities that will raise the standard of living for many Arkansans.

Journal Impact Factors

Table 11.6 provides evidence that ABI's research products are growing in quality as well as quantity with each year. Consistent with its mandate of performing research that will contribute to the health of Arkansans, the vast majority of its publications in each year are in journals that are given a Journal Impact Factor ranking. The number of publications in journals with a top-five subject ranking has increased by more than 50 percent each year. This growth demonstrates that the continued funding of research projects by ABI is leading to contributions that are well regarded by the international scientific community.

Table 11.6
Journal Impact Factor Rankings for ABI Publications

Ranking	2002–2003	2003–2004	2004–2005
Top five	18	32	52
Six through ten	13	8	33
Ranked below ten	40	38	107
Not ranked	19	31	55
Total	90	109	258

NOTE: Ranks based on highest within-subject ranking of Journal Impact Factor for each published article.

Remarkably, ABI articles are published in journals in more than 80 fields, from to agricultural engineering to zoology. Several subjects, including biochemistry and molecular biology, food science and technology, immunology, oncology, and pharmacology and pharmacy, have 20 or more published articles by ABI-funded researchers. ABI researchers have published in the top journal in 13 different fields as diverse as horticulture, ornithology, and substance abuse. Agriculture (multidisciplinary) and pediatrics lead the list with seven and six publications, respectively, in the top journal in their field. The JIF analysis demonstrates that the ABI research has broad strength.

Qualitative Analysis of Exemplary Projects

The two ABI projects chosen for review (1) a project that received a large amount of funding to examine birth defects, specifically the relationship between nicotine and congenital heart defects and (2) a project that received seed funding to initiate research into the impact of nicotine on memory. Projects of different sizes were intentionally selected to determine whether investments in projects of either size could produce benefits for the state of Arkansas.

The birth defects study was reviewed by a physician from RAND who specializes in public health genetics and a professor in the Utah State Nutrition and Food Sciences Department. The physician states, "Ultimately the results of [this project] should facilitate the development of effective strategies and tools designed to improve risk assessment for congenital heart defects…[and] millions of health dollars saved." She concludes, "I am confident that ABI is fulfilling its mission through the funding of the research program in birth defects."

The memory effects study was reviewed by a human geneticist from RAND and a cytogeneticist the Molecular Medicine and Genetics program at Wayne State University School of Medicine. The first reviewer noted that "with a minimal amount of funding" the research "contributed to new knowledge by building on previous studies, contributing novel ideas, and disseminating research results to the scientific community." The second reviewer added, "The PI's choice of a mice model with Down syndrome is an excellent model to perform studies that would have an impact on…product development, health sector benefits, and broader economic benefits for the community." Although both reviewers expressed some concern whether such a

259

small, "isolated" project can produce outcomes that will "directly improve health outcomes for the citizens of Arkansas," they both found merit in the project.

SUMMARY

This year, we have updated some studies from past reports, reviewed data collection and analysis efforts by several of the service-based programs, and presented initial results on two new types of outcome measures for the academic programs. In future years, we will continue to update and extend these analyses as the data permit and to the extent that they can provide useful feedback to the policies undertaken by the commission and the activities of the programs themselves.

Chapter 12
Synthesis and Recommendations

The Initiated Act created the Arkansas Tobacco Settlement Commission (ATSC) to oversee the funded programs, assess their performance, and recommend program funding changes to the Arkansas General Assembly. Less formally, the ATSC facilitates the programs and is responsive to the political environment regarding public health and tobacco use in Arkansas. In Chapter 1 of this report, we provided the origins and the goals of the ATSC, and in Chapter 2, we described the policy context within which the ATSC has worked the past two years. We then examined, in individual chapters, the progress of each of the seven programs in fulfilling its mandates, as it developed and expanded its programming. Finally, in Chapters 10 and 11 we presented up-to-date results from our outcome analyses regarding program effects on trends in tobacco use, health measures associated with tobacco use, and other outcomes that could result from the seven programs established by the Initiated Act. In this concluding chapter, we bring together all of these individual evaluation results in a synthesis of the critical aspects of this biennial evaluation. Those aspects include the following:

- Program progress goals

- Program progress on the common themes and issues that were the focus of this evaluation, which include collaboration and coordination among programs, program governance and strategic direction, monitoring and quality improvement, financial management, and contracting

On the basis of these overarching aspects and our examination of the Tobacco Settlement Program as a whole, we offer recommendations for consideration by the ATSC, the governing boards that oversee the individual programs, and the Arkansas General Assembly.

SUMMARY OF PERFORMANCE THROUGH FISCAL YEAR 2006

The Initiated Act stated basic goals to be achieved by the funded programs through the use of the Tobacco Settlement funds, and it also defined indicators of performance for each of the funding programs—for program initiation, short-term actions, and long-term actions. The basic goals are listed in Chapter 2. During FY2005, the RAND team worked with each of the funded programs to establish long-range goals that define targets for future program activity. We also worked with each program to establish outcome measures that will enable us to assess the effects of the program on outcomes relevant to it. Both the long-range goals and outcome measures are intended to move each program toward the long-term actions defined for it in the Initiated Act. Last year, the ATSC formally approved the program long-term goals and agreed to monitor the programs' progress toward those goals in their regular reports to the ATSC. The monitoring is a two-step process, starting with tracking how well programs are moving toward their operational goals, and then assessing how much effect this progress is having on their outcome measures. If those levels of operation are not affecting outcomes, then the long-term goals may have to be revised to target stronger interventions to ultimately affect outcomes. The long-range goals were incorporated into the ATSC's own report of 2005, and the outcome measures provide the basis for the evaluations of outcomes in Chapters 10 and 11 of this report.

In the 2004 evaluation, we reported our assessment of the status of the programs on the program initiation goals and short-term actions defined for them in the Initiated Act. At that time, all the programs except the MHI and the Medicaid Expansion Programs had achieved their initiation goals. Within the past year, the Medicaid program has, after extensive negotiations with CMS, obtained approval of the AR-Adults program (see Chapter 9 for details).

The Minority Health Initiative had not yet prepared a list of priority health problems for minority populations. Soon after completion of our 2004 report, the MHI released a list of priority health problems for African Americans; however, it is not clear whether MHI is yet using this list to help them plan its activities. It has not put together the biographical database that the act specified. Although it provides counts of TV show airings, handouts distributed, etc., MHI has not linked these efforts to the awareness that such efforts are supposed to engender. The provision of screening and access to screening has been minimal at best, especially outside of the Hypertension Initiative. The contribution of MHI's effort to screening is not demonstrated. Additionally, we noted that growth in enrollments in MHI service delivery programs had been slow. In the last two years, while growth has improved, that growth has been uneven and is still below targets.

Progress of the Programs on Short-term Goals

For the present, however, evaluation must examine the short-term goals that are the intermediate steps towards the long-term objectives. To that end, we worked with the programs on short-term actions to be accomplished during FY2006. These are reported in detail in the respective evaluations of the seven programs (Chapters 3 through 9) and synthesized here. We summarize in Table 12.1 updated findings regarding performance of the seven programs on their short-term goals (divided into subgoals for three of the programs). Last year, we reported that all except two of the programs had achieved their short-term goals. The two exceptions were the Minority Health Initiative and the Medicaid Expansion Programs. This year, four programs have met all of their goals and subgoals, while three programs did not achieve all of their goals. AAI fell short on their goals of providing opportunities for professional education and putting together a database of funding opportunities. MHI did not submit an application for survey funding, increase enrollment in the Hypertension Initiative, or expand the Eating and Moving for Life Initiative. The Medicaid Expansion Programs did not achieve desired utilization of benefits in the AR-Seniors program or increase enrollment in that program.

Table 12.1
Program Status on the Short-Term Goals Established for 2005–2006

Program	Status
Arkansas Aging Initiative	3 of 5 goals and subgoals met
Arkansas Biosciences Institute	3 of 3 goals met
College of Public Health	4 of 4 goals met
Delta Area Health Education Center	9 of 9 goals and subgoals met
Medicaid Expansion Programs	2 of 4 goals met
Minority Health Initiative	5 of 8 goals and subgoals met
Tobacco Prevention and Education	5 of 5 goals met

In summary, most of the programs are on track with regard to their short-term goals. Medicaid Expansion Programs is not reaching the seniors as per their stated goals, but it is unclear whether this is due to anything that the program itself could do. MHI is falling short in both of its treatment provision goals. The remainder of the shortfalls are more in terms of internal processes and can be remediated without too much difficulty.

PROGRAM RESPONSES TO COMMON THEMES AND ISSUES

Some common themes and issues emerged from the first evaluation cycle that apply across the programs. For those issues, we offered recommendations in the 2004 evaluation report for actions to strengthen the programs in the future. We are monitoring the progress of the programs in carrying out these recommendations as part of our quarterly telephone updates with each program. We recapitulate these recommendations here, and we highlight activities undertaken by the programs for each recommendation. Relevant issues that merit consideration by the ATSC are identified.

Collaboration and Coordination across Programs

Collaborative activities among the programs would strengthen their ability to serve the goals of the act, to use the Tobacco Settlement funds efficiently, and to enhance needed health services for Arkansans. Some programs had been working together early in the program, and other opportunities were identified for additional collaborative programming.

Recommendation: We encourage the programs to pursue opportunities for collaboration as their work continues.

Program Responses: The amount of cross-program collaboration has been growing during the past two years. The programs most actively engaged in collaboration thus far have been TPEP, COPH, Delta AHEC, MHI, and AAI, all of which are working with one or more of the other programs. We present here some key examples of collaborative efforts, which we believe can serve as building blocks for further expansion of these activities:

- TPEP is working with the Delta AHEC and MHI to coordinate and reinforce their respective tobacco cessation services. It also recently awarded COPH the new contract to run the statewide smoking cessation network.

- For TPEP, the Delta AHEC sits on Hometown Health committees in Phillips, Lee, and Monroe counties in the Delta, and the Delta AHEC staff helps these committees with their initiatives.

- AAI is planning to collaborate with COPH to evaluate parts of its program.

- COPH students are participating in AAI activities that have led to publications.

- The Delta AHEC and AAI have shared activities through some shared staffing in AHEC and COA in Monroe County.

- The Delta AHEC is providing some technical support to the MHI Hypertension Initiative in Lee County.

- A commissioner on AMHC is also on the Delta AHEC advisory board, to better link activities between two programs.

- COPH is doing cultural diversity training in the Delta, and Delta AHEC staff members are attending these training sessions.

Governance Leadership and Strategic Direction

The diversity of the programs is reflected in their wide variety of governing bodies. Now that the start-up period is over, the governing bodies should play active roles in guiding the future strategic direction for the programs. They also provide an important vehicle for linking a program to its environment so the program hears the views of its stakeholders and has access to vital resources. Regardless of their structures, all the funded programs are accountable to the public, and it is appropriate for records of governance decisions and actions to be made publicly available to document policy oversight of the programs. Previously, we made the following two recommendations in this regard:

Recommendation: The governing boards or advisory boards of the funded programs should work with program management in defining a clear direction for the program, and should perform a constructive oversight function to ensure that the program is accountable for quality performance.

Recommendation: Individuals who can provide expertise on the goals defined for the program by the Initiated Act should be included in the membership of the program governing boards or advisory boards.

Program Responses: We asked each program to specify its governing and advisory boards and to rate the degree of involvement of these boards in providing oversight, monitoring program performance, and providing an interface with communities. These ratings are provided in the individual chapter reports of the programs; here, we summarize those results and discuss potential issues over programs.

264

- TPEP. The TPEP Advisory Board was created as mandated in the Initiated Act to provide oversight for the tobacco prevention and cessation program. This board, which meets quarterly, is minimally involved in the program, mostly engaging on community needs and interactions. The Arkansas State Board of Health, which oversees the Division of Health within DHHS, has only tangential oversight and is rarely if ever engaged with TPEP. Given that TPEP is several levels down in the hierarchy of the Board of Health's oversight responsibilities, this is neither surprising nor cause for concern.

- COPH. COPH has no advisory boards. Formal governance comes from the University of Arkansas Board of Trustees, from which COPH receives little or no attention. Again, given the nature of the University of Arkansas hierarchy, this is not surprising.

- Delta AHEC. This program is also formally governed by the University of Arkansas Board of Trustees, from which it receives little or no attention. On the other hand, the Delta AHEC has formed advisory boards at each of its three sites, and these boards are active in oversight and community interfaces but less so in program monitoring.

- AAI. AAI is officially governed by the University of Arkansas Board of Trustees, but it receives no attention from this board. The Reynolds Institute Community Advisory Board discusses AAI along with other Reynolds activities, but it too is minimally involved. Each of the regional Centers on Aging has its own advisory board, and the boards have varying degrees of involvement.

- MHI. MHI is supervised by the Arkansas Minority Health Commission, which exercises a great deal of directive oversight over the MHI program. The commission has one physician and two nurses among its members and therefore provides clinical expertise to the program, but it is not clear whether the commission has members with public health expertise. The Hypertension Initiative has a medical advisory board, which is only minimally involved in MHI.

- ABI. ABI has a governing board that meets regularly and is closely involved with the program. It also has scientific and advisory committees, which concern themselves with goals and priorities and monitor the program's progress toward these goals and its quality. The ABI board is specified in the Initiated Act, so its membership is fixed ex officio. The advisory committee members bring a breadth of expertise to the program.

- Medicaid Expansion Programs. The Medicaid activities are within two DHHS divisions—the Division of Medical Services (for claims payments) and the Division of County Operations (for application processing and eligibility determination). Although there is no governing board, the management of the two divisions provides oversight.

- ATSC. The commission oversees the activities arising out of the Tobacco Settlement Initiated Act. Although, because we report to ATSC, we cannot in a formal sense assess its own composition and nature of its governance, we note

265

that it does meet regularly and considers all aspects of the program, including our own evaluation reports.

Conclusion: Among all the programs, the natural differences in governance patterns make simple generalization difficult. None of the programs has much board involvement in fundraising; as budgets tighten, assistance could be helpful in this area. Programs that are several levels down in the organizational hierarchy from their official oversight organs can find themselves at the mercy of policies that have nothing to do with themselves, without recourse to effective intervention; in these instances, some way of officially communicating up and down the hierarchy should be explicitly arranged. Programs that do not have advisory groups should consider forming some groups as vehicles for eliciting community input, developing strategy on pertinent issues, and identifying potential funding opportunities.

Monitoring and Quality Improvement

As of the end of FY2004, few of the programs had internal accountability mechanisms for regularly monitoring and providing feedback on the program's progress; or, where mechanisms were in place, they relied on local program staff who often did not have sufficient training or resources to fully comply. Such a monitoring process, when well implemented, enables programs to perform regular quality improvement and assess how well each program component is meeting its goals. This capability also can help the programs fulfill their external accountability for performance to legislators and other state policymakers. Therefore, we made the following recommendation to all programs:

Recommendation: To monitor and improve quality and to assess program effects on health outcomes, the funded programs should have in place an ongoing quality monitoring process that has valid measures of performance, regular data collection on the measures, corrective actions to address problems, and regular reporting of data to management. The internal performance indicators and corrective actions should change over time to bring about ongoing, incremental improvements in program operation.

Program Responses: In the spring 2006, we asked each of the programs to report on their quality improvement activities. Their responses are elaborated upon in the respective program reports in Chapters 3 through 9. Here, we provide brief summaries.

- **TPEP.** TPEP has no formal quality monitoring or improvement processes. It has data collection and evaluation mechanisms in place for monitoring the work of its contractors and grantees, and it has obtained external evaluations. However, there is no process to synthesize all of these quality assessments and no continuous improvement mechanisms.

- **COPH.** COPH has had a quality management process in place since its establishment that appears to function well.

- **Delta AHEC.** The Delta AHEC does not have a formal written quality improvement process for the organization as a whole, but it does have processes in place for the diabetes clinic and established assessment processes under way for other activities. Overall, the criteria for quality performance and information collection procedures are in place, but analyses and formulating recommendations need improvement.

- **AAI.** AAI does not have a formal quality management process in place. Although it tracks activities for each Center on Aging, it does not have the capacity for monitoring performance or taking quality improvement actions.

- **MHI.** MHI has no quality improvement process in place for the initiative as a whole, nor does it have one for any of its components except the Hypertension Initiative. The latter needs improvement in data collection and analysis.

- **ABI.** ABI has a quality management program in place and does well on most aspects of quality management.

- **Medicaid Expansion Programs.** MEP does not have a quality management process per se, but it does have in place oversight mechanisms for detecting areas where quality in service delivery could be improved. A formal mechanism that includes quantitative measures of consumers' experience and ways of disseminating quality recommendations would be useful.

- **ATSC.** The commission does not have a quality management system in place to track its own functioning or that of its secretariat.

Conclusion: The information provided by the programs on their quality improvement activities is uneven and reflects the tradition of quality within the type of agency running the program. The more purely academic programs (COPH, ABI) have mature processes; line agencies within departments (TPEP, MEP, Delta AHEC) have no formal processes but have reporting requirements that could be the basis of processes; and specialized agencies (AAI, MHI, ATSC itself) would benefit from establishing official quality improvement regimes.

Financial Management

In the 2004 evaluation report, our analysis of the spending of the Tobacco Settlement funds identified issues in two areas: budgeting for the appropriations process and the program financial management and accounting systems and capabilities.

Appropriations Process and Fund Allocations. During the initial budgeting and appropriations process, several programs had appropriation allocations across expense classifications that did not fully match their operational needs. The program leaders were reluctant to make substantial changes to the fund allocations in the second biennial appropriations because doing so brought the risk of opening up the entire package to funding changes or reductions. Thus, the spending constraints experienced by the programs in the first two fiscal years were perpetuated in the FY2004–2005 biennial appropriations, a fact that hindered several programs from using their funding effectively. We therefore made the following recommendation:

Recommendation: For the upcoming appropriations process, the state should provide the programs with clear definitions of the appropriation line items as well as guidance for the budgeting process, so that programs understand clearly how they can use funds in each line item to support their activities. In addition, the programs should restructure the budgets they submit to the state for the next appropriations process so that allocations of spending across line items reflect actual program needs and are consistent with the appropriations definitions.

Program Responses: The four programs that are part of the UAMS system—AAI, COPH, Delta AHEC, and the UAMS portion of ABI—were having the greatest problem with poorly allocated appropriations. UAMS submitted a proposal for reallocation of the FY2005 budgeted line items for these programs to the Peer Review Committee of the Arkansas General Assembly, which approved the reallocation. The approved reallocations are shown in Table 12.2. The patterns of reallocations differed for the programs, but a common element was expansion of the operating expense line items, accompanied by reductions in other line items.

Conclusion: For the FY2006–2007 biennial appropriations, which were completed in April 2005, the programs modified their line item allocations as needed. This step should help ensure that future program appropriations do not place artificial constraints on the programs' ability to spend according to operational needs.

Table 12.2
Reallocation of Program Budgeted Line Items in the FY2005 Appropriations

	Authorized Appropriation	Reallocated Appropriation
Arkansas Aging Initiative		
Salaries	$ 1,278,527	$ 1,175,000
Personal services match	232,733	300,000
Operating expenses	198,515	604,475
Travel and conferences	56,500	20,000
Professional fees and services	0	150,000
Capital outlay	558,200	75,000
Total	$ 2,324,475	$ 2,324,475
College of Public Health		
Salaries	$ 2,500,613	$ 2,350,000
Personal services match	484,316	525,000
Operating expenses	196,784	376,713
Travel and conferences	40,000	60,000
Professional fees and services	100,000	100,000
Capital outlay	165,000	75,000
Total	$ 3,486,713	$ 3,486,713
Delta AHEC		
Salaries	$ 1,347,405	$ 1,195,000
Personal Services Match	245,270	280,000
Operating Expenses	340,800	539,475
Travel and conferences	41,000	25,000
Professional fees and services	0	85,000
Capital outlay	350,000	200,000
Total	$ 2,324,475	$ 2,324,475
Arkansas Biosciences Institute (UAMS)		
Salaries	$ 1,926,987	$ 785,000
Personal services match	350,773	185,000
Operating expenses	524,144	1,556,904
Travel and conferences	60,000	35,000
Professional fees and services	300,000	100,000
Capital outlay	1,000,000	1,500,000
Arkansas Children's Hospital	1,994,772	1,994,772
Total	$ 6,156,676	$ 6,156,676

Financial Management and Accounting. Several of the programs have been lacking in some aspect of the accounting and bookkeeping skills needed for effective financial management. Additional training and support should be provided to the programs to strengthen their ability to document their spending accurately and to use this information to guide program management.

Recommendation: Every program should have a *local* automated accounting system to record expenditures as they occur and to report spending monthly to its governance and management. This system would provide the detailed financial information needed for program management that is not provided by the larger systems within which many of the programs operate (e.g., the state or UAMS financial systems). Within this system, the programs should ensure they have the following:

- Personnel who are qualified to perform accounting or bookkeeping functions, and who are trained in use of the external accounting systems to which their programs report expenditures

- Separate accounts for each key program component so that the program can budget for and monitor spending by component

- Monthly monitoring of program spending along with reporting of financial statements and explanations of variations from budget to the program governing body at every meeting

Program Responses: From a strictly structural perspective, all of the programs are supported by well-established financial systems, although multiple systems are involved, as shown in the following list:

ABI	Each of the member universities has its own financial system
COPH	UAMS financial system
AAI	UAMS AHEC financial system
Delta AHEC	UAMS AHEC financial system
ADH	State financial management system
MHI	State financial management system
MEP	State financial management system

Conclusion: From an operational perspective, few of the programs are using these accounting resources for proactive monitoring and reporting of financial data to program management and governance. In RAND's more recent analysis of program spending, we were able to obtain the needed data much more easily than we could in previous years. However, for the programs with multiple components (ABI and AAI), we still had to go to the individual components for their financial data, rather than obtaining it from the leadership of the overall program. We would be able to get the information from the program leads if the individual components were submitting regular financial statements to them.

Other programs with multiple program components (e.g., Delta AHEC, MHI, and possibly COPH) do not yet appear to be establishing separate accounts for individual

270

components. This capability would not only provide more useful data for program planning, but it also would strengthen the program accountability in reporting to stakeholders and external funders. It is not clear whether the financial systems being used might hamper the programs' ability to establish accounts by program components, or whether there are other barriers. MHI claims to have a system in place to track component spending, but our own examination of this system did not lead to the conclusion that it was comprehensive enough.

Contracting

We asked each of the programs to provide information about how they contract for services. Most of the programs, including COPH, Delta AHEC, AAI, ABI, and Medicaid Expansion Programs, report having no contracts.

- **TPEP.** TPEP has some subgrants for service delivery and personal service contracts for needed expertise. For these contracts, TPEP reports monthly financial tracking, monitoring of quality, and comparison of spending to reported activities.

- **MHI.** MHI issues contracts for implementation of the Hypertension and Eating and Moving for Life initiatives, as well as a number of personal service contracts for needed expertise. The financial tracking of contracts ranges from monthly to annually, depending on the contract. There is some formal quality management for the hypertension activity but not for other contracts. There is no comparison of spending to activity.

- **ATSC.** The ATSC issues grants to community agencies, the evaluation contract to RAND, and various personal services contracts. Quarterly financial accounting is required, including spending to activity. Quality management is informal, but a system is being put into place for the community grants.

Conclusion: In summary, contract management appears largely to be adequate, with the exception of the Minority Health Initiative. This problem was flagged by RAND in the interim report in 2004–2005 (Farley et al., 2005b), and some improvements have been made, but performance is not yet satisfactory.

POLICY ISSUES AND RECOMMENDATIONS

We continue to believe, as we stated in the 2004 evaluation report (Farley et al., 2005a), that the programs supported by the Tobacco Settlement funds provide an effective mix of services and other resources that respond directly to many of Arkansas' priority health issues. In addition, the College of Public Health and the Arkansas Biosciences Institute are building educational and research infrastructure that can be expected to make long-term contributions to the state's health needs. With another two years of operation, the programs have achieved the initial and short-term goals defined in the Initiated Act, with but one exception. The programs' impacts on health needs also can be expected to grow as they continue to evolve and increasingly leverage the Tobacco Settlement funds to attract other resources. In this section, we take a bird's-eye view of the ATSC and provide new observations and recommendations for consideration that are addressed to the commission, the governor, or the Arkansas General Assembly, as opposed to the individual programs.

Program Funding

In an ideal world, we would again recommend that Tobacco Settlement funding continue to be provided to the seven funded programs according to the percentages in the Initiated Act. However, the world is not as anticipated, much less ideal. Chapter 2 documented the eroding contribution of the tobacco companies through the Master Settlement Agreement. Prudent planning on the part of the Arkansas General Assembly, the governor, and the ATSC requires at least a contingency for significant reductions in tobacco funding—perhaps as much as 50 percent.

Recommendation: Aggressively seek funding to supplement the Tobacco Settlement funds. Some of the shortfall should be made up for by aggressively seeking other funding sources. This has been most successfully done to date—as part of the original plan—by the College of Public Health and the Arkansas Biosciences Institute, and of course with the matching federal funds for Medicaid Expansion Programs. Other programs have either no or minor percentages of additional funding.

Recommendation: Consider potential revisions to the funding allocations of Tobacco Settlement funds. It is distinctly possible that external funding cannot replace the Tobacco Settlement losses. While it is still too early to panic, alternatives should be entertained and contingency plans made. We do not recommend any specific alternatives, but among the policies that might be considered are the following:

- Restructure the percentage allocation of funds among the different programs, maintaining levels of programs that are deemed (because of mission, performance, or both) to be worthy and reducing the allocation of others.

- Eliminate some programs and redistribute some of their tasks among other programs, or move these tasks to outside the Tobacco Settlement arena.

- Change funding rules from fixed grants to conditional matching of external funding (perhaps up to a certain level of performance).

None of these alternatives is pain-free, but the default of fixed reductions in funding if MSA funds decrease by 50 percent or so seems even worse. In summary, out of the threat of reduced funding can come the opportunity of revisiting the mechanisms of funding in order to bring the goals of the ATSC in line with developments over the past six years.

Leveraging Funding

Recommendation: Especially given the anticipated funding crunch, rethink the direct service delivery components of programs that have them, and either justify the contribution of these components to people beyond the direct recipients, or eliminate these components. While it may appear hard-hearted, this way of thinking provides better care for the targeted populations in the long term.

Even if the MSA provided a steady cash flow of $60 million per year, this is not what the late Senator Everett Dirksen would have termed "real money" in terms of what is spent in Arkansas on health care services delivery. This means that Tobacco Settlement money is perhaps best utilized to leverage existing care-delivery efforts. Leveraging can be accomplished in a number of ways—as evidenced by the Initiated Act itself:

- Increase the skills of care providers and policymakers. This is accomplished now by the activities of, among others, COPH, Delta AHEC, and AAI.

- Increase knowledge of how to provide care. This is the raison d'être of ABI, and it is also done by COPH. Needs assessment and other survey work by the other programs also accomplish this goal.

- Leverage other funds. The Medicaid Expansion Programs, using the 290 percent matching contribution of federal Medicaid dollars and focusing funding on a tightly defined subpopulation, accomplish this.

- Address public health. COPH, by its very name, does this. It is also a major component of outreach and policymaking efforts of AAI, MHI, Delta AHEC, and TPEP.

Technical Capacity

Recommendation: Programs should be urged to develop data collection and analysis plans and to dedicate resources for implementing these plans. The ATSC should provide funds to train program staff to accomplish these goals. These funds should be appropriated in the next general assembly appropriations cycle.

A theme that runs through both the process and outcome evaluations of many programs is that data collection and analysis are not yet adequate to fully track the programs' effects or to determine quality deficiencies and what to do about them. Because this theme is not isolated to one or two programs, it should be taken on by the ATSC as a whole. Last year, we recommended that the ATSC use some of its own budget to buy technical expertise to train programs. This was not accomplished because, although the money was there, the general assembly appropriation was not large enough to permit this expenditure. If the programs are to assess performance through regular monitoring of trends in their process indicators, progress toward the newly established long-term goals, and trends in effects on relevant outcomes, then they have to develop and use better data collection and analysis techniques. Technical capacity developed through the commission has the added advantage of serving multiple programs and enabling more joint activity.

Joint Activity

Recommendation: The collaboration among the seven Tobacco Settlement programs should be intensified, especially as programs experience challenges where expertise from potential partners would be beneficial. The ATSC can help in this regard by serving as an "honest broker," identifying potential collaborative efforts and bringing together programs.

As we noted earlier, collaborative activity across the programs is growing. We applaud and encourage this work. Of the seven programs established by the Initiated Act, only ABI and the Medicaid Expansion Programs have not yet been engaged in joint activities with other programs. While it might be said that these programs differ substantially from the others, there is still room for collaboration. ABI might consider paying special attention to proposals from other

Tobacco Settlement programs, or even soliciting proposals. The Medicaid Expansion Programs' difficulties with AR-Seniors might find some solutions in collaboration with AAI.

The joint activity already established can be fruitfully increased. The service programs all require assistance with data collection, management, and analysis, as well as quality management. The College of Public Health has expertise in all these areas.

Ubiquitous Quality Improvement

Recommendation: By the end of the next fiscal year, each Tobacco Settlement program and the ATSC itself should have in place a documented formal quality management program that includes explicit criteria for quality performance, collects information on measures of technical and perceived quality, has quantified measures that derive from the information collected, has analysis plans for addressing the measures, and formulates quality recommendations that are addressed to whoever needs to take action. The annual report of each program and the ATSC should include the results of quality analyses, a set of internal recommendations, and a statement of actions on previous years' recommendations.

Another theme running through most of the programs was that formal quality management systems were not in place. As discussed above, there was a range from fully mature quality management to virtually none. To be effective, quality management must be in place not only for the activities overseen by the programs, but for the central program management itself. This applies to the ATSC as much as to its constituent programs.

Issues for Individual Programs

Here, we revisit some of the findings for the seven individual programs in order to make recommendations that fall outside the purview of the programs themselves. We discuss three programs—TPEP, Medicaid Expansion Programs, and MHI—as well as the ATSC itself.

Tobacco Prevention and Education Program

Recommendation: The funding share for TPEP should be increased to return its funding for tobacco prevention and cessation activities, at an absolute minimum, to the percentage share stated in the Initiated Act.

As of the end of FY2004, TPEP continued to be funded at levels below the CDC-recommended *minimums* for tobacco prevention and cessation programs. Although Arkansas is ranked fifth nationally in terms of spending according to CDC recommendations, this is still less than the minimum, and it cries out for remediation. With the new appropriations adopted for FY2006–2007, TPEP's authorized funding declined both in absolute terms and relative to the other programs receiving Tobacco Settlement funds. Thus, its share of the total Tobacco Settlement dollars, which already was below what the Initiated Act had designated for tobacco prevention and cessation activities, will be yet smaller in the second biennium.

Recommendation: The Arkansas General Assembly and state administration are encouraged to increase other financial resources for tobacco control programming, which should be designed to complement TPEP programming so that shortfalls in CDC-recommended levels of funding for individual program components can be alleviated.

As we discussed in the 2004 evaluation report, both inadequate tobacco control policy by the state and erosion of financial resources for TPEP weaken the ability of this otherwise well designed and -managed program to affect smoking behaviors by Arkansans. As discussed in Chapter 10, our outcome evaluation is starting to detect reductions in smoking rates among some population groups, but these gains may not be sustained in future years if support for this programming continues to erode.

Another key component of a comprehensive tobacco control program is legislation that bans smoking in public areas and increases taxes on tobacco products, and here significant progress can be reported. Arkansas should be applauded for increasing tobacco taxes and for passing the Indoor Clean Air Act.

Minority Health Initiative

Recommendation: MHI should be reassessed in six months (as opposed to the normal annual cycle of assessment). If, at that time, performance has not improved to the point where there is confidence that full functionality of the program can be achieved in a reasonable amount of time, then MHI programming should be redistributed to other programs within the Tobacco Settlement framework.

MHI is uniquely positioned to address directly the health needs and priorities of the state's minority populations. It has made some real progress in programming growth and financial reporting during FY2005, and it is spending more of its funds than it did in the previous biennium. However, as discussed in Chapter 7, issues of declining enrollments, quality problems, and extremely high unit costs have been identified for the MHI Hypertension Initiative. The cost issues surfaced for the first time this year when the RAND evaluation team was finally able to obtain spending data for each of the contracts executed by the AMHC with outside entities. These issues could well be related to how MHI contracts are structured, with no provision for matching spending to actual performance. Earlier, we recommended that the ATSC work with the Arkansas Minority Health Commission to help strengthen MHI programming. We also suggested that, if MHI continues to underspend its Tobacco Settlement funding, this funding be reduced. Finally, we suggested that if the service delivery components of MHI cannot achieve appropriate service volumes at reasonable unit costs, then other providers should be considered.

In the year since those recommendations were made, MHI has improved slightly on all fronts, but it is still not functioning adequately. We are reluctant to repeat recommendations that have not been fully followed in the past. At the same time, the inherent value of much of the MHI programming and the important role filled by the AMHC make us reluctant to recommend closing the program or moving it elsewhere. We therefore have adopted a compromise recommendation.

Medicaid Expansion Programs

Recommendation: The Medicaid Expansion Programs should intensity their efforts to meet spending targets for the expansions they support. Unspent funds mean services are not provided to low-income people in need of health care, and the ability of the Medicaid programs to leverage federal funds for these services means that assets that would otherwise be available are not being tapped. While the Medicaid programs are to be applauded for their intense effort in bringing the four expansion programs on board, they should ensure that all four programs spend the funds available.

ATSC Management of Program Progress

Recommendation: The ATSC should continue to work toward establishing a complete reporting package through which the funded programs provide it with performance information on both their program activities and spending, which it should use for monitoring program performance on a regular basis. This package should include quarterly reports that contain the items specified in our 2004 evaluation report, as well as quarterly financial statements, quarterly data that extend trends in the process indicators of service activity, and annual reports on progress toward long-term goals.

During the first years of the Tobacco Settlement program, the RAND evaluation served to assess the progress of the funded programs in the start-up and early operation of their activities, as well as to work with the programs to establish goals and measures to monitor their continued operation and growth. In the 2004 evaluation report, we recommended actions the ATSC could take to reinforce reporting for accountability by the programs. In Chapter 2 of this report, we summarize the actions the ATSC has implemented thus far and its plans for continued development of monitoring and technical support for the programs.

The RAND evaluation team believes that at this point in the Tobacco Settlement program, it is appropriate to begin gradually to shift the role of monitoring the performance of the programs' activities away from the external evaluator into the hands of the ATSC. An external evaluator will remain necessary for the foreseeable future, but its role will shift over time. One of the responsibilities of the external evaluator is to support the sponsoring organization (the ATSC) in making this evaluation function an integral part of its ongoing operation. RAND, if chosen to continue in this role, will serve as an objective observer, reviewing performance reports the programs submit to the ATSC and assessing data on the programs' process indicators. However, over the next few evaluation cycles, the emphasis of the external evaluator should shift toward on analysis of program effects on outcomes, a function that requires the modeling and statistical expertise that are not yet within the capacity of the ATSC. Finally, even if the ATSC is fully capable of evaluating the programs, an external organization must "watch the watchers" and provide oversight of the ATSC itself.

DISCUSSION

The Arkansas General Assembly and Tobacco Settlement Commission continue to have much to be proud of in the investment made in the seven programs supported by the Tobacco Settlement funds. COPH and ABI are particularly to be acknowledged for their contributions to improving the public health skills of Arkansans and increasing the national and global visibility of Arkansas as a locus of research applied to improving the health of the population. All programs continue to make substantial progress in expanding and strengthening the infrastructure to support the health status and health care needs of Arkansas residents. We have begun to observe effects on smoking outcomes, and with time, we believe the prospects are good for the programs to achieve observable impacts on other health-related outcomes.

Arkansas has been unique among the states in being responsive to the basic intent of the Master Tobacco Settlement by investing its funds in health-related programs with a focus on reducing smoking rates. We encourage state policymakers to reaffirm this original commitment in the Initiated Act to dedicate the Tobacco Settlement funds to support health-related programming. To do justice to the health-related services, education, and research these programs are now delivering, they must be given the continued support and time they need to fulfill their mission of helping Arkansas to significantly improve the health of its residents. In addition, they must take actions to ensure that issues identified in this evaluation are addressed to reinforce the effectiveness of Arkansas' investment in the health of its residents.

Appendix A.
Initiated Act 1 of 2000:
The Tobacco Settlement Proceeds Act

SECTION 1. TITLE. This Act may be referred to and cited as the "Tobacco Settlement Proceeds Act."

SECTION 2. DEFINITIONS. (a) The following terms, as used in this Act, shall have the meanings set forth in this section:

(1) "Act" shall mean this Arkansas Tobacco Settlement Funds Act of 2000.

(2) "ADFA" shall mean the Arkansas Development Finance Authority.

(3) "Arkansas Biosciences Institute" shall mean the Arkansas Biosciences Institute created by Section 15 of this Act.

(4) "Arkansas Biosciences Institute Program Account" shall mean the account by that name created pursuant to Section 11 of this Act to be funded from the Tobacco Settlement Program Fund and used by the Arkansas Biosciences Institute for the purposes set forth in this Act.

(5) "Arkansas Healthy Century Trust Fund" shall mean that public trust for the benefit of the citizens of the State of Arkansas created and established pursuant to Section 7 of this Act.

(6) "Arkansas Tobacco Settlement Commission" shall mean the entity that administers the programs established pursuant to this Act, also known as "ATSC", which is described and established in Section 17 of this Act.

(7) "Arkansas Tobacco Settlement Commission fund" shall mean the fund by that name created pursuant to Section 8(f) of this Act to be used by the Arkansas Tobacco Settlement Commission for the purposes set forth in Section 17 of the Act.

(8) "Bonds" shall mean any and all bonds, notes, or other evidences of indebtedness issued by ADFA as Tobacco Settlement Revenue Bonds pursuant to the terms of this Act.

(9) "Capital Improvement Projects" shall mean the acquisition, construction and equipping of land, buildings, and appurtenant facilities, including but not limited to parking and landscaping, all intended for the provision of health care services, health education, or health-related research[,] provided that each such Capital Improvement Project must be either set forth in this Act or subsequently designated by the General Assembly pursuant to legislation.

(10) "Debt Service Requirements" shall mean all amounts required to be paid in connection with the repayment of Bonds issued pursuant to this Act, including, but not limited to, the principal of and interest on the Bonds, amounts reasonably required for a debt service reserve, amounts reasonably required to provide debt service coverage, trustee's and paying agent fees, and, to the extent reasonably necessary, capitalized interest on the Bonds.

(11) "Initial MSA Disbursement" shall mean the first disbursement from the MSA Escrow to the State, consisting of Arkansas' share of payments from Participating Manufacturers due under the Master Settlement Agreement and designated as the 1998 First Payment, the 2000 Initial Payment, and the 2000 Annual Payment, which amounts, along with any accumulated interest, represent all money due to the State and attributable to payments prior to January 1, 2001.

(12) "Master Settlement Agreement" or "MSA" shall mean that certain Master Settlement Agreement between certain states (the "Settling States") and certain tobacco manufacturers (the "Participating Manufacturers"), pursuant to which the Participating Manufacturers have agreed to make certain payments to each of the Settling States.

(13) "Medicaid Expansion Programs Account" shall mean the account by that name created pursuant to Section 12 of this Act to be funded from the Tobacco Settlement Program Fund and used by the Arkansas Department of Human Services for the purposes set forth in this Act.

(14) "MSA Disbursements" shall mean all amounts disbursed from the MSA Escrow pursuant to the Master Settlement Agreement to the State of Arkansas.

(15) "MSA Disbursement Date" shall mean any date on which MSA Disbursements are made to the State of Arkansas pursuant to the Master Settlement Agreement at the request of the State.

(16) "MSA Escrow" shall mean those escrow accounts established to hold the State of Arkansas' share of the Tobacco Settlement proceeds prior to disbursement to the State pursuant to the Master Settlement Agreement.

(17) "MSA Escrow Agent" shall mean that agent appointed pursuant to the Escrow Agreement entered into between the Settling States and the Participating Manufacturers pursuant to the Settlement Agreement.

(18) "Participating Manufacturers" shall mean those entities defined as Participating Manufacturers by the terms of the Master Settlement Agreement.

(19) "Prevention and Cessation Program Account" shall mean the account by that name created pursuant to Section 9 of this Act to be funded from the Tobacco Settlement Program Fund and used for the purposes set forth in this Act.

(20) "Program Accounts" shall mean, collectively, the Prevention and Cessation Program Account, the Targeted State Needs Program Account, the Arkansas Biosciences Institute Program Account, and the Medicaid Expansion Programs Account.

(21) "State Board of Finance" shall mean the entity created pursuant to Arkansas Code Annotated § 19-3-101, as amended.

(22) "Targeted State Needs Programs Account" shall mean the account by that name created pursuant to Section 10 of this Act to be funded from the Tobacco Settlement Program Fund and used for the purposes set forth in this Act.

(23) "Tobacco Settlement" shall mean the State of Arkansas' share of funds to be distributed pursuant to the Master Settlement Agreement between the Settling States and the Participating Manufacturers.

(24) "Tobacco Settlement Cash Holding Fund" shall mean the Fund established as a cash fund outside of the State Treasury pursuant to Section 4 of this Act, into which all MSA Disbursements shall be deposited on each MSA Disbursement Date.

(25) "Tobacco Settlement Debt Service Fund" shall mean the Fund established as a cash fund outside of the State Treasury pursuant to Section 5 of this Act.

(26) "Tobacco Settlement Program Fund" or "Program Fund" shall mean the Tobacco Settlement Program Fund established pursuant to Section 8 of this Act, which shall be used to hold and distribute funds to the various Program Accounts created by this Act.

(27) "Trust indenture" or "indenture" shall mean any trust indenture, ADFA resolution, or other similar document under which Tobacco Settlement Revenue Bonds are to be issued and secured.

SECTION 3. GRANT OF AUTHORITY TO STATE BOARD OF FINANCE.

The State Board of Finance is hereby authorized and directed to perform the following duties with respect to the Tobacco Settlement:

(a) The State Board of Finance is authorized and directed on behalf of the State of Arkansas to receive all authorized disbursements from the MBA Escrow. The Initial MBA Disbursement and each subsequent MSA Disbursement shall be immediately deposited into the Tobacco Settlement Cash Holding Fund, and distributed from there as prescribed in this Act. The Office of the Attorney General is directed to take all action necessary to inform the MBA Escrow Agent that the Board of Finance is authorized to receive such disbursements on behalf of the State.

(b) The State Board of Finance shall manage and invest all amounts held in the Tobacco Settlement Cash Holding Fund, the Tobacco Settlement Debt Service Fund, the Arkansas Healthy Century Trust Fund, the Tobacco Settlement Program Fund, the Arkansas Tobacco Settlement Commission Fund, and the Program Accounts, and shall have full power to invest and reinvest the moneys in such funds and accounts and to hold, purchase, sell, assign, transfer, or dispose of any of the investments so made as well as the proceeds of the investments and moneys, pursuant to the following standards:

(1) with respect to amounts in the Arkansas Healthy Century Trust Fund, all investments shall be pursuant to and in compliance with the prudent investor and other applicable standards set forth in Arkansas Code Annotated §§ 24-3-408, 414, 415, and 417 through 425, and Arkansas Code Annotated § 19-3-518;

(2) with respect to amounts in the Tobacco Settlement Debt Service Fund, all investments shall be pursuant to and in compliance with the prudent investor and other applicable standards set forth in Arkansas Code Annotated §§ 24-3-408, 414, 415, and 417 through 425, and Arkansas Code Annotated § 19-3-518[,] provided further that the types and manner of such investments may be further limited as set forth in Section 5 of this Act; and

(3) with respect to amounts held in the Tobacco Settlement Cash Holding Fund, the Tobacco Settlement Program Fund, each of the Program Accounts, and the Arkansas Tobacco Settlement Commission Fund, all investments shall of the type described in Arkansas Code Annotated

§ 19-3-510 and shall be made with depositories designated pursuant to Arkansas Code Annotated § 19-3-507; or such investment shall be in certificates of deposit, in securities as outlined in Arkansas Code Annotated § 23-47-401 without limitation or as approved in the Board of Finance investment policy. The State Board of Finance shall insure that such investments shall mature or be redeemable at the times needed for disbursements from such funds and accounts pursuant to this Act.

(c) The State Board of Finance is authorized to employ such professionals as it deems necessary and desirable to assist it in properly managing and investing the Arkansas Healthy Century Trust Fund, pursuant to the standards set forth in Arkansas Code Annotated § 24-3-425.

(d) The State Board of Finance is authorized to use investment earnings from the Arkansas Healthy Century Trust Fund to compensate the professionals retained under subsection (c), and to pay the reasonable costs and expenses of the State Board of Finance in administering the funds and accounts created under this Act and performing all other duties ascribed to it hereunder.

(e) On the last day of each month, the State Board of Finance shall provide the Department of Finance and Administration, Office of Accounting with the current balances in the Tobacco Settlement Cash Holding Fund, the Arkansas Healthy Century Trust Fund, the Tobacco Settlement Program Fund, the Tobacco Settlement Debt Service Fund, the Arkansas Tobacco Settlement Commission Fund, and each Program Account.

(f) The State Board of Finance is authorized and directed to perform all other tasks that may be assigned to the State Board of Finance pursuant to this Act.

SECTION 4. CREATION AND ADMINISTRATION OF TOBACCO SETTLEMENT CASH HOLDING FUND.

(a) There is hereby created and established a fund, held separate and apart from the State Treasury, to be known as the "Tobacco Settlement Cash Holding Fund," which fund shall be administered by the State Board of Finance.

(b) All moneys received as part of the Tobacco Settlement are hereby designated cash funds pursuant to Arkansas Code Annotated § 19-6-103, restricted in their use and to be used solely as provided in this Act. All MSA Disbursements shall be initially deposited to the credit of the Tobacco Settlement Cash Holding Fund, when and as received. Any and all NSA Disbursements received prior to the effective date of this Act shall be immediately transferred to the Tobacco Settlement Cash Holding Fund upon this Act becoming effective. The Tobacco Settlement Cash Holding Fund is intended as a cash fund, not subject to appropriation, and, to the extent practical, amounts in the Tobacco Settlement Cash Holding Fund shall be immediately distributed to the other Funds and Accounts described in this Act.

(c) The Initial MSA Disbursement shall be distributed from the Tobacco Settlement Cash Holding Fund to the Arkansas Healthy Century Trust Fund as an initial endowment pursuant to Section 7 of this Act.

(d) After the Initial MSA Disbursement has been transferred as set forth in Section 4(c), the State Board of Finance, beginning with MSA Disbursements for years 2001 and thereafter, shall receive all amounts due to the State from the MSA Escrow. In calendar year 2001, there shall first be deposited to the Arkansas Healthy Century Trust Fund from the MSA Disbursements attributable to calendar year 2001, the amount necessary to bring the principal amount of the Arkansas Healthy Century Trust Fund to one-hundred million dollars ($100,000,000). The remainder of any MSA Disbursements attributable to calendar year 2001 shall be deposited into the Tobacco Settlement Program Fund and distributed pursuant to Section 8 of this Act. Beginning in 2002, and for each annual MSA Disbursement thereafter, all MSA Disbursements shall be immediately deposited in the Tobacco Settlement Cash Holding Fund and then distributed, as soon as practical after receipt, as follows:

(1) The first five million dollars ($5,000,000) received as an MSA Disbursement in each calendar year beginning in 2002 shall be transferred from the Tobacco Settlement Cash Holding Fund to the Tobacco Settlement Debt Service Fund; and

(2) After the transfer described in Section 4 (d) (1), the amounts remaining in the Tobacco Settlement Cash Holding Fund shall be transferred to the Tobacco Settlement Program Fund.

(e) While it is intended that the Board of Finance will transfer funds from the Tobacco Settlement Cash Holding Fund immediately upon receipt, to the extent that any amounts must be held pending the transfers described in Sections 4(c) and 4(d), the State Board of Finance is authorized to invest such amounts in suitable investments maturing not later than when the moneys are expected to be transferred, provided that such investments are made in compliance with Section 3(c) of this Act.

SECTION 5. CREATION AND ADMINISTRATION OF TOBACCO SETTLEMENT DEBT SERVICE FUND.

(a) There is hereby created and established a fund, designated as a cash fund and held separate and apart from the State Treasury, to be known as the "Tobacco Settlement Debt Service Fund," which Fund shall be administered by the State Board of Finance. All moneys deposited into the Tobacco Settlement Debt Service Fund are hereby designated cash funds pursuant to Arkansas Code Annotated § 19-6-103, restricted in their use and to be used solely as provided in this Act.

(b) There shall be transferred from the Tobacco Settlement Cash Holding Fund to the Tobacco Settlement Debt Service Fund, the amount set forth for such transfer in Section 4(d) of this Act. All amounts received into the Tobacco Settlement Debt Service Fund shall be held until needed to make payments on Debt Service Requirements. The State Board of Finance is authorized to invest any amounts held in the Tobacco Settlement Debt Service Fund in suitable investments maturing not later than when the moneys are needed to pay Debt Service Requirements, provided that such investments comply with Section 3(c) of this Act, and further provided that the investment of such moneys may be further limited by the provisions of any trust indenture pursuant to which Bonds are issued or any related non-arbitrage certificate or tax regulatory agreement.

(c) Amounts held in the Tobacco Settlement Debt Service Fund shall be transferred to funds and accounts established and held by the trustee for the Bonds at such times and in such manner as may be specified in the trust indenture securing the Bonds. If so required by any trust indenture pursuant to which Bonds have been issued, amounts deposited to the Tobacco Settlement Debt Service Fund may be immediately deposited into funds or accounts established by such trust indenture and held by the trustee for the Bonds. The State Board of Finance is authorized to execute any consent, pledge, or other document, reasonably required pursuant to a trust indenture to affirm the pledge of amounts held in the Tobacco Settlement Debt Service Fund to secure Tobacco Settlement Revenue Bonds.

(d) On December 15 of each calendar year, any amounts held in the Tobacco Settlement Debt Service Fund, to the extent such amounts are not needed to pay Debt Service Requirements prior to the following April 15, shall be transferred to the Arkansas Healthy Century Trust Fund. At such time as there are no longer any Bonds outstanding, and all Debt Service Requirements and other contractual obligations have been paid in full, amounts remaining in the Tobacco Settlement Debt Service Fund shall be transferred to the Arkansas Healthy Century Trust Fund.

SECTION 6. ISSUANCE OF TOBACCO SETTLEMENT REVENUE BONDS BY ARKANSAS DEVELOPMENT FINANCE AUTHORITY.

(a) The Arkansas Development Finance Authority ("ADFA") is hereby directed and authorized to issue Tobacco Settlement Revenue Bonds, the proceeds of which are to be used for financing the Capital Improvement Projects described in Section 6(b) of this Act. The Bonds may be issued in series from time to time, and shall be special obligations only of ADFA, secured solely by the revenue sources set forth in this section.

(b) The Capital Improvement Projects to be financed shall be:

(1) University of Arkansas for Medical Sciences, Biosciences Research Building[,] provided, however, that no more than two million, two hundred thousand dollars ($2,200,000) of the annual transfer to the Tobacco Settlement Debt Service Fund shall be allocated in any one year to pay Debt Service Requirements for this project, and provided further that no more than twenty-five million dollars ($25,000,000) in principal amount of Tobacco Settlement Revenue Bonds may be issued for this project;

(2) Arkansas State University Biosciences Research Building[,] provided, however, that no more than one million, eight hundred thousand dollars ($1,800,000) of the annual transfer to the Tobacco Settlement Debt Service Fund shall be allocated in any one year to pay Debt Service Requirements for this project, and provided further that no more than twenty million dollars ($20,000,000) in principal amount of Tobacco Settlement Revenue Bonds may be issued for this project;

(3) School of Public Health[,] provided, however, that no more than one million dollars ($1,000,000) of the annual transfer to the Tobacco Settlement Debt Service Fund shall be allocated in any one year to pay Debt Service Requirements for this project, and provided further that no more than fifteen million dollars ($15,000,000) in principal amount of Tobacco Settlement Revenue Bonds may be issued for this project; and

(4) Only such other capital improvement projects related to the provision of health care services, health education, or health-related research as designated by legislation enacted by the Arkansas General Assembly[,] provided that the deposits to the Tobacco Settlement Debt Service Fund are adequate to pay Debt Service Requirements for such additional projects.

(c) Prior to issuance of any series of Bonds authorized herein, ADFA shall adopt a resolution authorizing the issuance of such series of Bonds. Each such resolution shall contain such terms, covenants, conditions, as deemed desirable and consistent with this Act together with provisions of subchapters one, two, and three of Chapter Five of Title 15 of the Arkansas Code Annotated, including without limitation, those pertaining to the establishment and maintenance of funds and accounts, deposit and investment of Bond proceeds and the rights and obligations of ADFA and the registered owners of the Bonds. In authorizing, issuing, selling the Bonds and in the investment of all funds held under the resolution or indenture securing such Bonds, ADFA shall have the powers and be governed by the provisions of Arkansas Code Annotated §§ 15-5-309-15-5-310.

(d) The Bonds shall be special obligations of ADFA, secured and payable from deposits made into the Tobacco Settlement Debt Service Fund created pursuant to this Act. In pledging revenues to secure the Bonds, the provisions of Arkansas Code Annotated § 15-5-313 shall apply.

(e) If so determined by ADFA, the Bonds may additionally be secured by a lien on or security interest in facilities financed by the Bonds, by a lien or pledge of loans made by ADFA to the user of such facilities, and any collateral security received by ADFA, including, without limitation, ADFA's interest in and any revenue derived from any loan agreements. It shall not be necessary to the perfection of the lien and pledge for such purposes that the trustee in connection with such bond issue or the holders of the Bonds take possession of the loans, mortgages and collateral security.

(f) It shall be plainly stated on the face of each Bond that it has been issued under this Act, and subchapters one, two and three of Chapter 5 of Title 15 of the Arkansas Code Annotated, that the Bonds shall be obligations only of ADFA secured as specified herein and that, in no event, shall the bonds constitute an indebtedness of the State of Arkansas or an indebtedness for which the faith and credit of the State of Arkansas or any of its revenues are pledged or an indebtedness secured by lien, or security interest in any property of the State.

(g) The Bonds may be issued in one or more series, as determined by ADFA. Additional Bonds may be issued in one or more series to fund additional Capital Improvement Projects subsequently designated pursuant to Section 6(b) (4) of this Act, so long as ADFA determines that revenues transferred to the Tobacco Settlement Debt Service Fund, in combination with other revenues available to secure the Bonds pursuant to Section 6(e) of this Act; will be sufficient to meet all Debt Service Requirements on such additional Bonds and any other Bonds then outstanding.

(h) Any funds remaining and available to ADFA or the trustees under any indenture or resolution authorized herein after the retirement of all Bonds outstanding under such indenture or resolution, and the satisfaction of all contractual obligations related thereto and all current expenses of ADFA related thereto, shall be transferred to the Arkansas Healthy Century Trust Fund.

(i) ADFA may issue Bonds for the purpose of refunding Bonds previously issued pursuant to this Act, and in doing so shall be governed by the provisions of Arkansas Code Annotated § 15-5-314.

(j) All Bonds issued under this Act, and interest thereon, shall be exempt from all taxes of the State of Arkansas, including income, inheritance, and property taxes. The Bonds shall be eligible to secure deposits of all public funds, and shall be legal for investment of municipal, county, bank, fiduciary, insurance company and trust funds.

(k) The State of Arkansas does hereby pledge to and agree with the holders of any Tobacco Settlement Revenue Bonds issued pursuant to this Act that the State shall not (1) limit or alter the distribution of the Tobacco Settlement moneys to the Tobacco Settlement Debt Service Fund if such action would materially impair the rights of the holders of the Bonds, (2) amend or modify the Master Settlement Agreement in any way if such action would materially impair the rights of the holders of the Bonds, (3) limit or alter the rights vested in ADFA to fulfill the terms of any agreements made with the holders of the Bonds, or (4) in any way impair the rights and remedies of the holders of the Bonds, unless and until all Bonds issued pursuant to this Act, together with interest on the Bonds, and all costs and expenses in connection with any action or proceeding by or on behalf of the holders of the Bonds, have been paid, fully met, and discharged. ADFA is authorized to include this pledge and agreement in any agreement with the holders of the Bonds.

SECTION 7. CREATION AND ADMINISTRATION OF ARKANSAS HEALTHY CENTURY TRUST FUND.

(a) There is hereby created and established on the books of the Treasurer of State, Auditor of State, and Chief Fiscal Officer of the State, a trust fund, to be created as a public trust for the benefit of the State of Arkansas, to be known as the "Arkansas Healthy Century Trust Fund," which Trust Fund shall be administered by the State Board of Finance. Such fund shall be restricted in its use and is to be used solely as provided in this Act.

(b) The Arkansas Healthy Century Trust Fund shall be a perpetual trust, the beneficiary of which shall be the State of Arkansas and the programs of the State of Arkansas enumerated in this section. The State Board of Finance, as it may from time to time be comprised, is hereby appointed as trustee of the Arkansas Healthy Century Trust Fund. Such trust shall be revocable, and subject to amendment.

(c) The Arkansas Healthy Century Trust Fund shall be administered in accordance with the provisions of this Section 7, which shall, for all purposes, be deemed to be the governing document of the public trust.

(d) The Arkansas Healthy Century Trust Fund shall be funded in an initial principal amount of one hundred million dollars ($100,000,000) as provided in Section 4 of this Act. All earnings on investments of amounts in the Arkansas Healthy Century Trust Fund, to the extent not used for the purposes enumerated in Section 7(e) of this Act, shall be redeposited in the Arkansas Healthy Century Trust Fund, it being the intent of this Act that the Arkansas Healthy Century Trust Fund shall grow in principal amount until needed for programs and purposes to benefit the State of Arkansas.

(e) The Arkansas Healthy Century Trust Fund shall be held in trust and used for the following purposes, and no other purposes:

(1) investment earnings on the Arkansas Healthy Century Trust Fund may be used for:

(A) the payment of expenses related to the responsibilities of the State Board of Finance as set forth in Section 3 of this Act; and

(B) such programs, and other projects related to health care services, health education, and health-related research as shall, from time to time, be designated in legislation adopted by the General Assembly.

(2) the principal amounts in the Arkansas Healthy Century Trust Fund may only be used for such programs, and other projects related to health care services, health education, and health-related research as shall, from time to time, be designated in legislation adopted by the General Assembly, it being the intent of this Act that the principal amount of the Trust Fund should not be appropriated without amendment of this public trust.

(f) It is intended that the beneficiaries of the Arkansas Healthy Century Trust Fund be the State of Arkansas and its programs, and other projects related to health care services, health education, and health–related research, as such are now in existence or as such may be created in the future.

(g) The State Board of Finance, as trustee of the Arkansas Healthy Century Trust Fund, is authorized to invest all amounts held in the Arkansas Healthy Century Trust Fund in investments pursuant to and in compliance with Section 3(c) of this Act.

SECTION 8. CREATION AND ADMINISTRATION OF THE TOBACCO SETTLEMENT PROGRAM FUND.

(a) There is hereby created and established on the books of the Treasurer of State, Auditor of State and Chief Fiscal of the State a trust fund to be known as the "Tobacco Settlement Program Fund," which fund shall be administered by the State Board of Finance. All moneys deposited into the Tobacco Settlement Program Fund are hereby restricted in their use and to be used solely as provided in this Act. All expenditures and obligations that are payable from the Tobacco Settlement Program Fund and from each of the program accounts, shall be subject to the same fiscal control, accounting, budgetary and purchasing laws as are expenditures and obligations payable from other State Treasury funds, except as specified otherwise in this act. The Chief Fiscal Officer of the State may require additional controls, procedures and reporting requirements that he determines are necessary to carry out the intent of this act.

(b) There shall be transferred from the Tobacco Settlement Cash Holding Fund to the Tobacco Settlement Program Fund the amounts set forth for such transfer as provided in Section 4 of this Act.

(c) Amounts deposited to the Tobacco Settlement Program Fund shall, prior to the distribution to the Program Accounts set forth in Section 8(d), be held and invested in investments pursuant to and in compliance with Section 3(c) of this Act[,] provided that all such investments must mature, or be redeemable without penalty, on or prior to the next succeeding June 30.

(d) On each July 1, the amounts deposited into the Tobacco Settlement Program Fund excluding investment earnings shall be transferred to the various Program Accounts, as follows:

(1) thirty-one and six-tenths per cent (31.6%) of amounts in the Tobacco Settlement Program Fund shall be transferred to the Prevention and Cessation Program Account;

(2) fifteen and eight-tenths per cent (15.8%) of amounts in the Tobacco Settlement Program Fund shall be transferred to the Targeted State Needs Program Account;

(3) twenty-two and eight-tenths per cent (22.8%) of amounts in the Tobacco Settlement Program Fund shall be transferred to the Arkansas Biosciences Institute Program Account; and

(4) twenty-nine and eight-tenths per cent (29.8%) of amounts in the Tobacco Settlement Program Fund shall be transferred to the Medicaid Expansion Programs Account.

(e) (1) All moneys distributed to the Program Accounts set forth above and remaining at the end of each fiscal biennium shall be transferred to the Tobacco Settlement Program Fund by the State Board of Finance. Such amounts will be held in the Tobacco Settlement Program Fund and combined with amounts deposited to such Fund from the annual MSA Disbursements, and then redeposited on July 1 pursuant to the formula set forth in Section 8(d).

(2) However, if the Director of any agency receiving funds from the Tobacco Settlement Program Fund determines that there is a need to retain a portion of the amounts transferred under this section, the Director may submit a request and written justification to the Chief Fiscal Officer of the State. Upon determination by the Chief Fiscal Officer of the State that sufficient justification exists, and after certification by the Arkansas Tobacco Settlement Commission that the program has met the criteria established in Section 18 of this Act, such amounts requested shall remain in the account at the end of a biennium, there to be used for the purposes established by this Act[,] provided that the Chief Fiscal Officer of the State shall seek the review of the Arkansas Legislative Council prior to approval of any such request.

(f) The State Board of Finance shall invest all moneys held in the Tobacco Settlement Program Fund and in each of the Program Accounts. All investment earnings on such funds and accounts shall be transferred on each July 1 to a fund hereby established and as a trust fund on the books of the Treasurer of State, Auditor of State and Chief Fiscal Officer of the State and designated as the "Arkansas Tobacco Settlement Commission Fund." Such fund is to be a trust fund and administered by the State Board of Finance. All moneys deposited into the Arkansas Tobacco Settlement Commission Fund are hereby restricted in their use and to be used solely as provided in this Act. Amounts held in the Arkansas Tobacco Settlement Commission Fund shall be used to pay the costs and expenses of the ATSC, including the monitoring and evaluation program established pursuant to Section 18 of this Act, and to provide grants as authorized in Section 17 of this Act.

SECTION 9. CREATION OF PREVENTION AND CESSATION PROGRAM ACCOUNT.

(a) There is hereby created a trust fund on the books of the Treasurer of State, Auditor of State and Chief Fiscal Officer of the State within the Tobacco Settlement Program Fund maintained by the State Board of Finance an account to be known as the "Prevention and

Cessation Program Account." Such account shall be used by the Arkansas Department of Health for such purposes and in such amounts as may be appropriated in law.

(b) On each July 1, there shall be transferred from the Tobacco Settlement Program Fund to the Prevention and Cessation Program Account the amount specified in Section 8(d) (1).

(c) All moneys deposited to the Prevention and Cessation Program Account except for investment earnings shall be used for the purposes set forth in Section 13 of this Act or such other purposes as may be appropriated in law.

(d) Moneys remaining in the Prevention and Cessation Program Account at the end of the first fiscal year of a biennium shall be carried forward and used for the purposes provided by law. Such amounts that remain at the end of a biennium shall be transferred to the Tobacco Settlement Program Fund pursuant to Section 8(e) of this Act.

SECTION 10. CREATION OF THE TARGETED STATE NEEDS PROGRAM ACCOUNT.

(a) There is hereby created a trust fund on the books of the Treasurer of State, Auditor of State and Chief Fiscal Officer of the State within the Tobacco Settlement Program Fund maintained by the State Board of Finance an account to be known as the "Targeted State Needs Program Account." Such accounts shall be used for such purposes and in such amounts as may be appropriated by law.

(b) On each July 1, there shall be transferred from the Tobacco Settlement Program Fund to the Targeted State Needs Program Account the amount specified in Section 8(d) (2)[.]

(c) All moneys deposited to the Targeted State Needs Program Account except for investment earnings shall be used for the purposes set forth in Section 14 hereof, or such other purposes as may be appropriated in law. Of the amounts deposited to the Targeted State Needs Program Account, the following proportions shall be used to fund the programs established in Section 14 of this Act:

(1) Arkansas School of Public Health - thirty-three per cent (33%);

(2) Area Health Education Center located in Helena - twenty-two per cent (22%);

(3) Donald W. Reynolds Center on Aging - twenty-two per cent (22%); and

(4) Minority Health Initiative administered by the Minority Health Commission - twenty-three per cent (23%).

(d) Moneys remaining in the Targeted State Needs Program Account at the end of the first fiscal year of a biennium shall be carried forward and used for the purposes provided by law. Such amounts that remain at the end of a biennium shall be transferred to the Tobacco Settlement Program Fund pursuant to Section 8(e) of this Act.

SECTION 11. CREATION OF ARKANSAS BIOSCIENCES INSTITUTE PROGRAM ACCOUNT.

(a) There is hereby created a trust fund on the books of the Treasurer of State, Auditor of State and Chief Fiscal Officer of the State within the Tobacco Settlement Program Fund maintained by the State Board of Finance an account to be known as the "Arkansas

Biosciences Institute Program Account." Such account shall be used by the Arkansas Biosciences Institute and its members for such purposes and in such amounts as may be appropriated in law.

(b) On each July 1, there shall be transferred from the Tobacco Settlement Program Fund to the Arkansas Biosciences Institute Program Account the amount specified in Section 8 (d) (3).

(c) All moneys deposited to the Arkansas Biosciences Institute Program Account except for investment earnings shall be used for the purposes set forth in Section 15 hereof, or such other purposes as may be appropriated in law.

(d) Moneys remaining in the Arkansas Biosciences Institute Program Account at the end of the first fiscal year of a biennium shall be carried forward and used for the purposes provided by law. Such amounts that remain at the end of a biennium shall be transferred to the Tobacco Settlement Program Fund pursuant to Section 8(e) of this Act.

SECTION 12. CREATION OF MEDICAID EXPANSION PROGRAMS ACCOUNT.

(a) There is hereby created a trust fund on the books of the Treasurer of State, Auditor of State and Chief Fiscal Officer of the State within the Tobacco Settlement Program Fund maintained by the State Board of Finance an account to be known as the "Medicaid Expansion Programs Account." Such account shall be used by the Arkansas Department of Human Services for such purposes and in such amounts as may be appropriated in law. These funds shall not be used to replace or supplant other funds available in the Department of Human Services Grants Fund Account. The funds appropriated for this program shall not be expended, except in conformity with federal and state laws, and then, only after the Arkansas Department of Human Services obtains the necessary approvals from the federal Health Care Financing Administration.

(b) On each July 1, there shall be transferred from the Tobacco Settlement Program Fund to the Medicaid Expansion Programs Account the amount specified in Section 8 (d) (4).

(c) All moneys deposited to the Medicaid Expansion Programs Account except for investment earnings shall be used for the purposes set forth in Section 16 hereof, or such other purposes as may be appropriated in law.

(d) Moneys remaining in the Medicaid Expansion Programs Account at the end of the first fiscal year of a biennium shall be carried forward and used for the purposes provided by law. Such amounts that remain at the end of a biennium shall be transferred to the Tobacco Settlement Program Fund pursuant to Section 8(e) of this Act.

SECTION 13. ESTABLISHMENT AND ADMINISTRATION OF PREVENTION AND CESSATION PROGRAMS.

(a) It is the intent of this Act that the Arkansas Department of Health should establish the Tobacco Prevention and Cessation Program described in this section, and to administer such programs in accordance with law. The program described in this section shall be administered pursuant to a strategic plan encompassing the elements of a mission statement, defined program(s), and program goals with measurable objectives and strategies to be implemented over a specific timeframe. Evaluation of each program shall include performance based measures for accountability which will measure specific health related results.

(b) The Arkansas Department of Health shall be responsible for developing, integrating, and monitoring tobacco prevention and cessation programs funded under this Act and shall provide administrative oversight and management, including, but not limited to implementing performance based measures. The Arkansas Department of Health shall have authority to award grants and allocate money appropriated to implement the tobacco prevention and cessation program mandated under this Act. The Arkansas Department of Health may contract with those entities necessary to fully implement the tobacco prevention and cessation initiatives mandated under this Act.

Within thirty (30) days of receipt of moneys into the Prevention and Cessation Program Account, fifteen percent (15%) of those moneys shall be deposited into a special account within the prevention and cessation account at the Department of Health to be expended for tobacco prevention and cessation in minority communities as directed by the Director of the Department of Health in consultation with the Chancellor of the University of Arkansas at Pine Bluff, the President of the Arkansas Medical, Dental and Pharmaceutical Association, and the League of United Latin American Citizens.

(c) The Tobacco Prevention and Cessation Program shall be comprised of components approved by the Arkansas Board of Health. The program components selected by the Board of Health shall include:

(1) community prevention programs that reduce youth tobacco use;

(2) local school programs for education and prevention in grades kindergarten through twelve (K-12) that should include school nurses, where appropriate;

(3) enforcement of youth tobacco control laws;

(4) state-wide programs with youth involvement to increase local coalition activities;

(5) tobacco cessation programs;

(6) tobacco-related disease prevention programs;

(7) a comprehensive public awareness and health promotion campaign;

(8) grants and contracts funded pursuant to this Act for monitoring and evaluation, as well as data gathering; and

(9) other programs as deemed necessary by the Board.

(d) There is hereby created an Advisory Committee to the Arkansas Board of Health, to be known as the Tobacco Prevention and Cessation Advisory Committee. It shall be the duty and responsibility of the Committee to advise and assist the Arkansas Board of Health in carrying out the provisions of this Act. The Advisory Committee's authority shall be limited to an advisory function to the Board. The Advisory Committee may, in consultation with the Department of Health, make recommendations to the Board of Health on the strategic plans for the prevention, cessation, and awareness elements of the comprehensive Tobacco Prevention and Cessation Program. The Advisory Committee may also make recommendations to the Board on the strategic vision and guiding principles of the Tobacco Prevention and Cessation Program.

(e) The Advisory Committee shall be governed as follows:

(1) The Advisory Committee shall consist of eighteen (18) members; one (1) member to be appointed by the President Pro Tempore of the Senate and one (1) member to be appointed by the Speaker of the House of Representatives, and sixteen (16) members to be appointed by the Governor. The Committee members appointed by the Governor shall be selected from a list of at least three (3) names submitted by each of the following designated groups to the Governor, and shall consist of the following: one (1) member appointed to represent the Arkansas Medical Society; one (1) member shall represent the Arkansas Hospital Association; one (1) member shall represent the American Cancer Society; one (1) member shall represent the American Heart Association; one (1) member shall represent the American Lung Association; one (1) member shall represent the Coalition for a Tobacco-Free Arkansas; one (1) member shall represent Arkansans for Drug Free Youth; one (1) member shall represent the Arkansas Department of Education; one (1) member shall represent the Arkansas Minority Health Commission; one (1) member shall represent the Arkansas Center for Health Improvement; one (1) member shall represent the Arkansas Association of Area Agencies on Aging; one (1) member shall represent the Arkansas Nurses Association; one (1) member shall represent the Arkansas Cooperative Extension Service; one (1) member shall represent the University of Arkansas at Pine Bluff; one member shall represent the League of United Latin American Citizens; and one (1) member shall represent the Arkansas Medical, Dental and Pharmaceutical Association. The Executive Committee of Arkansas Students Working Against Tobacco shall serve as youth advisors to this Advisory Committee. All members of this committee shall be residents of the State of Arkansas.

(2) The Advisory Committee will initially have four (4) members who will serve one (1) year terms; four (4) members who will serve two (2) year terms; five (5) members who will serve three (3) year terms; and five (5) members who will serve four (4) years. Members of the Advisory Committee shall draw lots to determine the length of the initial term. Subsequently appointed members shall be appointed for four (4) year terms and no member can serve more than two (2) consecutive full four (4) year terms. The terms shall commence on October 1st of each year.

(3) Members of the Advisory Committee shall not be entitled to compensation for their services, but may receive expense reimbursement in accordance with Ark. Code Ann. § 25-16-902, to be paid from funds appropriated for this program to the Arkansas Department of Health.

(4) Members appointed to the Advisory Committee and the organizations they represent shall make full disclosure of the member's participation on the Committee when applying for any grant or contract funded by this Act.

(5) All members appointed to the Advisory Committee shall make full and public disclosure of any past or present association to the tobacco industry.

(6) The Advisory Committee shall, within ninety (90) days of appointment, hold a meeting and elect from its membership a chairman for a term set by the Advisory Committee. The Advisory Committee shall adopt bylaws.

(7) The Advisory Committee shall meet at least quarterly[;] however, special meetings may be called at any time at the pleasure of the Board of Health or pursuant to the bylaws adopted by the Advisory Committee.

(f) The Arkansas Board of Health is authorized to review the recommendations of the Advisory Committee. The Arkansas Board of Health shall adopt and promulgate rules, standards and guidelines as necessary to implement the program in consultation with the Arkansas Department of Health.

(g) The Arkansas Department of Health in implementing this Program shall establish such performance based accountability procedures and requirements as are consistent with law.

(h) Each of the programs adopted pursuant to this act shall be subject to the monitoring and evaluation procedures described in Section 18 of this Act.

SECTION 14. ESTABLISHMENT AND ADMINISTRATION OF THE TARGETED STATE NEEDS PROGRAMS.

(a) The University of Arkansas for Medical Sciences is hereby instructed to establish the Targeted State Needs Programs described in this section, and to administer such programs in accordance with law.

(b) The targeted state needs programs to be established are as follows:

(1) Arkansas School of Public Health;

(2) Area Health Education Center (located in Helena);

(3) Donald W. Reynolds Center on Aging; and

(4) Minority Health Initiative administered by the Minority Health Commission.

(c)(1) Arkansas School of Public Health. The Arkansas School of Public Health is hereby established as a part of the University of Arkansas for Medical Sciences for the purpose of conducting activities to improve the health and healthcare of the citizens of Arkansas. These activities should include, but not be limited to the following functions: faculty and course offerings in the core areas of public health including health policy and management, epidemiology, biostatistics, health economics, maternal and child health, environmental health, and health and services research; with courses offered both locally and statewide via a variety of distance learning mechanisms.

(2) It is intended that the Arkansas School of Public Health should serve as a resource for the General Assembly, the Governor, state agencies, and communities. Services provided by the Arkansas School of Public Health should include, but not be limited to the following: consultation and analysis, developing and disseminating programs, obtaining federal and philanthropic grants, conducting research, and other scholarly activities in support of improving the health and healthcare of the citizens of Arkansas.

(d) Area Health Education Center. The first Area Health Education Centers were founded in 1973 as the primary educational outreach effort of the University of Arkansas for Medical Sciences. It is the intent of this Act that UAMS establish a new Area Health Education Center to serve the following counties: Crittenden, Phillips, Lee, St. Francis, Chicot, Monroe, and Desha. The new AHEC shall be operated in the same fashion as

293

other facilities in the UAMS AHEC program including training students in the fields of medicine, nursing, pharmacy and various allied health professions, and offering medical residents specializing in family practice. The training shall emphasize primary care, covering general health education and basic medical care for the whole family. The program shall be headquartered in Helena with offices in Lake Village and West Memphis.

(e) Donald W. Reynolds Center on Aging. It is the intent of this Act that UAMS establish, in connection with the Donald W. Reynolds Center on Aging and its existing AHEC program, healthcare programs around the state offering interdisciplinary educational programs to better equip local healthcare professionals in preventive care, early diagnosis and effective treatment for the elderly population throughout the state. The satellite centers will provide access to dependable healthcare, education, resource and support programs for the most rapidly growing segment of the State's population. Each center's program is to be defined by an assessment of local needs and priorities in consultation with local healthcare professionals.

(f) Minority Health Initiative. It is the intent of this Act that the Arkansas Minority Health Commission establish and administer the Arkansas Minority Health Initiative for screening, monitoring, and treating hypertension, strokes, and other disorders disproportionately critical to minority groups in Arkansas. The program should be designed:

(1) to increase awareness of hypertension, strokes, and other disorders disproportionately critical to minorities by utilizing different approaches that include but are not limited to the following: advertisements, distribution of educational materials and providing medications for high risk minority populations;

(2) to provide screening or access to screening for hypertension, strokes, and other disorders disproportionately critical to minorities but will also provide this service to any citizen within the state regardless of racial/ethnic group;

(3) to develop intervention strategies to decrease hypertension, strokes, and other disorders noted above, as well as associated complications, including: educational programs, modification of risk factors by smoking cessation programs, weight loss, promoting healthy lifestyles, and treatment of hypertension with cost-effective, well-tolerated medications, as well as case management for patients in these programs; and

(4) to develop and maintain a database that will include: biographical data, screening data, costs, and outcomes.

(g) The Minority Health Commission will receive quarterly updates on the progress of these programs and make recommendations or changes as necessary.

(h) The programs described in this section shall be administered pursuant to a strategic plan encompassing the elements of a mission statement, defined program(s), and program goals with measurable objectives and strategies to be implemented over a specific timeframe. Evaluation of each program shall include performance based measures for accountability which will measure specific health related results.

(i) Each of the programs adopted pursuant to this section shall be subject to the monitoring and evaluation procedures described in Section 18 of this Act.

SECTION 15. ESTABLISHMENT AND ADMINISTRATION OF THE ARKANSAS BIOSCIENCES INSTITUTE.

(a) It is the intent of this Act to hereby establish the Arkansas Biosciences Institute for the educational and research purposes set forth hereinafter to encourage and foster the conduct of research through the University of Arkansas, Division of Agriculture, the University of Arkansas for Medical Sciences, University of Arkansas, Fayetteville, Arkansas Children's Hospital and Arkansas State University. The Arkansas Biosciences Institute is part of a broad program to address health issues with specific emphasis on smoking and the use of tobacco products. The Arkansas Biosciences Institute is intended to develop more fully the interdisciplinary opportunities for research primarily in the areas set forth hereinafter.

(b) Purposes. The Arkansas Biosciences Institute is established for the following purposes:

(1) to conduct agricultural research with medical implications;

(2) to conduct bioengineering research focused on the expansion of genetic knowledge and new potential applications in the agricultural-medical fields;

(3) to conduct tobacco-related research that focuses on the identification and applications of behavioral, diagnostic and therapeutic research addressing the high level of tobacco-related illnesses in the State of Arkansas;

(4) to conduct nutritional and other research focusing on prevention or treatment of cancer, congenital or hereditary conditions or other related conditions; and

(5) to conduct other research identified by the primary educational and research institutions involved in the Arkansas Biosciences Institute or as otherwise identified by the Institute Board of the Arkansas Biosciences Institute and which is reasonably related, or complementary to, research identified in subparagraphs (1) through (4) of this subsection.

(c) Arkansas Biosciences Institute Board. (1) There is hereby established the Arkansas Biosciences Institute Board which shall consist of the following: the President of the University of Arkansas; the President of Arkansas State University; the Chancellor of the University of Arkansas for Medical Sciences; the Chancellor of the University of Arkansas, Fayetteville; the Vice President for Agriculture of the University of Arkansas; the Director of the Arkansas Science and Technology Authority; the Director of the National Center for Toxicological Research; the President of Arkansas Children's Hospital; and two (2) individuals possessing recognized scientific, academic or business qualifications appointed by the Governor. The two (2) members of the Institute Board who are appointed by the Governor will serve four (4) year terms and are limited to serving two consecutive four (4) year terms. The terms shall commence on October 1 of each year. These members appointed by the Governor are not entitled to compensation for their services, but may receive expense reimbursement in accordance with Ark. Code Ann. § 25-16-902, to [be] paid from funds appropriated for this program. The Institute Board shall establish and appoint the members of an Industry Advisory Committee and a Science Advisory Committee composed of knowledgeable persons in the fields of industry and science. These Committees shall serve as resources for the Institute Board in their respective areas and will provide an avenue of communication to the Institute Board on areas of potential research.

(2) The Arkansas Biosciences Institute Board shall establish rules for governance for Board affairs and shall:

(A) provide overall coordination of the program;

(B) develop procedures for recruitment and supervision of member institution research review panels, the membership of which shall vary depending on the subject matter of proposals and review requirements, and may, in order to avoid conflicts of interest and to ensure access to qualified reviews, recommend reviewers not only from Arkansas but also from outside the state;

(C) provide for systematic dissemination of research results to the public and the health care community, including work to produce public service advertising on screening and research results, and provide for mechanisms to disseminate the most current research findings in the areas of cause and prevention, cure, diagnosis and treatment of tobacco related illnesses, in order that these findings may be applied to the planning, implementation and evaluation of any other research programs of this state;

(D) develop policies and procedures to facilitate the translation of research results into commercial, alternate technological, and other applications wherever appropriate and consistent with state and federal law; and

(E) transmit on or before the end of each calendar year on an annual basis, a report to the General Assembly and the Governor on grants made, grants in progress, program accomplishments, and future program directions. Each report shall include, but not be limited to, all of the following information:

(i) the number and dollar amounts of internal and external research grants, including the amount allocated to negotiated indirect costs;

(ii) the subject of research grants;

(iii) the relationship between federal and state funding for research;

(iv) the relationship between each project and the overall strategy of the research program;

(v) a summary of research findings, including discussion of promising new areas; and

(vi) the corporations, institutions, and campuses receiving grant awards.

(d) Director. The director of the Arkansas Biosciences Institute shall be appointed by the President of the University of Arkansas, in consultation with the President of Arkansas State University, and the President of Arkansas Children's Hospital, and based upon the advice and recommendation of the Institute Board. The Director shall be an employee of the University of Arkansas and shall serve at the pleasure of the President of the University of Arkansas. The Director shall be responsible for recommending policies and procedures to the Institute Board for its internal operation and shall establish and ensure methods of communication among the units and divisions of the University of Arkansas, Arkansas Children's Hospital and Arkansas State University and their faculty and employees engaged in research under the auspices of the Institute. The Director shall undertake such administrative duties as may be necessary to facilitate conduct of research under the auspices of the Arkansas Biosciences Institute. The Director shall perform such other duties as are established by the President of the University of Arkansas in consultation with the President of Arkansas State University, the President of Arkansas Children's Hospital and with the input of the Institute Board.

(e) Conduct of Research. Research performed under the auspices of the Institute shall be conducted in accordance with the policies of the University of Arkansas, Arkansas Children's Hospital, and Arkansas State University, as applicable. The Institute Board and the Director of the Institute shall facilitate the establishment of centers to focus on research in agri-medicine, environmental biotechnology, medical genetics, bio-engineering and industry development. Such centers shall be established in accordance with procedures adopted by the Institute Board, and shall provide for interdisciplinary collaborative efforts with a specific research and educational objectives.

(f) In determining research projects and areas to be supported from such appropriated funds, each of the respective institutions shall assure that adequate opportunities are given to faculty and other researchers to submit proposals for projects to be supported in whole or in part from such funds. At least annually the Institute Board shall review research being conducted under the auspices of the Institute and may make recommendations to the President of the University of Arkansas and the President of Arkansas State University and President of Arkansas Children's Hospital of ways in which such research funds may be more efficiently employed or of collaborative efforts which would maximize the utilization of available funds.

(g) The programs described in this section shall be administered pursuant to a strategic plan encompassing the elements of a mission statement, defined program(s), and program goals with measurable objectives and strategies to be implemented over a specific timeframe. Evaluation of each program shall include performance based measures for accountability which will measure specific health related results.

(h) Each of the programs adopted pursuant to this Section shall be subject to the monitoring and evaluation procedures described in Section 18 of this Act.

SECTION 16. ESTABLISHMENT AND ADMINISTRATION OF MEDICAID EXPANSION PROGRAMS.

(a) It is the intent of this Act that the Arkansas Department of Human Services should establish the Medicaid expansion programs described in this section, and to administer such program in accordance with law.

(b) The Medicaid expansion programs shall be a separate and distinct component of the Medicaid program currently administered by the Department of Human Services and shall be established as follows:

(1) expanding Medicaid coverage and benefits to pregnant women;

(2) expanding inpatient and outpatient hospital reimbursements and benefits to adults aged nineteen (19) to sixty-four (64);

(3) expanding non-institutional coverage and benefits to adults aged 65 and over; and,

(4) creating and providing a limited benefit package to adults aged nineteen (19) to sixty-four (64). All such expenditures shall be made in conformity with the State Medicaid Plan as amended and approved by the Health Care Financing Administration.

(c) The programs defined in this section shall be administered pursuant to a strategic plan encompassing the elements of a mission statement, defined program(s), and program goals with measurable objectives and strategies to be implemented over a specific timeframe. Evaluation of each program shall include performance-based measures for accountability which will measure specific health related results.

(d) Each of the programs adopted pursuant to this Section shall be subject to the monitoring and evaluation procedures described in Section 18 of this Act.

SECTION 17. ESTABLISHMENT OF THE ARKANSAS TOBACCO SETTLEMENT COMMISSION.

(a) There is hereby created and recognized the Arkansas Tobacco Settlement Commission, which shall be comprised of the following: the Director of the Arkansas Science and Technology Authority, or his designee; the Director of the Department of Education or his designee; the Director of the Department of Higher Education or his designee; the Director of the Department of Human Services or his designee; the Director of the Arkansas Department of Health or his designee; a healthcare professional to be selected by the Senate President Pro Tempore; a healthcare professional to be selected by the Speaker of the House of Representatives; a citizen selected by the Governor; and a citizen selected by the Attorney General.

(b) The four (4) members of the Commission who are not on the Commission by virtue of being a director of an agency, will serve four (4) year terms. The terms shall commence on October 1st of each year. Committee members are limited to serving two (2) consecutive four (4) year terms. Members of the Commission shall not be entitled to compensation for their services, but may receive expense reimbursement in accordance with Ark. Code Ann. § 25-16-902, to be paid from funds appropriated for this program.

(c) Members appointed to the Commission and the organizations they represent shall make full disclosure of the member's participation on the Commission when applying for any grant or contract funded by this Act.

(d) All members appointed to the Commission shall make full and public disclosure of any past or present association to the tobacco industry.

(e) The Commission shall, within ninety (90) days of appointment, hold a meeting and elect from its membership a chairman for a term set by the Commission. The Commission is authorized to adopt bylaws.

(f) The Commission shall meet at least quarterly[;] however, special meetings of the Commission may be called at any time at the pleasure of the Chairman or pursuant to the bylaws of the Commission.

(g) ATSC is authorized to hire an independent third party with appropriate experience in health, preventive resources, health statistics and evaluation expertise to perform monitoring and evaluation of program expenditures made from the Program Accounts pursuant to this Act. Such monitoring and evaluation shall be performed in accordance with Section 18 of this Act, and the third party retained to perform such services shall prepare a biennial report to be delivered to the General Assembly and the Governor by each August 1 preceding a general session of the General Assembly. The report shall be accompanied by a recommendation from the ATSC as to the continued funding for each program.

(h) The Commission is authorized to hire such staff as it may reasonably need to carry out the duties described in this Act. The costs and expenses of the monitoring and evaluation program, as well as the salaries, costs and expenses of staff, shall be paid from the Arkansas Tobacco Settlement Commission Fund established pursuant to Section 8 of this Act.

(i) If the deposits into the Arkansas Tobacco Settlement Commission Fund exceed the amount necessary to pay the costs and expenses described in Subsection (h) of this Section, then the ATSC is authorized to make grants as follows:

(A) Those organizations eligible to receive grants are non-profit and community based.

(B) Grant criteria shall be established based upon the following principles:

(i) all funds should be used to improve and optimize the health of Arkansans;

(ii) funds should be spent on long-term projects that improve the health of Arkansans;

(iii) Future tobacco-related illness and health care costs in Arkansas should be minimized through this opportunity; and

(iv) funds should be invested in solutions that work effectively and efficiently in Arkansas.

(C) Grant awards shall be restricted in amounts up to fifty-thousand dollars ($50,000) per year for each eligible organization.

SECTION 18. MONITORING AND EVALUATION OF PROGRAMS.

(a) The ATSC is directed to conduct monitoring and evaluation of the programs established in Sections 13, 14, 15, and 16 of this Act, to ensure optimal impact on improving the health of Arkansans and fiscal stewardship of the Tobacco Settlement. ATSC shall develop performance indicators to monitor programmatic functions that are state and situation specific and to support performance-based assessment for governmental accountability. The performance indicators shall reflect short and long-term goals and objectives of each program, be measurable, and provide guidance for internal programmatic improvement and legislative funding decisions. ATSC is expected to modify these performance indicators as goals and objectives are met and new inputs to programmatic outcomes are identified.

(b) All programs funded by the Tobacco Settlement and established in Sections 13, 14, 15 and 16 shall be monitored and evaluated to justify continued support based upon the state's performance-based budgeting initiative. These programs shall be administered pursuant to a strategic plan encompassing the elements of a mission statement, defined programs, program goals with measurable objectives and strategies to be implemented over a specific timeframe. Evaluation of each program shall include performance-based measures for accountability that will measure specific health related results. All expenditures that are payable from the Tobacco Settlement Program Fund and from each of the Program Accounts, therein, shall be subject to the same fiscal control, accounting, budgetary and purchasing laws as are expenditures and obligations payable from State Treasury funds, except as specified otherwise in this Act. The Chief Fiscal Officer of the State may require additional controls, procedures and reporting requirements that he determines are necessary in order to carry out the intent of this act.

(c) The ATSC is directed to establish program goals in according with the following initiation, short and long-term performance indicators for each program to be funded by the Tobacco Settlement, which performance indicators shall be subject to modification by the ATSC based on specific situations and subsequent developments. Progress with respect to these performance indicators shall be reported to the Governor and the General Assembly for future appropriation decisions.

(1) Tobacco Prevention and Cessation: The goal is to reduce the initiation of tobacco use and the resulting negative health and economic impact. The following are anticipated objectives in reaching this overall goal:

(A) Initiation: The Arkansas Department of Health is to start the program within six (6) months of available appropriation and funding.

(B) Short-term: Communities shall establish local Tobacco Prevention Initiatives.

(C) Long-term: Surveys demonstrate a reduction in numbers of Arkansans who smoke and/or use tobacco.

(2) Medicaid Expansion: The goal is to expand access to healthcare through targeted Medicaid expansions thereby improving the health of eligible Arkansans.

(A) Initiation: The Arkansas Department of Human Services is to start the program initiatives within six (6) months of available appropriation and funding.

(B) Short-term: The Arkansas Department of Human Services demonstrates an increase in the number of new Medicaid eligible persons participating in the expanded programs.

(C) Long-term: Demonstrate improved health and reduced long-term health costs of Medicaid eligible persons participating in the expanded programs.

(3) Research and Health Education: The goal is to develop new tobacco-related medical and agricultural research initiatives to improve the access to new technologies, improve the health of Arkansans, and stabilize the economic security of Arkansas.

(A) Initiation: The Arkansas Biosciences Institute Board shall begin operation of the Arkansas Biosciences Institute within twelve (12) months of available appropriation and funding.

(B) Short-term: Arkansas Biosciences Institute shall initiate new research programs for the purpose of conducting, as specified in Section 15: agricultural research with medical implications; bioengineering research; tobacco-related research; nutritional research focusing on cancer prevention or treatment; and other research approved by the Institute Board.

(C) Long-term: The Institute's research results should translate into commercial, alternate technological, and other applications wherever appropriate in order that the research results may be applied to the planning, implementation and evaluation of any health related programs in the State. The Institute is also to obtain federal and philanthropic grant funding.

(4) Targeted State Needs Programs: The goal is to improve the healthcare systems in Arkansas and the access to healthcare delivery systems, thereby resolving critical deficiencies that negatively impact the health of the citizens of the state.

(A) School of Public Health:

(i) Initiation: Increase the number of communities in which participants receive public health training.

(ii) Short-Term: Obtain federal and philanthropic grant funding.

(iii) Long-term: Elevate the overall ranking of the health status of Arkansas.

(B) Minority Health Initiative:

(i) Initiation: Start the program within twelve (12) months of available appropriation and funding.

(ii) Short-Term: Prioritize the list of health problems and planned intervention for minority population and increase the number of Arkansans screened and treated for tobacco-related illnesses.

(iii) Long-term: Reduce death/disability due to tobacco-related illnesses of Arkansans.

(C) Donald W. Reynolds Center on Aging:

(i) Initiation: Start the program within twelve (12) months of available appropriation and funding.

(ii) Short-Term: Prioritize the list of health problems and planned intervention for elderly Arkansans and increase the number of Arkansans participating in health improvement programs.

(iii) Long-term: Improve health status and decrease death rates of elderly Arkansans, as well as obtaining federal and philanthropic grant funding.

(D) Area Health Education Center:

(i) Initiation: Start the new AHEC in Helena with DHEC offices in West Memphis and Lake Village within twelve (12) months of available appropriation and funding.

(ii) Short-Term: Increase the number of communities and clients served through the expanded AHEC/DHEC offices.

(iii) Long-Term: Increase the access to a primary care provider in underserved communities.

SECTION 19. Arkansas Code Annotated § 19-4-803 is amended to add a new subsection to read as follows:

"(e) The Tobacco Settlement Cash Holding Fund administered by the State Board of Finance shall be exempt from the provisions of this subchapter."

SECTION 20. The Director of the Department of Human Services, after seeking approval of the Chief Fiscal Officer of the State and review by the Arkansas Legislative

Council, shall implement the Medicaid Expansion Programs established in Section [16] of this Act with such existing funds and unobligated appropriation as may be available during the biennial period ending June 30, 2001.

SECTION 21. The Director of the Department of Human Services shall use six hundred thousand dollars ($600,000) of existing funds and unobligated appropriation as may be available during the biennial period ending June 30, 2001, to offset federal cuts in the Meals on Wheels Program.

SECTION 22. If any provision of this Act or the application thereof to any person or circumstance is held invalid, such invalidity shall not affect other provisions of this Act which can be given effect without the invalid provision or application, and to this end the provisions of this Act are declared to be severable.

SECTION 23. All laws and parts of laws in conflict with this Act are hereby repealed.

Appendix B.
RAND Evaluation of the Arkansas Tobacco Settlement
Program Evaluation Methods

The evaluation approach we have designed responds to the intent of the Tobacco Settlement Commission to perform a longitudinal evaluation of the development and ongoing operation of its funding program. We employ an iterative evaluation process through which information is tracked on both the program implementation processes and effects on identified outcomes. This information can be used to inform both future funding decisions by the Commission and decisions by the funded programs on their goals and operations. Presented below is a description of each of the three major evaluation components: policy analysis, process evaluation, and outcome evaluation.

POLICY EVALUATION

The policy evaluation was performed to achieve two purposes. First, we documented the policy issues confronting the state of Arkansas, which was the context within which the Coalition for Healthy Arkansas Today (CHART) process and the Initiated Act were developed, and we identified the priorities and rationale for the funding decisions implemented in the Initiated Act. Second, the results of the program evaluation were synthesized and interpreted in the context of the state's policy issues to provide the Commission and other policymakers with additional information to assist future decisions on Tobacco Settlement policy and funding priorities.

Sources of information for the policy evaluation included existing documents produced by various state agencies, federal agencies, or relevant policy research organizations, as well as interviews with stakeholders involved in or affected by the use of the Tobacco Settlement funds or relevant programs. We conducted individual and group interviews with key stakeholders, through which we learned and documented their perspectives regarding priorities and activities being undertaken by the Tobacco Settlement programs.

PROCESS EVALUATION

Process evaluation refers to a set of evaluation activities that document the development, implementation, and ongoing activities of a program (Devine, 1999) and its level of quality. We performed a process evaluation for each of the programs funded by the Arkansas Tobacco Settlement Commission.

Process evaluations provide a rich context in which to interpret outcome results—a context that ties these results to the levers that produce them. Without a process evaluation, outcome evaluators may find themselves trying to explain outcomes as a function of services that may not have been delivered or that are different from what the program intended to deliver (Scheirer, 1994). Process evaluation also has a formative function (i.e., providing insights and understandings that can be continuously fed back to those involved in setting up the delivery of services) (Browne and Wildavsky, 1987). When performed as a continuous, collaborative, and iterative activity, an activity that draws upon multiple sources of data on an ongoing basis over the lifetime of the study, a process evaluation can grow and change as a program matures (Dehar,

Casswell, and Duignan, 1993; Shadish et al., 1991). Finally, a well-designed process evaluation can provide critical findings on facilitators and barriers to program implementation—findings that will be invaluable for future replication of an innovative program model.

The framework used to perform the process evaluation for each of the funded programs was the FORmative Evaluation, Consultation, and Systems Technique (FORECAST) model. In this process evaluation system, program staff and evaluators collaboratively decide what needs to be monitored and how (Goodman and Wandersman, 1994). It is especially well suited for this evaluation because the funded programs are pursuing very distinct program activities and interventions.

As the first step in the FORECAST process, we worked with the programs to develop logic models depicting what the program has identified as the underlying issues and how it will operate to successfully address those issues. In this case, the definition of issues was guided by the performance mandate that the Initiated Act defined for each program. The action plans built upon work already begun by the programs, as well as the priorities defined for each program in the initiation, short-term, and long-term performance indicators defined in the Initiated Act.

Documenting Program Development and Progress

To monitor the development and progress of the funded programs on a regular basis, we are using a combination of annual site visits and quarterly conference calls. At the site visits, we are able to observe the programs in operation at their facilities, engage in dialogue with program leaders and participants, and conduct interviews with other stakeholders outside of the program management. The site-visit information represented annual "data points" in a longitudinal collection of data on a program's status over time. Through the quarterly conference calls, we collect data for intervening points in time between the site visits, through which we document trends in program development along with changes in the issues the programs face over time and how the programs manage those issues.

Annual Site Visits. The first annual site visits were conducted in March and April 2003, the second site visits were in April 2004, and the third visits were in February and March 2005. In the first two years, the site visit for each program consisted of two parts—meetings with the program management and staff to gather information on the program scope and operation, and interviews with other stakeholders who are users of the program or community leaders to learn their perspectives on the program. In the third year, the site visits were limited to meetings with program management and staff to gather information on program progress and issues encountered, and to work with them in developing long-term goals for each program.

Each site visit was planned in advance in consultation with the program lead. After each site visit, the RAND site-visit team prepared a report summarizing what we learned from the discussions, interviews, and associated documents.

Quarterly Conference Calls. Regular contact with the programs between site visits is maintained through quarterly telephone conferences. During these calls, the programs inform RAND staff of significant events that have taken place over the past three months, including significant achievements and successes that should be given special notice, as well as ongoing barriers and challenges they face. At the initial site visits, we identified sets of key issues for each program that we followed. At each quarterly call, we document the status of the program in managing these issues, and we identify other new issues that have emerged. Collectively, these reports yielded a description of the evolution of each program over time.

The quarterly conference calls are conducted with each program in July, October, and January of each evaluation cycle. The fourth contact in the cycle is the annual site visit in March or April of each year, at which the program's full year of activities are assessed.

Process Indicators

A set of process indicators was developed for each of the funded programs. The purpose of the indicators is to provide information for the Arkansas General Assembly, Arkansas Tobacco Settlement Commission, and the funded programs about the programs' progress in achieving the aims established in the Initiated Act. The process indicators consist of the following:

- *Longitudinal measures* that can be evaluated on a periodic basis to track program trends over time (e.g., percentage of residents in a county who participated in an educational program)*Single-event measures* that document the achievement of key program achievements (e.g., completing a needs assessment)

The process indicators were generated at the start of the evaluation through an interactive process with the funded programs. As RAND developed the indicators, we consulted with the program leads to ensure that the programs (1) were kept fully aware of the contents of the evaluation, (2) could assess the validity of the indicators from the program perspective, and (3) had an opportunity to identify key process measures they felt had been overlooked.

The indicators address policy-level aspects of the programs that relate directly to the program mandates specified in the Initiated Act. Differing numbers of indicators were developed for each program, depending on the complexity of the program and the level of detail the program preferred for tracking its progress. RAND selected the process indicators using the following criteria:

1. Closely related to the most important program outcomes
2. Early indicators of performance
3. Easy to measure
4. Create incentives that are aligned with the goals of the program
5. Diverse in order to cover the range of markers
6. Either longitudinal to show change from year to year or a key program endpoint

The programs' performance on the process indicators has been monitored on a semiannual basis for the two six-month periods of January through June and July through December of each year. We gathered the data retrospectively for the time from initial program funding to the start of the evaluation, so that programming trends can be tracked from inception. The data collection has continued prospectively as part of the longitudinal evaluation. Trends in the indicators have been reported to the Arkansas Tobacco Settlement Commission. This information is reported for each program as part of the process-evaluation results in Chapters 3 through 9.

Long-range Goals

As described above, the RAND evaluation team worked with the funded programs in the FY2005 evaluation cycle to develop long-range goals that define the direction and level of activity that each program is planning to achieve. Many of these goals build upon the process indicators established for the programs; others address other desired achievements. Whenever possible, the long-range goals are quantified to enable their achievement to be measurable. In some cases, however, the goals are stated in qualitative terms, usually reflecting uncertainty in the feasibility of achieving a goal or inadequate data to be able to measure it yet. The goals established for each program are stated in Chapters 3 through 9 and summarized in Chapter 12.

Analysis of Program Spending Trends

An important part of the process evaluation is documenting and assessing trends in the programs' spending of the Tobacco Settlement funds. The pace at which spending grew in the early months of the funding reflects the speed at which a program was able to initiate its new programming and bring it to full operational status. In addition, the extent to which the programs spent the available funds on the mandated services or other programming is a measure of their success in applying these valuable resources to addressing the health-related needs of Arkansans.

In early 2005, we requested monthly financial data from all the funded programs on their spending of the Tobacco Settlement funds they had received. Using the information provided, we prepared schedules of appropriations, funds received, and actual expenditures for each program. Monthly patterns of spending by line items were analyzed to identify any variances from trends, with particular attention to the line items with the largest expenditures. Wherever possible, we tracked spending by key program components so that trends could be followed for the mix of services provided by each program. The results of the spending analysis are reported in Chapters 3 through 9 as part of the process-evaluation results for each program.

Analysis of Mature Program Functioning

In 2005, we administered a survey to all programs to examine their functioning along four important dimensions: (1) governing and advisory boards, (2) financial and accounting, (3) contracting and oversight, and (4) quality improvement. The survey instrument is included as Appendix C of this report. These areas were deemed important at this stage of program development. The programs were sufficiently mature that we could move our focus from measures of basic functioning to these areas that are required for the maintenance and evolution of program activity in a changing environment. After the programs provided the requested information, the RAND team members reviewed the responses to clarify any issues that remained unclear. The information that was gathered is analyzed in this report.

OUTCOME EVALUATION

For an effective outcome evaluation, we examine program results relative to the overarching goals to be achieved through application of the Tobacco Settlement money. For example, we examine whether the expenditures had a positive impact on the health of Arkansans. Such an analysis requires knowledge of counterfactuals: What would the health of Arkansans have been in the absence of the funded programs? What would the outcomes have been if the money had been spent on other programs instead?

The outcome evaluations presented in Chapters 10 and 11 use data from a variety of sources to measure the effect of the funded programs on the smoking-related outcomes and non-smoking outcomes of Arkansans. We describe here the data and methods used in the analyses, making references to particular sections of the chapters that provide examples of where these methods are used.

Measuring Outcomes

The scope of the outcome evaluation was defined by the outcome measures we selected for analysis. The first step in this process was to review the goals of the Tobacco Settlement expenditures. The measures selected had to be capable of providing information on how well the programs are meeting those goals. Then we worked with the program leads in identifying outcomes that would be expected to change as a result of the program interventions they were implementing. We used this information to define candidate measures, and we then assessed the availability of data needed to analyze each measure.

Two sets of outcome measures were defined for the evaluation: overall measures that addressed global outcomes for the state as a whole, and program-specific measures that addressed outcomes specific to the types of services provided by each program. All of the overall measures were measures of smoking behaviors and related health outcomes, which address one of the fundamental goals of the Initiated Act—reducing use of tobacco products across the state.

To accurately estimate program effects, two values of each outcome measure must be compared: the actual outcome that occurs in the presence of the program and a counterfactual value of the outcome that would have occurred if the program had not been implemented. Many outcome measures would change even without the program as a result of trends in demographics and economic conditions. Therefore, simple baseline outcome measures often do not provide adequate counterfactuals by which to measure program impact.

It is well documented that program changes require time to be translated into health outcomes for a given population. Furthermore, localized program activities will affect only the population exposed to the program. Some of the programs supported by the Tobacco Settlement funds are state-level programs. However, in many cases, the program interventions are not applied equally across the entire state but are focused on specific geographic areas or on a designated population subgroup. Therefore, state- and national-level data from such instruments as the Behavioral Risk Factor Surveillance System (BRFSS) and Youth Risk Behavior Surveillance System (YRBSS) are not specific enough to detect and assess program effects for some of the funded programs. Other data sources had to be sought to address these outcomes.

Assessment of program impacts requires the ability to connect the effort undertaken by a program to the expected outcome in a way that takes into account other factors that influence the outcome. If this is not done, changes in an outcome could be attributed incorrectly to a program's interventions when in fact the changes were due to other factors. Examples of other factors include the following:

- Broader (nationwide or regional) trends that are independent of local program efforts

- Continuation of trends that pre-date the program and reflect effects of earlier actions or interventions

- Changes in the demographic composition of the population

- Efforts by other related programs

Assessment also requires that findings be presented with an indication of their statistical precision. Whenever survey data are collected and analyzed, it is important to report not only the size of the effect, but also the degree of certainty. The degree of certainty can be reported as a margin of error (+/- so many percent), as a confidence interval (the narrower the interval, the more precise the estimate), or as a significance level on a hypothesis test (whether or not the finding is reliable or could be expected by chance). Without this additional information, the reader does not know whether an apparent impact reflects changes in the underlying behavior or merely variability in the data or model.

The Use of Population Measures

In this appendix, we discuss the data and methods related to outcome measures for the entire target population rather than for program participants alone. For example, we measure changes in smoking rates for all adults in Arkansas rather than for a group who participated in a particular education or cessation program. In many cases the target population is restricted to a particular demographic group (e.g., youth) or a specific geographic region (e.g., the Delta), but in all cases we measure outcomes for that entire target population and not for a specific group of program participants.

There are several advantages of this approach. First, some program components, either alone or in combination with other program components that have similar goals, have sufficient size that an impact should be measurable at a population level. In such a case, it is important to demonstrate that the program affects a broad segment of the population. Second, some components, such as media campaigns and other educational outreach efforts, do not have participants per se but are targeted at everyone in a particular population. Third, many programs have an impact that extends beyond the immediate participants. For example, programs that attempt to change the behavior of program participants through education can affect the behavior and health outcomes of other people who are in contact with the immediate participants. Finally, and perhaps most important from an evaluation standpoint, it is very difficult to distinguish between pre-program tendencies and the impact of the program under study if only outcomes for program participants are considered. The people who participate in a specific program frequently are the most motivated individuals in the population, and many would improve their outcomes even without participating in the program.

Only through comparison to a control group or through careful statistical modeling is it possible to determine whether the outcomes for a group of program participants are due to the program or simply reflect a high level of motivation on the part of program enrollees. Creating a randomized control group is neither cost-effective nor politically feasible. Collecting voluminous background information on participants to use in statistical modeling is also expensive and intrusive. Therefore, we focus our outcomes evaluation on programs that we judge to be sufficiently large to have a measurable impact on an identifiable target population and for which we have population outcome measures.

Data Sources and Outcome Definitions

Smoking-related Outcomes

Table B.1 lists the main sources of data used for the analysis of outcomes in the target populations. The primary outcome of interest, smoking behavior, is measured by several of these data sources. The Behavioral Risk Factor Surveillance System is a survey that asks a random sample of each state's population a series of questions about behaviors related to health outcomes, including whether or not they smoke. The Youth Risk Factor Surveillance System records the answers to similar questions for a sample of youth. The Natality Data Public Use File records the answers to questions about smoking for all women who give birth.

The BRFSS is the primary source of information regarding smoking behavior for the adult population. The sample size of approximately 3,000 Arkansans per year is adequate to obtain a fairly precise estimate of smoking prevalence among the adult population in the entire state, but precision drops considerably when using these data for analysis of specific subpopulations within the state.

The YRBSS is of similar size, so the same comments apply. An additional limitation of the YRBSS is that it is only collected every two years and in the most recent collection the response rate in Arkansas was sufficiently low that it did not meet the CDC requirements for valid data.

Table B.1
Data Sources and Outcome Measures

Outcome	Figure	Data
Tobacco Prevention and Cessation		
Adult smoking prevalence[a]	10.2, 10.3, 10.11	Behavioral Risk Factor Surveillance System
Cigarette Consumption	10.4	Cigarette Excise Tax Revenue; Adult Tobacco Survey
Pregnant women smoking prevalence[a]	10.5, 10.6, 10.8, 10.11	Natality Data Public Use File (Birth Certificates)
Pregnant teenager and young adult smoking prevalence	10.7, 10.8	Natality Data Public Use File (Birth Certificates); Behavioral Risk Factor Surveillance System
Sales to minors	10.9	Synar inspections
Delta AHEC		
Adult smoking prevalence	None	
Pregnant women smoking prevalence	10.11	Natality Data Public Use File (birth certificates)
Teen pregnancy		
Medicaid Expansions		
Adequate prenatal care	11.2	Natality Data Public Use File (birth certificates)

a. Also analyzed for association between county programming activity and smoking.

The other source of smoking prevalence information has a different set of limitations. The information on the smoking behavior of pregnant women is collected for all women who give birth, which produces a sample of approximately 35,000 observations per year in Arkansas. This sample size is adequate for producing precise estimates of smoking prevalence of this population and many subpopulations defined by age, race, and county of residence. However, the unique circumstances of this special population limit its usefulness as an indicator of changes in smoking behavior among the general population.

Two other direct data sources also provide information on smoking activity. Monthly revenue reports from the sales of cigarette tax stamps by the Arkansas Department of Finance to cigarette wholesalers allows for the calculation of the number of packs of cigarettes sold each month. Similar information is available annually for all other states. The Synar amendment requires random inspection of tobacco retailers to determine compliance with laws prohibiting sales to minors. Data from these inspections provide information regarding the success of a state in preventing such violations.

A final source of information regarding smoking behavior and attitudes toward smoking and smoking regulation is the Arkansas Adult Tobacco Survey (AATS). Conducted in 2002 and 2004, it asked a battery of questions of randomly selected adults. Unfortunately, comparisons with BRFSS and cigarette excise tax collection data suggest that the AATS undersampled smokers in 2004. Presumably, tobacco cessation and prevention programming had heightened awareness about smoking and more smokers than nonsmokers declined to participate in the 2004 study. Other states have had similar difficulties. Although we report some findings from the AATS, we think they should be interpreted cautiously.

Nonsmoking Outcomes

We also use data sources that provide health status and health care utilization information in order to examine the effect of funded programs on these outcomes. The birth certificate data provide information on expectant mothers' use of prenatal care and on infant birth weight. As noted above, the birth certificate data also provide information on the age, race, and residential location of the mother, thereby allowing analysis of health and healthcare differences along these dimensions. When used in conjunction with population counts from the U.S. Census Bureau, the birth certificate information can provide estimates of teen pregnancy rates by residential location (i.e., counties or zip code within Arkansas or by state and metropolitan area for other states) and by demographic group.

The hospital discharge data provide information on the primary and secondary diagnosis as well as basic demographics, residential location, and type of payer for all hospital stays. These can be used to identify hospitalizations for smoking-related illnesses such as asthma, strokes, and acute myocardial infarctions as well as hospitalizations that are likely to be the result of inadequate primary care (McCall et al., 2001). Counts of these events are used in conjunction with census data to estimate rates for subpopulations that are targeted by funded programs.

Program and Policy Information

As described below, these outcomes data are most useful when used with information that measures the program and policy efforts that have an impact on smoking and related health outcomes. We have assembled data on ATSC-funded program efforts within the state for the major community-based programs (TPEP, MHI, Delta AHEC, and AAI). For interstate comparisons, we have annual spending on prevention and control activities by state for years 2000 through 2005. We also have data on cigarette taxes by state for 1970 through 2003.

Analytic Framework

This section describes a common analytic framework that we apply to the evaluation of many of the smoking-related and nonsmoking outcomes. For many of these outcomes, we analyze administrative or survey data that provide information on individuals in the populations targeted by the funding programs. Although the analyses for each of the programs have many idiosyncratic features, most share four basic steps. The first step is to calculate the prevalence of a behavior or a condition in each year for which data are available. The second step is to use multivariate analysis to adjust for changes in demographic composition in order to isolate changes in behavior or health status for people of similar characteristics. In the third step, we estimate the baseline trend in the outcome for the adjusted population and compare the observed outcomes following program implementation to what would be expected based on this trend. Finally, in some cases we are able to investigate whether deviations from this baseline trend differ from those observed in other states or in other portions of the state with less intense programming.

Prevalence

The analyses require a stable sample frame for a sequence of years. For example the BRFSS annually surveys a national random sample of all adults age 18 and over. From this sample, a consistently measured outcome is obtained. For example, the BRFSS used the same question about smoking behavior starting in 1996. Using the sample weights, which adjust for variation in sampling rate by demographic category, the estimated prevalence in the population can be defined, along with a measure of precision that indicates how much variation in the estimate would be expected if the sampling process was repeated. This most simple of analyses is reported in Figure 10.2 for adult smoking prevalence in Arkansas.

A modification of this approach is used for the prevalence of smoking among pregnant women (Figure 10.6). In this case, the sample frame is all pregnant women, so no sampling weights are needed and sampling precision is not an issue.

Adjusting for Demographic Composition

Smoking prevalence, the proportion of a population who smoke, is not useful for measuring the effectiveness of anti-smoking programs when other factors are affecting this proportion. The first factor we address is the changing composition of the population. From year to year, the aging process as well as migration in and out of the sample frame changes the identity of the people in the sample frame. Since smoking rates differ among people of different ages, different racial and ethnic identities, and between men and women, it is important to account for demographic changes that could influence smoking trends.

We do this by performing multivariate analysis of the outcome measures for individuals as a function of their demographic characteristics. We create measures of age, race, sex, and pregnancy status and include these as explanatory variables in a regression. The regression also includes measures of time, which allow us to measure the change in the outcome after controlling for changes in population demographics.

This multivariate analysis takes into account the sampling design using STATA 8's commands for clustered sampling. We use appropriate functional forms, such as logit for binary outcomes (smoking versus not smoking) or least squares regression for continuous outcomes that have approximately normal distributions.

Table B.2 presents the odd ratios from the logit estimates that are used to adjust for demographic changes. The coefficients indicate that men smoke more than women; African Americans smoke less than whites or than people from other racial/ethnic groups. The relationship between age and smoking is captured by the coefficients on age and age squared with prevalence reaching its maximum at age 34. Throughout the period of study, the average age of the population increasing is getting older and the percentage of the population from other racial/ethnic groups is increasing, both of which have effects on smoking prevalence. Performing multivariate analysis isolates the changes in smoking prevalence that are related to these demographic changes, allowing us to focus on changes in prevalence that are unrelated to demographic changes.

Table B.2
Logit Estimates for Figure 10.3

	First Regression Model		Second Regression Model	
	Odds Ratio	Standard Error	Odds Ratio	Standard Error
Male	1.172**	0.040	1.172**	0.040
Pregnant	0.485**	0.110	0.483**	0.110
Black	0.714**	0.042	0.714**	0.042
Other race	1.300**	0.121	1.309**	0.122
Age	1.071**	0.007	1.071**	0.007
Age squared	0.999**	0.000	0.999**	0.000
Year 1997	1.164	-0.106		
Year 1998	1.039	-0.085		
Year 1999	1.09	-0.088		
Year 2000	0.989	-0.081		
Year 2001	1.005	-0.082		
Year 2002	1.031	-0.082	1.027	-0.068
Year 2003	0.961	-0.075	0.97	-0.072
Year 2004	0.992	-0.079	1.013	-0.088
Year			0.988	-0.013
Observations	27,555		27,555	

SOURCE: Arkansas BRFSS, 1996–2004.

NOTES: Dependent variable: currently smoking = 1, 0 otherwise. Significant levels: significant at 10 percent; ** significant at 5 percent.

The coefficients on the dummy variables for each year in the first column in Table B.2 provide an estimate of the difference between prevalence in that year and in the omitted year (1996) after adjusting for demographic changes. In this case, the prevalence in any year is not significantly different from the prevalence in 1996. The adjusted prevalence estimates that are graphed in Figure 10.3 (i.e., the points around the line) are based on this equation evaluated at the sample means of the demographic variables and the appropriate year dummy.

Baseline Trend Extrapolation

We also use multivariate analysis to estimate the baseline trend and to test whether the years following program initiation are significantly different from the baseline trend. The third column of Table B.2 contains logit estimates that are similar to those in the first column except the pre-program years are captured by the linear trend rather than yearly dummies. The coefficient on the trend is negative but not significant, indicating that the decrease during the baseline period is negligible. Evaluating this equation at the sample means of the demographic variables creates the linear trend graphed in Figure 10.3.

The equation also includes dummy variables for each post-initiation year. The test statistics associated with these coefficients test the null hypothesis that the adjusted outcome is equal to the extrapolated baseline trend. This hypothesis is not rejected for any of the post-initiation years in this example, which suggests that the program has not had an impact on smoking behavior for the general adult population.

It is also possible to estimate a new trend line for the post-initiation years. We create a spline variable that takes on the value zero for all years up to program initiation and then counts the positive integers for each year following program initiation. The coefficient on this variable indicates the change from the baseline trend in the years following initiation. This approach is used in Figure 11.2 tocreate lines that have a kink at program initiation.

Comparative Analysis

The above analyses are based on a pre-/post-design. Inference about the effect of a program is based on deviations from the pre-program trend, making a comparison only between the target population prior to program implementation and the same population following implementation. An alternative is to make comparisons between the target population and a similar population at the same time. This could be done by completely relying on cross-section information, comparing the level of the outcome between populations with and without program exposure. This approach requires that all confounding factors that differ among the populations be measured and included in the analysis. Because this strong requirement is seldom met, we prefer alternative methods whenever available.

An alternative is to combine both longitudinal and cross-sectional variation. This improves upon the simple longitudinal design presented above because changes over time in unmeasured confounding factors (e.g., economic conditions or health care access) are accounted for as long as they change in the same way in both the target and non-target population. However, if these unmeasured confounding factors change in ways that differ between the target and comparison populations, then this method can lead to erroneous inferences.

We make use of this type of analysis in two circumstances. We use this type of analysis for within-state comparisons between areas with and without program activity and among areas of varying levels of program activity. We also use it to compare outcomes in Arkansas with outcomes in other states.

Figure 11.2 presents the first type of analysis comparing teen pregnancy trends in Delta counties with trends in the rest of the state in order to evaluate the effect of Delta programs to prevent teen pregnancy. In this type of analysis a similar estimation to that presented in Table B.2 is performed using a sample that combines the treatment population (i.e., teenage women in Delta counties) and the comparison population (i.e., teenage women in other counties). Separate trend lines are fit for the two populations and a kink in each trend is permitted at the time of program initiation. It is possible that the trend in the comparison population might turn more positive or more negative at the time of program initiation for reasons unrelated to the program (e.g., unmeasured changes in the availability of contraception throughout the state). In fact, as shown in Figure 11.2, the trend in the comparison area does become more negative at the time of program implementation in the Delta. The trend in the Delta also becomes more negative, but by a similar amount to the trend in the comparison area. Therefore, we conclude that the change in the trend in the Delta is due to factors that are affecting the entire state rather than efforts that are specific to the Delta. This conclusion is supported by a hypothesis test of the null hypothesis that the Delta trend does not change at the time of program implementation by a different amount than the change in the trend elsewhere.

Another type of comparative analysis is to compare outcomes in Arkansas with outcomes in other states. We do this by performing an analysis similar to that presented in Table B.2, only using information on all respondents to the BRFSS for Arkansas and the six surrounding states from 1996 through 2003. Our assumption is that if unobserved factors such as national and regional advertising campaigns by cigarette companies and anti-smoking groups have a similar affect throughout the region, then smoking prevalence in Arkansas will change in a similar way as smoking prevalence in the surrounding states. Any divergence between Arkansas and the surrounding states can be attributed to differences in tobacco control programming and cigarette taxes. We track these two factors and control for demographic factors. The results are presented in Figure 10.11.

Other Analyses

The above section describes the analysis of data that contain outcomes information at the individual level. We also perform analyses at the county or state levels. Our analysis of teen pregnancy and cigarette sales require the event counts from outcome data sources to be combined with population counts from census data. The rates formed from combining these data sources are for particular subpopulations such as targeted age groups or counties with varying levels of program effort. Trends in these rates are analyzed in a similar fashion to that described above. That is, we look for changes in the trends in these rates following program initiation and compare changes in trends between areas with varying levels of program activity. Unlike the analyses of individual data, the analyses of subgroup rates does not control for changing demographic characteristics. These subgroup rate analyses are presented in Figures 10.4 and 11.2.

Appendix C.
Program Component Process Evaluation Information Request for 2005–06 Arkansas Tobacco Settlement Evaluation
fill in program name here

WHAT IS THIS INFORMATION REQUEST?

With this form, we request information regarding four critical aspects of the *fill in program name here* program of the ATSC. RAND's orientation is that, after four years of funding, the overall structures of the programs are largely in place, and our attention is turning to looking at how the programs are functioning (i.e., process evaluation). We are beginning to turn towards directly assessing the desired outcome measures, but for now, the major part of the evaluation will be looking at whether the processes necessary to promote successful outcomes are in place. Our examination requires information regarding the process of the four following components of program functioning, namely:

- Governing and advisory board

- Financial and accounting

- Contracting and oversight

- Quality improvement

For each of these four components, we ask for each component in turn, what the *fill in program name here* has in place to administer the components, and then how well the processes in place are doing. We will do this with a combination of "circle the best answer" questions and short open-ended questions.

In addition to these four components, we ask for short answers with regard to two aspects of continuous program monitoring, namely

- Progress on program goals (as specified in the RAND progress report of last year) (Farley et al., 2005b), and

- Responses to RAND recommendations (as specified in that same document)

Whereas the four components are designed to apply to all ATSC programs, the continuous program monitoring and information we are asking for here are specific to the goals and RAND recommendations of *fill in program name here*. We do recognize that each of the programs funded by Tobacco Settlement dollars is different and that some of the component questions may not fully apply to some programs. Although we have attempted to tailor this request *to fill in program name here*, it is possible that a question may not apply to your program. If that is the case, please place an "N/A" (not applicable) instead of answering.

HOW DO WE WANT YOU TO PROVIDE THE INFORMATION REQUESTED AND WHAT WILL WE DO WITH IT?

We would like the program director, together with principal program staff, to develop an official program response to this questionnaire. If we provide factual information, please confirm that we have it correctly and up-to-date. If we request factual information, please provide the most recent information you have according to your records. For matters that contain an element of subjectivity, please confer among yourselves to produce a single joint consensus response. Please tell us which program staff participated in any such discussions.

Participating staff:

_____

_____

_____

_____

_____

_____

_____

The responses you send us will be used as part of the formal evaluation by RAND that is incorporated into the legislature's overview of the ATSC. The information will also be used to help inform RAND staff in preparation for their annual site visits during April 2006.

Because of the need to have this information before the site visits, the information requested **must** be received by *fill in your own name here* at RAND no later than *put specific date here*.

If you have questions regarding this questionnaire, please contact *fill in your own name, telephone number and e-mail address here* and you will receive a response within two days of your contact.

1. Governing and advisory boards

The functioning of boards affiliated with *fill in program name here* is vital to the program's effectiveness. There are two types of boards that we are interested in learning about: governing and advisory. We define a ***governing board*** as an officially appointed body that oversees a program. This type of board has authority over the program, with formal responsibility for approving many aspects of program functioning such as spending, strategic objectives, contracts, and major staffing decisions (not all governing boards address all of these aspects). It may be called a board of directors or a commission, or other such name. The board meets a minimum of once a year, but possibly more often. A program may have no governing board or one governing board, but will not have more than one governing board.

We define an ***advisory board*** as an appointed body that has the purpose of offering advice to a program but has no official role in approving the actions of the program. Advisory boards may be called advisory boards, community advisory boards, advisory groups, feedback groups, or some other title that conveys the sense of the definition. The advice may include commenting on spending/fundraising, strategic objectives, contracts, etc. The advice may be in the form of feedback from stakeholder or community groups on how the program is perceived as functioning. A program may have none, one, or more than one advisory board. The advisory groups may be general (crossing stakeholder and community interests) or may represent a specific constituency (for example, health providers, community recipients, local governance).

The information requested in this section refers specifically to boards that govern or advise the *fill in program name here*, and not to boards that are connected to local efforts that may be fully or partially funded by the program.

1.1   Does *fill in program name here* have a governing board?

☐ Yes   ☐ No

1.1.a. If the program does not, do you believe it would be useful to have a governing board? Why or why not? Please answer this question and then go to item 1.2.

1.1.b. How many members does the governing board have and how are they appointed? How long are the terms of office of the members?

if we have this information (e.g., from the Act), provide it here. similarly for all questions where we already know the answers. put our answers in italics.

1.1.c. How many times a year does the governing board meet?

1.1.d. Please list the current governing board members, what their "real" jobs are, what special role, if any, they represent on the governing board, and, if relevant, what committees within the governing board they belong to.

_____

_____

_____

_____

_____

_____

_____

_____

_____

_____

1.1.e. Does the governing board have standing subcommittees? If so, please provide the names of these subcommittees. Do they meet at times other than general governing board meetings, and if so, when are these meetings?

Subcommittee Meetings

_____   _____

_____   _____

_____   _____

_____   _____

_____   _____

_____   _____

1.2   Does the *fill in program name here* have any advisory boards?

☐ Yes ☐ No

1.2.a. If the program does not, do you believe it would be useful to have advisory boards? Why or why not? Please answer this question and then go to item 1.3.

1.2.b. For each advisory board the *fill in program name here* has, please copy and paste the set of questions below for each advisory board separately.

1.2.b.1. Name of Advisory Board _____

1.2.b.2. What constituency, if any, does this Advisory Board represent?

_____

1.2.b.3. How many members does it have and how are they appointed? How long are the terms of office of the members?

1.2.b.4. How many times a year does the advisory board meet? _____

1.2.b.5. Please list the current board members, what their "real" jobs are, and what special role, if any, they represent on the advisory board.

_____

_____

_____

_____

_____

_____

_____

_____

_____

If the program has neither any governing board nor advisory boards, skip the remainder of section 1 of this request for information. If there are governing or advisory boards, please read the definitions below and then, with this page available for reference, answer item 1.3 for each such board.

We define the work a board does as falling into three general categories:

(1) Oversight of policy matters, which we call "P-functions":

P-1: Overarching goals and strategic planning. To what extent does the board involve itself with the program's overarching goals and strategic planning?

P-2: Program priorities. To what extent does the board involve itself with the priorities of the program that are meant to implement its goals?

P-3: Budget. To what extent does the board involve itself with how the program determines how to spend its annual budget, including internal staffing, contracting, and non-labor expenditures?

P-4: Quality management. To what extent does the board involve itself with the program's quality management activities?

(2) Monitoring program performance, which we call "M-functions":

M-1: Progress towards goals. To what extent does the board monitor the program's progress towards its goals?

M-2: Spending. To what extent does the board monitor the program's spending, including whether or not it is following its budget?

M-3: Quality performance. To what extent does the board monitor the program's quality of performance, using either the program's own quality management criteria or alternative criteria used by the board?

(3) Providing an interface between the program and the community, which we call "C-functions":

C-1: Community needs. To what extent does the board provide information to the program regarding the community's needs, or evaluate the validity of the program's community needs assessments?

C-2: Community interactions and collaborations. To what extent does the board involve itself in the program's interactions with the community and with collaborative arrangements the program makes with agencies within the community?

C-3: Fundraising. To what extent does the board participate in the guidance or actual conduct of program fund raising beyond the money provided by the Master Tobacco Settlement and the legislature?

1.3 For each governing board and advisory board, please make a copy of this page and use the ratings form below to assess how the board functions with respect to each of the ten

aspects. For each aspect, rate the board by circling the most descriptive number on a five-point scale, as follows:

1 = This aspect is not part of the board's mandate, so the board is not involved.

2 = The board is minimally involved with this aspect. It makes a general review at best.

3 = The board can get involved with this aspect. Most of the time, its involvement is not intense, but if the board believes that there may be problems or that it can help in a detail, it will choose to get more involved.

4 = The board fully considers this aspect in detail, and may modify or suggest modifications to decisions made by program management.

5 = The board is directive for this aspect, formulating what the program should do.

Name of board: _____

	Not involved	Minimally involved	Not intense	Fully considers	Directive
P-1: Goals and planning	1	2	3	4	5
P-2: Priorities	1	2	3	4	5
P-3: Budget	1	2	3	4	5
P-4: Quality management	1	2	3	4	5
M-1: Progress toward goals	1	2	3	4	5
M-2: Spending	1	2	3	4	5
M-3: Quality performance	1	2	3	4	5
C-1: Community needs	1	2	3	4	5
C-2: Community interactions	1	2	3	4	5
C-3: Fundraising	1	2	3	4	5

Note that there is not a single correct assessment for any board; the degree of involvement in each of the functions depends on the nature of the board.

2. Financial Management and Accounting

Financial awareness is crucial to the proper performance of a program. In order to have this awareness, proper financial management and accounting systems need to be in place, and the *fill in program name here* should have (either in-house or outsourced) people who know how to use those systems. In the case of the ATSC programs, as is true for many programs that ultimately are responsible to governmental oversight, there can be special systems for meeting the governmental financial and accounting requirements. Additionally, a program must supervise the financial and accounting practices of independent components, contractors, etc. that it may oversee.

2.1   What is the name of the accounting system that the fill in program name here uses to report spending to the state for the Tobacco Settlement program (Note: there are multiple accounting systems in use within Arkansas.)?

_____

2.2   How does the program work with that system? That is, does *fill in program name here* core staff run the system, or are accounting specialists hired to do the job, or is the task of financial management outsourced (to whom)?

2.3   Does the program also have a local automated accounting system (that is, an accounting system that is used by the *fill in program name here* to record expenditures and report spending to its management and boards)?

    Yes   No

2.3.a. If no, would it be desirable to acquire such a system? Why or why not?

2.3.b.1. If yes, what is the name of this system (if it has a name)?

_____

2.3.b.2. How does the program work with that system? That is, does *fill in program name here* core staff run the system, or are accounting specialists hired to do the job, or is the task of financial management outsourced (to whom)?

2.4.   Does the *fill in program name here* program management believe that it is adequately informed about matters of financial management and accounting?

☐ Yes ☐ No

2.4.a. If no, what information does it consider to be lacking?

2.5.   Have the *fill in program name here* governing and advisory boards expressed the belief that they are adequately informed about matters of financial management and accounting?

☐ Yes ☐ No ☐ N/A (no such boards)

2.5.a. If no, what information does they consider to be lacking?

2.6   Has the *fill in program name here* established separate accounts for the key program components so that the program can budget for and monitor spending by component?

Yes, on the state system   Yes, on the local system   No

2.6.a.   If no, why has the program not established separate accounts?

2.7   Do the personnel who perform the *fill in program name here* program's financial management and accounting functions have the required qualifications, including training in bookkeeping or accounting as well as in the accounting systems being used?

Yes, all personnel   Yes, some personnel   No

2.7.a.   If there are financial personnel that do not have these qualifications, is the *fill in program name here* planning to train existing personnel or hire qualified personnel?

3. Contracting and Oversight

The *fill in program name here* may have responsibility for individuals, agencies, or other programs. The responsibility may arise from contracts (formal written agreements between the two parties) the *fill in program name here* has made with these entities, or the responsibility may be part of an organizational structure (for example, when the line of authority is established by the Initiating Act or ATSC implementation rules). As an example of contracts, a program may provide health services to communities by contracting with individual or organizational providers to offer those services. As an example of organizational structure, a research-oriented program may have oversight (but not direct management) responsibilities for research organizations scattered throughout the state.

In this section, our focus is on contracting and oversight that is directly related to the *fill in program name here's* core activities (as defined by the Initiating Act and possibly subsequently revised). We are not addressing possible contracting for ancillary services, such as secretarial support, transportation, provision of office space, etc.

3.1   Does the *fill in program name here* contract with other organizations to perform some or all of the program activities supported by the Tobacco Settlement funding?

☐ Yes ☐ No

3.1.a   If yes, List the contractors and the functions to be performed under each contract.

_____

_____

_____

_____

_____

_____

_____

3.1.b   If yes, are the contracts specific to each individual contractor, or can they be sorted into standard types of contracts (for example, to community health agencies, individual practitioners, outreach agencies). If they can be sorted, list the different types of contracts.

_____

_____

_____

_____

_____

_____

3.2 Does the *fill in program name here* have oversight for agencies or other programs that perform some or all of the program activities supported by the Tobacco Settlement funding?

☐ Yes ☐ No

3.2.a If yes, list these agencies or other programs and the functions to be performed by each.

_____

_____

_____

_____

_____

_____

If the answers to both 3.1 and 3.2 are no, then skip the remainder of this section and go to section 4.

Contracting and oversight involves four processes or specifications to contracting. These are (1) basing contract or oversight on performance, (2) monitoring financial reporting, (3) monitoring quality performance and reporting, and (4-only for contracts) having a payment structure that reflects the nature of the service. The questions below are for these specifications.

For the following four questions, please answer separately for each contract type (or each contract if they are unique types) and each oversight arrangement the information items 3.3 through 3.6. To do this, please copy this and the next page and fill it in separately for each contract or oversight arrangement.

Name of Contract type/Oversight Arrangement _____

3.3   **Performance basis.** Does this contract type or oversight arrangement have provisions that tie payments, contract continuation, or oversight assessments to the output or effects that the contractor, agency, or program is expected to achieve (e.g., number of clients enrolled, smoking cessation rates, community changes achieved, consumer satisfaction with service, research grants won, research publication rates)?

☐ Yes ☐ No

3.3.a   If yes, please provide a list of the outputs or effects used in the assessments.

3.4   **Financial reporting.** Does this contract type or oversight arrangement have a financial reporting requirement?

☐ Yes ☐ No

3.4.a   If "yes", does that requirement include:

3.4.a.1. comparisons of actual to planned spending?

☐ Yes ☐ No

3.4.a.2. explanations of reasons for variances from budget?

☐ Yes ☐ No

3.4.a.3. comparison of spending to program activity?

☐ Yes ☐ No

3.4.a.4. How often each year are finances reported? _____ times

3.5 **Quality performance and reporting**. Does this contract type or oversight arrangement have requirements that:

    3.5.a the contractor agency or program establish a quality management process through which the contractor establishes quality measures?

        ☐ Yes ☐ No

    3.5.b monitor its own performance relative to those measures?

        ☐ Yes ☐ No

    3.5.c take corrective actions to improve performance when needed?

        ☐ Yes ☐ No

    3.5.d regularly report performance and actions to your program?

        ☐ Yes ☐ No

3.6 **(For contracts only) Payment structure reflecting the nature of the service**. Does this contract type have payments so the program pays the contractor only for services that are actually provided, such as payment per unit of service for distinct services provided to individual consumers or patients (e.g., per office visit or for per package of services for each program enrollee)?

        ☐ Yes ☐ No

    3.6.a If no, does the contract specify aggregate budgets to cover the costs for services to population groups (e.g., community education initiative, health fair, telephone helpline?

        ☐ Yes ☐ No

4. Quality management

Next, we would like you to tell us about the *fill in program name here's* quality management by which it keeps track of its own activities. If you have contractual or organizational responsibility for oversight of another party's activities (for example somebody provides care or other services for the program), quality management refers to how you maintain awareness of that other party's quality, not the actual quality management of the other party.

We define quality management as a written process used to continuously improve program performance over time. The management process may appear under a variety of possible names, including Quality Management, Continuous Quality Improvement, Quality Assurance, ISO Standards, or the like. It may or may not be governed by a Quality Management Committee or similarly-named body. In order to qualify as a formal quality management process, we require that the following be included:

- Definition of the criteria for quality performance. For each aspect of quality, what constitutes adequate performance?

- Collection of quality information. Based upon the definitions, there should be a quality information collection plan.

- Quality deficiency identification. From the information about quality that has been collected, there should be analyses that identify where/if the program is falling short of its quality objectives.

- Recommendations for improvement. The quality management process should formulate recommendations for overcoming the deficiencies that have been identified. These recommendations should be specific as to what deficiencies should be overcome and who should be responsible for implementing the recommendations.

4.1   Does the *fill in program name here* have a formal quality management process?

☐ Yes   ☐ No

4.1.a.   If not, why isn't there a formal quality management in place? Do you believe that a quality management process is not appropriate for your program? After answering this question, please skip the remainder of section 4.

4.1.b.   If yes, how long has the formal quality management process been in place?

_____

4.2.   Is there an entity within the *fill in program name here* responsible for quality management? Here, we will call it the quality management committee, although you may use a different name for it.

☐ Yes   ☐ No

If no, please go directly to question 4.3.

4.2.a.   If yes, who serves on the quality management committee, and how are these people appointed?

4.2.b.   What is the relationship between the quality management committee and program management?

4.2.c. How many times a year does the quality management committee meet?

_____

4.2.d. Does the quality management committee produce formal documents?

☐ Yes   ☐ No

4.3 What does the quality management process entail?

For each of the aspects of quality management listed below, indicate how well the *fill in program name here* **quality management process performs this aspect.**

	N/A	Needs improvement	Does satisfactorily
4.3.a. Specifies criteria for quality performance			
4.3.b. Collects information on technical quality measures			
4.3.c. Collects information on consumers' experience with service			
4.3.d. Collects data on program enrollments, demographic characteristics of enrollees, service encounters			
4.3.e. Has quantified quality measures for technical aspects of service			
4.3.f. Has quantified measures of consumers' experience with service			
4.3.g. Has quantified measures on program enrollments, demographic characteristics of enrollees, and service encounters that may be compared to targets			
4.3.h. Analyzes technical quality data to identify potential quality deficiencies			
4.3.i. Analyzes consumer experience data to identify potential quality deficiencies			
4.3.j. Analyzes measures on program enrollments, etc., to identify potential quality deficiencies			
4.3.k. Formulates quality recommendations that are addressed to who needs to take action			
4.3.l. Reports results of quality analyses to executive management/boards			
4.3.m. Reports results of quality analyses to relevant committees			
4.3.n. Disseminates quality recommendations to the public ("report cards")			

4.4 To what extent does the fill *in program name here* demand that independent components, contractors, etc. have their own quality management processes that mirror those of the program?

Program has no such subordinate bodies

Subordinate bodies have no quality management processes in place

Subordinate bodies have their own quality management processes in place, which may differ from body to body

Program requires common quality management approach

4.5 To what extent have the *fill in program name here* quality measures and corrective actions changed over the last two years within the program?

4.6 Name up to three quality improvement recommendations within the last two years that were successful in that improvements resulted as a result of the recommendations. For each recommendation, describe how quality improved as the result of the recommendation.

5. Progress on program goals

Your program set a number of goals a year ago during our last site visit. These goals are:

INSERT AND NUMBER THE PROGRAM GOALS HERE

Goal 1.

Goal 2.

...

For each of the goals listed above (plus any we may have missed), please answer the following questions:

5.1　　Has that goal been met or is progress toward the goal going as planned?

Goal 1.　☐ Yes　☐ No

Goal 2.　☐ Yes　☐ No

Goal 3.　☐ Yes　☐ No

Goal ...　☐ Yes　☐ No

5.2　　For each goal that has not yet been met and progress is slower than expected, why has progress varied from the anticipated rate?

Goal ___

Goal ___

5.3　　For each goal where progress has exceeded expectations, why has this happened?

Goal ___

Goal ___

6. Responses to RAND recommendations

In the RAND first Biennial Evaluation Report (delivered in 2004) and the RAND interim evaluation delivered in 2005, we made recommendations to the program. These were:

INSERT AND NUMBER THE RAND RECOMMENDATIONS HERE. Indicate for each recommendation whether it was delivered in 2004, 2005 or both.

RAND Recommendation 1.

RAND Recommendation 2.

RAND Recommendation ...

6.1   For each RAND recommendation, please state how the program has responded. You need not repeat information provided last year, but if there is no updating since then, please state that fact. If you anticipation further response between the time you prepare this answer and June 2006, please tell us what you anticipate.

References

Abt Associates Inc. for the Massachusetts Department of Public Health. *Independent Evaluation of the Massachusetts Tobacco Control Program.* Fourth Annual Report. Cambridge, Mass.: Abt Associates Inc., 1997.

American Association of Diabetes Educators, *The Scope of Practice, Standards of Practice, and Standards of Performance for Diabetes Educators.* Chicago, Illinois: American Association of Diabetes Educators, 2005.

American Heart Association, American Cancer Association, Campaign for Tobacco-Free Kids, and American Lung Association, titled *Broken Promise to Our Children: The 1998 State Tobacco Settlement Seven Years Later. A Report on the States' Allocation of the Tobacco Settlement Dollars* (2005).

Arkansas Tobacco Settlement Commission (ATSC). *Biennial Report to the General Assembly and Governor on the Tobacco Settlement Act of 2002 Program Performance and ATSC Recommendations.* Little Rock, Ark., August 1, 2002.

Arkansas Tobacco Settlement Commission (ATSC). *Agency Strategic Plan for the Fiscal Years 2005–2009.* Little Rock, Ark., 2004.

Baroud, T. *Arkansas County-Specific Smoking and Other Tobacco Use.* Arkansas Department of Health, Tobacco Prevention and Education Program. As of July 24, 2006:
http://www.stampoutsmoking.com/pdf/county_specific_tobacco_use.pdf

Bindman, A.B., K. Grumbach, D. Osmond, M. Komaromy, K. Vranizan, N. Lurie, J. Billings, and A. Stewart. "Preventable hospitalizations and access to care." *JAMA* 274 (1995): 305–311.

Booth, G.L., and J. E. Hux. "Relationship between Avoidable Hospitalizations for Diabetes Mellitus and Income Level." *Archives of Internal Medicine* 163 (2003): 101–107.

Browne, A., and A. Wildavsky. "What Should Evaluation Mean to Implementation?" in D.J. Palumbo, ed., *The Politics of Program Evaluation* Newbury Park, Calif.: Sage, 1987, pp.146–172.

California Department of Health Services. *Adult Smoking Trends in California.* As of July 24, 2006:
http://www.dhs.ca.gov/ps/cdic/ccb/tcs/documents/FSAdulttrends.pdf

Center for Substance Abuse Prevention, SAMHSA. Tobacco/Synar Home Page. As of July 24, 2006:
http://prevention.samhsa.gov/tobacco/01synartable.asp

Center for Substance Abuse Prevention, SAMHSA. *Arkansas Annual Synar Report.* 42 U.S.C. 300x-26. OMB 0930-0222, FFY2003. As of July 24, 2006: http://www.state.ar.us/dhs/dmhs/2003%20Annual%20Synar%20Report.doc

Center for Substance Abuse Prevention, SAMHSA. *Arkansas Annual Synar Report.* 42 U.S.C. 300x-26. OMB 0930-0222, FFY2004. As of July 24, 2006: http://www.state.ar.us/dhs/dmhs/2004%20Annual%20Synar%20Report.doc

Center for Substance Abuse Prevention, SAMHSA. *Arkansas Annual Synar Report.* 42 U.S.C. 300x-26. OMB 0930-0222, FFY2005. As of July 24, 2006: http://www.arkansas.gov/dhs/dmhs/FFY2005ASRfinal%2010%2027%2004.pdf.

Centers for Disease Control and Prevention (CDC). "Guidelines for School Health Programs to Prevent Tobacco Use and Addiction." *MMWR* 43 (No. RR-2) (1994), pp. 1-18.

Centers for Disease Control and Prevention (CDC). "Decline in Cigarette Consumption Following Implementation of a Comprehensive Tobacco Prevention and Education Program—Oregon, 1996–1999." *MMWR* 48 (1999a):140–143.

Centers for Disease Control and Prevention (CDC). *Best Practices for Comprehensive Tobacco Control Programs—August 1999.* Atlanta, Ga.: U.S. Department of Health and Human Services, Centers for Disease Control and Prevention, National Center for Chronic Disease Prevention and Health Promotion, Office on Smoking and Health, August 1999b.

Chatila, W., W. Wynkoop, G. Vance, and G. Criner. "Smoking Patterns in African Americans and Whites with Advanced COPD." *Chest* 125(1) (2004): 15–21.

Dehar, M., S. Casswell, and P. Duignan. "Formative and process evaluation of health promotion and disease prevention programs." *Evaluation Review* 17(2) (1993): 204–220.

Devine, P. *A Guide to Process Evaluation for Substance Abuse Treatment Services.* Fairfax, VA: National Evaluation Data and Technical Assistance Center (NEDTAC), Caliber Associates, 1999.

Emery, S. M.M. White, and J.P. Pierce, "Does Cigarette Price Influence Adolescent Experimentation?" Journal of Health Economics 20: 261-270, 2001.

Farley, D.O., M.J. Chinman, E. D'Amico, D.J. Dausey, J.B. Engberg, S.B. Hunter, L.R. Shugarman, and M.E.S. Sorbero. *Evaluation of the Arkansas Tobacco Settlement Program: Progress from Program Inception to 2004.* No. TR-221-ATSC. Santa Monica, Calif.: RAND Corporation, 2005a.

Farley, D.O., M.J. Chinman, E. D'Amico, J.B. Engberg, S.B. Hunter, S. Lovejoy, D. Schultz, and L. R. Shugarman. *Evaluation of the Arkansas Tobacco Settlement Program: Progress from Program Advancement in 2005.* No. WR-272-ATSC. Santa Monica, Calif.: RAND Corporation, 2005b.

Farrelly, M.C., Davis, K.C., Haviland, M.L., Messeri, P., Healton, C.G., "Evidence of a dose response relationship between 'Truth' antismoking ads and youth smoking prevalence." *American Journal of Public Health* 95 (2005): 425–431.

Fiore, M.C., W.C. Bailey, S. J. Cohen, S.F. Dorfman, M.G. Goldstein, E.R. Gritz, et al. *Treating Tobacco Use and Dependence.* Clinical Practice Guideline. Rockville, Md.: U.S. Department of Health and Human Services, Public Health Service, June 2000.

Floreani, A.A., and S.I. Rennard. "The Role of Cigarette Smoke in the Pathogenesis of Asthma and as a Trigger for Acute Symptoms." *Current Opinions in Pulmonary Medicine* 5 (1999): 38–46.

Geobel, K. "Lesbians and gays face tobacco targeting." *Tobacco Control* 3 (1994): 65–67.

Goodman, R.M., and A. Wandersman. "FORECAST: A formative approach to evaluating community coalitions and community-based initiatives." *Journal of Community Psychology* (Center for Substance Abuse Prevention Special Issue) (1994): 6–25.

Hamilton, J.L. "The demand for cigarettes: Advertising, the health scare, and the cigarette advertising ban." *Rev Econ Stat* 54 (1972): 401–11.

Harris, J., and S. Chan. "The Continuum-of-Addiction: Cigarette Smoking in Relation to Price Among Americans Aged 15–29." *Health Economics Letters* 2(2) (February 1998): 3–12.

Institute of Medicine, *Access to Health Care in America.* Washington, DC: National Academy Press, 1993.

Lewin Group, *Arkansas Aging Initiative: Final Program Evaluation.* Washington, DC.: Lewin Group, 2005.

Lightwood, J.M., and S.A. Glantz. "Short-Term Economic and Health Benefits of Smoking Cessation: Myocardial Infarction and Stroke." *Circulation* 96 (1997): 1089–1096.

Lightwood, J.M., C.S. Phibbs, and S.A. Glantz. "Short-term Health and Economic Benefits of Smoking Cessation: Low Birth Weight." *Pediatrics* 104 (1999): 1312–1320.

Ling, P.M., and S.A. Glantz. "Why and how the tobacco industry sells cigarettes to young adults: Evidence from industry documents." *American Journal of Public Health* 92 (2002): 908–916.

McCall N, Harlow J, Dayhoff D. Rates of hospitalization for ambulatory care sensitive conditions in the Medicare+Choice population. *Health Care Financing Review.* 22(3), 2001, 127–145.

National Center for Biotechnology Information. *Community-based Participatory Research: Assessing the Evidence.* 2004. As of July 24, 2006: http://www.ncbi.nlm.nih.gov/books/bv.fcgi?rid=hstat1a.chapter.44133

Nuorti, J.P., J.C. Butler, M.M. Farley, L.H. Harrison, A. McGeer, M.S. Kolczak, R.F. Breiman, and the Active Bacterial Surveillance Team. "Cigarette Smoking and Invasive Pneumococcal Disease." *New England Journal of Medicine* 342 (2000): 681–689.

Robinson, R.G., M. Barry, M. Bloch, S.J. Glantz, J. Jordan, K.B. Murray, et al. "Report of the Tobacco Policy Research Group on marketing and promotions targeted at African Americans, Latinos, and women." *Tobacco Control* 1 (1992): S24–S30.

Robinson, R.G., M. Pertschuk, and C. Sutton. "Smoking and African Americans: Spotlighting the effects of smoking and tobacco promotion in the African American community." In *Improving the Health of the Poor,* edited by S.E. Samuels and M.D. Smith. Menlo Park, Calif.: Henry J. Kaiser Family Foundation, 1992, pp. 123-181.

Scheirer M.A. "Designing and Using Process Evaluation," in J.S. Wholey, H.P. Hatry, and K.E. Newcomer, eds., *Handbook of Practical Program Evaluation.* San Francisco: Jossey-Bass, 1994, pp. 40-66.

Senner, J. (Director of the Division of Health, Center for Health Statistics). Phone conversation about the SAMHSA audit and findings, 2006.

Shadish W.R., T.D. Cook, and L.C. Levito. *Foundations of Program Evaluation: Theories of Practice.* Newbury Park, Calif.: Sage, 1991.

Siegel M. and L. Biener. "The impact of an antismoking media campaign on progression to established smoking: results of a longitudinal youth study." *American Journal of Public Health* 90(3) (2000): 380–386.

Tauras J. "Public Policy and Smoking Cessation among Young Adults in the United States." *Health Policy* Vol. 68, 2004m pp. 321–332.

Thompson, J.W., F.W. Boozman, S. Tyson, K.W. Ryan, S. McCarthy, R. Scott, and G.R. Smith, "Improving health with tobacco dollars from the MSA: The Arkansas experience." *Health Affairs* 23(1) (January–February 2004a): 177–185.

Thompson, J.W., K.W. Ryan, S. Tyson, and C. Munir. "Arkansas Tobacco Settlement Proceeds Act of 2000: Results from education and engagement with policy makers and the public." *Health Promotion Practice.* 5(3 Suppl) (July 2004b): 57S–63S.

Thompson J.W., G.R. Smith, M.K. Stewart, P. Card-Higginson, C.R. Nash, S.G. McCarthy, et al. *Position Paper on Spending the Tobacco Settlement Funds in Arkansas.* Little Rock, Ark.: Arkansas Center for Health Improvement, February 9, 1999.

Tobacco Advisory Group of the Royal College of Physicians. *Going Smoke-Free: The Medical Case for Clean Air in the Home, at Work and in Public Places.* London: Royal College of Physicians of London, 2005.

Tobacco Settlement Proceeds Act of 2000 (Initiated Act). Ark Stat. Ann. Secs. 19-12-101. As of July 24, 2006: http://www.achi.net

U.S. Department of Health and Human Services (US DHHS). The health benefits of smoking cessation: A eport of the Surgeon General. DHHS Publication No. (CDC) 90–8416. Atlanta, Ga.: U.S. Department of Health and Human Services, Centers for Disease Control and Prevention, 1990.

U.S. Department of Health and Human Services (US DHHS). *Preventing Tobacco Use Among Young People: A Report of the Surgeon General.* Atlanta, Ga.: U.S. Department of Health and Human Services, Public Health Service, Centers for Disease Control and Prevention, National Center for Chronic Disease Prevention and Health Promotion, Office on Smoking and Health, 1994.

U.S. Department of Health and Human Services (US DHHS). *Tobacco Use Among U.S. Racial/Ethnic Minority Groups—African Americans, American Indians and Alaska Natives, Asian Americans and Pacific Islanders, and Hispanics: A Report of the Surgeon General.* Atlanta, Ga.: U.S. Department of Health and Human Services, Centers for Disease Control and Prevention, National Center for Chronic Disease Prevention and Health Promotion, Office on Smoking and Health, 1998.

U.S. Department of Health and Human Services (US DHHS). *Reducing Tobacco Use: A Report of the Surgeon General.* Atlanta, Ga.: U.S. Department of Health and Human Services, Centers for Disease Control and Prevention, National Center for Chronic Disease Prevention and Health Promotion, Office on Smoking and Health, 2000.

U.S. Department of Health and Human Services (US DHHS). *Women and Smoking 2001: A Report of the Surgeon General.* Atlanta, Ga.: U.S. Department of Health and Human Services, Centers for Disease Control and Prevention, National Center for Chronic Disease Prevention and Health Promotion, Office on Smoking and Health, 2001.

Wooding S., S. Hanney, M. Buxton, and J. Grant. *The Returns from Arthritis Research.* No. MG-251-ARC. Santa Monica, Calif.: RAND Corporation, 2004. As of July 24, 2006:
http://www.rand.org/publications/MG/MG251/

Yerger, V.B., and R.E. Malone. "African American leadership groups: Smoking with the enemy." *Tobacco Control* 11 (2002): 336–345.